THE CULTURAL INFRASTRUCTURE OF CITIES

URBAN WORLDS

Urban areas are dynamic spaces where people come together in close proximity to live, work, learn and be entertained. They are also places of great contrast, extremes and inequalities. At a time of enormous global pressures, not least the vulnerability of urban areas and their populations to the effects of climate change, the Urban Worlds series interrogates the challenges – from governance and planning to consumption and sustainability – facing urban areas today and examines how the drivers of urbanization continue to shift and change.

Published

The Cultural Infrastructure of Cities
Edited by Alison L. Bain and Julie A. Podmore

THE CULTURAL INFRASTRUCTURE OF CITIES

Edited by

ALISON L. BAIN AND JULIE A. PODMORE

agenda
publishing

We dedicate this book with love and respect for their ongoing support, guidance, and care to our respective families, Anne and Tony Bain, Camden Bain, Cathy Clarke, Gail and John Podmore, and Laudan Vaezmir.

First published in 2023 by Agenda Publishing

Agenda Publishing Limited
PO Box 185
Newcastle upon Tyne
NE20 2DH
www.agendapub.com

ISBN 978-1-78821-491-9 (hardcover)
ISBN 978-1-78821-492-6 (paperback)

British Library Cataloguing-in-Publication Data
A catalogue record for this book is available from the British Library

Typeset by Newgen Publishing UK
Printed and bound in the UK by CPI Group (UK) Ltd, Croydon, CR0 4YY

CONTENTS

Part III – Consuming Culture

Part IV – Collecting Culture

LIST OF CONTRIBUTORS

Chan Arun-Pina is a doctoral candidate in the Faculty of Environmental and Urban Change, York University, Ontario.

Alison L. Bain is a professor of geography in the Faculty of Environmental and Urban Change, York University, Ontario.

Taylor Brydges is a research principal at the Institute for Sustainable Futures, University of Technology Sydney.

Luke Dickens is a senior lecturer in the Department of Geography, King's College London.

Phil Hubbard is a professor of urban studies in the Department of Geography, King's College London.

Megan A. Johnson is a research associate for Re•Vision: the Centre for Art and Social Justice, University of Guelph.

Lily Kong is a professor of social sciences at Singapore Management University.

Friederike Landau-Donnelly is an assistant professor in the Department of Geography, Planning and Environment, Radboud University.

Deborah Leslie is a professor in the Department of Geography and Planning, University of Toronto.

Bryan Mark is a master's student in the Faculty of Environmental and Urban Change, York University, Ontario.

Antonio Moya-Latorre is a doctoral candidate in the Department of City and Regional Planning, Cornell University.

Julie A. Podmore is an affiliate assistant professor in the Department of Geography, Planning and Environment, Concordia University and a professor in Geosciences at John Abbott College, Montreal.

Bernadette Quinn is a senior lecturer in the School of Tourism and Hospitality Management, Technological University Dublin.

Martha Radice is an associate professor in the Department of Sociology and Social Anthropology, Dalhousie University.

Norma M. Rantisi is a professor in the Department of Geography, Planning and Environment, Concordia University.

Suntje Schmidt is a professor at the Leibniz Institute for Research on Society and Space, and at the Humboldt-Universität zu Berlin.

Marlis Schweitzer is a professor in the Department of Theatre and Performance, York University, Ontario.

Rhian Scott is a postdoctoral research fellow in the Department of Geography, King's College London.

Jessie Stein is a doctoral candidate in the Department of Earth and Environmental Sciences, CUNY Graduate Center.

Rianne van Melik is an associate professor at the Institute for Management Research, Radboud University.

Aidan Wong is an assistant professor at the College of Integrative Studies, Singapore Management University.

CHAPTER 1

INTRODUCTION: CONFIGURING URBAN CULTURAL INFRASTRUCTURE

Alison L. Bain and Julie A. Podmore

INTRODUCTION

Cities are works of art. They are imaginative objects. They have life forces of their own that bring into view colliding individual and collective needs and ambitions and "heterogeneous views of functions and requirements of administering, of instituting, and distributing resources" (Blum 2003: 5). As centres of commerce, transportation and government, where large numbers of people live and work, cities are dense gathering places, sites where cultures intersect and collide (Bain & Peake 2022). It is from the emblematic co-presence of strangers, social interactions and critical engagements that collective life is built through institutions, public spaces, workplaces and homes within neighbourhoods (Miles 2007). But that density also brings with it socio-political conflicts, inequality brought by struggles over resources and infrastructure, as well as the threat of terrorism and disease transmission (Anheier *et al.* 2021).

In recent years, the global Covid-19 pandemic has, within a short period of time, produced a counter to the historical role of cities as sites of population concentration and social interaction. It has spurred urban exoduses and the digitization of many urban education and medical institutions, workplaces and retail and entertainment environments. Through information communication technologies (ICTs), the domestication of urban social relations has intensified, potentially eroding and reconfiguring long-established public-private spatial binaries that inform the meanings of urban places and the social structures and morphologies of cities. While ICTs enable spatio-temporal transcendence, meaning that "fewer relationships or transactions require ... copresence", they also increase the capacity for centralized surveillance and social control from various corporate and state actors (Calhoun 1992: 221). A constrained urban public life is concomitantly the product of this dramatic and rapid reworking made possible by the continual malleability of the material and human cultural infrastructure of cities that are ever-open to such change.

Often treated as superficial in contrast with the frameworks of urban economies, material and human cultural infrastructure is what makes cities themselves archives and works of art. In their diversity and multiplicity, cities are also synonymous with the production and consumption of culture. Early scholarship on "world" or "global cities", for example, noted that in addition to centralizing and controlling the political economy, the more worldly cities were "cultural" hubs, centres for professional talent (e.g., in universities, hospitals and libraries) and entertainment (e.g., in media, theatre, film and music) (Hall 1966). As Zukin (1995: 264) argues, "culture is ... what cities 'do' best" because "they so clearly mark a human-made sense of place and a human-sized struggle with scale". The "cultures of cities", therefore, are embedded in, and negotiated through, urban political and symbolic economies whose seductive imagery facilitates competitive urban redevelopment while obscuring underlying strife and conflict wrought by exclusion, surveillance and displacement (Zukin 1995).

This book strives to critically re-examine this long-established relationship between the urban and its cultures by developing the concept of urban cultural infrastructure across its cycles and value chains as spatially embedded in a range of cities. The collection expands scholarly understandings of the concept and highlights the foundational role of culture to the materiality and sociality of urban life and the governance of cities. As a framework for the collection, this chapter provides a theoretical overview of the cultural and infrastructural turns in urban studies scholarship. It then grapples with definitions of cultural infrastructure and its "hard" and "soft" dimensions before critically considering the vulnerabilities generated in the cultural sector by the Covid-19 pandemic. It concludes with an outline and justification for the book, describing its key questions.

THE CULTURAL TURN IN URBAN STUDIES

The late-1980s cultural turn in urban studies was later exemplified by theories of the creative city and its emerging economy. Following Charles Landry, Peter Hall and Richard Florida, "creative" and "creativity" have become two of the most (over)used words in contemporary English language, applied to activities, objects, individuals and places (from cultural venues to neighbourhoods to cities and their suburbs) to signal agility, progressiveness and novelty (Mould 2018). The ensuing "creative city" metaphor became a major intellectual current in urban studies that captured the culture-economy nexus. As a "global policy meme", it was incorporated into urban neoliberal policy scripts (Whiting *et al.* 2022). Creative cities were initially framed as incubators of innovation with the goal of relaunching urban growth through interdisciplinary partnerships based on accountability and justice that could enhance social inclusion (Landry 2008; Hall 1998). Creative city solutions were imagined as bold, and far-sighted, breaking with formula and tradition, but ultimately, they reinforced neoliberal entrepreneurial appropriation and its unequal embrace of market-driven individual success to regenerate urban economies at the neglect of collective flourishing (Mould 2018).

As a field of study, the creative city has proliferated. Yet it is based in an economistic interpretation of culture and a reductionist understanding of what constitutes urban creativity. When applied sweepingly by Florida to a whole "creative class" of problem-solving professionals in business, law, engineering, science and healthcare who value individuality, difference and merit and are attracted to cities that offer the 3Ts (technology, talent and tolerance), everyone and every city has the potential to be creative. Such conceptual "fuzziness" (Markusen 2006, 2014) is critiqued for its aggregation of unrelated occupational groups with very different work-based cultures, skills and incomes (Krätke 2010). Moreover, it minimizes how central social reproduction is to creative labour (Parker 2008) and glosses over the exclusions wrought by whiteness and heteronormativity (Catungal & Leslie 2009; Oswin 2014) while privileging middle-class, rather than working-class, cultural capital (McLean 2014). The malleability of the creative class concept makes it a politically expedient policy tool, but one that aggravates social exclusions and selectively instrumentalizes culture for economic growth (Krivý 2013).

So definitive has creativity been for urban futures that it now shapes class-based aspirations, social mobility and cultural capital. As McRobbie (2016) asserts, young people aspire to be creative and unique, to have autonomy and to "make a difference" in society, yet these markers of cultural capital remain unattainable in unbalanced creative labour markets that are characterized by informality and precarity. The creative cities theory is also marred by the assumption that regardless of size, all cities "can somehow create an infrastructure to attract the right calibre of talented people" (McRobbie 2016: 7); but small cities may not be able to sustain large cultural infrastructure (Dova *et al.* 2022). This fallacy obscures urban hierarchies of cultural infrastructure wherein global cities continue to concentrate their power, resources and highly skilled labour, and specialized urban centres emerge in music, film, fashion and media. "Being creative" also requires a location in a major urban centre and embedding oneself in its specialized creative economy, localized networks and infrastructure.

Within the "creative city" framework, culture's urban benefits are calculated according to the sector's economic footprint. Its value is determined by increases in property, business and tax revenues generated by tourism and "entrepreneurial creativity" (e.g., arts districts, public art installations, contemporary art museums, festivals, night markets, street food and hipster retail) in the service of "developing a new, modern, globally oriented public culture" (Zukin 2012: 22). Many urban residents – migrants, low-wage workers, homeless – inhabit the city without playing a part in its public consumer culture. Seldom incorporated into its emerging symbolic economy and long subject to urban redevelopment's displacements, they build their own homes, neighbourhoods and cities through complex cultural "strategies and calculations", "improvisation and bricolage" and "constant imagination" on peripheries (Caldeira 2017: 5). In contrast to the spectacular and polished cultural products and amenities geared towards the supposed "creative class" (Florida 2002) that are showcased in the media as the essence of contemporary global urban culture, cultures of peripheral urbanization are formed in unfinished spaces where infrastructure is "never quite done, always being altered, expanded, and elaborated upon" (Caldeira 2017: 5–6).

Urbanism's productive organization makes cities places that underscore the variance in interpretations of culture. Cities have long been crucibles of culture synonymous with hierarchical, sanctioned "high culture" (Hall 1998). Dating back to a time when urban elites valued the city, this "arts and letters" view of culture equates cultural institutions (e.g., concert hall, theatres, museums, archives, universities and libraries) with urban "civilization" (Hall 1998). This formal and refined world of high culture is based in aesthetic aspirations and legitimizing practices that confer status on social groups with "cultural capital" who appear superior "even to those who do not participate" and who, "through a negative process of inculcation", see their own practices as inferior (Bourdieu 1993: 24). The cumulative built heritage of cities – its architecture, landscapes, toponymy, memorials – are the cultural remnants of differing urban ideals and technological innovations, serving both as testament and witness of past urban cultures and reflecting state and private philanthropic patronage (Findley 2005). This built heritage substantively informs the image and uniqueness of cities. In a competitive global world, cities market themselves through their distinctive cultural amenities, reorienting their economies towards the revenues generated by cultural and creative industries (e.g., advertising, architecture, graphic and industrial design, film, radio and television, software and gaming, publishing and print media, fashion and food, music and performing arts), entrepreneurially fusing local character with a global symbolic economy that stresses authenticity and creativity in a never-ending quest for unique cultural investments (Zukin 2010). In contemporary urban economies, it is culture that "attracts, sells, brings people together, entertains, appeals, and impresses" because it bridges divides of the local-specific and the global-universal through "a dialogue that transcends language and imperfect translations, as well as codes, beliefs, religions, and differences of all manners" (Brault & Kaplansky 2010: 6). In these different ways, then, culture has been understood as a symbolic resource for urban political and economic agendas, as a framework defining human experiences or as a source of agency and interpretation through heterogeneous practices and infrastructure (Chen & Kanna 2012: 8).

CULTURE IN THE URBAN "INFRASTRUCTURAL MOMENT"

Urban infrastructure and its renewal have come to the fore in the contemporary "hard" and "large" public "infrastructural moment" of city (re)making (Amin 2014), but a notable infrastructural gap remains with regards to culture. Urban infrastructure scholarship trains on municipal public goods and engineering assets, platforms that connect people through material and virtual spaces. It focuses on substantive multi-level government and private sector financial and symbolic investments, prioritizing the construction and maintenance of engineered transportation, communication, sanitation and energy systems (see Graham & McFarlane 2015; McFarlane & Rutherford 2008). According to Calhoun (1992), this "infrastructure of modernity" is what undergirds the expansionary impetus of capitalist urbanization, making possible the urban era's large-scale social relationships (Lefebvre 2003). Embedded in wider processes of rationalization and technoscientific expertise, infrastructure is "presented as modernity itself", becoming integral to the development of the modern state and the very functionality of cities (Gandy 2014: 4). A Latin-based French word meaning "underneath or below the structure" (Merriam-Webster Dictionary 2022), infrastructure was first used in the 1870s to refer to the substructure of a railroad bed and then later extended to Anglo-American hydrologic systems (Gandy 2014). Infrastructure refers to those often-hidden systems that create the material, political and cultural conditions upon which human action plays out and urban everyday life is built (Bingham-Hall & Kaasa 2018).

In urban planning and international development studies, infrastructure is treated as a fundamental driver of urban growth that is critical to reducing poverty and enhancing social welfare (Beall *et al.* 2019). After having initially treated infrastructure as technocratic and "mundane to the point of boring", these social facets of infrastructure came to the fore through a critical social science perspective (Star 1999: 376). Largely about engineering and macro-scale government projects, infrastructure had been associated with "unexciting ... lists of numbers and technical specifications, and hidden mechanisms subtending those processes more familiar to social scientists" (Star 1999: 377). Star's social critique identifies nine key properties of infrastructure, including its embeddedness, transparency and scope, but also its capacity to be learned through conventions of practice and standards, while also being dependent upon a local fixity for its base installation, only becoming visible when deteriorating. Building on Star, Gandy (2011) views infrastructure as a material manifestation of social norms that give physical form to the common needs of citizens yet skew towards biopolitically managed majority interests. Similarly, Furlong (2020) signals how infrastructure's users become disembodied urban subjects due to the universal and generic way that it serves social needs.

Inspired by science and technology studies, Graham and Marvin's (2001) now classic book *Splintering Urbanism* initiated such critical perspectives in urban studies. Infrastructure's networks and technical (im)mobilities reinforce urban inequalities through the geographically uneven distribution of resources and services, the circulation of knowledge, meaning and power, and the mobility of people and goods (Graham & Marvin 2001). Infrastructural inequalities also derive from the different rationalities and political choices of governance actors, urban categorizations and management practices and the affordances of technical objects (Pilo 2021). Graham and Marvin's (2022: 170) work catalysed "the politics of material infrastructure [as] a central focus of critical urban studies" within and beyond the social sciences and humanities.

As critical urbanists moved infrastructure into the methodological arena, more specific subfields have developed. An initial and key arena was the understanding of infrastructure as an instrument of power (Gandy 2004; Graham 2004). Highway overpasses, water conduits and electricity grids, for example, materialize power dynamics by reinforcing social inequities and making new ones (Datta & Ahmed 2020; Siemiatycki *et al.* 2020). Later research directed attention toward how governance unevenly shapes infrastructural provision and creates deficits and practices of disinvestment (Keil 2009; McFarlane & Rutherford 2008; Peck 2012). As "long-term, capital-intensive" objects of local and national state governance, the ownership, control, management, funding, finance and governance of urban infrastructure systems determines what infrastructure is provided, its costs, and "which people and places can access it and on what terms" (O'Brien *et al.* 2019: 1292). As the "setting and stake of social struggle" in the injustices and inequities of "the detritus of yesterday's spatial fixes", infrastructural objects are locally embedded while the regionalized multi-scalar jurisdictions that govern their provision simultaneously connect citizens to the wider region (Addie *et al.* 2020: 10–11).

In urban planning and policy, infrastructure is framed as a public good requiring careful planning, procurement, delivery and maintenance (Dodson 2009). Whether the common infrastructure is social housing, sewage, telecommunications, subways or airports, infrastructure is provided predominantly by a combination of public and private actors, but neoliberal entrepreneurialism emphasizes profit-driven public–private partnerships at the expense of the provision of the common good (Steele & Legacy 2017). Such infrastructural public goods "condition the social world by shaping subjects and publics" and "bringing new subject types into being" through individual encounters with their systems (Angelo & Hentschel 2015: 307). Built into infrastructure's production are assumptions about who will use it and how. But this "obduracy" of "infrastructural settlement" can also be challenged through inhabitation (Latham & Wood 2015).

Interdisciplinary urban scholarship, therefore, understands infrastructure not just as systems that provide the services that people rely on in their daily lives (O'Brien *et al.* 2019), but also as an everyday lived experience in and of itself (Graham & McFarlane 2015). In what Simone (2021: 1341) initially treated as a "'throw-away' formulation", "people as infrastructure" theoretically extended understandings of infrastructure by linking its materiality to everyday urban activities (Simone 2004). It theoretically extended infrastructure to include the urban conjunctions between "complex combinations of objects, spaces, persons, and practices" and their fluid, mobile and provisional intersections (Simone 2004: 407–8). Departing from a sociological emphasis on social bonds, ideology, and habitus and emphasizing "a 'mathematics' of continuous recombination of people's experiences and practices", Simone (2021: 1341) had rendered "people's actions as technical".

People thus become infrastructure when they act collectively to create possibilities outside of the generic intentions of formal planning and governance frameworks, when they make subaltern embodied spatial claims and fend for themselves by improvising tasks in the crevices and discards of the mainstream (Wilson & Jonas 2021). In their different material and political universes, they "find new ways of doing, thinking, and relating in response to everyday problems that are usually taken for granted", demonstrating cultural practices that resourcefully disturb urban orders (Hamdi 2010: 35). Exemplified by the makeshift urbanism of the subaltern, informal infrastructure is a malleable, mobile and continuous effort to build a future without a future, to make infrastructure political through acts of displacement and translation (McFarlane & Vasudevan 2014). Underpinning social action, infrastructure is "a political process that delivers and dispossesses citizenship rights and responsibilities" (Lemanski 2022: 667), providing the venues for infra-political claims-making through negotiation, disobedience and contestation (Kleinman 2014; Sizek 2021). These spatial claims are, however, often discounted by the state unless "they are manifested in behaviours that can be measured, subjected to the probabilities of specific outcomes, and ally with political and economic projects that seek to define and mobilize them" (Simone 2021: 1344).

Despite this attention to people and their everyday practices as infrastructure, the dominant streams of infrastructural analysis privilege social, political and environmental concerns rather than cultural. When culture is addressed, it is largely through ethnographic interpretations of everyday infrastructural practices rather than the analysis of *cultural infrastructure* on its own terms. Amin's (2014) "lively" infrastructure, for example, refers to what he calls the "culture of the commons", a communal landscape that emerges from the interplay between collective culture, the infrastructural aesthetics of place and social praxis. Amin explains how the aesthetics, curation and discursive meanings of such communal landscapes inform sociality, but their cultural role as infrastructure remains undefined. In *Seeing like a City*, Amin and Thrift (2017) argue that the globally accelerated upscaling and densification of infrastructure in cities has rendered it "no longer an effect but a cause", its many layers contributing to the new, human-driven geological era known as the Anthropocene (Amin & Thrift 2017: 34). Theorized indirectly as cultural in terms of being "the bedrock of civilization" and a "structure of contact", for Amin and Thrift (2017: 49, 27) infrastructure's expression as culture is "what shows up as real at any juncture" (Amin & Thrift 2017: 27). The real takes material form (the stones, bricks, woods, plastics, metals and glass entangled in urban building, road, railway and computer networks, water, waste and electricity systems) (Gandy 2014), but includes the procedural and political elements of infrastructure that enable the rationalization of urban space. In its "standardization, technical compatibility, professional rivalry, bureaucratic imperatives, regulatory competences and general dispositions" infrastructure "allow[s] thing[s], quite literally, to fit together" while practices of repair maintain infrastructure, working to guarantee its presence (Amin & Thrift 2017: 27). Infrastructure becomes the Anthropocene by providing cities with a sense of direction that both channels human life and determines access to its various paths. Its cultural resonance only emerges in its temporal registers: where infrastructure "provides the trails from the past into the future" it does "not just locate us but tell[s] us *what* we are" (Amin & Thrift 2017: 65, emphasis in original).

Within this infrastructural turn, where then is culture found and how has it been addressed? Crossing between the visible and invisible domains of urban space, infrastructure is understood to simultaneously unify and divide communities through its accomplishments and failures, to resolve but also create urban environmental problems, and to produce uneven patterns of socio-spatial (dis)advantage and (in)equity (Steele & Legacy 2017). Critical infrastructure is "a multidimensional and lived phenomenon" that is "as much about space, place, ecology and culture, as it is about pipes, scaffolding, wire and concrete" (Steele & Legacy 2017: 3). Indeed, Graham and McFarlane (2015) underscore how urban infrastructure becomes cultural because it mediates everyday life. It imbricates in subtly important ways not just technology, nature and politics through socio-political agendas that materialize and concentrate power, control and access, but also culture through the organization and representation of space. In Dourish and Bell's (2007: 428) work on computation, space is infrastructural, organized both practically and culturally. In cultural terms, "space becomes infrastructure for the collective production and enactment of cultural meaning" (Dourish & Bell 2007: 415). Cultural understandings provide a frame for meaningful spatial encounter that relates to human activities, an idea that corresponds with Star's (1999: 379) ethnographic understanding of infrastructure as coming with cultural "points of view". While these interpretations suggest that infrastructure is itself cultural – that it is a representation of universalized cultural norms but also a way of seeing and inhabiting cities – infrastructure is also definitively a set of cultural products contingent upon the struggles to materialize different and competing urban imaginaries (Gandy 2011). Within the infrastructural turn, therefore, culture has been treated primarily as a representational by-product of the social without considering cultural infrastructure as its own fundamental networked system that is no less subterraneously foundational to the life of cities.

THEORETICAL FRAGMENTS OF URBAN CULTURAL INFRASTRUCTURE

As the infrastructural turn accelerated, proliferating into many realms of urban studies, attention to cultural infrastructure was largely absent (Duxbury *et al.* 2008). Unable to gather theoretical momentum, the infrastructure of urban culture has been treated as secondary to other more economistic planning and policy priorities of culture-led redevelopment in the informing fields of study – creative cities, cultural capitals, cultural districts, cultural industries, cultural ecosystems and cultural mapping – that do not address infrastructure directly. When cultural infrastructure is addressed, it is often from the vantage point of the empirically grounded specificities of place-, discipline- or venue-based case studies.

Within the competitive creative city dynamics of twenty-first-century global urbanism, "aspirational cultural strategies" instrumentalize culture and cultural infrastructure in financial terms as recognizable "cultural amenities, for the discerning 'global eye' of the transnational corporate class" (Zukin 2012: 31). The spectacular cultural infrastructure of flagship museums, art galleries, theatres and opera houses have provided data for indexing and ranking creative cities relative to one another, inviting them to enviously compete for a higher status in global hierarchies. As Florida's (2002) comparative methodology gained international popularity, its critics asserted: "Who would not want their city to be scientifically ranked as the coolest on earth: the most creative city? It makes the residents feel good, politicians feel even better, and makes outsiders envious: so much so that they might even visit" (Pratt 2008: 109). But these rankings obscure the contradictions of the culture-capital compromise and the ways in which creative cities also incubate their own rapidly disappearing vernacular culture in fragmented networks of neighbourhood and community spaces. The very grassroots cultural infrastructure used to promote the uniqueness of each city is eclipsed by commodified global cultural flows and gentrification processes. The creative people and places that buttress this new centrality are displaced due to the lack of affordable land and buildings that reduce financial risk and make practices of experimentation and creativity possible (Bain 2010). Culture is created by creative people and projects that need to be based somewhere within "creative cities" or "cultural capitals", requiring dedicated cultural infrastructure.

Among European cities, policies promoting cultural infrastructure and making it an investment priority became a source of inter-urban competition with the establishment in 1983 of the European City of Culture programme. Adjudicated by the European Commission, it provides annual awards to different European cities in recognition of their cultural vibrancy. It is one of the most comprehensive initiatives to establish "cultural space" in European cities (Sassatelli 2008). More than an annual festival that showcases a city's culture, the initiative is also a "venue for exchange, debate, and reflection" about cultural "unity in diversity" (Sassatelli 2008: 234). Heritage-rich, high cultural cities like Athens, Florence, Berlin, Paris and Amsterdam were some of the first to receive this designation. After Glasgow leveraged the title in 1990 to initiate culture-led regeneration, subsequent awardee cities have continued the competitive practice of publicly investing in "new cultural infrastructure" (Džupka & Gróf 2021) to enhance arts space capacity and audience development, but often without legacy planning for ongoing cultural programming, management and access by local populations (Dova *et al.* 2022). Rebuilding cities as capitals of creativity and culture, however, meant large-scale urban redevelopment schemes of purpose-built cultural infrastructure and cultural district clustering in adaptively reused industrial infrastructure that simultaneously displaced communities formed in previous eras (Gallen 2015).

Case studies of specific cultural districts highlight these synergies and displacements at a micro-scale. Zukin's (1982) case study of SoHo, New York, inspired the place-based study of culture and capital by demonstrating how the reproduction of an artistic lifestyle initiated the gentrification of the city's industrial infrastructure. Hae (2011) demonstrates how the "spatial fix" of designated nightlife districts in Lower Manhattan stimulated the successive gentrification of surrounding districts. Mommaas' (2004: 510–11, 516) study of the Rotterdam Museum Quarter describes how the creation of "a mixed cultural infrastructure of bistros, bars, galleries and arts education centres" resulted in overinvestment in consumption-oriented "physical 'hardware'" to the neglect of the production-oriented "cultural 'software'". Driven by the common physical and communicative culture, leisure and tourism amenity priorities of the "new middle class" (museums, theatres, cafes, bars, restaurants and "interesting" architecture), such cultural clusters have played a key role in "the recentralisation or recommodification of urban space, turning old and often forgotten vernacular places into vibrant, fashionable spaces" (Mommaas 2004: 526), but the spatial pressure they exert crowds out the "critical cultural infrastructure" needed to support the local creative economy and the "city's ambience or image of creativity, openness, and/or cosmopolitanism" (Mommaas 2004: 523). As Leslie and Rantisi (2011) have interpreted, the success of cultural districts depends upon the development of a "critical infrastructure" that mediates risk and uncertainty in cultural production for creative workers by delivering a mix of "spatial, professional and cultural qualities" that allow for "contexts of trust, socialisation, knowledge, inspiration, exchange and incremental innovation" (Mommaas 2004: 521).

The concept of cultural and creative industries stems from neo-Marxist critiques of the rise of mass culture and its impacts on production and commodification of creative practices such as visual arts, music production, performance and literature under industrial capitalism (Hartley *et al.* 2012). Adorno and Horkheimer (1979 [1947]) coined the term "cultural industries" to direct attention towards the debasement of art and culture brought by industrialization and promoted through mid-century cultural policies (Hesmondhalgh & Pratt 2005). Rising prosperity, literacy and leisure in the global North along with new media and "hardware" for the dissemination and consumption of culture accelerated the growth of cultural industries. By the 1980s, urban policymakers began to emphasize the economic dimensions of local cultural industries and direct urban planning towards their incubation in dedicated but short-lived cultural quarters (Hesmondhalgh & Pratt 2005). For example, through a seeming "magical injection of culture" London's Hoxton Square – once home to marginalized social populations and a centre for furniture and textile production – was temporarily regenerated by British artists of the 1990s "Cool Britannia" era who were later displaced as it became the epicentre of Britain's new media industry (Pratt 2009: 1042). Clusters of cultural industries in quarters, Pratt (2009: 1043) argues, are the starter fuel for private residential property development that generates "precious little redistribution, or spread effect, and little space or opportunity for cultural producers" themselves.

As academic and policymaking interest in cultural and creative industries accelerated at the turn of the twenty-first century, it continued to raise fundamental questions about the shifting relationships between culture, economics, governance and public policy under successive waves of the neoliberal marketization of creative labour and instrumentalization of culture (Hesmondhalgh & Pratt 2005). Foord's (2009: 98) analysis of public policies and strategic plans to promote city-regional development of creative industries in Barcelona, Berlin and London, demonstrates that most infrastructural development is for cultural consumption with limited "higher level interventions in technology infrastructure" and an emphasis on public–private partnerships where investment was higher risk. Despite these common characteristics, the development of cultural industries within cities is strongly place-based. As Leslie and Rantisi's (2011: 1774) research on the Cirque du Soleil in Montreal attests, creative industries draw heavily on "place-specific resources" and "place-based images" which provide a localized comparative advantage to the creation of distinctive cultural products, synergistically generating city-regional revenue and employment. Educational synergies between the National Circus School and the Cirque du Soleil, for example, have produced qualified circus arts performers but also storage and rehearsal opportunities which were "particularly significant in the early years when this kind of infrastructure was cost-prohibitive for the Cirque" (Leslie & Rantisi 2011: 1783). This delicate balance between art and commerce was compromised as the Cirque became a global corporation internationally sourcing talent and staging more standardized productions that favoured shareholder value to the diminishment of skill development and tacit knowledge exchange (Leslie & Rantisi 2019). Local synergies in the creative industries foster cultural infrastructural development and innovation as part of wider urban cultural ecosystems.

A place-based understanding of cultural infrastructure and resources is reflected in scholarship that adopts a networked "ecology" approach. For Comunian (2011: 1174), a city's cultural infrastructure is part of the historically embedded "complex adaptive system" that emerges locally through dense sector-based actor and agency-based networks rather than through top-down universal cultural policies. Cultural ecologists treat culture in networked terms as "cultural ecosystems" or "cultural systems". This analogy is derived from early twentieth-century social Darwinist arguments that drew parallels between human and natural habitats to holistically appreciate the "complex of physical factors" forming environments (Schippers 2016: 13). In the 1960s, anthropologists used this analogy to conceptualize the complex web of people, organizations, events and institutions that shaped "intangible cultural heritage" (Schippers 2016: 10). With the ensuing establishment of cultural studies and accelerating interest in urban cultural economies, a systems approach to culture gathered conceptual traction as a way to understand how different actors who produce, distribute, present and consume arts and culture interact and collaborate across different administrative domains within and beyond the visual, design and performing arts (Dameri & Demartini 2020). In cultural ecology terms, these include artists and cultural workers across different fields and genres, in conjunction with leaders of small, independent organizations, non-profit community groups and large established public institutions with their board members, volunteers, sponsors and participants who together "produce, present, organize, guide, regulate, and serve the cultural economy" (Markusen 2010: 814). Subsidized by public funds (municipal, regional and national), cultural ecosystems are connected, overlapping and heterogeneous with different degrees of cohesion and scales of interconnection (Borin & Donato 2015). With their complex interdependencies and heavy reliance upon public sector funding, cultural ecosystems are unstable and continuously changing, yet their infrastructure is regenerative as culture cycles from initial creativity, through curation, consumption and collection and, over time, becoming the heritage that stimulates innovation (Holden 2015).

Embedded in these cultural ecosystems are practitioners – arts organization administrators, artists and cultural planners – and activists, sometimes in concert with scholars, who interpret the cultural sector, script reports and inventory local cultural infrastructure for different levels of government from the municipal to the national (e.g., Ang *et al.* 2016; Duxbury *et al.* 2008). Such reports are often place-specific, classifying and mapping venues in cities or profiling singular facilities, and concluding with a series of recommendations for cultural policy and practice. They often leverage versions of cultural resource mapping to visualize cultural assets within communities with the goal of contributing to the creation of cultural infrastructure databases that can document the volume, visibility and analysis of spatial data (Ang *et al.* 2016). Nevertheless, such reports remain important for their pragmatic definitions of cultural infrastructure as well as their attention to interdependencies of hard and soft infrastructure. "Hard infrastructure" is usually treated as the physical bricks and mortar of facilities while "soft infrastructure" refers to the "physical, human, financial, cultural, and artistic resources" that operationalize and sustain cultural resources as community hubs (Duxbury *et al.* 2008: 39–40). Reporting on cultural infrastructure and its problems is not just a matter of ensuring that museums, theatres, libraries and archives are on government investment agendas (and negotiated alongside, but usually in competition with, roads, sewers, water pipes, recreation facilities and public transit); it is also about ensuring that cultural policies directly address cultural infrastructure as a distinctive policy issue.

It is only within the last few years that many Anglo-European cities have begun to more comprehensively inventory and plan for cultural infrastructure on a municipal and regional basis. In London, England, the Mayor issued a manifesto committing to the development of a cultural infrastructure strategy "to identify what we need in order to sustain London's future as a cultural capital" that was debated by academics and practitioners well before its release as an official plan (Theatrum Mundi 2019). Theatrum Mundi – a platform for learning about city-making through cross-disciplinary conversations between artists and urbanists founded by Richard Sennett and Adam Kaasa in 2012 – for example, ran three genre-based roundtable discussions (performance, making, the virtual) in 2016 with thought-leaders. Hosted by arts organizations that provide cultural infrastructure and using their *in situ* experience as a starting point for discussion, participants (artists, architects, writers, scholars, publishers and institutional leaders) debated whether the conditions for culture can be designed, leading to new questions about "the effects of cultural infrastructure on artists and the condition of their work" in London (Bingham-Hall & Kaasa 2018: 4). Three years later, the London Authority's Cultural Infrastructure Plan was released, detailing that the city's cultural infrastructure is at risk and identifying five specific issues contributing to losses of cultural venues: land value increases, the national planning system, business rate increases, licensing restrictions and funding reductions (Greater London Authority 2019b). By "recognizing the importance of production", the report signalled a shift in emphasis, an understanding that "a healthy cultural infrastructure is founded on production, on artistic creation, which is never quite as glamorous as imagined by those who do not make art; and cherished with a vengeance by those who do" (Green 2020: 245). The plan is complemented by an online, interactive Cultural Infrastructure Map inventorying 30 different categories of cultural spaces never previously cohered (Greater London Authority 2022b). It places individual venues alongside transportation routes and demographic data and indicates geographical clusters and permits a spatial understanding of agglomeration economies. What constitutes "cultural infrastructure" is wide-ranging, including archives, pubs, artists' studios and residences, community centres, music venues, built heritage at risk and even LGBTQ+ nightlife. The map is crowdsourced and interactive, enabling the public to share their cultural knowledge by adding new categories and venues. Such a dynamic mapping methodology is intended to capture how "ever changing and evolving" and "difficult to locate" cultural infrastructure is (Greater London Authority 2022b).

London's approach to cultural infrastructure has been interpreted more widely by Kim (2020: 201) as part of a municipal "infrastructural paradigm shift" that de-emphasizes the instrumentalization of culture as a "city-making" tool (Courage & McKeown 2018), instead offering the potential of "a more substantial and lasting set of urban conditions to transform and support the contribution of artists and the inhabitants of a given community over the long run". One of the drawbacks of an infrastructural approach to culture is that it creates local competition between cultural groups and organizations, initiating a zero-sum game where any limited investments in larger projects syphon away available investments for smaller initiatives and groups (Sennett 2018). Both London, England and Amsterdam, Netherlands, Kim (2020: 202) argues, have championed an infrastructural approach because of its potential to safeguard and nurture arts and culture by envisioning "the city in its entirety as a kind of cultural district". By de-emphasizing the monetization and consumption of culture and instead privileging artistic production, the cultural infrastructure approach broadens the scope of culture, to include "the provision of a wider set of physical, and social, infrastructural conditions to support this activity, rather than the construction of a set of buildings: the creation of potential rather than actualities" (Kim 2020: 202–3). To sustain urban cultural production requires spaces and infrastructure that can enhance connections between cultural producers and consumers through their coexistence in shared time and provides the instruments, resources and spaces for the exchange of ideas and creativity.

COHERING AND DEFINING URBAN CULTURAL INFRASTRUCTURE

From these fragmentary and indirect references to infrastructure in studies of urban culture emerges a new paradigm that coalesces the creative and cultural elements of cities as forming a distinct infrastructure. Urban cultural infrastructure is a relatively recent term that refers to a combination of buildings, facilities, spaces, practices, funding and legal frameworks, personal and institutional networks, and social media sites that support a common localized urban culture (Ang *et al.* 2016; Bingham-Hall & Kaasa 2018; Kim 2020). Synergistically aligned with Markusen's (2014) more place-based understanding of a cultural ecology, cultural infrastructure provides an integrated framework that "encompasses the many networks of arts and cultural creators, producers, presenters, sponsors, participants, and supporting casts embedded in diverse communities" and their "complex interdependencies" (Holden 2015: 6). Situating urban culture within the "wider political, social and economic environment with both proximate and remote connections" of culture, it parallels Holden's (2015: 22) "cultural environment", but avoids limiting cultural infrastructure to the built environment (theatres, concert halls, streets and parks). Live music venues are, for example, built infrastructure because they provide the space for performances, but they also serve as "physical, social and enabling spaces within a city that foster creative and cultural practices" (Gallen 2015: 557). Urban cultural infrastructure is thus more heterogeneous in its configuration, shaped through soft networks of people and places (Lawhon *et al.* 2018). By treating urban culture itself as an infrastructure, it becomes as serious and integral as water, electricity or transportation to the functioning of metropolitan areas while also circumventing the highly selective attachments of culture to specific parts of the city that drive cycles of neighbourhood economic revalorization (Kim 2020). If infrastructure is a way of seeing cities, it is based in an imagination that provides researchers of urban culture with the conceptual, theoretical and methodological tools for understanding how crucial culture is to city life, weaving its way "ubiquitously through time, space and place" (Steele & Legacy 2017: 1).

More concrete definitions of cultural infrastructure from detailed studies by scholar-practitioners working with different levels of government to define the cultural field are also useful for the strategic ways they operationalize the concept. The 2008 international symposium co-organized in Canada by the Centre of Expertise on Culture and Communities (CECC) at Simon Fraser University and the City of Ottawa entitled "Creative Construct: Building for Culture and Creativity" is a case in point. The intent was to address "the largely neglected infrastructural realm of *cultural infrastructure*" within "mainstream" reports and studies in the arena of cultural policy and planning scholarship on urban creative economies and communities (Duxbury *et al.* 2008: 2, emphasis in original). A follow-up report co-authored by the then director of CECC, Nancy Duxbury, focuses on the Canadian context, summarizing the state of the nation's cultural infrastructure, cultural policy-funding frameworks and supporting partnership models (Duxbury *et al.* 2008). This report attributes growing public interest in cultural infrastructure to different factors: economic restructuring, changing demographics (particularly the divergent interests of older adults, youth and ethno-culturally diverse populations), cultural sector growth and changing multi-disciplinary creative needs, and aging infrastructure. The main issues they identify are municipal cultural infrastructural deficits in conjunction with cultural facility obsolescence (the use of unsafe or non-compliant spaces), and jeopardized public legacies (due to under-resourcing the budgets required to maintain cultural assets). The report advocates rethinking governance approaches to cultural infrastructure, directing "greater attention to issues of lifecycle, productivity, the interaction of social and built infrastructure, and long-term sustainability" (Duxbury *et al.* 2008: 10) because, as facilities age (especially beyond 35 years), they become expensive to operate, refit and replace.

The "Creative Construct" report also provides a pragmatic understanding of cultural infrastructure (Duxbury *et al.* 2008). By counting, measuring and inventorying Canada's cultural infrastructure, it provides comparable and policy-relevant statistical data about type, quantity, location, condition and use. It treats cultural infrastructure as "physical assets and spaces whether they are full time or part time, single purpose or multipurpose, historic or contemporary that have cultural products and accommodate and satisfy the requirements of cultural activities and cultural industry" within wider cultural and community ecosystems (Duxbury *et al.* 2008: 17). Although a lack of standardization and consistency within inventories is acknowledged, from a performance/exhibition perspective, five categories of cultural infrastructure (e.g., defined-cultural-use facilities, multi-disciplinary spaces, multi-function centres, multi-use venues and adaptive reuse of unconventional spaces) are proposed. This fivefold typology also acknowledges practical distinctions between cultural facilities including spaces of presentation, production, live-work, multi-functionality, preservation/collection, education/training and administration/ancillary. In the Australian context, Ang *et al.* (2016) have developed a parallel "spatial domain" framework for Sydney that distinguishes between spaces of: community and participation; practice, education and development; commerce and enterprise; performance and exhibition; and festivals and events. They also use the dimensions of the relational value chain (creation, production, dissemination, use and education) to identify types of cultural venues and networks of cultural flows facilitated through digital networks.

Together, the definitions, categories and classifications of cultural infrastructure reflected in Duxbury *et al.*'s (2008) and Ang *et al.*'s (2016) reports determine what is seen, counted, planned for, and funded within cultural governance frameworks while also informing what is discussed as infrastructure by academics and city leaders. Moreover, these pragmatic spatial approaches to cultural infrastructure reflect Larkin's (2013) arguments about the "conceptually unruly" character of infrastructure. Larkin asserts that this unruliness stems from an ontological duality between infrastructure as "things" and as "the relation between things". For Larkin (2013: 329), infrastructure is distinctive because its "objects ... create the grounds on which other objects operate, and when they do so they operate as systems".

This more relational understanding of infrastructure as more than spaces, buildings and venues is echoed in cultural infrastructural research that emphasizes networks of creativity. Borrup's (2011: 21) research on Silicon Valley, for example, defines "new cultural infrastructure" as "loose networks of practicing artists along with large, medium, and small non-profit organizations and facilities designed to encourage various forms of cultural expression and group activities". It uncovers the unique ecosystem of a more "decentralized, nonhierarchical, participatory, and culturally diverse" infrastructure within which many American urban arts organizations struggle to survive (Borrup 2011: 18). To characterize the cultural infrastructure of this spatially dispersed, rapidly growing and ethno-culturally diverse yet socially polarized and disenfranchising city-region notorious for its high cost of living and entrepreneurial support for technological innovation, the idea of cultural infrastructure is broadened to include a wider array of activities beyond what is usually considered "cultural" (e.g., "educational, religious, civic, recreational, commercial, neighborhood, family, and social settings") (Borrup 2011: 21). Others embrace such a holistic approach, stressing the importance of creating spaces and integrating cultural identities into the definition of cultural infrastructure beyond artistic production itself. For example, *Making Space for Culture in Sydney: Cultural Infrastructure Study 2020* recently stated that "cultural infrastructure is increasingly being thought of not as specific types of buildings, but as the spaces in which diverse, multicultural populations exercise their own creative practices and create common cultural identities" (City of Sydney 2020: 4). In Canada, the Vancouver's *Making Space for Arts and Culture: 2018 Cultural Infrastructure Plan* (City of Vancouver 2018) reinforces the necessity of a holistic understanding of cultural infrastructure precisely because the main issue that cultural providers identify is shared by many marginalized communities – a dearth of affordable spaces to live and work and a consequent displacement from existing spaces and neighbourhoods because of a lack of property ownership.

In cities around the world, cultural infrastructure is under threat of diminishment from urban (re)development real estate incursions by housing, retail and tourism sectors. Pollio *et al.* (2021: 780) examine how the "fragile existence" of cultural infrastructure evolves under displacement pressure from waves of gentrification and super-gentrification. They underscore the "makeshift economies" and "spatial strategies of survival" and physical, organizational, and economic transformations that "creative workers embrace to maintain cultural infrastructure that is endangered rather than driven by urban redevelopment" (Pollio *et al.* 2021: 780). Cultural policy is often identified as the key tool municipalities can leverage to "protect" and "support" cultural infrastructure in the face of increasing land values and demands for public funds and to reinforce its continued socio-economic importance to urban life (Džupka & Gróf 2021). It is only by treating the provision of adequate and suitable cultural infrastructure as vital to competitive urban regeneration strategies – on par with managing roads, energy and waste – that municipalities and metropolitan authorities bring them to light as integrated, already-existing systems, with lifespans and vulnerabilities in the face of waning active participation and global health crises, like the Covid-19 pandemic (Gallen 2015).

COVID-19 AND THE FRAGILITY OF CULTURAL INFRASTRUCTURE

The Covid-19 public health crisis with its many non-medical social and economic impacts has wreaked havoc on an already fragile cultural ecosystem and its urban cultural infrastructure, exposing systemic problems of precarity and injustice (see Bain & McLean 2013). The pandemic not only reduced private spending on culture (Anheier *et al.* 2021), it presented "a stark 'new normal'" in which most cultural activity was "paused" (Pratt 2020: 1). Fluctuating lockdowns, prolonged confinements and the reduced use of public spaces and closure of venues meant dramatic losses of incomes for creative workers, self-employed freelancers within the gig economy (often the first to be cut in economizing measures), along with casual, temporary and part-time workers who are often ineligible for government support packages (Khlystova *et al.* 2022). There were also differential impacts on the various components of urban cultural infrastructure.

Many exhibitions, concerts, festivals, tours and solo performances were cancelled and then later moved online through video-conferencing and screencasts. Publicly funded cultural venues that traditionally offered face-to-face services (e.g., museums, archives, libraries, theatres and concert halls) were sustained, in part, by financial aid from the state and philanthropists. Such aid helped finance the rapid adoption of digital technologies and the development of digital infrastructure, permitting a reorganization of interactions with clientele (Khlystova *et al.* 2022). It also provided the technical support needed to adapt to health and safety requirements for physical distancing and changing business models. Libraries, for example, demonstrated strong resilience during the pandemic while also attracting more readers, in part because the development of a "digital safety net" gave them more affordable access to shared digital technologies through consortia membership (Khlystova *et al.* 2022: 1200). Many smaller companies and independent cultural producers survived by relying upon digital tools and services to keep their businesses operating in a socially distanced manner (Escalona-Orcao *et al.* 2020). As a pandemic mitigation tool, the rapid uptake of digitization and video-conferencing along with reliance upon websites and social media enabled some continuity in work, education, medicine, social lives and creative output, but, as Pratt (2020: 2) asserted, "recovery from this may well do fatal damage to our cultural infrastructure (hard and soft)". Emergency relief job support for cultural workers was recommended in international reports like the OECD's *Culture Shock* (Travkina & Sacco 2020) and *Culture in Crisis* (UNESCO 2020) and mirrored in local measures that offered rent holidays for buildings, job retention wage subsidies, self-employment income support, and digital capabilities training (Yue 2022).

However, "[t]he cultural economy of cities is not something that can simply be rejuvenated with the 'flick of a switch'" (Pratt 2020: 1). Moreover, the uneven resilience of cultural infrastructure is often closely aligned with place-specific urban governance capacities, namely the extent of funding, types of decisions made, and the kinds of policies implemented (Anheier *et al.* 2021).

Early in the crisis, a Brookings Institute report (Florida & Seman 2020) estimated the impacts of Covid-19 on the American creative economy (including industries such as film, advertising and fashion and creative occupations such as musicians, artists, performers and designers). In a limited four-month study period in 2020, the losses included sales, employment and earnings in these fields at various scales (national, state and metropolitan) totalling 2.7 million jobs and $150 billion in sales nationally (Florida & Seman 2020: 3). It predicted that the Covid-19 crisis would bring the greatest employment losses in the American south and the greatest loss in sales revenues in the west and northeast. Those city-regions with dense clusters of creative industry employment and sales such as New York and Los Angeles would experience the greatest absolute losses while smaller metropolitan areas with clusters of creative industry jobs such as Las Vegas, Nashville or New Orleans would experience greater proportional losses in overall employment and sales revenues (Florida & Seman 2020: 4).

What might be read as an atomized interpretation of cultural industries that never mentions cultural infrastructure and reduces it to descriptive statistics, the Brookings Institute report does make recommendations that have infrastructural dimensions. Proposing that "the crisis provides an opportunity 'to shift to locally sourced culture'", the report suggests civic re-localization to harness multi-scalar funding networks and public–private partnerships (Florida & Seman 2020: 4). It advocates support for the sector's soft infrastructure by addressing the immediate economic needs of artists and developing an equivalent federal recovery response to that of other industries by providing greater financial investment in arts, culture and creative organizations with particular attention to smaller non-profits and businesses that have limited financial cushions. Regarding harder infrastructural elements, it suggests that municipalities might also temporarily reduce retail and commercial real estate prices in city centres, creating "a window of opportunity" by "making studio, gallery, and small-scale performance spaces available … in neighborhoods and districts where there is increased vacancy due to COVID-19" (Florida & Seman 2020: 21). While the study recognizes the heterogeneity and centrality of the cultural sector to regional economies and urban liveability, the temporary character of the proposed funding in conjunction with the inevitable volatility of property markets means that they are only stop-gap measures. Cultural infrastructure is no more stable or viable with what this report proposes than it was under pre-pandemic conditions of exclusivity and displacement.

In this new urban cultural landscape of Covid-induced uncertainty, the patterns of consumption, entertainment, tourism and commuting that drove creative cities abruptly stopped, calling into question the very purpose of city centres and their cultural districts (Whiting *et al.* 2022). As emergency and recovery have fused together, seeming to stretch indefinitely across unanticipated time horizons, the pandemic has both re-domesticated and privatized creative lives while simultaneously laying bare systemic vulnerabilities within the cultural sector (Pacella *et al.* 2021). This global crisis, as refracted through different urban contexts, illuminated "in all-too-lurid detail" its destructive impact on cultural livelihoods and institutions, reconfiguring governments' and policymakers' understandings and valuations of arts and culture and "what they are prepared to do, on what grounds and with what capacity" (Banks & O'Connor 2021: 4). In an ambiguous position between public service (social development) and innovative industry (economic development), throughout the pandemic the cultural sector asserted its communal value above and beyond economic metrics, offering comfort, community, distraction, beauty and insight. While the richest of nations were able to offer fiscal bailouts and commitments to ongoing reinvestment to shore-up cultural infrastructure and "'save' culture" with different degrees of responsiveness and comprehensiveness, many of the poorest had to abandon it to its own devices in the face of competing and more pressing demands (Banks & O'Connor 2021: 7). The entry to a post-pandemic world is a critical juncture for cultural infrastructure because it is not inevitable that "what came earlier [will] continue to underpin what follows" (Lefebvre 1991: 229). Neither the spatial arrangements of cultural institutions nor the flexible and mobile human creativity that animate and connect them have proved to be as durable and resilient as once imagined, reinforcing an informed and strategic policy interventionist role for city governments if culture is to remain foundational to the urban fabric of the future (Anheier *et al.* 2021).

CONFIGURING URBAN CULTURAL INFRASTRUCTURE

This book investigates the infrastructuring of culture through its grounding in heterogeneous socio-spatial arrangements of the urban, both pre- and post-Covid-19. Such an infrastructural lens cuts across urban spaces from centres to peripheries. It brings to the fore the entanglements of infrastructural objects within urban landscapes that tend to "recede from view and become part of people's sense of being ... tangled through time in multiple relations" (Castán Broto *et al.* 2021). Treating cultural infrastructure as networks of dynamic artefacts that spatially and temporally organize culture in cities, it argues that urban cultural infrastructure emerges from tense entanglements of "hard" capital investments in facilities (e.g., public libraries, museums, archives, theatres, studios and galleries) and "soft" revenue investments in people and their work (e.g., funding for artistic projects, information and knowledge networks, outreach programming, educational collaborations and events). While the former is visibly leveraged within many urban regeneration toolkits through rapid capital investment, the latter is processual, relatively invisible, and less likely to be maintained over longer periods of time. Despite their different temporalities and visibilities, the permanence of hard cultural infrastructure is necessarily dependent upon the fluctuations of its soft counterparts which sustain its viability over the long term. The book analytically enriches cultural planning and creative city policy traditions that heretofore have made municipal recommendations based upon mapping and classifying cultural venues to quantify cultural assets and clusters. To counter the instrumentalization of culture as entrepreneurial capital asset, this book pragmatically investigates the interplay between the "hard" and "soft" dimensions of urban cultural infrastructure across a range of different sites, cities, and scales.

The collection addresses four central and related questions regarding the cultural infrastructure of cities. First, to attend to the "hard" infrastructure underlying cultural production, it asks how is urban culture produced in particular physical and virtual venues and with what dynamics of creativity, innovation and ensuing spatial politics? Second, it considers how is the cultural infrastructure of cities animated by "soft" networked and digital flows and relations that create tensions for governance, design and usage? Third, what adaptations and responses to systemic challenges of austerity, exclusion and inequality have occurred in urban cultural infrastructure to articulate forms of solidarity, care and community within and beyond crises like Covid-19? Finally, with respect to durability and maintenance, what capacities does the cultural infrastructure of cities have to foster more resilient and hopeful urban futures? While not the only questions to consider, these four do represent important trajectories in the resurgent interest in urban cultural infrastructure.

Offering a renewed focus on cultural infrastructure, this book provokes urban planners, policymakers, architects, developers and scholars to (re) consider the (im)material and (in)visible ways that culture is produced and expressed within cities as parts of cultural cycles and value chains (Ang *et al.* 2016). According to UNESCO (2009), a "cultural cycle" integrates the five dimensions of cultural production that include creation (authoring of new creative content), production (creating cultural products with specialist tools), dissemination (bringing cultural products to consumers), exhibition/reception/transmission (creating cultural consumption experiences and transmitting knowledge), and consumption and participation (consumption of cultural products and activities). These dimensions of the cultural cycle parallel elements within the value chain of creative industries, which cycle through the creative process from making to dissemination to exhibition/reception to archiving/preserving to education/understanding (Ang *et al.* 2016). The themes of the collection borrow from these categories and develop in progression, focusing on the role of cultural infrastructure in producing, performing, consuming and collecting culture. While based on an extensive literature in arts, education and sociology about professional arts education within "art worlds" (that provide training, collective communities of practice and emphasize knowledge exchange while addressing issues of representation, equitable participation in, and the valuing of culture) (Becker 1982), the educational component of the value chain does not have its own section. Rather, (in)formal educational elements figure within different chapters, underscoring that cultural production never occurs in a void but rather is "necessarily related to the work of others ... within communities of affiliation" inside and outside of cultural institutions (Irwin & Springgay 2008: xxiv). To render the actions of production, performance, consumption and collection more active, the section titles have been transformed into gerunds. Each section enacts cultural infrastructure through activity and addresses a series of related urban micro-geographical spatial configurations ranging from building venues to streets to neighbourhoods, to districts, to entire cities.

Each section begins with original artwork by the Canadian-based and Indian-born architect, visual artist and geographer Chan Arun-Pina. This section art provides a cultural infrastructural palimpsest that progressively builds conceptual relationships between the chapters. It is followed by short introductions that facilitate regional dialogues between contributors, accentuating differences in levels of urban cultural resourcing, governance and vulnerability. First, *Producing Culture* considers spatial infrastructural settings, both purpose-built and adapted venues, where the labour of cultural production takes place and the conditions for creative action are established. Second, *Performing Culture* foregrounds the sometimes (in)visible and (in)audible urban backstages that variously support the uncertainties, vulnerabilities and experiments that are part of cultural performance in theatres, community centres and public spaces. Third, *Consuming Culture* returns to the more established field of urban consumptive cultures, considering the (in)formal production and appropriation of urban space by everyday consumers, hipster retailers, independent fashion designers and street vendors. Fourth, *Collecting Culture* analyses grassroots and civic institutions such as museums, libraries and community archives to appreciate the "hard" and "soft" synergies that support the adaptation of these repositories of culture. While these sections highlight the many components of urban cultural infrastructure, the fluid boundaries between them challenge binaries such as production and consumption or performance and collection. Inevitably, the ideas about urban cultural infrastructure in the various chapters overflow their sectional boundaries.

A lateral approach to the many components of urban cultural infrastructure shapes the book's geographical vision. With a "light touch", it "comparatively gestures" to cities embedded in different regional contexts (Robinson 2016: 196). Rather than reinforcing the spatial and temporal hierarchies implied by the pejorative binary of an "advanced" global North and a colonized and "lagging" global South, the book adopts a middling logic informed by provincialization (Leitner & Sheppard 2016). The objective is to map alternative cartographies through the already familiar terrain of the culture of cities by finding new pathways between them and looking sideways at their similarities regardless of size and centrality within global urban hierarchies (Chen & Kanna 2012). As such, the collection modestly responds to the call to disrupt hegemonic urban theory by avoiding the universalism of the paradigmatic city as the implied standard of measure through the juxtaposition of case studies that connects major world cities to less familiar, secondary ones (Robinson 2016). It assembles a diverse repertoire of cities from different regions, including Europe and the United Kingdom (Berlin, Dublin, Leipzig, London, Munich and Utrecht), Oceania (Melbourne and Sydney), North America (Hamilton, Montreal, New Orleans and Toronto), Latin America (Medellín, Oaxaca and São Paulo) and South and Southeast Asia (Ahmedabad and Singapore).

Paralleling comparative urbanism's goal of moving away from authoritative theory generated in dominant urban centres to "think" different cities together (Robinson 2016), this collection draws a variety of cities into open-ended conversation. To extend research on urban cultural infrastructure, it emphasizes "shared features and variation across different cities, drawing cities around the world into analytical juxtaposition" (Robinson 2016: 190). Following Robinson (2016) and Caldeira (2017: 5), we treat juxtaposition, then, as a kind of comparison; rather than abstracting "the representative, typical, similar, or repetitive", the collection proceeds inductively, using juxtaposition to explore "the differential and internal conditions of cases, looking for a wide range of variation". By generating place-specific concepts with the possibility of wider applications, the collection valorizes more "provisional, modest and revisable claims about the nature of the urban" (Robinson 2016: 196).

CONCLUSION

The role of culture in cities around the world is a topic that has garnered significant traction within urban studies scholarship (Landry 2020). Culture and its infrastructure and activities are used through planning and policy governance frameworks to reimagine cities in the present and into the future, contributing financially to urban economies, socially to individual and community well-being and politically to justice (Redaelli & Stevenson 2022). Infrastructure, with its hubs, nodes and pathways that move people and goods while also reinforcing the circulation of knowledge and power, remains elemental to the urban, in its myriad forms, but also to culture. Infrastructure's hard artefacts and soft networked systems are what lie beneath and have long held together an ancient relationship between human culture and urbanism, making cities themselves archives and works of art. Across formal/informal, high/low and professional/amateur divides, people produce, perform, consume and collect culture in material spaces that are underpinned and shaped by infrastructural systems (Bingham-Hall & Kaasa 2018). While these infrastructural systems enfold, channel and even protect and defend culture, exposure to unanticipated conditions like the Covid-19 virus reveal both the sector's material vulnerability and its unpredictable future.

When an infrastructural imaginary is layered onto understandings of the cultures of cities, it offers a shift away from economistic and unevenly valorizing interpretations of culture as simply "cultural industries" or "creative economies". With its emphasis on providing the basis for the flourishing of multiple forms and practices of culture, cultural infrastructure has the potential to supersede the selective channelling of specific aspects of urban culture or the agglomeration of cultural activities within a single cultural district. It, therefore, offers "a genuine advance in arts and city-making strategy" that "moves beyond the creative placemaking approach" by providing a "breadth of vision" and potentially a deeper "commitment to supporting artistic practice in meaningful ways" (Kim 2020: 203). Attention to cultural infrastructure reveals urban culture's distinctive ecosystem that crosses internal physical boundaries within cities and includes a wider array of activities within its networks (Borrup 2011). Such an expanded view of urban culture based in networked infrastructure, specifically resonates with the fragilities revealed by the collapse and rebuilding of the cultural sector and its networks during and into the extended aftermath of the Covid-19 pandemic. This event has "rendered more visible and stark the significant diversities in urban dwellers' capacity to navigate the challenges of urban life" but has also underscored "the centrality of infrastructure and politics to this differentiation" for cultural workers and the cultural sector as a whole (Lemanski 2022: 664). By seeing the entire city as a cultural district, one that requires, produces and connects people to an infrastructure for culture, urban culture itself is broadened across space and horizontally to reveal what lies beneath. Finding and mapping new sites and revealing the sector's resourceful synergies demonstrates culture's utility for the common good, its just place at the centre of urban life and its importance beyond markets.

I

PRODUCING CULTURE

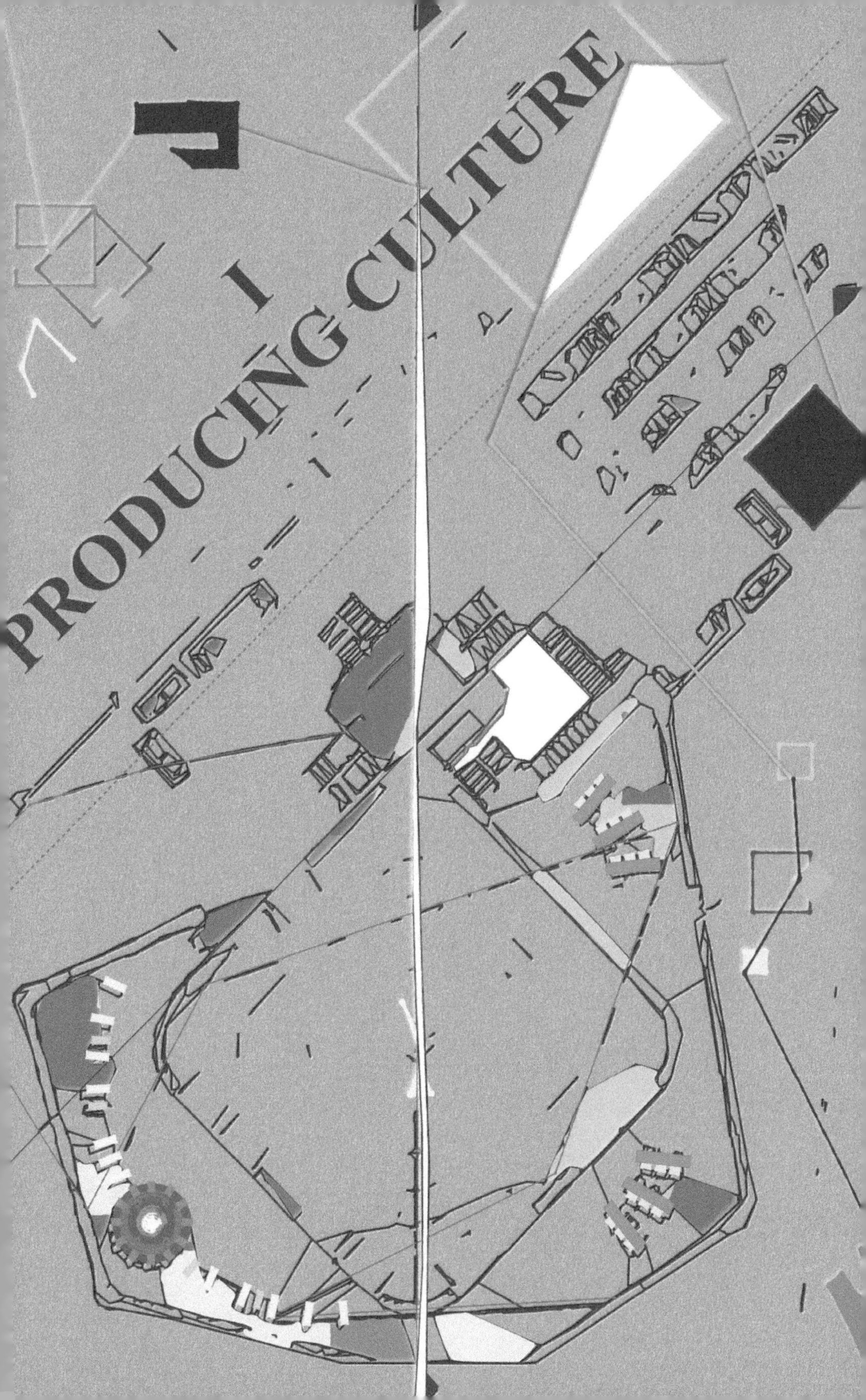

PART I

PRODUCING CULTURE

Cultural production – its services, activities and networks – are embedded in, and transformative of, places. Within cities, residential, industrial and commercial neighbourhood sites that fall into disrepair are revalorized through creative activity (Rantisi & Leslie 2010). Contemporary urban planning and policy solutions have leveraged the culture-capital compromise wherein the "authenticity" of artistic labour and the appeal of creative lifestyles (Zukin 1982) are employed to breathe new life into decaying urban industrial infrastructure – store fronts, strip malls, schools, religious institutions, factories and warehouses (Zukin 2010).

Sites of cultural production – where the process of artistic creation and art-making result in the fabrication of objects or activities – are often mythologized in the public imagination, yet they have straightforward infrastructural requirements. Spaces of cultural production demand the permanent storage of, and access to, tools, equipment and materials which suggests the need for stable locations that do not necessarily require the co-presence of audiences (Bingham-Hall & Kaasa 2018). Art schools are one such key site of cultural production, that resemble laboratories or factories of research, experimentation and innovation. In art schools, emerging communities of artists work at the avant-garde edge of their disciplines, looking "to the past and tradition for inspiration" but their "main currency" is "hip coolness, progressive ideas and place in the contemporary art scene" (Becker 2009: 38). Within this world of culture-making, it is the makers themselves who are highly esteemed, and those cultural workers – those artists – who gain critical attention for their labour who are most admired, along with the spaces they inhabit (Becker 2009).

Beyond art schools, art studios have long been privileged as sites for undisturbed experimentation with materials, sound, light, movement and ideas that constitute the making of cultural work as well as the formation of professional identities (Bain 2004, 2005). The studio is celebrated as a "space for ongoing as well as finished projects, colour, paintings, scraps, scribbles, prototypes, ideas, chaos, order, language" (Sjöholm 2014: 505–6). As a site to showcase oneself to curators and collectors, studios are not just places to make and store artwork. Rather, artists are collectors of objects and archivists of their own work and studios become places "where careers are stored and developed" and "where artists look both forward and backward in their practice" (Hawkins 2017: 91). Studios can just as easily be improvised within the multi-functional spaces of homes, on kitchen and dining room tables, in living rooms and in basements, where reproductive care and domestic lives intersect with creative practices (Bain 2007). In many respects, studios are mobile spaces connected to wider artistic networks of production and consumption (Daniels 2011) – to neighbourhoods, art scenes and cultural districts – through "space[s] of practice in relation to a whole series of other sites of collection, documentation, rumination, development and information" (Hawkins 2017: 97).

Cultural production is part of spatial networks that extend beyond individual studio needs to include a city's employment structure and housing market. Given the minimal employment regulation in the cultural sector, artists are some of the most vulnerable workers who lack regular working hours, minimum wage, benefits, funded holidays and parental leave. Accordingly, such informality plays a role in shaping the provision and location of studio space, further isolating and individuating the search for and retention of affordable working space. Artists' tenures in studios are individuated through lease agreements, which encode "an assumption of the artist as a lone actor or even art practice as a personal pursuit rather than a form of employment" (Bingham-Hall & Kaasa 2018: 23). Thus, precarity is normalized as part of how culture is produced with direct implications for the provision of affordable housing as another form of key urban infrastructure.

As cities capitalize on culture to regenerate themselves, they accelerate the exclusionary intensification of property markets, challenging the provision of secure housing for artists which, beyond the studio, remains "a fundamental requirement for all aspects of cultural production" (Bingham-Hall & Kaasa 2018: 25). While celebrated as urban change agents, the precarity of artistic labour positions artists alongside other low-income workers in need of adequate shelter. Neither cultural districts nor what Bingham-Hall and Kaasa (2018: 25) refer to in the context of London, England as "Creative Enterprise Zones" will be meaningful "unless they are tied directly to affordable housing for a range of workers and the tackling of low pay and precarious contracts". Aggregating artists in live-work studio complexes only serves to increase the cultural capital of neighbourhoods, leading to their revalorization and increasing the artists' risk of future economic displacement, especially when leases are short-term. Cross-sectoral solidarity in affordable housing provision and smaller, multi-purpose entrepreneurial spaces may be more sustainable given that cultural production is always already spatial and infrastructural.

This section considers how culture as the arts and as a way of life is produced within arts districts, open creative labs and creative land trusts. Arts districts within revalorized mixed-use neighbourhoods, are one such example (Bain & March 2019). They offer a density of proximate cultural assets, such as organizations, businesses, artists and visitors within differently sized artistic production and consumption venues and are instrumentalized as spatial strategies to reinforce the economic and symbolic value of art and culture by transforming an urban area into a destination for tourists and art world stakeholders (Bain 2018; Bain & Landau 2019b). In Chapter 2, Bain provides case studies of cultural districts from four cities in Germany and Canada examining how the current economic uncertainty within the cultural sector variably impacts their vitality. Such districts, it is argued, are shaped by a core tension between their designation as centres of culture and the artistic livelihoods where their infrastructure is based. The examples demonstrate that while Berlin, Leipzig, Toronto and Hamilton differ in their spatial forms and governance, the ubiquity of the cultural district and its economic dynamics result in common challenges to their vitality via the question of affordability for cultural producers.

Coworking spaces and open creative labs are often features of arts districts, but they can also be found elsewhere, extending their synergistic and collaborative practices across and between cities and into "creative economy" labour markets (Schmidt 2019). In Chapter 3, Schmidt examines "open creative labs", curated sites designed to enhance the creativity, synergy and productivity of mobile, independent and/or freelance workers in the districts of Kreuzberg, Neukölln and Mitte in Berlin, Germany. While these sites permit freelancers to share the costs of "hard" office infrastructure (Wi-Fi fees, software, office furniture and equipment) and create communities of practice, softer "atmospheric" elements of their infrastructure that stress particular forms of creativity may foreclose other worker embodiments and practices. The advantageous, intermittent use of open creative labs provides the creative economy with significant flexibility in labour and space, but the impermanence and constant displacement of productive space for artists remains a perennial concern.

In large cities worldwide, artists struggle to obtain long-term, affordable space to create their cultural products. Adaptively reusing the urban commons by creating land trusts – more traditionally used to provide affordable housing and community gardens – for artistic production can support the use value of urban space over its neoliberal economic value as capitalist property (Bunce 2018). Land trusts act as "a land value capture mechanism" because they separate “ownership of land from building infrastructure”, prevent “profit-making through resale from legal contracts”, and promote “long-term ... affordable land and building stock for community purposes” (Bunce 2018: 415). The promise of creative land trusts is explored in Chapter 4 by Scott, Dickens and Hubbard through a case study of London, UK. They argue that while the land trusts can support low-cost creative workspaces, such models generally are based on short leasehold tenure models that render artists’ spaces nothing more than “borrowed infrastructure”, a testament to the precarity of artistic livelihoods and studio spaces. Exacerbated by the Covid-19 pandemic, the chapter examines creative land trusts as remedial policy intervention into the infrastructural crisis of affordable cultural production space in creative cities.

From arts districts to open creative labs to creative land trusts, together, these variegated sites of cultural production illustrate the infrastructural heterogeneity of contemporary urban cultural configurations and their rootedness in more collective cultural ecologies of education and spatialized acts of creation. The communities and generations of artists and makers who inhabit this networked infrastructure of cultural production – spaces that are both purpose-built and adapted and animated by creative labour – are what regenerates cycles of culture within cities in its iterative move through performance, consumption and collection.

CHAPTER 2

CLUSTERING CULTURAL INFRASTRUCTURE IN DISTRICTS

Alison L. Bain

INTRODUCTION

A cultural district (or cultural quarter in Britain and mainland Europe) is a location within a city where cultural and artistic infrastructure, services, activities and networks are concentrated and embedded (Roodhouse 2006). Informally emergent in mixed-use urban neighbourhoods from the embryonic and *ad hoc* presence of cultural practitioners, cultural districts revalorize built heritage as "hubs, nodes, and workplaces for creative production" in lifecycles that extend from spatialization to recommodification (Zukin & Braslow 2011: 132). In the cultural industries, a cultural hub in a single building is the most "extreme" form of clustering (Pratt 2021). Such cultural hubs, and the industries and practitioners who animate them with their labour, have become important urban economic change agents in cities around the world grappling with industrial decline and restructuring. They adaptively reuse redundant industrial infrastructure (e.g., harbour areas, elevated rail corridors, shipyards, factories, warehouses and storage facilities), offices, schools, hospitals, churches and prisons, turning it into cultural infrastructure that can foster creativity through human co-presence (Pratt 2021). These "creative brownfields" – "aesthetically distinct, derelict and flexible industrial premises" that have attracted the attention of artistic communities and youth subculture – have become formalized as place-making anchors of cultural infrastructure, contributing to structural changes in neighbourhoods and cities (Andres & Golubchicov 2016: 758).

This chapter considers the informal and formal dimensions of cultural districts as urban infrastructure. It traces the historical roots of cultural districts to the precarity of artistic careers and the socio-spatial strategy of clustering as a means of professional survival. In the contemporary period, shaped by pandemic lockdowns, venue closures and event cancellations to control the spread of Covid-19, it demonstrates that economic uncertainties have deepened across the culture sector for practitioners and organizations alike, undermining the vitality and viability of cultural districts. Despite the seeming global ubiquity of cultural districts as an urban economic development tool, examples of this cultural infrastructure from Berlin and Leipzig in Germany and Toronto and Hamilton in Canada showcase intermediation in practice, demonstrating the range of cultural district spatial forms, programmes and rationales. The chapter concludes by reflecting upon the infrastructural challenges cultural districts face in remaining affordable and accessible spaces of cultural production for cultural practitioners whose very livelihoods are at stake.

AN (IN)FORMAL INFRASTRUCTURE TO CLUSTER CULTURE: THE CULTURAL DISTRICT IN THEORY

The "organic" generation of "natural" cultural districts in the absence of urban planning and policy intent depends upon a density of cultural assets (organizations, businesses, artists and audiences) (Stern & Seifert 2007). From eighteenth-century Covent Garden in London (Gatrell 2013), to nineteenth-century Montmartre in Paris with its mix of can-can dancers, prostitutes and impressionist and surrealist painters (Wilson 2000), to the twentieth century's Bohemian enclaves of Paris's Left Bank or New York City's Greenwich Village (Lloyd 2010), cultural districts have historically emerged in marginalized neighbourhoods as informal socio-spatial strategies used by cultural practitioners to sustain precarious and uncertain artistic careers. Geographical clustering encouraged artists and cultural entrepreneurs to "interact, learn, compete, and test out their ideas on one another" (Stern & Seifert 2007: 7). Moreover, the spatial concentration of creatives and participants, cultural producers and consumers in a delimited area generated community spill-overs such as increased business clients, an atmospheric "buzz", or a neighbourhood's counter-cultural identity (Martí-Costa & Pradel i Miquel 2012). The creative networks formed through the coexistence of different social and (sub)cultural groups, genres of music and art, in conjunction with leftist politics that "redefine the edges of dominant culture" (Shaw 2005: 150) create stimulating synergies across mediums, offering opportunities for inspiration and collaboration. Nevertheless, the cultural avant-garde invariably face the threat of institutionalization and market commodification within "in" (mainstream)/"off" (alternative) cultural systems (Vivant 2010).

Into the twenty-first century, the symbolic and economic value generated by the concentration of culture has become ever more explicitly capitalized upon by urban planners, policymakers and real estate developers in top-down strategies to revitalize declining central cities. Cultural districts – "well-recognized, labeled, mixed-use area of the city in which a high concentration of cultural facilities serves as the anchor of attraction" (Frost-Kumpf 1998: 7) – have become sites of direct local government intervention through public–private partnerships (Mommaas 2004). Non-profit and commercial cultural facilities can include, but are not limited to, performance spaces, galleries, museums, artist studios, music or media production studios, dance studios, libraries, public art and arts-related retail shops. With their attendant administrative and marketing services and festivalized programmes of activities, cultural districts are intended as sites where residents and tourists can spend their disposable income in cultural venues and adjacent restaurants, cafes, bars and other local businesses, increasing the tax base. With their mix of land uses (often including office, commercial and residential) and property owners, cultural districts take many different forms and invariably contend with multiple and conflicting stakeholder opinions about how they should be used, marketed and managed (Frost-Kumpf 1998). Cultural districts, then, are "inherently, irreducibly hybrid", contingent and "negotiated agonistically" across time (Pierce & Martin 2015: 1287).

Cultural districts may have an explicit focus on a particular arts and design sector (e.g., gallery, museum or theatre district) or they may be multi-sectoral and culturally hybrid (Mommaas 2004). The mix of activities within a district varies from a monofunctional focus on cultural consumption/exchange/presentation to a multifunctional combination inclusive of cultural production. While the outputs and processes of cultural production do vary considerably, cultural practitioners share complex and differing needs for tacit and informal knowledge exchange, learning, social labour organizing and value generation (Pratt 2021). As such, one of the key functions of cultural districts is *intermediation* (O'Connor 2013).

Through an intermediation lens, cultural districts can be understood as *creative ecosystems*; living networks composed of complex assemblages of interdependencies between profit and non-profit tenants – curated individual cultural practitioners who operate, in many respects, as micro-enterprises and small and medium-sized businesses – that need to connect to different audiences and markets (variously local, regional, national and international) while also building synergistic on-site relations of value exchange (e.g., "ideas, inspiration, trust, contacts, technology know how, employment, excitement, access to markets, start-up support, publication, ideas for new research bids and new teaching programmes"; Dovey *et al.* 2016: 88). Such intermediation between creative practitioners "aggregated together in co-located spaces, times, and social media constitute networks of creativity and innovation" (Dovey *et al.* 2016: 93). These networks rely upon soft infrastructure that frequently remains underreported and invisible within property-led frameworks prioritizing site redevelopment, building management and profit generation to maximize economic returns on investment.

To determine what activities and elements make for cultural district economic success, urban cultural planning scholars have offered typologies. For Montgomery (2007), for example, it is a combination of activities, built form and meaning that combine to create a "successful" cultural district. Cultural activities reference the range and size of cultural venues and businesses; built form addresses the urban morphological grain, building stock adaptability, streetscape permeability, layout legibility, public space accessibility, street front activity and people attractors; and meanings considers the historical and place-identity distinctiveness of the site as well as local and visitor knowledgeability and familiarity. Through targeted programming initiatives (e.g., a range of rent-controlled venues to protect activities associated with cultural production from displacement with rising land values and rents; integration of artist studios and craft/design workshops in underused properties; stimulation of cultural economic development; provision of workspace to incubate creative industries; augmenting site legibility with public art and signage; marketing the area locally, nationally and internationally; using the night-time economy and cafe culture to foster pedestrian uses; developing a place brand and profile; connecting to the local community through programming), the economic viability of a cultural district can be enhanced (Montgomery 2007). Such programme prescriptions are useful for appreciating the multi-faceted dimensions of cultural districts as well as the relationship between art and commerce, understanding how the consumptive embrace of aspects of the marketplace is key to cultural district survival (Caust 2021). It is equally important, however, as I have argued elsewhere (Bain & Landau 2019b, 2022), to be able to assess the local socio-spatial embeddedness of cultural districts within their immediate neighbourhoods and to consider their relationships to one another within, across and beyond a given city.

As place-embedded-yet-relational cultural infrastructure, cultural districts are not merely singular, discrete entities. They vary in terms of their degree of embeddedness in place and depend upon relational networks. Cultural districts exist not only in spatial intra- and inter-city relation to other cultural districts (with one potentially influencing the physical, social and affective character of another), but also often in temporal relation, fostering continuities between industrial pasts and coexisting presents. "Contrasting temporalities" is the "stuff of all places" (Massey 2005: 159). Different histories converge in urban landscapes shaped by the accumulation logics of redevelopment, gentrification and displacement. The "afterlives of infrastructure" – a "palimpsest of memories", stories and practices – have political significance that are leveraged by different urban actors with varying stakes and motives (Newman 2021: 2). Like other networked infrastructural systems – energy, sanitation, transportation, communication – cultural districts are palimpsests of socio-technical layers with multiple spatialities and temporalities (Monstadt 2022; Moss 2020). To appreciate a cultural district's contemporary relevance as infrastructure and longer-term sustainability it is necessary to understand its past. Moreover, a cultural district's viability in the present is contingent upon maintaining "what it is good at" but also being "flexible, highly adaptive and embrac[ing] change, new ideas, new ways of doing things and new work" (Kim 2011: 142). The transformative capacities of adaptation and innovation are enhanced by the intermediatory place-based function of cultural districts as rich, yet variable, infrastructural "middlegrounds" of social encounter, interaction and exchange in public spaces and across geographical distances (Cohendet *et al.* 2011: 153). In what follows, a selection of German and Canadian formal and informal cultural districts is briefly discussed to demonstrate how intermediation occurs across a diversity of infrastructural forms, uses and governance models.

CULTURAL DISTRICTS IN PRACTICE: FROM BERLIN TO LEIPZIG AND TORONTO TO HAMILTON

As transformative and transformed urban infrastructure, cultural districts have locally specific geographies and histories. Their intermediary embeddedness and function within particular urban neighbourhoods varies considerably as does the means by which they were realized and their longevity within the urban landscape. Nevertheless, cultural districts call attention to new possibilities for redundant industrial infrastructure and buildings. Such possibilities for leveraging culture to reanimate urban spaces and revitalize urban economies necessitate a range of social networking, ownership and power relations from both within and outside of the state (Lawhon *et al.* 2018), as the following examples illustrate.

Zentrum für Kunst und Urbanistik

As Germany's post-reunification capital and most cosmopolitan city, Berlin is marked by urban reinvention while also having the country's greatest concentration of political and arts institutions (Bain & Landau 2018). North and west of Berlin's central city arts scene in the borough of Mitte is the district of Moabit, a twentieth-century manufacturing and transportation hub at a railway and port nexus. With upwards of 75,000 residents (nearly 50 per cent of which are immigrants from upwards of 60 countries including prominent Turkish and Arabic communities), the loss of manufacturing jobs has brought poverty and unemployment to many families. Beginning in 2008, the municipality collaborated with the cultural sector to address urban decline. The industrial railway land (Güterbahnhof Moabit, formerly owned by Deutsche Bahn) was redeveloped as a public park, playground, community garden and cultural hub at the centre of an emerging informal cultural district.

The municipality granted a 40-year lease for two renovated railway buildings on the site to the artist collective Zentrum für Kunst und Urbanistik (ZK/U, www.zku-berlin.org/de/). Since locating there in 2012, ZK/U has leveraged their creativity and social networks to produce a space for artistic experimentation that explicitly reflects critically upon the intersection between art, the urban and neighbourhood development (Bain & Landau 2019a). On behalf of the political stakeholders, ZK/U's lease requires them as an artist-tenant to produce culture for and with local newcomer and long-time residents through socially engaged arts-led event programming (Figure 2.1).

In this cultural hub that functions as a micro cultural district with its gallery, studios, bar and outdoor community film, recreational, gardening and social spaces, ZK/U occupies a blurry cultural intermediary space between producing, performing, mediating and consuming culture. During

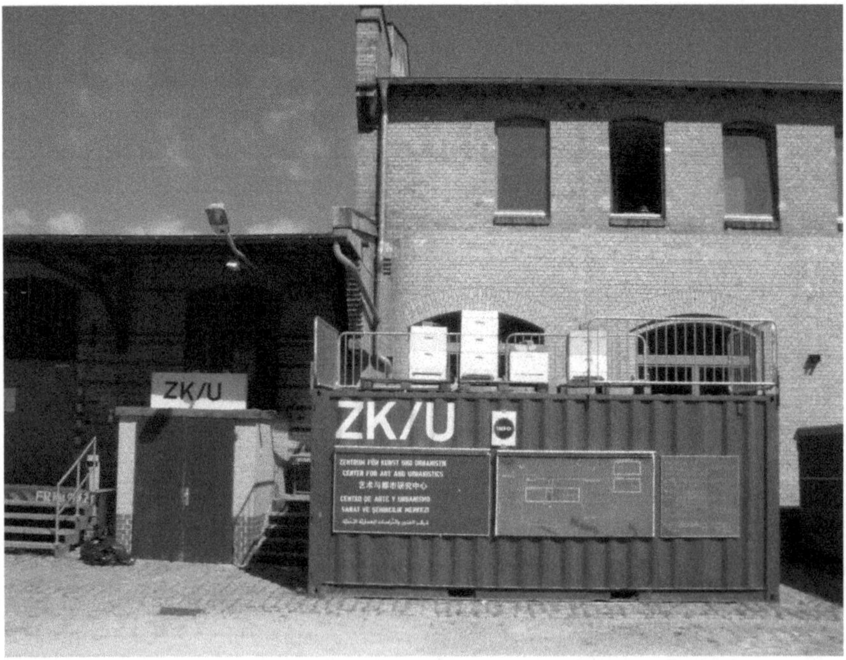

Figure 2.1 Exhibition, programming and artist residency spaces at the Zentrum für Kunst und Urbanistik (ZK/U) in Berlin

Source: Alison L. Bain.

Covid, the artist residencies remained open, however many ZK/U events to showcase the work-in-progress of its artists-in-residence to a wider audience (e.g., *Openhaus* (Openhouse)) were more irregular or went digital, using social media platforms like Instagram to display art and offer workshops and tutorials. In response to city-wide regulations to contain the spread of the disease and as Berlin shifted towards a new state of public life, hybrid event formats (individual, small group and online) were experimented with. ZK/U exemplifies a small cultural district realized through municipal funding and a mandate to be strategically embedded in a working-class, immigrant neighbourhood to transform this dilapidated transportation infrastructure into cultural infrastructure that could foster newcomer inclusion through artistic presence and programming.

Baumwollspinerei, Tapetenwerk, Westwerk and Kunstkraftwerk

Southwest of Berlin by 200 kilometres is Leipzig, a post-industrial city that many Berlin artists have relocated to in search of more affordable studio space. Once characterized as "shrinking" due to socialist state protectionism within the German Democratic Republic, Leipzig is now a fast-growing city. Arts and culture are as central to Leipzig's contemporary urban revitalization as they once were in framing its "foundational narrative" "as a 'book city' and as a 'music city'" in reference to internationally renowned publishing houses and composers (Mace & Volgmann 2018: 810). Successive cultural plans have identified four proximate and differently sized cultural districts in West Leipzig – "independent cultural centres" and "off-spaces" of cultural production and consumption – that strengthen Leipzig's national and international image as a "pulsating centre of visual and applied arts" (Bain & Landau 2022: 1623).

Constructed from 1884 to 1907 as a 20-building cotton mill on a 10-hectare site, the Baumwollspinnerei was bought in 2001 by a private shareholder company and redeveloped as a cultural district under a slogan that encapsulates this transformation – "from cotton to culture" (Figure 2.2). A visitor's centre, archive, and museum leverage and re-narrate this industrial past, documenting its infrastructural transformation into a site internationally renowned for artistic production and presentation with over 100 artist studios, numerous private art galleries and creative industries, including many innovation labs and business start-ups (Bain & Landau 2019b). The *Spinnereirundgang*, a bi-annual open-studio and gallery event with between 20,000 and 30,000 people, has increased this cultural district's profile and helped to formalize on-site intermediation between cultural institutions and producers.

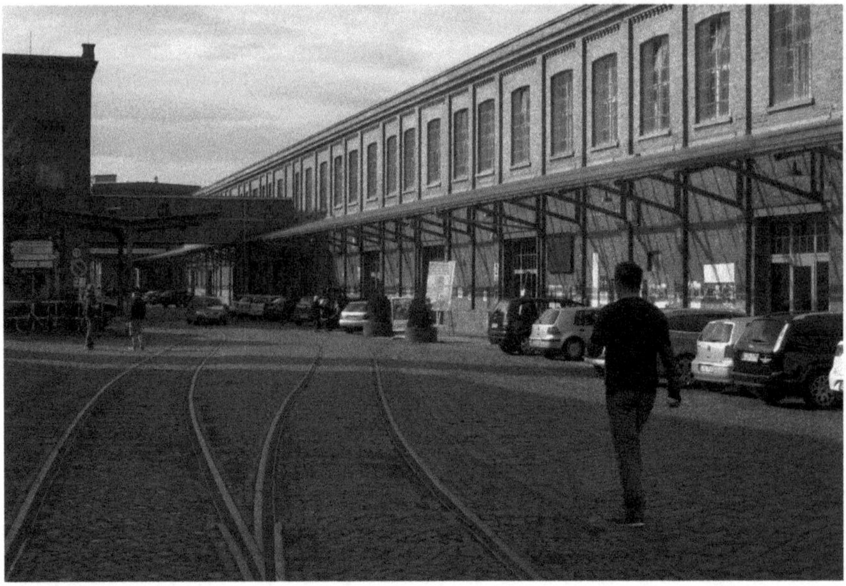

Figure 2.2 The adaptively reused interior public and built spaces of the Baumwollspinnerei cultural district in Leipzig

Source: Alison L. Bain.

Nearby smaller cultural districts, like Tapetenwerk in a former wallpaper factory, have also capitalized on visitor inflow to the Baumwollspinnerei by hosting concurrent events. With approximately 60 tenants, Tapetenwerk has 45 creative and artisanal businesses (e.g., architectural firms, artist studios, media companies and designers), a coworking space, a cafeteria and an exhibition/workshop space for tenants and local art school students. Since founding in 2007 by its architect owners, and in the ensuing years of gradual site renovations, arts-related usage remains at 30 per cent. In contrast to the Baumwollspinnerei, this cultural district hosts regular meetings for its tenants to foster organizational and decision-making transparency, which has produced numerous grant-writing and creative project synergies.

To the south of Tapetenwerk and east of the Baumwollspinnerei is Westwerk, a former heavy machine foundry built in 1882 which became a cultural district in 2007 with approximately 120 tenants (ranging from about 40 artists to businesses such as a coffee roasting company, a yoga studio, artisanal workshops, civic associations and architects). With its minor and low-budget renovations, flexible rental agreements, and subsidies, this cultural district has a reputation as the "last bastion of independent ateliers" (Bain & Landau 2022: 1627). A large hall supports tenant- organized events and the courtyard hosts a regular farmers' market. As part of a commercial usage survival strategy, a supermarket chain has become an anchor tenant.

The most recent and smallest addition to West Leipzig's cultural district fabric is Kunstkraftwerk. This privately owned former heating plant was bought in 2012. Following renovations, it opened in 2016 as an international and collaborative digital art-science exhibition space for tourists that also hosts weddings, high school diploma dances, business events and trade shows. Entrepreneurially leveraging the cultural consumption and experience economy, the owners of this site appreciate the locational synergies made possible by relational proximity to the Baumwollspinnerei, Tapetenwerk and Westwerk cultural districts. As in the other three cultural district locales, here too, former industrial buildings have not been sanitized; instead, infrastructural artefacts – old heating pipes, conveyor belts, dust filters, brick walls and wooden beams – are all exposed to visually and experientially capitalize on a working-class heritage.

Across all four sites, Covid-19 brought cancellations and closures to exhibitions and large-scale events in interior museum, gallery and studio spaces. Contemporary art galleries remained open for private bookings and scheduled visits, while tenants retained access to studios and other sites of cultural production, but the complexes were off-limits for long periods of time to visitors. The conjunction of national and municipal pandemic restrictions rendered the courtyards of these West Leipzig cultural districts – normally intermediation sites of serendipitous sociability, networking and consumption – quiet and desolate places. Nevertheless, these four adjacent, yet differently sized, funded and governed cultural districts in West Leipzig relationally persist, gradually becoming revived again as public spaces. Realized predominantly through private capital, they have each experimentally transformed and aestheticized the unsanitized industrial infrastructure of factories into urban cultural infrastructure that variously supports in different proportions production, performance, consumption and collection. Their spatial proximity and programming synergies create opportunities for differentiation while also reinforcing their collective infrastructural role as conduits of culture, appreciated by civic leaders and enfolded through cultural planning into the city's place-brand.

Distillery District and 401 Richmond

In Toronto, Canada's pre-eminent commercial centre for art, central city cultural districts like the Distillery District or 401 Richmond remain sites of cultural intermediation, but in the face of rampant real estate market speculation, it is questionable for how long. The 40 mid-nineteenth-century former Gooderham and Worts distillery buildings on an underused brownfield site, were privately redeveloped as a planned cultural district. "[S]tripped of their machinic impulses, industrial parts, and working-class histories" these buildings were "repackaged as aesthetic backdrops for consumption, housing retail, and cultural goods and services" (Mathews 2014: 1020). When the original developer, and now partner in the site, Cityscape, bought the property in 2001 they offered a 20-year lease below market rate to Artscape, a Toronto-based non-profit real estate organization with a mandate to provide affordable studio, performance and living space for artists, as their "community amenity" in exchange for increased building densities. The Artscape lease was used to attract sub-tenants in two connected buildings: one became ground floor storefront studios for artists and artisans and upper floor private studios and offices for arts organizations; and a second became rehearsal space for local performing arts groups. With the termination of their leases, 70 of these artists and arts organizations (who were joined in 2006 on the north side of the site by a theatre company and theatre school on a 120-year lease) have been displaced from this once model site of arts-led brownfield redevelopment and cultural tourism. In the face of steady development pressure, the City of Toronto has been slow to learn that you "don't exchange density that lasts forever for finite community amenities" in the form of leased spaces of cultural production that provide little in the way of permanent cultural infrastructure (Taylor 2021, n.p.). While smaller in scale than the Distillery District, 401 Richmond (like the previous four examples in Leipzig) illustrates the important role played by "philanthrocapitalism" (Bishop & Green 2008) in the cultural sector. Cultural philanthropist-developers can help to mitigate against the displacement of cultural practitioners from central city cultural districts.

Although benevolence in arts and culture is distributed unevenly across time and space, the cultural philanthropist-developer remains a key urban actor allied with the real estate market and property development who through their individualized commitments to specific neighbourhoods, buildings and local relationships can provide cultural districts, and the art scenes they nurture, some spatial stability (Bain & March 2019). Built between 1899 and 1923 as a canning factory, 401 Richmond is an industrial warehouse in downtown Toronto that was bought in the mid-1990s by an architect-developer-philanthropist-activist. Her portfolio of renovated and managed buildings has curated tenant mixes designed to function as cultural hubs while countering the predominant surrounding use of real estate by finance, insurance and real estate occupations. Although rental rates are kept below market-value for artists and non-profit arts organizations (and neither standardized nor publicized), Covid-19 increased the once slow pace of tenant turnover. Despite being described as an oasis, a utopia, a heaven and a haven for artists (Bain & March 2019), questions remain about how sustainable 401 Richmond will be post-Covid and with the eventual retirement of its benefactor. As in many cultural districts, the divergent values and needs of tenants within this cultural hub make for a complex arts ecology that can be difficult to manage in the face of widespread sectoral decimation. "There is only so much that one building and one person can do to financially buffer and spatially protect Toronto artists and arts organizations from displacement" without more strategic state urban planning and cultural policy support (Bain & March 2019: 187).

These two examples of Toronto cultural districts, more centrally located in the city than either of the two previous examples from Berlin and Leipzig, illustrate the precarity of cultural infrastructural claims by artists and arts organizations to prime urban real estate. While the vision and capital of individual philanthropist-developers in conjunction with cultural practitioner presence and artistic labour can transform industrial infrastructure into cultural infrastructure for production, performance, consumption and collection, it remains questionable for how long – certainly rarely in perpetuity. Cultural production is often exploited as interim practice undeserving of spatial protection, its material circumstances only supported over the short-term until a more profitable use for adaptively reused urban infrastructure can be found.

James Street North

In the face of continued rental and property increases in downtown Toronto (as in Berlin where artists have relocated to Leipzig), many cultural workers have moved to nearby mid-sized cities like Hamilton (75 kilometres southwest on the shores of Lake Ontario) in search of a more affordable lifestyle for themselves. In so doing, however, they have reduced housing affordability for local residents. Once a North American centre of steel manufacturing, this blue-collar city, like so many others, is grappling with deindustrialization and the poverty and socio-economic bifurcations that derive from rapid rent increases and gentrification (Dale 2021). As in other mid-sized cities, the challenge of inward migration and growing housing unaffordability predate the Covid-19 pandemic but have accelerated because of it (van der Merwe & Doucet 2021). These dynamics are especially apparent in two of Hamilton's 11 most deprived neighbourhoods that abut James Street North where the city's arts scene is concentrated, forming an informal cultural district locally branded "neighbourhood of the arts: a place where creativity lives" (https://supercrawl.ca/2021/11/visual-and-public-art/).

As was the case in Leipzig, Hamilton's civic leaders have also leveraged art and culture through cultural planning as an urban-economic development policy tool to rebrand the city's Steeltown image. In 2005, as part of Hamilton's Creative City Initiative they began further loosening zoning restrictions in support of the adaptive reuse of central city buildings. Prior to this official municipal land-use policy shift, artists had already leveraged their capital, sweat equity and tenant curatorship to transform the nineteenth-century buildings and storefronts along James Street North that once supported Jewish, Italian and Portuguese immigrant communities into cultural infrastructure. With the zoning change, the pace of infrastructural transformation accelerated. Property ownership by a network of small-scale artist-developers (who vary in their entrepreneurial, community engagement and social justice perspectives) in a range of different partnerships has helped to home-grow local artistic talent, foster intermediation, and incubate small businesses (Bain 2018).

Proximate to one another are small commercial and independent art galleries, non-profit artist-run centres, studios, artists' collectives, performance venues, independent arts-based businesses and creative business incubators, interspersed by social service agencies, ethnic grocers and restaurants. A large annual fall arts festival (*Supercrawl*) that showcases live music and public art happens here along with a monthly art crawl of synchronized gallery art openings (Bain & Rallis 2017). Together, the "cyclical rhythm[s] allow for fixity in the temporary" while building an arts-based place brand for the neighbourhood and city (Schaller & Guinand 2018: 62). During Covid-19, both events, however, were on hiatus. They relied instead upon supporting large-scale public works of art programming for local residents to enjoy during lockdowns to signal their future viability. As in many cities, the pandemic took its toll on independent retail and arts initiatives. Despite strong resident support for local businesses, small retailers and restaurants have been rendered vulnerable to bankruptcy, leaving storefronts empty but also sites of social-media-amplified "pop-up urbanism" (Schaller & Guinand 2018). Where James Street North differs from the Toronto, Leipzig and Berlin cultural districts is that property ownership is dispersed among a network of grassroots private property investment groups with local residents and artists at their core. Co-located on one downtown artery, these property project networks challenge the precarity of artists' careers by providing a steady source of alternative income through rising real estate values and centring artists as active agents in cultural district development.

CONCLUSION

This chapter has demonstrated that with the continued urban planning and policy valorization of agglomeration economies and the place-based economization of creativity and culture, cultural districts may appear to be a standardized element of large cities, celebrated as transformative and transformed urban infrastructure. However, the continued presence of cultural districts in urban landscapes, notably their support of cultural production, is not guaranteed. While a "transfer and copying of cultural policy models" has contributed "to the homogenisation of urban cultural landscapes", there remain, as this chapter has illustrated through its German and Canadian examples, a great variety of cultural district spatial forms, programs and rationales (Vivant 2010: 113).

The ZK/U in a more peripheral, working-class district of Berlin exemplifies a small, municipally funded, leased and mandated cultural district in a former train station strategically positioned to simultaneously revitalize the urban fabric and foster newcomer inclusion through arts programming. On a larger scale and across four neighbouring and networked cultural districts in West Leipzig, individual private investors have experimented with the transformation and aestheticization of unsanitized factory infrastructure into cultural infrastructure that supports different combinations of cultural production, performance, consumption and collection. It is the spatial proximity and programming synergies of the Baumwollspinerei, Tapetenwerk, Westwerk and Kunstkraftwerk that help to sustain these cultural districts in conjunction with cultural planning recognition by civic leaders. In Toronto, like Berlin, where central city real estate speculation continues apace despite the pandemic, cultural districts like the Distillery District and 401 Richmond (particularly as it prioritizes cultural production) struggle to persist outside of a performative and consumptive frame without investment by individual philanthropist-developers. When investment in more informal cultural districts is decentralized through heterogeneous networks of property ownership that centre local residents and artists and involve them in cultural planning and policymaking processes, as is the case in Hamilton's James Street North, greater potential exists for cultural practitioners to resist gentrification and displacement. Whether a stand-alone building or a building complex or a quarter or a network of locations dispersed across a city, this chapter has demonstrated that cultural districts as infrastructure prioritize intermediation, linking cultural activities and amenities with socio-spatial and economic policy goals (Mommaas 2004).

In cultural districts, productive cultural and creative power is generated through the interaction between social and material infrastructure.

They face, however, a threefold challenge. First, how can cultural districts avoid further individualizing the concentration of property ownership wealth? Second, in overheated property markets, how can the displacement of artists from cultural districts be prevented as neighbourhoods gentrify and central city rents rise? Third, what ensures that cultural districts remain more than curated destinations of independent consumption for young, educated and socially liberal creatives? The ever-present danger is that "art and cultural activities make a run-down area attractive for residential or new commercial incomers, and 'development ready'" (Pratt 2021: 3). When the real estate sector profits from the economic value of cultural districts, inevitably the material and symbolic basis for cultural production is eroded (Martí-Costa & Pradel i Miquel 2012). While cultural practitioners often possess the specialized knowledge to adapt prior infrastructural forms and create new working relationships with this materiality, they are still members of a "vulnerable" user group (in terms of their financial precarity within the vagaries of capitalist markets and their relative exclusion from normative funding, business and aesthetic systems) that requires access to affordable and secure workspace (Pratt 2021). Models of collective property ownership in formal and informal cultural districts offer a means for cultural practitioners to assert their agency in urban development processes and potentially to sustain their longer-term presence in central cities.

Like the arts and culture sector more generally, cultural districts are underpinned by network-based and precarious work practices that Covid-19 eroded. With unemployment and underemployment among arts workers continuing to soar, many cultural districts look and feel very different than pre-2020. The anchors of cultural districts – music venues, theatres, art galleries and museums – were forced to close for long periods and the exhibitions, concerts, plays, literary, art and music festivals that animate them were cancelled. Likewise, many artists, musicians, actors and dancers along with ticket-takers and arts administrators were put out of work or took significant salary cuts while the organizations that employed them may have drawn on federal subsidies, grants and donations to survive. When self-employed freelancer cultural practitioners are unable to pay the rent on their workspaces or are leaving their professions altogether and arts organizations cannot afford their overhead costs and close, this tenant turnover creates vacancies in and economic uncertainty for cultural districts. Moreover, as the economic gap between individual cultural practitioners and arts organizations (long a source of tension in this sector) continues to widen, it further destabilizes the intermediation capacities and economic viability of cultural districts. Certainly, arts, entertainment, culture, tourism and hospitality are all sectors central to the economies of cultural districts that have been hard-hit by a pandemic-induced economic downturn, raising fundamental questions of sustainability. But as infrastructural hubs for the convergence of, and mediation between, diverse communities of creative practice and their audiences, cultural districts are nothing without the cultural practitioners whose labour and imaginations animate them. The lives and livelihoods of individual artists, then, cannot be disregarded as they are central to any infrastructural future for cultural districts.

CHAPTER 3

THE RELATIONAL INFRASTRUCTURE OF OPEN CREATIVE LABS

Suntje Schmidt

INTRODUCTION

With the transformation towards knowledge and innovation societies, the share of solo- and micro-entrepreneurship, freelance work, gig work or digital entrepreneurship of the total workforce has increased. Likewise, the share of income-related employment organized in atypical forms of work (outside tenured full-time employment) has increased in Western industrialized countries supporting project-based work outside of a fixed workplace and various combinations of part-time employment. Knowledge, creative and/or digital workers often work from home, make use of third places (e.g., cafes, libraries, community centres), or use collaborative workspaces (e.g., coworking spaces or makerspaces). Over the past 15 years, coworking spaces have emerged as a new urban cultural infrastructure. Globally, Deskmag (2019) estimates that the number of coworking spaces has increased from 8,900 in 2015 (with 545,000 members) up to 26,300 in 2020 (with 2.7 million members). In addition to collaborative workspaces, mixed-used shared spaces for creative practices (e.g., hackerspaces, fab labs, open workshops) have also been established. Taken together, these two more general trends exemplify how digital affordances, technological development and economic as well as labour-market transformation processes have inspired the development of new material production settings that support collaboration, co-design, co-production, co-creation or sharing.

Platforms such as Deskmag or the Fab Lab Association, suggest that social-material infrastructure for sharing work environments, tools for creative projects and experiences are no longer novel and experimental in cities. Instead, such places have become established and expected material urban artefacts. Collaborative workspaces can be understood as "hard" cultural infrastructure that facilitate the production of culture in cities by promoting creative and digital entrepreneurship and practices (Bryson 2007). Likewise, they can also be considered "soft" cultural infrastructure because they provide access and contribute to diffusing information, generating knowledge, organizing learning experiences and fostering networks. This latter characteristic underscores that they are not just neutral platforms for social activities, but instead are "fundamentally relational concepts" (Star & Ruhleder 1996: 113). Collaborative workspaces develop, enable and spread organized practices and are composed of hard and soft infrastructural elements that contribute to building multiple forms of communities of practice by "connecting people and things in socio-material relations that sustain urban life" (McFarlane & Silver 2017: 463). However, creating, organizing and even curating communities, linkages and relations is also closely aligned with creating logics of inclusion and exclusion. Although most collaborative spaces promote openness to a wide range of creative user communities and uses, practices of access, appropriation, programming and design, they also exclude different groups and individuals.

Against this backdrop, the chapter addresses the plurality of shared social-material places for creative work in cities before elaborating on how such places have been investigated as "hard" and "soft" infrastructure in existing scholarly debates in ways that accentuate their social meaning for users and operators. Focusing on the soft dimensions of cultural infrastructure, this chapter critically engages with iterations of openness and closure. It concludes by discussing how these shared workspaces are locations for cultural production and creative actions.

OPEN CREATIVE LABS AS SHARED SPACES OF WORK AND EXPERIMENTATION

Knowledge and innovation societies thrive on the capacities of individuals, communities and organizations to continuously generate valuable, novel solutions. Creativity and innovation are collaborative processes requiring the interaction between individuals and organizations, collective sensemaking and learning as well as the ability to activate and assemble oftentimes trans-local resources and competencies (Schuessler *et al.* 2021). Attempting to provide fruitful social-material environments for creativity and innovation, and as a strategy to address the profound structural changes in the organization of knowledge intensive, creative and digital work, a multiplicity of collaborative workspaces has been established since the turn of the century, especially in Western economies. Preliminary empirical investigations also emphasize how iterations of open creative labs can foster entrepreneurship in the global South (Friederici 2018). Some spaces clearly address income-related knowledge work, such as coworking spaces, start-up accelerators or makerspaces. Others provide spaces for fostering creative initiatives and for sharing specialized interests (e.g., fab labs, hackerspaces or open workshops). This new urban cultural infrastructure provides access not only to novel tools (e.g., for digital tinkering or artesian work), desks or Wi-Fi, but also to communities with shared interests in creative practices or solving societal challenges (e.g., local energy solutions, neighbourhood development, civic participation). Some of these spaces and their communities have gained international recognition for their work, such as the c-base in Berlin, MIT's Center for Bits and Atoms in Cambridge, MA, or the Critical Making Lab in Toronto.

At first glance these collaborative places seem quite diverse, but a closer analysis reveals some shared infrastructural characteristics that are important prerequisites for collaborative, innovative and creative processes (Schmidt 2019). Therefore, Brinks, Ibert, Kuebart and Schmidt (Brinks 2019; Schmidt 2019; Schmidt & Brinks 2017; Schmidt *et al.* 2018), have proposed the umbrella concept of open creative labs (OCLs) to cover the diversity of spatial solutions for collaborative practices. Across the multiplicity of shared social-spatial arrangements, access is provided to users independently from formal qualifications (e.g., educational background or training) and includes using shared online and offline tools and material for user-driven interests and creativity. OCLs are also open with regards to how users make use of and modify the space. As Figure 3.1 illustrates, traces of existing and former users and their projects are often visible or even collected and exhibited in OCLs to foster and allow for an exchange among users.

OCLs frequently provide social-material environments for developing, changing, adjusting projects and careers. A case study of OCLs in German metropolitan regions, for instance, revealed that they are used for shaping pathways of user-driven innovation processes (Brinks 2019), igniting nascent entrepreneurship or providing time, space and distance from daily routines to refocus individual careers (Schmidt *et al.* 2018). OCLs also frequently create their own institutional configurations with regards to regulation and governance systems (e.g., setting up membership boards, codes of conducts, wiki-groups), creating distance from the outside world but also opportunities for selective openness and closure. Overall, OCLs that provide space for entrepreneurial, work-related projects of their users can be distinguished from those that provide space for creative tinkering and experimentation.

In German metropolitan regions, the highest density of OCLs can be found in central, often gentrifying neighbourhoods. The German capital region of Berlin-Brandenburg, for example, is comprised by the city of Berlin and the federal state of Brandenburg that to a large extend can be characterized as rural. Figure 3.2 indicates a high concentration of OCLs in the Berlin districts

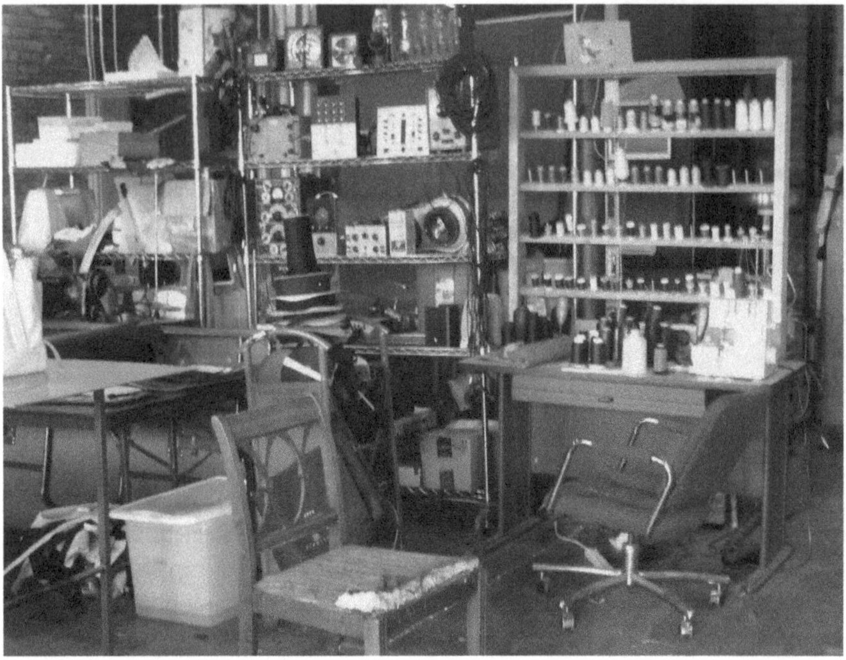

Figure 3.1 Showcasing a multiplicity of seemingly unrelated tools and materials (e.g., electronic devices, sewing equipment, spools of thread and work desks) in a Detroit-based makerspace

Source: Suntje Schmidt, IRS.

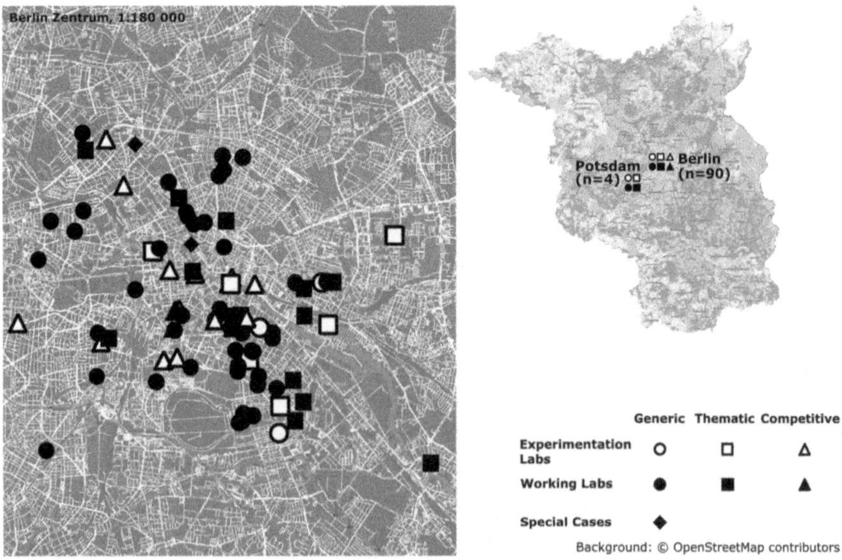

Figure 3.2 Open creative labs in Berlin and Brandenburg (2016)

Source: Andreas Kuebart, IRS.

of Kreuzberg, Neukölln and Mitte, while only very few labs can be found outside the urban agglomeration. Since the map was developed in 2016, more initiatives can be found in more peripheral regions in Brandenburg, often with ties to OCLs in Berlin.

OPEN CREATIVE LABS AS OPEN INFRASTRUCTURE

Work-related, entrepreneurial OCLs, especially in the form of coworking spaces, are treated by scholars as urban infrastructure. Ivaldi *et al.* (2018: 226), for instance, distinguish four types of coworking spaces: infrastructure, relational, network and welfare coworking. In their findings, infrastructure coworking spaces provide physical workplaces for independent professionals, offering basic tools and facilities with desks, Wi-Fi connection, computers, printers and fax machines. In contrast to the other three types of coworking spaces, infrastructure coworking spaces focus on the provision of hard infrastructure. In comparison, relational coworking spaces promote knowledge sharing among their users and networking coworking spaces support professional connections among the users and subjects outside the space (other professionals and organizations). Welfare coworking spaces address the specific needs and socio-cultural issues of their users, such as women and work, sustainability or fighting unemployment. Other authors suggest that these four types are seldom clearly delineated from each other and instead appreciate their mixed functions. Capdevila (2015) conceptualizes urban coworking spaces as micro-clusters embedded in entrepreneurial systems. Like industrial clusters that provide access to public and private infrastructures and services, coworking spaces as micro-clusters provide access to shared facilities and services, such as printers, internet connections and sometimes office services. In a similar vein, Bliemel *et al.* (2019) characterize start-up accelerators as infrastructure that actively engages with entrepreneurial clusters by providing access to and developing standardized seed funding, training in structured programmes and temporary co-location for the start-up-teams. Kuebart (2021), in comparison, understands OCLs as functional infrastructure for entrepreneurial ecosystems. He argues that OCLs operate as intermediaries in entrepreneurial clusters, offering the necessary entrepreneurial support to adapt to the shifting and changing demands of new employment ventures (Kuebart 2021: 9). Work-related OCLs do not just mediate links to valuable stakeholders, actors and services at the regional level for start-ups to become better embedded in regional entrepreneurial ecosystems, they also facilitate inter-ecosystem ties across distant ecosystems and regions.

In addition to such mediating practices, OCLs offer services for resource acquisition, incubation and peer learning. Against the background of these discourses, one could argue that OCLs do not only provide "hard" structures, but also actively create and curate entrepreneurial communities of practice (Schmidt 2019) that are comparable to the "soft" infrastructures described by Bryson (2007).

A second group of OCLs can be described as experimental labs, encompassing spaces such as fab labs, open workshops, repair cafes, hackerspaces, living labs or creative hubs (Schmidt & Brinks 2017). Like work-related, entrepreneurial OCLs, these labs have also been conceptualized as cultural infrastructure. Domanski *et al.* (2020), for instance, investigate social innovation labs and centres. Such labs are initiated and developed by civil society actors, often lacking public funding, for collaborative and oftentimes cross-sectoral problem-solving. For these actors, labs provide an infrastructure that enables collaboration by strategically bringing together people with diverse backgrounds for making sense of problems, challenges and situations and for collective solution finding. Similarly, living labs support actor-centred research and innovation and emphasize sustainability (von Geibler *et al.* 2014). Like entrepreneurial labs, living labs are embedded in larger infrastructural systems, namely research and innovation systems. Authors frame living labs as structures that improve access to the research and innovation systems of other institutions and organizations and related networks, integrating users and problem-affected social actors in processes of generating novel solutions. As such, living labs become nodes in processes of developing sustainable products and services (von Geibler *et al.* 2014: 593). While social innovation labs and living labs are associated with notions of innovation, sustainable development and novelty, makerspaces are framed as places for doing and creating things that eventually also lead to building and establishing local maker communities (Schmidt 2019). Thus, makerspaces can be regarded as providing access to shared resources and learning, comparable to libraries, YMCAs and community colleges (Holman 2015). Against this background, makerspaces seem to resemble public do-it-yourself facilities for training and cultural education.

These various manifestations of OCLs are conceptualized as infrastructure in that they provide access to shared material/physical resources (e.g., ranging from office spaces including desks, seats, meeting and workshop rooms, Wi-Fi-connections, to shared tools for artisanal creativity). Beyond these seemingly neutral materialities, OCLs also function as infrastructure for accessing services, networks and learning which underscores the relational nature of infrastructures highlighted by Star (1999). In addition, scholars demonstrate that experimental and entrepreneurial lab forms are embedded in larger systems such as research and innovation systems, entrepreneurial ecosystems, industrial clusters and diverse communities of practices such as, for instance, hacker or maker communities (Garrett *et al.* 2017). As such, OCLs are complementary structures within wider financial, social and material resources that support creative individuals, artisans, makers, hackers and entrepreneurs in organizing, developing and implementing their creative projects.

While OCLs seem to be open to various users and practices, they are simultaneously exclusive spaces that are either explicitly or implicitly closed to others. Labs are infused with social meanings and expectations regarding the vision of a particular space, the practices that are enabled by the space, its tools and social events, and what users are expected to contribute or how users are expected to behave (Howe *et al.* 2016). As Howe *et al.* (2016) point out, infrastructure is not just material, but is also connected to social trajectories that include institutions, social and economic regulatory systems, forms of social expression as well as philosophical trajectories within which imagined futures find concrete forms.

PRODUCING ITERATIONS OF OPENNESS AND CLOSURE IN OPEN CREATIVE LABS

OCLs have been associated with positive expectations regarding their impact on creative processes, practices and economies as they may support social community building (Spinuzzi *et al.* 2019), place-based learning (Capdevila 2015) and entrepreneurship (Friederici 2018), or access to technologies (Schmidt 2019). As such, OCLs seem to offer access to and for communities of practice, for instance freelancers, independent entrepreneurs, cultural workers and mobile professionals, makers, hackers and enthusiasts (Schmidt & Brinks 2017). Oftentimes, owners or managers of OCLs or the communities of these spaces will collectively formulate mission statements that stress openness for participation, shared values such as knowledge sharing and communal support or visions (e.g., of the future of work or creative tinkering). The betahaus Berlin, for instances, claims: "Let's take the time to explore. To seek out connections. To fall in love with work, at least once a day. To be innovators. Misfits. Try new things and make mistakes. We're not just a coworking space, but a community" (www.betahaus.com). Likewise, at national and international scales, communities of lab providers, too, create collective visions and meanings. The "Nation of Makers" vision "is to build a society where everyone has access to the tools, technologies, experiences and knowledge to make anything; to create a thriving, connected and inclusive community of practice where collaboration fosters a culture of abundance" (www.nationofmakers.us/mission-and-vision).

Despite these seemingly inclusive imaginaries, however, user participation is often limited by gender, age, ethnicity, class and/or association of their creative communities. Morgan (2020: 156), for instance, stresses that "these communities are often not open and egalitarian; instead, their membership is curated in ways that may serve to exclude people from certain social backgrounds". This curation takes place at various levels, such as their postulated vision statements, the spatial and visual design of a space, demonstrated community values, showcased practices of using a space, implicit rules lived by an existing user community (Virani & Gill 2019) and the micro-location within a city. A Berlin-based lab provider, for instance, reflected that his lab "attracts certain people anyway and not others. That's a selection that, that's like a filter, I think that happens through location [urban neighbourhood, explanation by author], people who are here, premises" (interview, translated by author).

A further level of actively curating the participation in OCLs can be identified in the practices of founders and managers of the spaces. Virani and Gill (2019: 132) describe how lab managers seek to build up the "right" lab community which they find to exhibit "intense segmentation and hierarchy along race and gender lines." The "right" community frequently includes participants and members of whom fruitful interactions might be expected, who seem to fit best into an existing community and who might likewise be attractive to future users. In an interview, a Berlin-based lab provider said "first of all, all are welcome who look in the same direction as we do" (interview, translated by author), meaning that they share working values and work within the broader context of "new work". Virani and Gill (2019) also underscore that users expect the lab managers to do so to make users feel comfortable. Against this background, curation becomes a practice of identifying suitable lab users who fit into an existing community but who also contribute to further establishing and developing the existing user community. However, active curation is neither inclusive, nor uncontested and poses the risk of creating homogeneous and socially homophilic lab communities as lab managers might tend to provide access to users who share similar identities and embodiments (Virani & Gill 2019: 144), reproducing predominantly white, middle-class, cis-male spaces.

In addition to the boundaries established by curation, user practices of appropriating labs spaces might also support closure to outsiders. Bingel (2019), for instance, describes how the practice of making use of the space in the material sense and the behaviour exhibited in particular artistic scenes, subcultures or political positions, either invite or further exclude users or members of the spaces. This includes active boundary constructions between different user communities such as independent artists and freelancers or between workers in creative or cultural professions. Boundary-making and curation practices eventually solidify images or profiles of OCLs as serving specific communities (e.g., bloggers and free journalists or sustainable social enterprises). Among the plurality of OCLs, hackerspaces seemingly exemplify creative experimentation, as sites where learning, tools, materials and projects are approached in an "adhocist" way (Toombs *et al.* 2014). Nevertheless, while these spaces appear creatively open, experiences of sexism, sexual harassment and discrimination by female-identifying hackers has also limited participation, inspiring the foundation of explicitly feminist hackerspaces in the United States as "safer spaces" (see Toupin 2014).

These examples demonstrate that a proclaimed openness is closely related to forms of closure and exclusion as manifest through practices of curation and founding principles. Both, work-related, entrepreneurial as well as experimentation-oriented OCLs claim to be open to diverse user groups or to various projects and initiatives that might evolve in their labs, as is manifest in narratives of creating communities that share a particular interest or practice. However, communities can be characterized by collective actions of community-building that create boundaries between community members and non-members wherein lab providers and existing users establish and reinvigorate a vision for the OCL and its community (Garrett *et al.* 2017). Furthermore, existing communities as well as newcomers observe social norms and identify potential for further development eventually resulting in more exclusive practices such as shared routines and responsibilities within particular lab spaces.

PRODUCING CULTURE IN OPEN CREATIVE LABS

Open creative labs are often located in central urban areas, in gentrifying neighbourhoods or proximate to higher education facilities. This also speaks to the area from which users are drawn. Holman (2015), for instance, points out that makerspaces draw their members from a limited geographic surrounding area, thus also addressing a limited social mixture living and working within these spatial constraints. Likewise, interviews and observations of OCLs in Berlin, Detroit and Amsterdam support this finding. Small coworking spaces, makerspaces and fab labs, in particular, tend to attract users from a reasonable inner-city commuting distance. Figure 3.2, for example, demonstrates that most Berlin-based OCLs are found along two subway lines in the city that connect gentrifying neighbourhoods in northern parts of Neukölln and southern areas of Wedding as well as Kreuzberg and Berlin-Mitte.

Work-related, entrepreneurial OCLs such as start-up accelerators and larger coworking spaces frequently choose more prestigious, central inner-city locations, making use of and contributing to business atmospheres and working cultures. From the perspective of knowledge intensive work, creative and digital professions who make use of work-related OCLs, labs provide a networked infrastructure focussed on coordinating work among like-minded peers. Similarly, work-related OCLs contribute to establishing shared entrepreneurial and social values, including working in volatile, often uncertain labour markets or accepting long working hours. OCLs thereby contribute to creating a culture of freelance, independent and individual work by offering resources that provide resilience in flexible labour markets, such as a working atmosphere, distance from the isolation of home-offices, and shared office costs (Merkel 2019; Schmidt *et al.* 2018). Likewise, experimentation-oriented labs contribute to creating cultures of creative tinkering and interacting for individual projects, especially by creating and cultivating their own communities based on implicit and explicit forms of social curation. Programmes, events, networking practices, engagement in local activities and mentoring are elements of localized learning and establishing specific social practices (Meyboom 2009). In Detroit, for example, an experimentation-oriented OCL set up governance boards and regulation systems to establish and cultivate practices of collectively accepting new members. The same culture of collective decision-making and sense-making was also extended outside the lab through interactions and engagements with neighbourhood initiatives.

Despite diverse forms of OCLs worldwide, what remains common and unifying among them is the practice of establishing rules to access or participate in these iterations of urban cultural infrastructure. While most OCLs are located in large city-regions, they are becoming increasingly present in and beyond their peripheries as important relational infrastructure variously serving communities of mobile professionals, tinkerers, creatives, artisans or hackers. These communities, too, can access spaces across the globe without necessarily needing to be acquainted with and learn new rules and social norms. Thus, OCLs provide a recognizable relational and increasingly transnational urban cultural infrastructure.

CONCLUSION

This chapter was inspired by Star's (1999) provocation to study infrastructure from a user perspective. It has offered a critical reflection on OCLs as urban cultural infrastructure, demonstrating how they are embedded in societal organization practices and thus contribute to producing cultures of collaboration, sharing and creative tinkering. Even though OCLs seem to have a quite local effect since most users are drawn from nearby central city neighbourhoods, OCLs are not isolated locations, but instead are highly networked among each other. Likewise, OCLs are embedded in other, complementary and trans-local structures of workplaces, entrepreneurial ecosystems, innovation systems or start-up accelerators. They are seemingly transparent – and thus "open" – to access given that practices of use extend beyond single events, qualification certificates or specific OCL venues. However, they are also bounded spaces, shaped by exclusions wrought by gender, age, ethnicity, class and community of practice participation.

Despite the postulated openness, becoming an active member of OCL communities depends upon learning and drawing boundaries. OCL users need to invest time and effort to learn how to use and contribute to this soft and hard urban cultural infrastructure. Doing so, some users may also generate knowledge that then enables them to make use of lab infrastructure in other locations due to the standards embodied in different types of OCLs (e.g., fab labs, coworking or makerspaces that often share mission statements across multiple locations). Hence, around OCLs exists a culture of sharing (namely resources, materials, tools and, to a limited extent, also knowledge), making use of facilities for creative projects, and of seeking a social and spatial context for project-driven work in independent professions. However, this also includes drawing boundaries since becoming a community member means associating with a particular place and its practices. While this seemingly benefits and nurtures an existing community, these practices also reinforce social homogeneity. Despite the commonalities and relationalities, OCLs as urban cultural infrastructure are not uniform across cities. Creative projects or entrepreneurial initiatives differ and are very place-dependent. Detroit-based makers, for instance, might develop a more entrepreneurial spirit than users of open workshops in Berlin-Brandenburg. As such, labs are urban cultural infrastructure that enable relations, practices, change and learning and thereby are themselves constantly evolving.

To date, OCLs have been established primarily in urban areas. In the case of work-related OCLs, this might be explained by the concentration of creative, knowledge-intensive and digital professions in urban centres. Furthermore, urban environments might tend to expose individuals to novel technologies, new ideas from distant locations earlier as compared to rural regions (which might explain the concentration of experimentation-oriented labs in cities as well). Many OCL initiatives were ignited by creatives or collectives, especially at the turn of the twenty-first century. Later, in contrast, larger associations (e.g., the fab lab association, tech-shops, Impact-Hub networks, Othello, to name a few) or companies (e.g., we works or techstars) further developed the model, but also at the cost of the initial openness to experimentation and transition. Furthermore, only a few OCLs have been established by or in cooperation with public organizations (e.g., Techtown Detroit, A^2 programme in Berlin), fostering a truly novel relation between public and private associations. Nevertheless, OCLs represent novel relational infrastructure for creativity and work that are growing in terms of numbers and with respect to ever-new variations and models of curating, enabling and foster relations among users and their surroundings.

CHAPTER 4

AFFORDABLE STUDIO SPACE AS CULTURAL INFRASTRUCTURE: LAND TRUSTS AND THE FUTURE OF CREATIVE CITIES

Rhian Scott, Luke Dickens and Phil Hubbard

INTRODUCTION

Creative policy in world cities has often focused on the development of spaces where culture is showcased, exhibited or sold, such as flagship museums, galleries and performance spaces. Yet studio spaces are also a vital part of the cultural infrastructure of cities, providing the basis of the networks and spaces where art is produced and disseminated. In the visual arts, for example, without studio spaces there is no possibility of developing an arts scene based on the co-location and networking of creative workers, with the physical space of the studio being particularly important for providing opportunities for coworking and socially engaged arts practice (Zilberstein 2019). Yet in the super-gentrified cities of the global North – London, Paris, New York, San Francisco and Sydney, for example – the declining affordability of spaces for cultural production has proved a major challenge for urban policy predicated on the cultural economy as a driver of regeneration and renewal (Shaw 2014).

In such world cities, manufacturing decline in the 1980s frequently left swathes of abandoned industrial units that leant themselves to artistic production practices and were available at relatively affordable rates. The emergence of vibrant and profitable art scenes in specific inner-city districts was often the instigator of neighbourhood changes associated with residential improvement and economic growth, providing the basis of a seemingly sustainable model of arts-based urban regeneration that was trumpeted as part of the "creative city" agenda. Indeed, it has been repeatedly noted that creative industries generate significant amounts of economic, social and cultural capital for their host cities; for example, recent, pre-Covid, figures from the UK show creative industries were growing at twice the rate of the rest of the economy (Creative Industries Council 2021), with the creative economy accounting for one in six jobs in London (Greater London Authority 2022a). Here, the sector contributes £52 billion a year, with the Greater London Authority (GLA) estimating that related supply chains generate an additional £40 billion a year for the city's economy (2019a).

There is, then, much evidence to suggest that arts-and-culture-based policy can provide something of a panacea for post-industrial urban decline. Yet even as this arts-based urban policy model has spread well beyond major world cities to smaller towns elsewhere in the global North, as well as cities of the global South (Prince 2012), its contradictions have become all too apparent: by "adding value" to specific urban neighbourhoods, the creative workers who live and practise there have been increasingly subject to displacement (Vivant 2013). Visual artists have been especially caught up in the processes of revalorization that they themselves appear to instigate: while their presence alongside studio spaces and arts-themed activity adds cultural cachet to previously run-down neighbourhoods, it frequently encourages corporate-led redevelopment of the industrial premises that attracted artists in the first instance (Moreton 2013), raising property values and displacing both formal and informal creative spaces as competition for land intensifies.

This chapter explores some of the policy models which have been used to embed affordable and sustainable artists' studios within the cultural infrastructure of increasingly unaffordable and often super-gentrified world cities. While much discussion has focused on the potential of "makeshift" and "meanwhile" spaces of art production (Ferreri *et al.* 2017; Pollio *et al.* 2021), the focus here is on a policy initiative in London designed to embed affordable studio spaces in the city for the longer-term. Adapting the land trust idea of holding land in perpetuity in the interests of local residents, the chapter considers the potential for London's Creative Land Trust to preserve artistic workspace despite extreme displacement pressures. It details the compromises required, including the sacrifice of flexibility – and creativity – in the name of stability and security.

ARTISTIC PRODUCTION IN THE FACE OF GENTRIFICATION

The relationship between artistic production and urban gentrification has been much researched in cities across the United Kingdom, Europe, North America and Australasia (Bain 2018; Harris 2012; Ley 2003). As early as the 1970s, Zukin (1982) documented the role of artists in attracting developers and investment to the derelict loft districts of New York, and their contribution to the transformation of areas like SoHo into high-priced neighbourhoods, which led to their eventual displacement. However, much less attention has been paid to the displacement of artists via inflated costs of housing and, crucially, studio space, in relation to different models of land tenure (Pratt 2018). Moreover, scholarship has yet to consider the studio and its displacement directly in relation to wider debates about cultural infrastructure. Yet the displacement of artists, either directly through eviction or rent hikes, or indirectly through forms of cultural exclusion, is intensifying and has become a crucial issue in many of the so-called "creative capitals" of the global North. Since the global recession of 2008, when the collapse of the sub-prime mortgage market in the US sent ripples through global property markets, the financialization of property has encouraged a rapacious expansion of investment in the built environment, leading to a pronounced housing crisis in those world cities regarded as the most profitable sinks for global investment capital (Potts 2020).

Alongside Hong Kong, San Francisco, Sydney, Toronto and Vancouver, London is one of the world's least affordable housing markets, and a notable "sink" for foreign investment. This has boosted house prices to ten times the median wage in even the most affordable boroughs, and as much as 40 times median wage in Kensington and Chelsea (ONS 2021). Rapidly rising land prices have had particular impact on artists. As studio rents and housing spiral in London, some have relocated to more affordable towns in the south-east of England (Ward & Hubbard 2019). Visual artists – a broad category including painters, sculptors, ceramic artists and graphic designers – are among the lowest earners in the creative industries, and hence highly susceptible to precarity and displacement (Scott 2018). In 2016, one survey suggested the average annual earnings of visual artists derived from art practice was as little as £6,020, with most reliant on additional jobs or financial support from family members to remain in the capital (TBR 2018).

In London, as in other cities around the world, affordable studios provide a cultural infrastructure that affords sociability (Zilberstein 2019) and affective properties – especially natural light alongside space to gather and experiment with material resources (Sjöholm 2018) – of vital importance to the process of artistic and creative knowledge production (Scott 2018; see Figure 4.1). The inability of creative workers to find affordable studio spaces of the right kind and in proximity to affordable housing hence threatens to have a direct impact on the level of creative production that London supports, as well as job creation in the wider "creative ecology" of the city (GLA 2014). Demand for creative workspace is thus very high, with continuous occupancy rates at 95 per cent plus and more than 13,000 artists on waiting lists (GLA 2018). Indeed, despite Covid-19 and the downturn in London's creative sector (Bull & Dickens 2021), continuous occupancy rates show no sign of slowing (CLT 2019).

In the UK, the national government has placed much emphasis on the ability of the market to meet this demand, deregulating and loosening planning

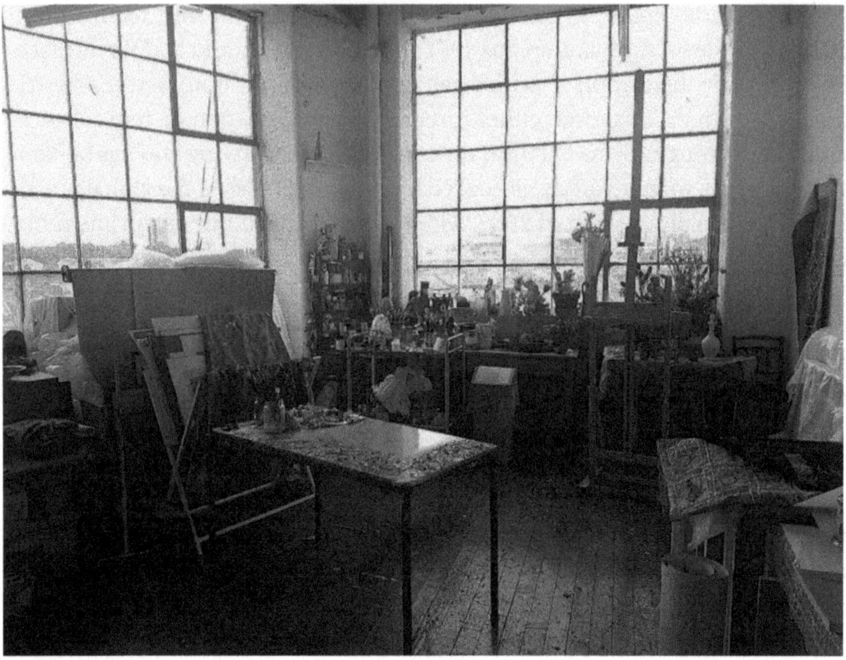

Figure 4.1 Interior of studio at Childers Street, Deptford, in London managed by Acme (studio provider)

Source: Rhian Scott.

controls to encourage more property development under the assumption that increased supply will meet demand while pushing prices down (Imrie 2021). However, this policy focus appears misplaced given that new developments tend to favour market rate over subsidized accommodation, with property increasingly standing empty because it has been purchased for investment not occupation, and land often held without building or selling it on for profit, a phenomenon known as "land banking". In 2015, the UK's biggest housebuilders were sitting on 600,000 plots of land with planning permission, four times the total number of homes built in 2016 (Wainwright 2017). This strategy is logical from the perspective of developers who can afford to wait for their proposals to work through the planning process, but removing such land from productive use has arguably compounded the difficulties of creating affordable property by gradually reducing the amount of market rate floorspace (Raco *et al.* 2018).

In this real estate context, numerous stakeholders, including some London boroughs, regard the failure of the market to provide affordable workspaces as a policy priority. Indeed, for want of alternatives, temporary occupation has become frequent, offering a degree of reprieve for artists in London.

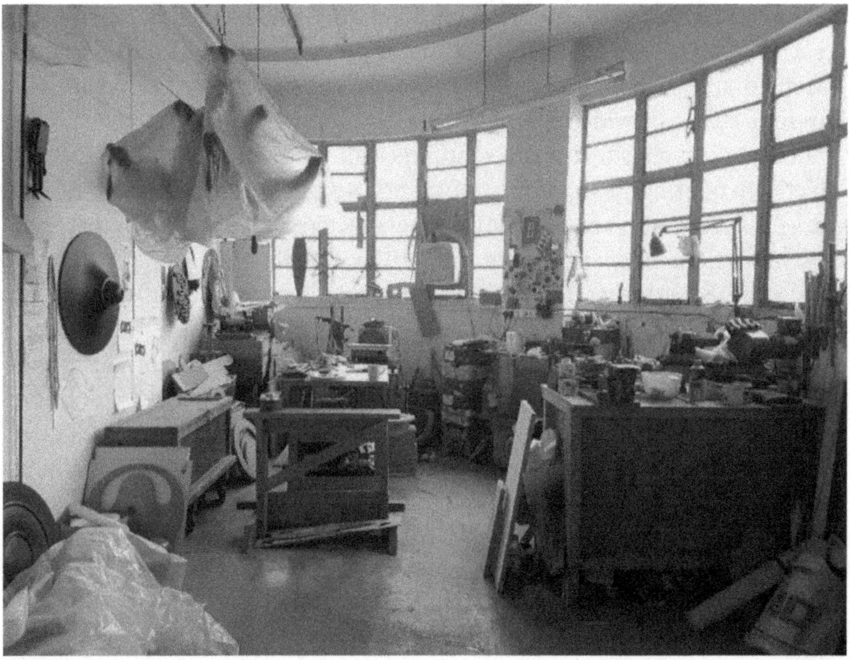

Figure 4.2 Interior of studio, Orsman Road, Haggerston, a former 1930s factory site in London, managed by Acme since 1983

Source: Rhian Scott.

Since the late 1960s, studio groups including SPACE and Acme began renting disused and semi-derelict space as an affordable workspace solution in the industrial East End of London (Figure 4.2), initiating what soon became a city-wide trend (Moreton 2013). In the early days these groups were able to negotiate "token rents" (sometimes as little as £1), taking on empty properties in inner-city areas affected by industrial decline, with the regional government gaining informal security on properties that would otherwise be susceptible to squatting and dereliction (Green 2001). Similar trends have been noted in cities outside of the UK, such as Amsterdam and Berlin, in which small informal collectives of artists came together to negotiate affordable rents on inner-city properties leased from the public sector (Bain & Landau 2018).

Over time, this trend has become known as the "borrowed infrastructure" model, encompassing other short-term solutions such as "meanwhile use" or "pop-up" schemes (Ferreri *et al.* 2017; Harris 2020; Scott 2018). This notion of "meanwhile" invokes the temporary and unstable nature of occupation – generally a short-term lease – and stresses this mechanism as a stop-gap solution to accessing low-cost workspace rather than a permanent response to the demand for affordable workspace needs. It is notable here that while the creative workspace/studio sector occupies premises with a range of tenures, leasehold still accounts for around 87 per cent of properties managed by London's studio providers (GLA 2018).

Although such short-term solutions can be attractive to developers, effectively offering guardianship of otherwise unused buildings while providing a source of revenue, from the perspective of artists they create serious limitations and exacerbate precarities (Scott 2022; see also Bain & Landau 2018; Ferreri *et al.* 2017). Having initially provided a useful strategy for growing a supply of studios while keeping costs low, the proliferation of this model has generated a sectoral dependency on fluctuations in the property market to produce under-utilized space: when market conditions change and developers want to exploit the value of land, artistic production is at best unstable and at worst displaced. This has prompted discussion on how to encourage developers to reduce costs and produce subsidized long-term studio space in developments which otherwise are devoted to commercial or residential market-rate property. For example, the early impacts of Covid-19 caused new voids to open-up in the market as retail and commercial space was abandoned, yet in the wake of these market shocks an increasing number of leasehold studios are again under threat, with studio organizations not always best equipped to negotiate rent reviews and lease renewals to secure their premises (CU 2016; GLA 2014). Across the UK, planning regime changes are also compounding these problems by making it easier for developers to repurpose existing commercial and retail properties for residential use (Scott 2018).

CREATIVE LAND TRUSTS: SUSTAINING CULTURAL INFRASTRUCTURE?

In recent years, the failure of both market-led and short-term leasehold models to secure affordable creative workspace has prompted discussion among urban authorities and cultural policymakers about alternative approaches. Noteworthy in London was the 2019 establishment of a Creative Land Trust (CLT) as part of a suite of cultural policy measures seeking to embed "good growth", led by the Mayor of London (Gasch & Dickens 2022; Mayor of London 2018). The CLT's stated mission was to secure 1,000 studio spaces within five years that would otherwise not exist and make these available for below-market rent to artists and makers via existing studio providers (Arts Council England 2019): its first acquisition, a property in Hackney Wick, was announced in March 2021. Initial funding was secured through £4 million from the Mayor of London, £2 million from Arts Council England and Bloomberg Philanthropies, and additional seed funding from the Outset Contemporary Art Fund. The hope was that, over time, the CLT would attract a mixed portfolio of public, philanthropic and social investment to purchase buildings capable of providing affordable workspace "in perpetuity" across the capital, increasing the supply of affordable workspaces and ensuring returns were reinvested in the Trust (CLT 2022). The long-term aims of the CLT are twofold: first, to purchase property which will be held and protected by the Trust in perpetuity for creative use; and second, to help studio providers to purchase their own properties. The Trust seeks to do this either by purchasing freehold properties or long-leases and then renting back to studio providers, or by part-purchasing buildings with a studio provider. The intention is to insulate artists' workspaces from the instabilities associated with property speculation, which, in theory, avoids studio providers having to continually negotiate short-term leases.

While the CLT is a local response, it was directly informed by the work of the Community Arts Stabilization Trust (CAST) in San Francisco, US. Established in 2013, CAST provides a vehicle for purchasing and leasing spaces for the exclusive use of non-profit arts organizations in perpetuity. Investors in CAST receive tax deductions, with the money being used to purchase property, which they lease back to the sector at below market rates using a "lease-to-own" model (WCCF 2022). Explicitly conceived as a means of testing affordability interventions into the provision of cultural infrastructure, CAST aims to be a "living laboratory that creates permanent, affordable space for artists, creative entrepreneurs and arts and cultural organisations" across one of the most expensive regions of the US following the "tech boom" (Stehlin 2015: 121).

Initiatives such as CAST, and similar, smaller, schemes in Scotland (e.g., the Wasps Trust which acquires properties and owns them in trust for the arts community), Toronto (e.g., the Parkdale neighbourhood land trust, a community land trust that acquires and maintains open and available spaces to protect the cultural diversity of the Parkdale neighbourhood), Vancouver (e.g., the Hogan's Alley Trust, a community land trust focused on protecting arts and cultural space for community building through art, dance, music and knowledge sharing), and elsewhere (Ross 2020), draw on principles of the community land trust concept, which involves non-governmental organizations mobilized by community collectives acquiring and holding land in perpetuity for the use of other low-income community members (Bunce 2018). While their origins in the US date back to the civil rights movement's response to black exclusion from land ownership in southern states, in more recent years land trusts have developed as a strategy for low-income communities to access affordable housing (DeFilippis *et al.* 2018; Thompson 2020). Despite the lack of specific legal definition in the US, it is generally understood that land trusts must make provision for a statutory "asset lock" to ensure that any land acquired can only be bought, sold or developed for the explicit benefit of the community. This means that upon dissolution, assets must transfer to another "asset-locked entity" on behalf of the present and future community, a key feature that distinguishes land trusts from other cooperative housing models (Thompson 2020). Ross (2020: 118) concludes that this model, based on property law, has significant potential for the "preservation of invaluable cultural and community space in the city".

In the case of London's CLT, it is too early to properly assess its effectiveness, not least because the impacts of Covid-19 within a year of its launch in 2019 caused short-term challenges as developers began to rethink their property portfolios. Nonetheless, given the long-term focus of this initiative, considerable work has been undertaken to develop detailed implementation plans and identify key issues likely to be encountered as it seeks to secure quality, affordable art-space. Here, the chapter turns to four specific infrastructural challenges raised in research-led workshops held with stakeholders in February 2022 (including representatives from the GLA, London boroughs, major developers, studio groups and visual artists) which, collectively, provide critical insight into CLT's long-term potential as a means of creating sustainable urban cultural infrastructure (Scott 2022).

Defining affordability

Defining affordability in terms of rent is a key challenge faced by the CLT. Typically, in a community land trust model, housing affordability is measured against the average annual income of future residents, which is possible because future residents usually control the trust. However, since CLT is directed by an executive team and a board of trustees comprised largely of sector professionals, rather than the artist-tenants themselves, defining affordable rent in this way is not possible. Indeed, it is notoriously difficult to assess artists' earnings given the precarious nature of artistic work, which is often supplemented by secondary employment or support from families. As such, the CLT have looked to existing studio providers to benchmark "affordability", based on comparable rents across the sector. However, given the complexity of such provision (e.g., property type, facilities on site, length of tenure and art practice), there is no consistent method of assessing this, with some studio providers arriving at a single figure inclusive of business rates and service charges while others separate out these costs. Moreover, even where benchmark measures have been used among existing studio providers, available data shows that rents above these are often still charged. For example, despite an informal 2021 "affordable rent" benchmark being set at £11 per square foot a year, the actual average rental charges in London had already risen from £13.73 in 2014 to £14.29 in 2018 (GLA 2014, 2018). Thus, comparing rents across the sector is not an effective way of measuring affordability.

In discussions with stakeholders, two potential solutions to this problem of measuring affordability have been noted. The first is to measure rent as a set percentage of an artist's annual turnover. While this would place additional resource pressure on studio providers to monitor artists' salaries as they fluctuate and require artists to follow an "open book" policy on their earnings, studio providers nonetheless see great potential in this approach since they already have relationships with artists and can build it into existing annual studio reviews. The second is to define affordability against a set percentage of market rent by introducing similar parameters to those used to define affordability in the housing sector, which stakeholders in the workshops agreed should be set at 30–60 per cent open market value. While this would require top-down coordination by the CLT, local and regional government officials also welcomed this approach, with one London borough already using it. Agreement was also reached on an important caveat: that discounted rents should be based on comparable rents in relevant markets (i.e., relative to studio space on the open market as opposed to office space, which is frequently the case), and further, that the amount of discount should also vary in relation to local land rent costs.

Although stakeholders were divided on which approach would be most effective, the general expectation was that the CLT should avoid replicating existing measures, and, to make a meaningful impact on long-term studio affordability and provide sustainable cultural infrastructure, it first needed to leverage its strategic position (working with regional government, property developers and studio providers) to find a mutual mechanism for measuring affordability that can then be rolled out across the sector.

Demonstrating the value of artists' studios to potential partners

A second challenge relates to demonstrating to developers that investing in cultural infrastructure is of value to them because, even if it is not profitable in the short-term, over the long-term it enhances the social sustainability of communities and neighbourhoods. Indeed, a recent review of residential property values over a ten-year period shows property values in cultural districts and/or "creative clusters" (situated close to studios) outperformed surrounding areas by 4.4 per cent per annum (CLT 2019). However, developers of new buildings frequently need to demonstrate the immediate added value of facilities beyond demarcated residential units, which includes any studio provision. Relatedly, local authorities are often under pressure to achieve "best value" when disposing of community assets such as land, which can lead to them prioritizing short-term financial gains over longer-term community value (Paddock & Partridge 2021). Both new-build developments and renewal projects bring higher and more immediate financial returns, often outcompeting studio developments.

Another dimension to this challenge – which partly points towards potential solutions – is considering the infrastructural value of studios beyond their financial worth, both as spaces where individual artists to develop creative practice (Sjöholm 2018), and as key sites of creative encounter, exchange and collaboration among wider communities of artists and others (Scott 2018). Indeed, workshop discussion raised the need to position studios as investments that sit within wider social infrastructure and cultural ecologies. Stakeholders felt there was sufficient evidence of the social value that studios add to their local areas, encouraging the CLT to move beyond advocacy for the sector in this regard. This was felt to be especially important for bringing social impact investors into London's creative sector while also allowing local authorities to support studio development plans with clear social returns. Relatedly, discussion with stakeholders raised the potential for the CLT to demonstrate how individual studio schemes contribute to wider regeneration and masterplan strategies. Developers felt that a longer and broader view of the delivery process would ensure greater flexibility for defining what viability looks like, and thus reduce the pressure to demonstrate short-term financial returns. A further benefit of such big-picture thinking raised by developers was that studios could be used as a placemaking strategy to "activate" ground floors rather than merely providing a rental return *per se*, since financial losses could be absorbed elsewhere in a larger development.

Artists and studio groups engaging with the CLT

Although borne out of a shared recognition of the need for securing affordable, long-term creative workspace, the CLT was not initiated by those it intends to support. This disjuncture creates a set of challenges around building meaningful engagement with both artists and studio providers. These relationships nonetheless matter because they provide the "soft", social infrastructure that supports and animates the cultural infrastructure of affordable spaces within Creative Land Trusts. Indeed, the relationship between the CLT and the artists it seeks to support is less clear than the case of community land trusts, which are typically initiated and led directly by a community to meet a specific local housing need. Thus, land trusts offer an alternative for communities to develop and manage assets for long-term benefits by taking them off the market and making them permanently affordable for the local community through collective ownership (UN HABITAT 2012; Thompson 2015). Driven by participatory, cooperative and mutual principles, land trusts are an opportunity for residents to reimagine themselves and their lives. By offering ontological security, and the promise of futurity, occupants of such developments believe that their investments in place (financial and otherwise) will have longevity, something important for grassroots movements seeking to resist urban enclosure and reclaim space for social reproduction (Thompson 2015).

Despite these obvious divergencies, the CLT still has scope to produce purposive relationships between community members who have organized around an expression of shared needs and interests in similar ways to land trusts. Indeed, some land trusts have proven inadequate for protecting land due to issues with volunteer management, since who takes responsibility for protecting or managing a property in a dynamic community is sometimes uncertain (Kruger *et al.* 2020). Thus, the London CLT has much potential in relation to arts-based community development as soft infrastructure, for example, by enlisting local residents into creative citizenship practices, and enhancing community participation while supporting creative city agendas. For both artists and studio providers, there was also much to be gained by the CLT being in a more enduring managerial position, particularly via the management of 999-year leases. Given that the CLT sits within a wider regional government agenda of delivering "good growth", it is well-placed to use its leverage to support bottom-up initiatives in ways that deliver benefits across London, such as by funding and supporting existing studio providers to secure and deliver their own workspace.

However, tensions around engagement also pertain to CLT's relationships with studio providers, who expressed hesitation about getting involved with the trust if there was a risk of replicating their existing work in negotiating long-term leases, or by being in competition with them for funding to secure long-term workspace. For the CLT to overcome this risk of duplicating the work that is already happening across the sector, stakeholders felt it needed to do more than provide studios: for example, by playing a more active role in advocating on behalf of the sector, producing new studio development mechanisms, establishing new funding streams and brokering relationships. One suggestion was for CLT to establish local branches that support both artists and studio providers to develop their bids, providing localized technical advice and support during the proposal and bidding stages. Relatedly, another suggestion was to ensure a balanced board structure that includes both artists and studio groups they seek to serve, ideally following the "magic formula" of US land trusts, composed of one third residents, one third local stakeholders and one third technical experts.

Creating a "third estate"

A fourth challenge is about the mechanisms that the CLT might use to deliver affordable workspace, and specifically how they can effectively bridge the gap between the market price of land in London and what artists can afford. In the UK, property tenure and law tend to be conceptually collapsed into either "leasehold" or "freehold" models, with the conventional land trust approach removing property and land from the market and breaking this freehold-leasehold binary. Land trusts thus create a "third estate": rather than inventing a new system, they combine elements of leasehold and freehold tenure in new, hybrid ways. In the US, there is a unique land trust model that splits ownership of land and property to create a "land lock", under which the land is owned by the trust and the property is leased by the individual (Thompson 2020).

The CLT is not such a radical intervention into property as the US model with split-ownership. However, it has secured its first property with a near-permanent 999-year lease and 33,000 square feet of ground-floor workspaces in Stone Studios, Hackney Wick (Figure 4.3). This lease is exceptionally long when compared to the 25-year leases that studio providers in London typically

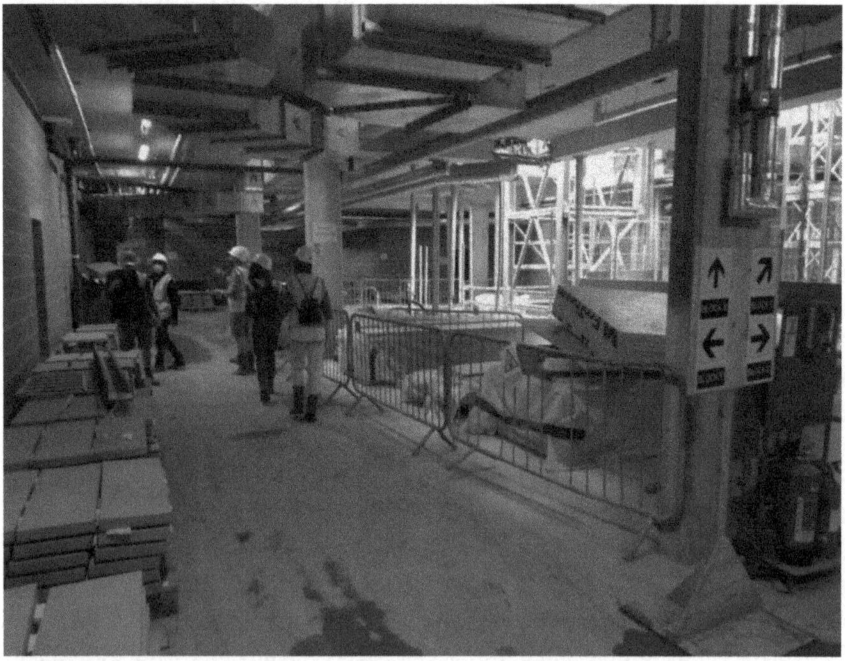

Figure 4.3 Stone Studios, Hackney Wick, London, under construction
Source: Luke Dickens.

negotiate, and effectively insulates the property from land value change. As was clear from workshop discussions, studio groups want to own their properties freehold but cannot access the funds needed due to the short-term leases under which property portfolios generally tend to be managed. With some lenders demanding leases of at least 25 years, the 999-year lease secured by CLT could provide an opportunity for studio providers to draw out bank loans against the value of the lease, allowing them to purchase freehold property in the future, and with the aim of eventually purchasing property independent of the CLT. The CLT is also experimenting with asset transfer at one site, which includes leveraging architectural heritage funds to restore two former accommodation blocks for firefighters (Alice Billings House, Newham) into 30 studio spaces. CAST in San Francisco has likewise proven that there is no single approach for securing long-term affordable workspace, meaning a key consideration for CLT is whether it can continue to be responsive to the situation on the ground and innovate within the opportunities available.

CONCLUSION

Much like other global and wannabe-global cities, London is a highly unaffordable capital city where artists have appeared somewhat powerless to reverse the lack of affordable studio space (see Bain 2018). In this context, the Creative Land Trust represents an important intervention in vital urban cultural infrastructure in a city where it has otherwise been frequently undermined or displaced by the machinations of a super-gentrified property market. Yet, while the CLT's long-term lease arrangements provide a strong element of security and predictability for artists in the face of capricious market changes, by maintaining a leasehold model it inevitably appears as a compromise. Nonetheless, it is important to recognize that the activities of community land trusts more generally are fraught with contradiction. While they appeal to community ownership and the creation of an (artistic) commons, they require legal arrangements, formalism and bureaucracy. Thus, as Thompson (2015: 1028) argues, "in seeking to develop and replicate successful common ownership institutions, we run the risk of diluting, paralysing, and fossilising into inflexible bureaucratic structures the informal, spontaneous, and creative energies of commoning which animate radical collective action". Similar debates surface in relation to CLT. There is a clear need for external intervention into the city's cultural infrastructure to insulate studios from rising land rents, but whether the CLT can foster the types of grassroots impulses that the creative workspace sector in London originated from and still aligns is uncertain.

However, while the CLT model seeks to build on the work of these earlier grassroots models and shows genuine commitment to providing new spatial and infrastructural opportunities for artists, it is currently being promoted as an economically efficient, affordable workspace strategy embedded within a wider policy agenda for achieving "good growth" (Rattu 2018). Significantly, the launch of CLT in 2019 coincided with the unveiling of a £38 million mayoral fund for residents across London to build and manage homes through cooperative and community land trust arrangements (Mayor of London 2018). In this context, political interest in land trusts represents an attempt to deliver affordable living space and workspace across the city in response to market failure, rather than promoting an organizational approach that might empower artists or other low-income groups to take control of specific local spaces and realize their value as commons. Given the land trust model has increasingly shifted into a formalized means to access affordable housing and now workspace, it is essential to consider the implications of losing its radical purpose as an effective intervention into the dominant leasehold-freehold dichotomy that facilitates accumulation through dispossession. Thus, while it is certainly pushing back against a hegemonic system of private property rights in the UK through collective land ownership, without strategic reflection, the CLT still risks replicating the power imbalances of a landlord–tenant relationship and, as a result, limiting the potential for their occupying artists to properly establish or maintain the kinds of creative ecologies upon which creative city agendas depend.

Internationally, this model of intervening in and supporting urban cultural infrastructure at the scale needed to ensure long-term stability is gaining in popularity. For instance, cultural policy strategists and urban planners in Sydney are looking to the land trust as a global best practice model for making space for culture and are undertaking their own research into the viability of developing a similar model to address the rapidly rising costs of creative workspace there (Left Bank Co. 2021). However, as it stands, and much like CAST in San Francisco, London's CLT is essentially taking on the role of a non-profit real estate development company. It is imperative that some form of intervention be taken to overcome the rampant inequalities of the London property market, and notwithstanding that the CLT is at an early stage of implementation, it nevertheless appears that earlier and insufficient trade-offs with "meanwhile use" are being replaced with a new series of compromises. These orientate around a tension whereby artistic workspace, often *perceived* as grassroots, is being *delivered* through increasingly formalized mechanisms aligned to top-down policy aspirations designed to prevent "creative flight" from the city. Any attempt to embed the cultural infrastructure of artistic workspace within cities – whose long-term potential to harbour artistic work currently appears questionable in the face of property financialization and gentrification – is to be welcomed. Whether London's CLT can continue to encourage the collective and inclusive urban futurities often envisaged by artists themselves, and upon which a meaningful creative city depends, remains to be seen. For now, CLT provides a critical point of reflection for other world cities as an infrastructure through which creativity and culture is produced, and the types of interventions that can best support and secure such infrastructure at the scale needed to counteract the creative flight happening in cities across the globe.

II
PERFORMING CULTURE

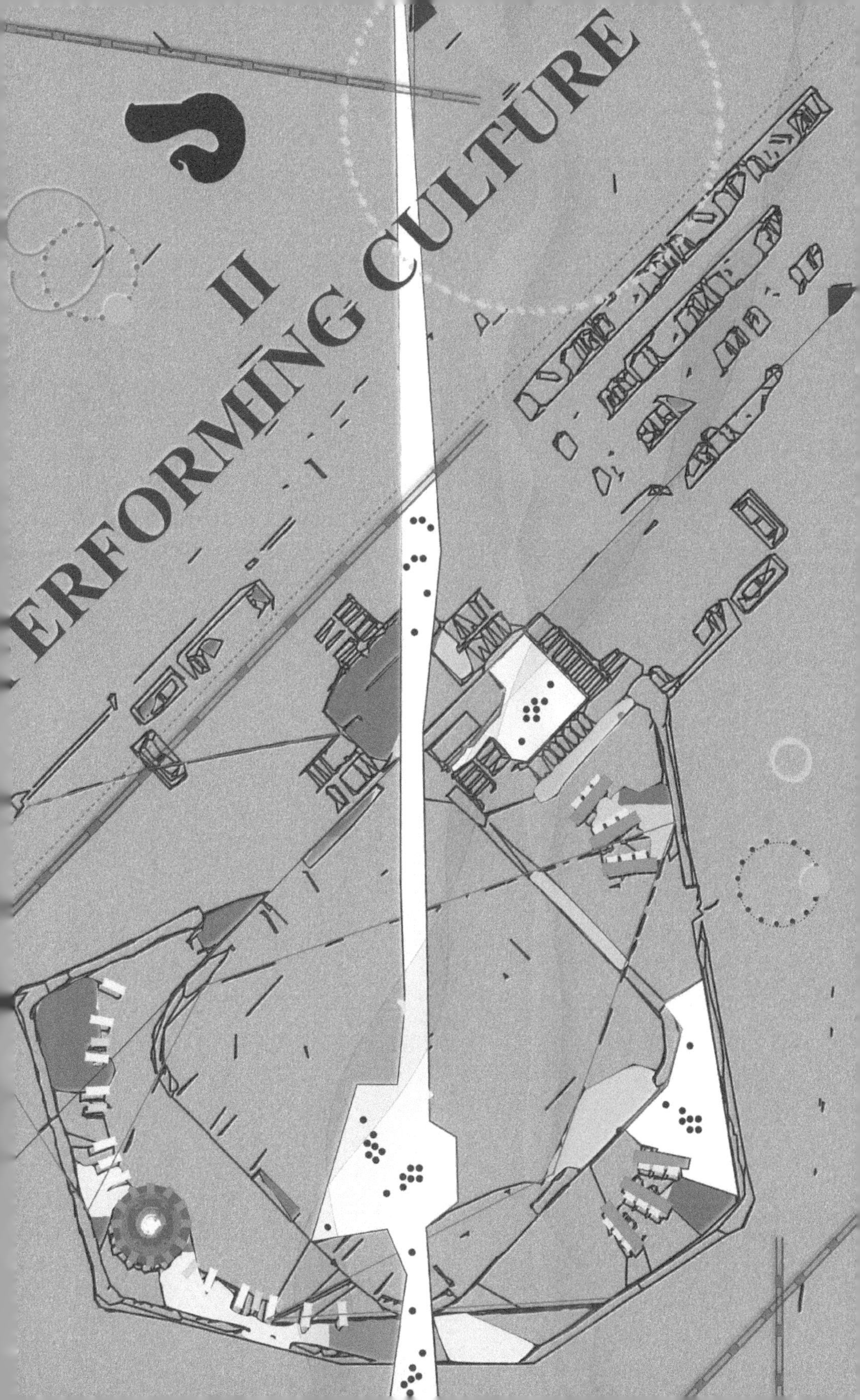

PART II

PERFORMING CULTURE

As a mode of cultural production, the performance of culture – whether high or low, formal or vernacular, material or digital – involves a series of embodied actions that unfold over time and at various scales in a range of purpose-built and adaptively reused spaces. It is by moving in different ways – physically, but also imaginatively, affectively, socially, culturally and politically – that bodies, individually and collectively, produce and perform culture and hence co-generate urban spaces. Performative actions may include instruments and props, be guided by scripts and scores, and culminate in distinct situations or events. On a spectrum from amateur to professional, performers are artists (e.g., actors, poets, musicians, dancers and Carnival krewes) who present their work publicly after it has been tested and refined through rehearsal.

Performances of urban culture, then, are supported by a distributed infrastructure of rehearsal spaces (as well as performance venues, the city streets and community and cultural centres) that are accessed across cities, often in a time-limited way through short-term rentals. Where they can still afford to operate in cities, rehearsal rooms and recording studios can be rented by the hour or day to individuals and small groups. Many larger cultural institutions like universities, colleges, theatres, museums, libraries, dance studios and music halls also offer rehearsal spaces through rentals and residency programmes, but these come at a cost and must be applied and budgeted for. Those performers with long-term institutional relationships and contracts usually have access to stable and affordable rehearsal facilities, but individuals and community groups often struggle to access such spaces and are forced to be more mobile. In a panoply of small rehearsal spaces in the backrooms of bars, suburban garages, strip-mall storefronts, abandoned warehouses and even on pavements, subway platforms and apartment balconies, the uncertainties and vulnerabilities underlying creativity and cultural experimentation play out. Yet, as Bingham-Hall and Kaasa (2018: 10) specify, "[i]f performers are mobile, use infrastructures for time-limited periods, and are less tied to specific locations", their infrastructural needs are less likely to be articulated in a unified political voice that can be amplified through media coverage, and they are less likely to be implicated in the contentious "politics of place" that contributes to neighbourhood-based gentrification.

In rehearsal and display there is always a political power to performances. This is the power to question, and if only fleetingly through different genres, reimagine and renegotiate the urban archive. Evidently performances take multiple forms, and in their intimate dialogues between performers and audiences provide moments and models of resistance; while they may be counterpoints to the urban consumer spectacle, they can also be co-opted to intensify and diffuse its production (Débord 1970). The cacophony of the spectacle is one of unending and all-encompassing consumerism that within urbanization histories marks the current triumph of the city that can only be evaded by breaking up and reconnecting urban spaces into a bricolage of fragments. With its networks of front and back stages, theatres, music spaces, night clubs and dance halls, urban cultural infrastructure reconnects creative spaces that support the performance of culture, its distribution, and its consumption (Schweitzer 2015). Most performances are mobile and ephemeral, leaving few material (yet potentially recorded digital) traces in urban landscapes that become their infrastructural stages. In networks of black-box sites across and between cities, where performances layer upon one another, culture is (re)imagined, given form, and comes to life through the repetitious rhythms of artistic practices that require technical, managerial and business skills (Hracs 2009). The performance of cultural infrastructure, then, is processual and networked yet grounded in urban spaces that can be both specific to cultural forms, but also adapted to accommodate them.

Performance takes place along a continuum of urban private and public spaces. Formal, privatized performances in purpose-built venues of institutionalized display and production, require a ticket for entry. From metropolitan opera houses to outdoor band shells, from proscenia and auditoria to back-street fringe theatres, these specialized and focused spaces for listening and watching have clear parameters for the relationship between performers and audiences. In their formalities, their performance expectations can be creatively constraining especially when they were combined with the stay-at-home and physical distancing orders of many Covid-19 pandemic protocols. As always, to expand and find new publics or escape infrastructural rigidity, performers adapt elements of the urban fabric to create theatrical opportunities. Particularly during the pandemic, the public spaces of parks, plazas, gazebos, squares and pavements offered invaluable and adaptable outdoor performance infrastructure where larger numbers of people could gather with less fear of disease spread. This "wild" infrastructure in conjunction with adapted semi-public spaces like churches, bars and former warehouses all become key sites of urban performance. While such spaces have their own range of logistical and technical challenges when vying for the public's "unfocused attention" and raise questions about their capacities to challenge audiences in terms of content and style, they nevertheless remain accessible venues wherein creative commitments to a city's people, histories and stories are expressed (Bingham-Hall & Kaasa 2018: 13).

Breaking boundaries between private and public, virtual performance in domestic spaces intensified through the pandemic. Computers and MIDI (musical instrument digital interface) instruments provide transgressive tools in non-institutional acoustic spaces contained by headphones. Without the necessity for soundproofing, in the basements and attics of cities, "bedroom producers" use TikTok, Instagram and cloud-based video conferencing platforms like Zoom, to rapidly bring as-yet-unknown performers instant and large audiences. The intimacy of analogue radio has been replicated through podcasting platforms like Podbean and Spotify that instantly infuse earbuds with pre-recorded and live performances. In places where there is less digital access, bidirectional DIY performances using citizens' band mobile radio systems (CB radio) provide a localized audible infrastructure through which music, political messages and culture can be shared. Sounds waves travel and files are streamed across power lines, optical fibres and wireless signals. This audible infrastructure is what makes music and sound happen in cities, but it is powerfully political in terms of its investments and subversively malleable in its innovation potential (Devine & Boudreault-Fournier 2021).

The chapters in this section explore the artistic, theatrical, audible and nocturnal cultural infrastructure of urban performance, demonstrating the centrality of artistic labour to resist state-driven urbanism (Bedford 2015). From the professional "dream factories" of London's West End and New York City's Broadway to informal performance venues, urban theatres are more than cultural production sites that build audiences; they are also linchpins of urban economic development that anchor zones of consumption (McKinnie 2007). In Chapter 5, Johnson and Schweitzer examine the infrastructural response of theatre companies to the Covid-19 pandemic. Detailing how "pandemic proofing" programming and virtual performances led to the evaluation of the weight of artistic infrastructure, they query whether a new malleability enhances accessibility and theatrical experimentation or simply reinforces the precarity of the performative in neoliberal cities that condition theatrical flexibility.

The performance of culture has very real visceral qualities – sonic, luminous, olfactory, gestured and rhythmic – that create intense atmospheres that are felt in the body, amplifying the livedness of cultural infrastructure where people adjust to one another in unpredictable relations in both formal and informal sites of cultural performance. The body, then, "is both a conduit and an effect – a locus of interconnected, shifting, fractured, and often indeterminate forces and factors" (Detamore 2010: 242). But bodies are part of social registers that mediate their regulation and possible spaces of encounter. Under conditions of oppression and exclusion, where citizenship rights come into question, many bodies are left with no alternative but to move and perform in informal and grassroots spaces to circumvent their own policing and displacement (Stanley Niaah 2008). In Chapter 6, the focus is on the precarious performative promise of cultural infrastructure. Stein asks what does cultural infrastructure do and what does it promise? Using the example of a Munich cultural institution's pop-up party called Plug in Beats, Stein evaluates the potential and pitfalls of intercultural art programming to perform expansive urban/national/and international belonging. While national and municipal cultural infrastructure can be used to fulfil the promise of solidarity between established locals and newly arrived refugees, cultural institutionalization works to carry, disperse and normalize territorialized dominant cultures, and rationalize violent exclusion from urban cultural spaces.

It is "the qualities of moving bodies", then, that can contribute "to the qualities of the spaces in which these bodies move" (McCormack 2008: 1823). Through New Orleans' public spaces, in Chapter 7 Martha Radice ethnographically considers the embodied performance infrastructure of new-wave Carnival "krewes". Whether throwing beads from a huge float hauled by a tractor, marching for miles playing tuba, dancing choreography between trash and potholes, pulling a tiny shoebox-sized float or marshalling the invisible line between spectators and performers, parading is an embodied performance art. The soft infrastructure of muscles and joints and neural pathways navigates the hard infrastructure of city streets in encounters that can be both ecstatic and brutal. Her investigation of the handmade aesthetics and progressive politics of smaller walking Carnival krewes illustrates how a seemingly fragile cultural performance infrastructure is sustained through a combination of embodied labour, "soft" sociality and creativity, and tactical appropriation of "hard" urban resources.

In more peripheral urban contexts, young people and their embodied performances are often marginalized and not celebrated or prioritized in the provision of cultural infrastructure. As Mullings and Habib (2022: 295) argue with respect to some of the poorest and most racialized youth in many cities around the world, young people are not considered "a social investment for the future, but rather a threat to the present – to be contained", "a surplus population" that is framed as "malevolent, criminal, or simply a nuisance". Turning to the peripheries of Latin American cities, in Chapter 8, Antonio Moya-Latorre foregrounds the performative insurgent citizenship practices of youth in Medellín, Oaxaca and São Paulo. He proposes the concept of "peripheral cultural infrastructure" to conceptualize youth-led pedagogic spaces of practice and activism that mobilize communities around urban social justice issues. Creative and artistic performances of citizenship by youth are used to challenge the daily stigmas and exclusions they experience and ultimately to make cities anew.

From formal theatrical performances to dance parties to Carnival parades to youth city-making interventions, this section focuses on the generative relationship between human bodies and urban cultural infrastructure of performance. The chapters complicate corporeal understandings and questions of exclusion, displacement and denial that performance in place brings to the fore. Whether attempting intercultural communication at pop-up dance parties in Munich or building creativity, sociability and solidarity on the streets of New Orleans as new wave "Carnival krewes" respond to the pandemic (Radice 2021), cultural infrastructure has crucial affective qualities. The reconfiguration of theatrical performances in Toronto brought by the Covid-19 pandemic or the practices of city-making by youth performers on the periphery of Latin American cities attest to the importance of performance to the animation and use of urban cultural infrastructure.

CHAPTER 5

THE INFRASTRUCTURAL POLITICS OF POST-PANDEMIC THEATRICAL PERFORMANCE

Megan A. Johnson and Marlis Schweitzer

INTRODUCTION

In March 2020, theatres around the world shuttered their doors in the face of the Covid-19 pandemic. Although it was not the first time that theatres had closed to contain viral spread, the scale and length of the closure was unprecedented. Unable to gather in person, theatre companies beyond and across Canada cancelled productions and postponed entire seasons. In Canada's largest city, Toronto, 12,000 public performances were cancelled between March 2020 and March 2021, leading to an estimated loss of CDN$58 million in ticket sales, a decline of 17 million audience members, and "CDN$16 million in lost artist and production salaries/fees" (Toronto Arts Council 2021). While some organizations found the demands of creating performance under pandemic conditions untenable, many theatres began pivoting, deploying diverse strategies to present new work and engage audiences safely. Aside from the almost universal move toward forms of digital dissemination, which involved adapting existing plays or commissioning new works for virtual platforms, companies reduced cast and crew size; collaborated with other theatres; reimagined the functionality of theatre spaces; and moved to outdoor private and public venues.

This chapter considers how the "pivots" made by Toronto theatres in response to the Covid-19 pandemic represent a significant infrastructural shift in how theatre is conceived, constructed and presented. The chapter consciously employs the word "pivot" – a term that became ubiquitous in North America during the pandemic – with the dual purpose of both celebrating the creativity and ingenuity of theatres and signalling the challenge of constant adaptation. Focusing on the first and second waves (March 2020–February 2021), while acknowledging that waves varied geographically according to a series of factors (including government policies and supports, public attitudes and access to vaccines, masks and other forms of personal protective equipment (PPE)), it identifies the wide variety of artistic strategies companies developed to foreground the infrastructural reappraisal that followed. As the realities of the first pandemic wave hit, companies had to rethink their infrastructure, not only in the turn from live to virtual presentations, but also as a means of guarding against the uncertainty of last-minute changes in public health restrictions. This reappraisal occurred in three primary domains: first, companies engaged differently with built space; second, they acknowledged the need for robust digital architecture; and third, they reconfigured their approach to administration and labour.

Although the pandemic necessitated adjustment, this chapter argues that such changes must be understood as more than temporary reactions. Rather, the pivots taken by theatres prompted an infrastructural reckoning that represents an industry-wide shift in how contemporary theatre engages and evaluates infrastructure both internally and externally. Thus, this chapter also considers how the pandemic has compelled theatres to reassess their infrastructural responsibility to the broader urban cultural fabric. Given that the Covid-19 pandemic is ongoing (as of this writing), with many lives and organizations in a state of flux, it is difficult to offer firm conclusions as to the full impact of these pivots. What remains clear is that as artistic and managing directors anticipate the future of post-pandemic performance, they must evaluate the "weight" of their artistic infrastructure, including the high costs associated with maintaining brick-and-mortar venues in central city locations, the need for robust digital architecture and revamped administrative practices. The many pivots demanded by the pandemic highlight a trade-off between the stability of "fixed" or "heavy" infrastructure and the nimbleness of infrastructure that are malleable and open to change. Companies must assess infrastructure for its responsiveness to shifting and unpredictable external circumstances and, ideally, remain "pandemic-proof". And they must engage artists, audiences and governments in collectively reimagining theatre's place as vital urban cultural infrastructure for twenty-first-century cities.

INFRASTRUCTURE/POLITICS/PERFORMANCE

Grounded in theatre and performance studies and cultural geography, this chapter approaches its topic with a keen interest in what Shannon Jackson (2011: 21) terms the "infrastructural politics of performance". All theatrical performance relies upon and is shaped by infrastructural dynamics that tend to be obscured until something breaks – an actor gets sick, a set piece breaks, the theatre burns down, the audience boycotts the production – at which point the inner workings of a theatre company are exposed. So too do theatres depend on the broader infrastructural support of local, provincial and federal governments; the ease of public transit; and the consistent application of public health regulations. When this support fails or changes radically, as it did during the pandemic, the infrastructural politics of performance come sharply into focus. Jackson's ideas resonate with scholarship in critical infrastructure studies that has broadened the purview of what "counts" as infrastructure – extending it past its historical roots in large public works systems to include networks and systems that are "heterogeneous ... configurations" of material, technical, human and administrative elements embedded with various ideologies, politics, and power relations (Carse 2017; Lawhon *et al.* 2018). This chapter understands infrastructure as "enablers"; structures and systems that "create conditions that promote the achievement of wider societal objectives" (Filion *et al.* 2019: 3). From this perspective, theatre is enabled and supported by various built/technical/human infrastructure and *is also itself* an infrastructure that enables the development of urban culture. The pandemic brought these infrastructural aspects to the foreground, enacting what Bowker and Star (2000: 34) term an "infrastructural inversion". An inversion counters "the tendency of infrastructure to disappear" and thus reveals our reliance on it that, despite its import and ubiquity, often escapes notice (Bowker & Star 2000: 34). Such infrastructural reliance also comes into sharp focus in the realm of performance, given that it is an art form that "requires a degree of systemic coordination" between many different systems and labouring bodies (Jackson 2011: 14).

In attending to theatre's place within an urban environment during a period of intense crisis, this chapter joins a strong strain of cultural materialist scholarship that examines the interconnections of government policy, urban architecture, infrastructure, labour practices and performance (Dickinson 2017; Harvie 2013; Knowles 2017; Jackson 2011; McKinnie 2007; Ridout 2013). Among this work, the City of Toronto has been a popular case study. Levin and Solga (2009), for example, usefully demonstrate how Toronto's cultural infrastructure has been deployed in service of the "creative city" ethos espoused by urban theorist Richard Florida (2002) – where the renovation of large cultural institutions and the promotion of high-profile arts and culture festivals sought to cinch the city's reputation as "world class". Michael McKinnie's (2007) historical study of the city similarly shows how Toronto theatres specifically became necessary to civic development; helping to transform, for example, Toronto's downtown manufacturing district into an entertainment district undergirding a leisure, service and tourism economy.

Although arising from events shaped by geographic location and artistic discipline, the model of analysis deployed in this chapter is applicable to other cultural sectors and to studies of urban cultural infrastructure in cities elsewhere. The specificity of local contexts cannot be ignored – theatre in Toronto is not theatre in New York or New Delhi, for example – and yet across varying urban contexts it is clear that theatre makes a vital contribution to the cultural dynamism essential to retaining a robust urban cultural ecology (see Bethel 2022 on the Bahamas; Bhattacharyya 2021 on India; Kruger 2021 and Young 2021 on South Africa; Serafini & Novosel 2021 on Argentina). The future of all cities will be profoundly shaped by how their artistic and cultural infrastructure adjust to pandemic and post-pandemic realities.

INFRASTRUCTURAL ADJUSTMENTS; OR, HOW DID THEATRES PIVOT?

The first wave of the pandemic brought into stark relief theatre companies' evolving relationship to and dependence on critical infrastructure, particularly in terms of physical space/built environment, digital capacity, and organizational/administrative models. With shifting public health directives, limits on venue capacity, nervous audiences, unpredictable revenue streams and increased responsibilities for the health and well-being of their staff and artists (among many other practical and administrative concerns), companies had to rethink how they conceived of, created and presented theatrical work. This section asks: How exactly did theatre companies pivot during the 2020–21 season? Any answer to this question cannot be an exhaustive list of the strategies developed by Toronto companies to continue producing theatre, but rather a list based upon observations of press releases, company websites and the productions themselves. It is important to note that these pivots are not unique to Toronto theatres; many companies across the world responded in similar ways (see Bhattacharyya 2021; Kruger 2021; Young 2020). Moreover, many of the strategies deployed were not necessarily new but were expansions of existing or emerging innovations that had been developing for some time, especially with regards to digital theatre. What was new was the intensity of the public health crisis and the economic factors compelling companies to respond quickly.

These strategies have been grouped into three categories based on the kind of pivots deployed. They include:

1. *A transposition of theatrical form* from the physical to the digital, which constituted a change in the formal register of theatre, relocated the audience and shifted audience–performer relations;
2. *A reconceptualization of theatre's spatial relations*, which prompted new considerations of how to use built infrastructure and also a reorienting of performers, crew/technicians/staff and audiences in performance venues; and

3. *A reimagining of how theatre was in service to its community,* which necessitated an interrogation of theatrical networks and how they were (or were not) being engaged.

Critically, these categories are not discrete (many strategies stretch across them), nor, again, are they unique to the Toronto or Canadian context. For example, in the Bahamas, Ringplay Productions returned to in-person theatre in December 2021 with a docudrama that restaged and recounted experiences of pandemic life (Bethel 2022). And New York-based performers Joshua William Gelb and Katie Rose McLaughlin developed Theater in Quarantine, livestreaming newly created performances that took up themes of loneliness, isolation and consolation (Scorese 2022). Acknowledging the moments where strategy categories overlap is also valuable because it allows for further insight into their infrastructural implications.

Transposition of theatrical form

- *Audio performance* – many companies produced audio dramas, podcasts or site-specific audio experiences; while some invested in audio recording equipment and software to produce the plays in-house, others contracted or partnered with experts. Examples include Tarragon Theatre's collaboration with Expect Theatre to produce an entire acoustic season; Factory Theatre's Winter 2021 audio drama series *You Can't Get There from Here*; Outside the March's *The Ministry of Mundane Mysteries*, an improvised show delivered via series of phone calls; and Soulpepper Theatre's multi-company collaborative summer season (2021), *Around the World in 80 Plays*. Although most productions focused exclusively on the audio experience, some incorporated visual elements (e.g., Nightwood Theatre and Native Earth Performing Art's *Embodying Power and Place*).
- *Move to film, television and social media* – some companies moved their productions to social media or other streaming platforms. One of the most innovative examples is Obsidian Theatre's *21 Black Futures*, a series of 21 commissioned solo plays, staged and recorded in Toronto's Meridian Hall theatre and then broadcast via the CBC Gem streaming service for 12 months. Buddies in Bad Times Theatre produced *Queer, Far, Wherever You Are* on Instagram Live. Individual artists also made the most of Instagram, TikTok and Twitter, writing, producing and staging their own solo productions from the safety of their homes.
- *Livestreaming performances from theatre spaces (without audience)* – downtown companies with access to their own theatres transformed their spaces into livestream studios. Examples include Factory Theatre's *Acts of Faith*, a

solo show by David Yee featuring Natasha Mumba, which was performed live every night for its run; and Theatre Passe Muraille's *Speculation*, a hybrid theatre/film which offered the option for spectators to "call in" at a scheduled time for a collective performance of John Cage's *4'33"*. Other companies opted to make archived recordings of older productions available to audiences, either for free or on a subscription basis (e.g., StratFest@Home).

Reconceptualization of theatre's spatial relations

- *Zoom plays* – some of the earliest responses involved companies adapting existing plays or writing new plays for online performance. Examples include Factory Theatre's Zoom production of Daniel MacIvor's solo play *House (The Isolation Version)*, which actor Kevin Hanchard performed from his home with technical support from his son; and Outside the March's *The Stream You Step In*, an anthology of three plays commissioned specifically for Zoom and written by Elena Eli Belyea, Karen Hines, David Yee and Marcus Youssef (co-produced with the University of Windsor).
- *Innovative use of theatre space* – companies with their own theatre buildings also experimented with new uses of the built structure. For *Ephemeral Artifacts*, an ĀNANDAṀ production in association with Theatre Passe Muraille, the two-storey Theatre Passe Muraille building in Toronto's Queen West was transformed into an outdoor installation, with projections of dancer Travis Knights appearing in top windows for audiences to view from the street below (Figure 5.1). Crow's Theatre, located in Toronto's East End, also made innovative use of their building, staging a free holiday window display in December 2020 for community members to enjoy.
- *Changing venues* – companies without their own buildings turned to other parts of the city, performing outside in parks, under tents, on porches, pavements and in parking lots. These *ad hoc* venues lent themselves to formal experiments in structure and audience interaction. Examples include Musical Stage Company's *Porchside Songs*; Tapestry Opera's *Box Concerts*; and Canadian Stage's *Dream in High Park*, which involved multiple performing arts companies performing in and around the High Park stage – not just theatre but dance, music and comedy (Figure 5.2). Given health restrictions, these performances played to small audiences, a structural limitation that director Alison Wong used to great effect in her site-specific production of *nowhen*, wherein individual audience members followed a solo performer along High Park pathways for at least half of the performance's duration.

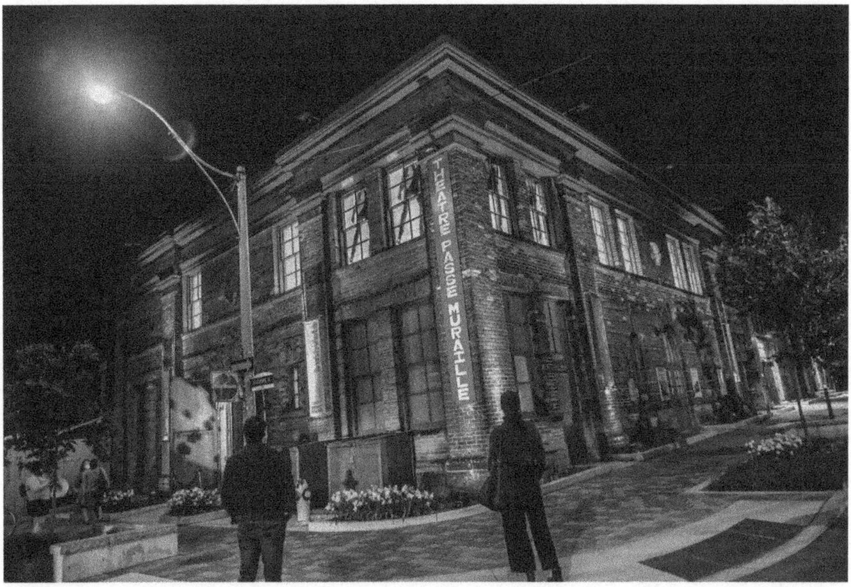

Figure 5.1 *Ephemeral Artefacts*, an ĀNANDAṀ Dancetheatre Production in association with Theatre Passe Muraille. In the photo: Travis Knights. Lighting designed by Siobhán Sleath. Co-creator: Brandy Leary

Source: Dahlia Katz.

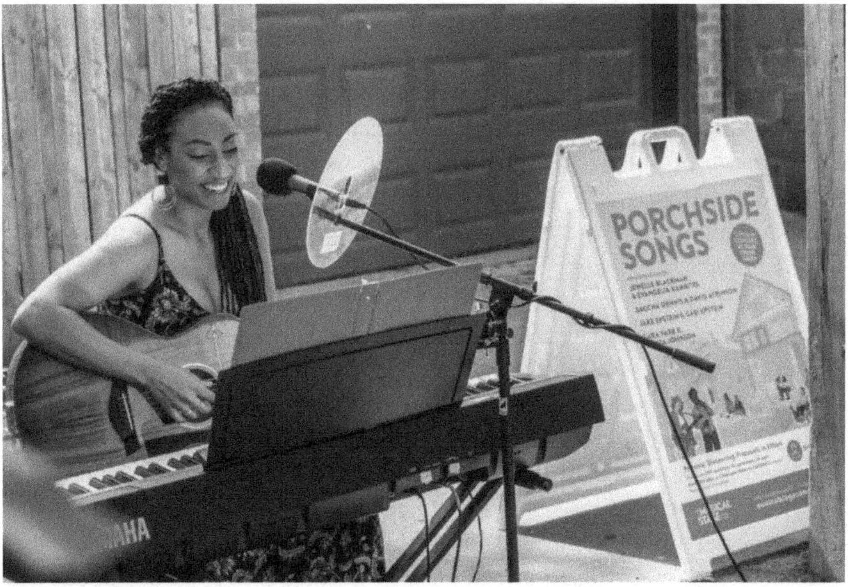

Figure 5.2 Evangelia Kambites in the Musical Stage Company's *Porchside Songs*

Source: Dahlia Katz.

Reimagination of theatre's service to community

- *Education, workshops and enhanced training* – although many Toronto-based companies had previously established programmes to support emerging artists and/or offer enhanced training (see, for example, Tarragon Theatre's Young Playwrights Unit, Nightwood Theatre's Write from the Hip, or Shakespeare in the Ruff's Young Ruffian Apprenticeship), other companies developed new training opportunities, launched "podcast in residence" programmes (see Crow's Theatre), or provided a series of digital tools to support the artistic community (see SpiderWebShow's ongoing series of tools, which led to the formation of #TODigital, a working group engaged to research and propose digital platforms for artists to use). New companies arose. In spring 2020, a group of artists led by actor-director Graham Abbey formed GhostLight as a "digital theatrical training ground and digital performance space" offering classes on a range of topics including clown, singing, directing and cultural dramaturgy (GhostLight 2020).
- *New publications: plays, postcards and books* – while publishers of Canadian plays engaged audiences via Zoom book launches (see Playwrights Canada Press' *Spring Launch*), several theatre companies also engaged audiences with new publications, providing scripts, postcards and other tactile materials for audiences to read or even perform at home. The Vancouver-based theatre company Boca Del Lupo commissioned four playwrights to write short plays as part of their Plays2Perform@Home series. These plays were packaged and mailed to audiences across the country to perform as they wished. This venture was so successful that multiple theatre companies from across the country partnered with Boca Del Lupo for a 2021–22 season, producing regional-focused boxes (e.g., Prairie Box, Ontario Box, Quebec Box, Eastern Box). In Toronto, Common Boots, Red Dress Productions and Theatre Passe Muraille reimagined Alex Bulmer's *May I Take Your Arm?* as a "7-part multidisciplinary follow-at-home experience", complete with a tactile book mailed to audiences ahead of time (Theatre Passe Muraille 2020).
- *Taking a pause* – not surprisingly, some companies decided to go dark, meaning that they postponed or cancelled productions to the end of 2020 and made only tentative plans for 2021. For some companies, these decisions were enabled by government wage subsidy programmes such as Canada Emergency Response Benefit (CERB), which supported many unemployed, furloughed or laid-off theatre artists during the first wave. Some companies paused in response to shifting conversations about the nature of work and precarious labour; others felt compelled to take time to reflect on future leadership and theatre's complicity in systemic, anti-black

racism following the murder of George Floyd in May 2020. The mass exodus from urban centres (and the resultant labour shortages) that accompanied remote work also impacted theatres, with many artists electing to move to smaller cities or rural areas once their jobs no longer tied them to Toronto (Sumi 2020).

Although this annotated list offers a small sampling of the pivots that theatre companies undertook during the first two waves of the pandemic, it showcases the extent to which the form, spatial relations and service provision of theatres were affected. The next section considers how each of these adjustments also required theatres to enact infrastructural shifts in three primary-yet-overlapping domains to support new ways of creating and presenting performance: built space, digital infrastructure, and administration and labour.

INFRASTRUCTURAL TRANSFORMATION IN THREE DOMAINS

The first and second waves of the pandemic performed an infrastructural inversion that recalled how cultural infrastructures are imbued with vulnerability (Landau 2020a), forcing many theatre companies to reconsider their use of, and relationship to, existing infrastructures and their place within the broader urban landscape. As theatre companies required different forms of support in this context, they began to evaluate their built/digital/administrative infrastructure through different lenses. Furthermore, companies were compelled to closely examine their internal mandates, value propositions and responsibilities to the communities they served. A range of new questions arose. What kinds of new infrastructural configurations were needed to support the assorted theatrical forms that companies were turning to? How could theatres develop infrastructure that could adapt to unsteady contexts that included varying levels of lockdown and highly inconsistent revenue streams? As one theatre CEO observed, with large-scale productions that require hundreds of thousands of dollars to be invested before the curtain ever rises, a sudden shut-down means the risk of bankruptcy. "How," this executive mused, "do you ever take that sort of risk in a climate where the rules change on you daily?" (Marcus 2022: n.p.).

Interestingly, the size and scale of a company did not necessarily predict a response, nor guarantee its artistic merit or economic success. In some ways, the pandemic's restrictions levelled the playing field for companies, and, in other ways, demonstrated the liability of elements that had once given companies a competitive advantage. Historically, companies situated in a permanent venue have had advantages over more itinerant companies – their fixed location meant they could outfit their space in specific ways, cultivate a consistent site from which to engage and interact with audiences and avoid the uncertainty of searching out new venues for each show. Although property ownership is a financial commitment – one that ties companies to the real estate market and forces them to weather a shifting urban political economy – many theatre companies in Canada have still sought to own their space, viewing the acquisition of a permanent venue as a measure of success (McKinnie 2007). In the context of the pandemic, however, brick-and-mortar venues became an increased financial liability in terms of cost, while companies without the burden of such "heavy" built infrastructure had an advantage. This inversion has prompted a critical reassessment of the value of theatre space, since theatrical venues significantly shape the theatre-going experience and its social meaning, not to mention companies' literal place within the urban landscape. While presenting theatre beyond the proscenium is not new, the pandemic has prompted new consideration of *how* we gather as theatre publics and *what* kinds of built infrastructure are needed (or not) to enable that.

In the future, companies may rely even more heavily on temporary, transient or novel venues – not only as a means of artistic experimentation, but as a way of retaining flexibility in their infrastructural commitments. Yet the shifting ground that has come with creating and producing theatre in a pandemic demands a level of adaptability that eerily resembles neoliberalism's push towards flexible and entrepreneurial cultural labour. As Jen Harvie (2013) argues, the cultural and artistic adjustments in response to neoliberalism's social and economic impact have produced benefits (such as democratizing art practices and empowering audiences) but also drawbacks (such as devaluing expertise and promoting individualization over social connection). Harvie is critical, for example, of transitory "pop-up" artistic venues for how they prey on the temporary, novel and consumptive ethos that is fetishized within neoliberalism – prompting surface-level engagement rather than true cultural investment. Yet this critique also registers differently in the context of the pandemic when pop-up performances became a viable means of presentation. The pandemic has recast how the flexibility demanded by neoliberalism (which arguably erodes meaningful work and social connections) instead might be harnessed to support the continued presentation of theatre in an unstable urban context.

Similar infrastructural queries emerge in relation to theatre's pandemic-induced shift to the digital. Buoyed by donors, arts foundations, corporate sponsors and government financial support programmes, many companies made substantial investments in their digital infrastructure: outfitting their spaces with livestreaming technology, providing technical training for staff and artists and engaging more fulsomely with various forms of social media.

Such investments expanded the geographical reach of companies, allowing them to develop artistic collaborations on a national or international level, and to take full advantage of the networking capabilities of Zoom, TikTok and other digital platforms to bring collaborators together and reach dispersed audiences in their homes. This immediately prompted questions about accessibility, the different communities that theatre was reaching and the kinds of audiences it was responsible to. Moves to the digital expanded the geography of where a performance could be broadcast, creating new opportunities for global connectivity (Kruger 2021), but it also necessitated a certain level of technological infrastructure and technical know-how on the part of audiences – something that could not be assumed in every community. Acknowledging this, some companies sought to create audio-based work that circumvented the need for high-speed internet, while others turned more consciously to the local and rededicated themselves to serving their immediate community by bringing performance to parking lots, porches and parks, or by collaborating with local businesses. Early in the pandemic Brendan Healy (2020: n.p.), artistic director of Canadian Stage, advocated for theatres to "embrace the local", arguing that "[o]ur relevance will be dependent on our ability to be problem-solving partners to our neighbours and by committing ourselves to improving the daily lives of those closest to us". In the summer of 2021, Canadian Stage modelled this approach to locality by inviting smaller theatre, dance and performing arts companies without permanent performance venues to present their work in an open-air amphitheatre as part of the company's revamped *Dream in High Park* (Wild 2021). Amid the many infrastructural pivots that companies were undergoing, therefore, they were also navigating a balance between investing in local communities and bolstering their digital infrastructure as a means of connecting with new audiences and artistic collaborators.

As theatres adjusted the creation and presentation of their work during the early stages of the pandemic, they also made amendments to administrative and labour infrastructure. Companies have been forced to develop contingency plans for every event and require additional human resources to implement and manage Covid-19 protocols. Staff had to acquire new skills in digital modes of working, which involved adjustments to remote work and the virtual creation and presentation of theatre. In some cases, staff learned on their own; in others, outside contractors had to be employed to train staff or address previously unanticipated needs (e.g., videographers for live streaming). Mitchell Marcus (2022: n.p.), CEO of Toronto's Musical Stage Company, outlines how staffing costs have risen exponentially for companies during the pandemic, since "every task takes 2–3 times longer than it did before, with significant new complexity". So too did artist contracts have to be rethought – partly in response to the possibility of cancellation, but also because digitally broadcasting a production brings in different union regulations and copyright considerations than live performance. Box office revenue – already a tenuous stream of income for many companies – became more unpredictable given the high possibility of cancellations and subsequent ticket refunds, not to mention audience expectations for reduced prices or free admission. In addition, companies rethinking the formal boundaries of theatre had to reckon with their place within a specific urban context. Those that produced "theatre by mail", for example, also found themselves beholden to other infrastructural systems such as the postal service that were likewise grappling with labour shortages, increased workloads, and time-consuming health and safety protocols. For some companies, the potential to reach new audiences outside the urban centre made efforts to overcome such infrastructural challenges worthwhile; whether they lead to long-term transformation and a redefined relationship to the city remains to be seen.

Other companies have had to reconsider the administrative supports they can provide artists, and, recognizing that the creation of digital or virtual forms of theatre will only increase, elected to offer training in digital media. As noted above, SpiderWebShow, a platform that had already been developing methods and technologies for digital performance, created a toolbox series of videos to support artists working in digital and remote forms of creation, and later launched #TODigital, a working group to research and propose digital platforms for artists. In September 2021, Theatre Passe Muraille announced their Digital Transformation Project and committed to outfitting their venue with technology to support digital, virtual and immersive theatre experiences. As artistic director Marjorie Chan observed, the innovations that emerged from early in the pandemic signalled that "Digital was not only for pandemic times" and that there is a need "to help artists augment their work with digital resources and equipment – while continuing to reach audiences who may not be able to attend in person" (Theatre Passe Muraille 2021: n.p.). In these cases, administrative, labour and training shifts are taking place beyond even the internal staff of a company, and also extending to the kinds of opportunities and experiences being offered to theatre artists and audiences.

CONCLUSION

Although it is difficult to know in what form theatre will emerge post-pandemic, and how exactly this might change theatre's relationship to the city, it is already clear that this experience has provoked radical infrastructural reckonings. Moving forward, it is imperative for theatre companies, arts foundations, donors, city planners, audiences, academics and other participants within and beyond Toronto's cultural ecosystem to consider ongoing questions related to the transposition of theatrical form, the reconceptualization of spatial relations and the reimagination of service that this chapter outlines. These questions include:

- *Transposition of theatrical form*: Is theatre's flexibility of form and adaptability to changing circumstances a virtue? Or will flexibility pull it off its centre and risk eroding its core values? How do companies develop robust administrative infrastructure that allows for nimbleness and flexibility without relying on contingent or precarious labour?
- *Reconceptualization of spatial relations*: How is built infrastructure enabling but also restricting theatre's ability to adapt to changing parameters and uncertain contexts?
- *Reimagination of theatre's service*: To which communities are theatre companies responsible, particularly if digital theatre can reach audiences worldwide? What would happen if theatre was treated as an "essential service", an endeavour that is much more than a fringe benefit but rather a vital component of urban life?

Together, these questions challenge stakeholders to be mindful of the symbiotic relationship between the continuing evolution of theatrical form and artistic outputs and, more broadly, urban culture. Theatre companies must not expect to return to pre-pandemic infrastructural configurations. The pandemic-era investments, innovations, collaborations and administrative adjustments that companies have made are no longer temporary. Most companies now recognize that their viability hinges on their ability to adjust, adapt and innovate with little or no advance warning. "Pivot-ability" must be embedded within a company's infrastructure. Guided by this realization, theatre companies are now making long-term decisions about resource allocation as it relates to: built infrastructure and digital competencies; administration and governance; audience outreach and community engagement; and season planning and artist contracts. This infrastructure-based decision-making will, and is already, affecting how companies uphold their values and realize their mandates.

Such infrastructural transformations are unfolding against a backdrop of much larger social, economic and cultural turmoil within the theatre and performing arts industries in Toronto, across Canada and around the world. As pandemic waves persist, some companies are going bankrupt, cancelling or closing productions early, or losing their spaces entirely because of ongoing urban redevelopment priorities. Living in a state of perpetual pivoting is exhausting, even for those with the resources to do so. Many theatre artists are seeking greater career stability and financial security than theatre can offer. Some are moving to film and television; others are returning to school to pursue graduate degrees or to reskill in another profession; many are leaving large urban centres because they can no longer afford the high cost of living (Sumi 2021). These industry-wide changes not only affect one individual or one company but the entire theatre ecosystem, not to mention restaurants, hotels, retailers and other businesses that prop up Toronto's CDN$10.3 billion tourism economy (City of Toronto n.d.) and the CDN$11.3 billion arts and culture sector (Toronto Arts Foundation 2018). The theatre industry does not merely rely on a strong urban infrastructure but is *itself* an essential node in the city's infrastructural network. How theatre companies and artists respond, the decisions they make – to pivot, to stay, to go and so on – will fundamentally reshape Toronto's urban landscape and cultural identity in the decade ahead. Reflecting on the impacts of the pandemic, playwright/director/producer Graham Isador (2022: n.p.) recently stated:

> The idea that people won't make theatre in Toronto, that it doesn't return in some capacity, is naive. People are going to make it in some capacity regardless of the conditions. But I want better than that for myself and my peers. I want a place where we can thrive, or I don't want to do it at all.

While Isador's words underscore the importance of artists and creators in maintaining a robust urban ecosystem, they also signal the need for an infrastructure that will allow those artists, who are vital elements of the cultural milieux, to enjoy a sustainable, fulfilled life.

CHAPTER 6

THE PERFORMATIVE CONTINGENCY OF CULTURAL INFRASTRUCTURE

Jessie Stein

On a Munich summer night in 2018, I attended a dance party. The music was all over the place: an Afghan *qataghani* was followed by German hip-hop, a Syrian *dabke* tune would play after a Turkish remix of an old recording of a tango track. It had been almost three years since: thousands of migrants had arrived in Munich's central train station; the city had erected refugee camps to receive newcomers; the asylum paperwork, the translation, the German lessons and the mutual aid networks had all been established.

The partygoers had grown up in many different parts of the world, many of them waiting on Germany's immigration apparatus to process their refugee claims, or their appeals after their status had been turned down. People were dancing, drinking, talking or smoking by the club door. Of the 50-plus people there, most had arrived in Munich since the proclamation of a so-called "European refugee crisis" – some by foot, by bus, by train and some, like me, by plane. We shared the same room that night because we knew the music would be diverse. While it can be challenging to dance to unfamiliar musical styles and the shift from one track to the next can be jarring, this was to be part of the night's beauty.

The party, called Plug in Beats, was billed as an "intercultural democratic dance party" (Figure 6.1). Each month, long-established Munich residents and newly arrived people came together in Orangehouse, one of the small clubs housed in Feierwerk, a city-funded cultural centre. Armed with smartphones, attendees would choose music for each other to dance to. The process, which borrowed from karaoke, followed a specific format. Attendees were greeted by Feierwerk staff and volunteers who passed around laminated cards with numbers on them. Translators were on hand, and instructions in six different languages (Arabic, Farsi, French, German, English and Spanish) were laid out around the room explaining that numbers would soon appear on a VJ screen above the stage, indicating

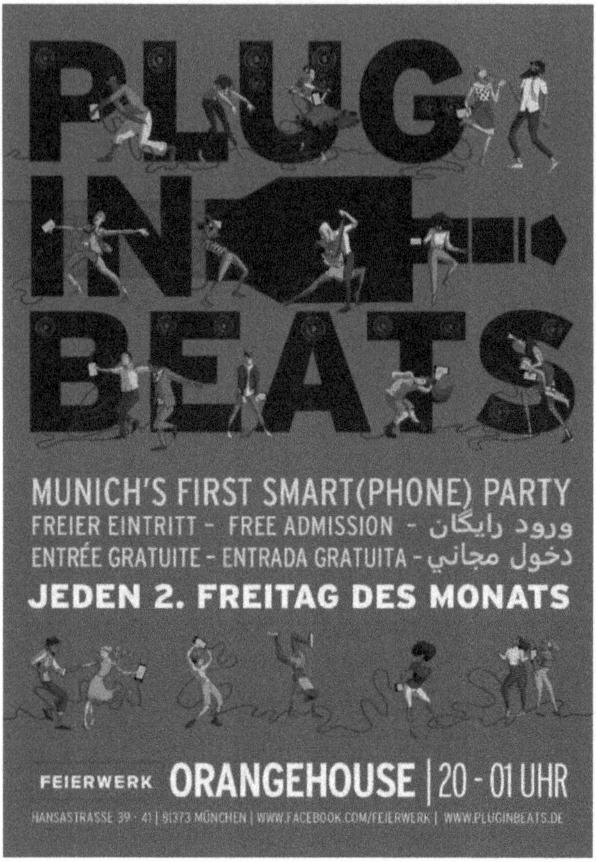

Figure 6.1 Promotional poster for Plug in Beats party, Munich

Source: Feierwerk.

the moment to bring one's smartphone to the DJ with a musical selection ready. And so, the night of music would go, with numbers changing above the booth and songs of all kinds blaring through speakers as the DJ played tracks chosen by attendees in a continuous stream to the dancing crowd.

Plug in Beats was started in response to a need – a camp had been installed on one of Feierwerk's neighbouring lots in 2015 and the people living there had nowhere to play music, and, at first, few places to socialize. Following the construction of the camp in 2016, the centre's organizers made a deliberate effort to open the institution to newly arrived refugee claimants. They offered free tickets and created events in collaboration with the newcomers. Some events, like Plug in Beats, were specifically intended to bring together newcomers and longer established residents. In addition to the party, Feierwerk's radio station, which broadcasts across the Munich area, created slots for multilingual and migrant-produced programming. The centre developed a "cultural companions" programme to introduce the new migrants to Feierwerk's offerings and local cultural norms. Through these efforts, Feierwerk became an important place for intercultural sociality between established locals and newly arrived migrants. This programming, like all Feierwerk's initiatives, directed a public funding infrastructure that we might think of as specifically *cultural*, and redistributed these public goods to a new public consisting of both citizens and people rendered precarious by insecure immigration status.

In the context of the European Union's (EU) heated immigration debate, such a move begs the question of how to think about these instances of the extension of belonging to people with politically contested and legally contingent immigration status and their unequivocal inclusion as valid recipients of public goods. Spaces like Feierwerk are nodes in a wider cultural infrastructure, their programming working with an expansive and inclusionary idea of "the public". While this programming may be considered transgressive, do the moments they create simply function as safety valves, ultimately stabilizing existing social relations? What does *cultural* infrastructure "promise" (Anand *et al.* 2018) and what, in its multivariate forms, can cultural infrastructure do? If infrastructure's politics and poetics are associated with a desire for (or the desire to profit from) a co-temporaneous global modernity founded on notions of progress (Larkin 2013), when urban infrastructure is "cultural", what is its role in the contest over the definition of belonging? This chapter engages these questions by thinking through the ambivalent politics of Plug in Beats, where dancing together becomes an act that is alternately solidaristic and fraught.

As the INCITE Collective (2017), the radical network of feminists of colour, made clear in their landmark anthology *The Revolution Will Not Be Funded*, significant shifts in power structures are unlikely to happen through non-profits funded by philanthrocapitalists or the state with vested interests in the maintenance of existing social relations. Municipal cultural infrastructure enables Feierwerk to exist, and inevitably influences its mandate. What space is there, then, between the goals of urban funders of cultural institutions, and the institutions that autonomously employ resources for their own ends? And, to what extent could such a gap accomplish a radical goal such as expanding the imaginary around citizenship and belonging? Cultural funding infrastructure – which, in Feierwerk's case in 2018, existed most markedly in the form of rent-free buildings and general grants from the City of Munich to cover their operating budget – are capacious and allow for these places of counter-cultural and intercultural life to emerge. This indeed can shape the consciousness of the people who participate at these interstices, but what do places and moments that seem to resist more hegemonic (nationally defined) understandings of cultural belonging do to the cultural infrastructure itself? Are there any feedback loops that change the system or reconfigure the unequal political ordering of humans?

This chapter considers these questions in the intercultural context of Plug in Beats. Building on research conducted at the party in 2018, including participant observation and 18 one-hour-long interviews with German and newly arrived participants, it frames Feierwerk as a node in a wider network of state-funded cultural spaces which together form an infrastructure that supports urban culture. It argues that in a limited way, these art spaces in cities are one place where the notion of national culture might be stretched. At the same time, these spaces are susceptible to capture. The Feierwerk case reflects on a question that has long plagued those interested in the relationship between arts and politics: in a highly socio-economically uneven, yet globally interconnected world, how can counter-cultures insurgently redefine dominant cultures?

INFRASTRUCTURE OF DOMINANCE

The notion of a singular dominant culture often generates national and then political belonging. States have a stake in reproducing hegemonic subjectivities that justify the boundaries of citizenship. How is this achieved and where might the terms of membership be resisted? What infrastructure bears "culture" and where might its power be redistributed? Could the plasticity of culture itself scratch at pseudo-ethnic cultural norms promulgated by nation-states to justify exclusions of all kinds? If cultural infrastructure is captured in ways that resist hegemonic notions of national belonging, they may play a role in destabilizing the routine exclusions endemic to the bordering and citizenship apparatus.

Clearly, none of this is guaranteed. Cultural infrastructure shares the contingency of all infrastructure and its emancipatory possibility must be continually fought for. The promise of *cultural* infrastructure may be found in the margins of cultural institutions, where cultural workers sometimes have the agency to adapt national funds to create spaces of expansive urban belonging. This expansion is neither accidental, nor necessarily aimed at reorienting the funding infrastructure *per se*. Nonetheless, it may be generative of openings or shifts in structures of collective feelings about who constitutes the public entitled to membership in society and stable access to public goods. To expand the project of cultural belonging to one of political belonging requires fundamental shifts in the well-funded, highly institutionalized cultural infrastructure, which carries and disperses, exports and normalizes notions of singular territorialized dominant cultures.

WHAT COUNTS AS CULTURAL INFRASTRUCTURE?

Infrastructure has received so much attention in recent years that it has earned the status of "a turn". The proliferation of metaphorical, commercial, colloquial and academic applications of the word are dizzying. In this chapter, infrastructure requires a specific definition not of what it categorically *is* or *is not*, but of how it will be used. Certainly, "the act of defining an infrastructure is a categorizing moment" in which political and epistemological choices are made to circumscribe "what one sees as infrastructural (and thus causal)" (Larkin 2013: 330).

With this caveat in mind and, for the purposes of this chapter, cultural infrastructure are major networks that enable the systematic flow and distribution of objects, actors, mores and ideals that are recognized and understood as "cultural". In this chapter, cultural institutions are not cultural infrastructure *per se* but rather access points in wider infrastructure that fund, circulate and enable cultural activities. The Feierwerk arts centre is not treated as an infrastructure, but as one piece among an infrastructure's many component parts. This distinction preserves two elements that are analytically useful: the network functioning at the urban or national scale; and the question of the public good (which invites the question of who constitutes the public and has access to the benefits of citizenship) (Anand 2017). The institutions that make up the "hard" expression of cultural infrastructure (e.g., schools, museums, arts centres) are the places where a cultural mandate ("soft infrastructure") finds its expression.

The infrastructure of state funding bodies and the programming mandates attached to them outline parameters for what counts as supportable cultural activity. What counts as culture, however, in a particular place is also a question of which people are constructed as the deserving beneficiaries of state support and what aims are supportable (Caust 2003). Studies of state-funded civil society institutions reveal the limits to purely co-optational views of the state's hold over social organizations (Rantisi & Leslie 2021). While organizations are regularly incorporated into the social, cultural or economic agendas of state funders, and often are complicit with state aims, recent work by Rantisi and Leslie (2021) suggests that funders' control is mediated in important ways that may be overlooked without careful attention to their everyday institutional practices. Institutional actors have a role to play in shaping how resources are used within civil society institutions. These workers, who are aware of funders' constraints, may seek institutional strategies to "push back in ways that may be overlooked when emphasizing co-optation" (Rantisi & Leslie 2021: 366).

Larkin (2013) details how many thinkers in science and technology studies follow Hughes' (1993) notion that an infrastructural analysis centres the system and system building. For science and technology studies scholars (Bowker & Star 2000), the gift of a systems approach is that it brings technological and non-technological networks into conversation to reveal both in the infrastructural apparatus (Larkin 2013). State cultural funding provides a networked infrastructure that participates in a nation-building project that touches people at the urban scale. The definition of European national belonging following the so-called refugee crisis has been charged around the politics of migration. Migration politics, in turn, bears a marked racial integument (Gutiérrez Rodríguez 2018). Indeed, as De Genova (2017: 75) argues, the question of European national identity has acquired a vexing quality as "presumptively self-evident, fundamental national identities have been destabilized in unprecedented and unforeseen ways by the mere presence and lived practices of migrants and their progeny". The capture and redirection of cultural funds by urban institutions may seem a small place to look at the cultural politics of national belonging, but the counter-cultural moves made by rebellious nodes of larger cultural infrastructure merits attention. These spaces have a role to play in shaping the apparatus of the politics of belonging.

In liberal societies, the promotion of cultural expression has often been employed to contain political struggle. In this context, the interface of the political and the cultural in bounded nations is vitally important, because the legal systems that enable the persistence of life-preserving (albeit insufficient) institutions, such as asylum, are bound up in and contested in the terms of both cultural politics (they do (not) belong) and the cost of social supports (public goods). When considering cultural infrastructure in relation to migrants, its role in the contest over taken-for-granted definitions of culture must be considered.

SCALING A CULTURAL INFRASTRUCTURE (TO MAYBE TEAR IT DOWN)

In many wealthy countries, cultural and political inclusion is perhaps most obviously defined at the nation-state scale. Nation-states depend on the creation of a community of members (citizens) to safeguard the salience of a "national" body – the "self" in "self-determination" (Anderson 2016). The ongoing debate around the concept of *leitkultur* (leading culture) is a salient example of the struggle over the cultural framing of national belonging (Pautz 2005). Of course, the citizenry of wealthy countries always contains multiple cultural groups, and while some celebrate this "diversity", the infrastructure that organizes culture – expansively defined or otherwise – seeks to cohere a citizenry around certain ideas at the expense of others (Moss 2009). The

German state uses the concept of integration to manage access to the nation's cultural infrastructure.

Examples of Germany's national cultural infrastructure includes state arts funding bodies, education systems and integration programmes, which are often accessed at an urban scale through public institutions and non-profits. While the institutions providing services are usually nominally independent, their supporting infrastructure offers contingent funding that frequently blunts the radical potential of local institutions and turns their more radical aims into reforms. This is because of what the INCITE! Collective (2017) call the "non-profit industrial complex", defined by Rodríguez (2017: 21–2) as "a set of symbiotic relationships that link political and financial technologies of state and owning class control with surveillance over public political ideology, including and especially emergent in progressive and leftist social movements".

For arts institutions in Germany, the funding of majority interests reproduces a tacitly white, bourgeois status quo as "culture" to the neglect of youth and migrant population needs. Political formations within non-profits (like Feierwerk) have historically defended the colonial, white supremacist status quo which benefits them (INCITE! Collective 2017). It is nevertheless also the case that urban cultural institutions are run and accessed by people acting at the human scale whose work practices accomplish outcomes other than those planned. The national infrastructural apparatus cannot fully control what happens in the everyday life of localized urban institutional nodes, where activists have agency to siphon power and to reinterpret how resources might be used, even as conformist pressures abound.

Cultural life in general, and artistic work specifically, can play a role in social consciousness building. Over time, in small ways, this can lead to feedback loops that speak back to the premises that undergird cultural infrastructure. Shifts in structures of feeling are worked through in the cultural sphere, sometimes making space for conversations that help people understand structural challenges that initiate alternate structural demands of the state. But infrastructure does not come cheap and is typically built to last a long time. It must be maintained, and from time-to-time rebuilt. If enough power is siphoned, if enough feedback loops are activated, and if the consciousness work that sometimes comes out of cultural spaces combines with social movements to mount a challenge to a power structure, cultural infrastructure may be eroded, renovated and lead to political transformation. Even if all these *ifs* fall into line, transformation is not guaranteed. Infrastructure, cultural or otherwise, holds ambivalent promises and cultural infrastructure is built to make space for and contain political and social difference in the cultural realm.

A NETWORK OF COMMUNITY ARTS AND CULTURAL CENTRES: FEIERWERK GELÄNDE IN MUNICH

Feierwerk is as a non-profit service organization in Munich, Germany with a mandate to empower people of all ages through cultural activities and social engagement. Many of the organization's initial cultural activities were music-related, and while today Feierwerk makes space for various cultural activities, it retains a strong music focus. In 1983, Feierwerk's founders were studying critical pedagogy, and were assigned to organize a youth culture project. They saw themselves as educators working with young people outside of the traditional school system engaged in performing and promoting cultural work. "The idea was to animate people to participate in cultural action" (interview, 27 August 2018). After Feierwerk obtained non-profit status, it became possible to partner with the city and to apply for funding to launch projects.

In Munich, 1985 was the "Year of the Youth", and Feierwerk asked the city to loan it a large building for the year. After a successful year, the city agreed to an expansion of the space and its operations. Feierwerk was always strategic in its interactions with the state, never presenting itself as an anarchist or anti-state organization. Its strong ties with the municipal government afforded the security of city permits and funding. The institutional legitimacy it built resulted in substantial material and financial benefits, culminating in the municipal gift of access to a large building complex on a main street. In 2018, Feierwerk occupied all of its buildings rent-free and received a substantial operating budget. The staff employed for "pedagogical" reasons have their full salaries paid by the City of Munich, and the institution accesses several other municipal programmes. At the time of study, 40 per cent of Feierwerk's budget came from municipal grants to support cultural activities and 60 per cent of the operating budget was generated through ticket sales for events. The Bavarian state government also contributed a small amount of money annually as cultural grants. This infrastructure of urban support was already in place when Feierwerk-Gelände gained a refugee camp as a neighbour.

Siphoning power

The arrival of the camp prompted a change of narrative in Feierwerk's approach to programming. The head cultural programmer, Thomas Lechner, identified Feierwerk as a progressive venue and one ultimately responsible for active inclusion.

> Before the migrant camp was set up Feierwerk said "we programme culture for everyone" ... Everyone is welcome [but] that doesn't necessarily mean that everyone shows up. It's a very passive attitude, so we changed that into something more active – and as a progressive cultural venue we did not want to exclude, but we had to learn the way to approach others.
>
> (interview, 27 August 2018)

He began to strategize about how to open Feierwerk's spaces to its new neighbours – 170 people initially housed in one big tent, with a smaller catering tent and some containers for washing and showers. German classes were held in the medical centre, but there was nowhere for people to spend their time during the day. The logic of providing neighbourhood support for artistic and cultural expression to a now-expanded group of people became a permissible frame through which to justify the use of Feierwerk's infrastructural funding.

Feierwerk's institutional mandate made it possible to have a conversation about accommodating a group of people who had unexpectedly appeared and were not yet part of the local community and dedicating a portion of the space for these newcomers. Feierwerk's approach looks a lot like integration in that it opens its spaces and creates the possibility of interactivity between locals and migrants. However, the programming did not bear the assimilationist tinge carried by many integration programmes. Instead, Feierwerk's programming attempted to make space for people with various cultural backgrounds to access their infrastructure and produce or share their culture.

Through trial and error, Feierwerk staff created programming where different cultural backgrounds and experiences would be useful, appreciated, and wanted. The first project, *Kultur Begleiter*, was a cultural companion initiative that offered local Feierwerk attendees free entry to shows with the condition that they spend the evening with a group of five refugees. All Feierwerk's shows had at least 12 tickets set aside for these purposes and migrants could apply for the tickets at their camp. Next, the centre's gallery hosted an exhibit of the films and photos that the camp residents took during their migrations and a radio programme, *Babel FM* (a multilanguage radio show broadcast across Munich which regularly features people who lived at the camp), was initiated. After DJing at a big welcome party for refugees in a large venue in the city centre, Lechner got the idea for an intercultural dance party where a mixed audience of established locals and "new-citizens" could choose the music and dance together.

Dancing at Plug in Beats

As the numbers on the VJ screen change at Plug in Beats, wildly different songs are played in quick succession. Each musical selection demands a different kind of movement and both music and dance bely complex weavings of national cultures and practices. Simultaneously, the dance movements signal membership as well as otherness (Reed 1998). Plug in Beats created a context where no single national culture dominated the speakers, but each dancer experienced both the comfort of familiar sounds and movement and the discomfort of the unfamiliar (Figure 6.2).

The dancers assembled in different formations depending on the music. They formed circles when the music called for it. If an Afghan song played, some semblance of a *qataghani* would begin, with those who knew the dance lifting their heels behind them and holding their arms out wide, crossing their legs in tiny, graceful steps. Others did their best to mimic. They tried to move their feet in better unison and were made to feel welcome as they stumbled along in good faith. Soon the music would change, maybe bringing a new challenge or maybe something more immediately accessible to the body.

The shared responsibility for the soundtrack gave the people in the room an opportunity to collaborate in the setting of the sonics and movement culture of the party. A young refugee who had been to more than 20 Plug in Beats parties said that he preferred this party to others for this reason. He could hear music he loved, and he liked the intercultural aspect of getting to dance with diverse people to music from elsewhere in the world, with everyone

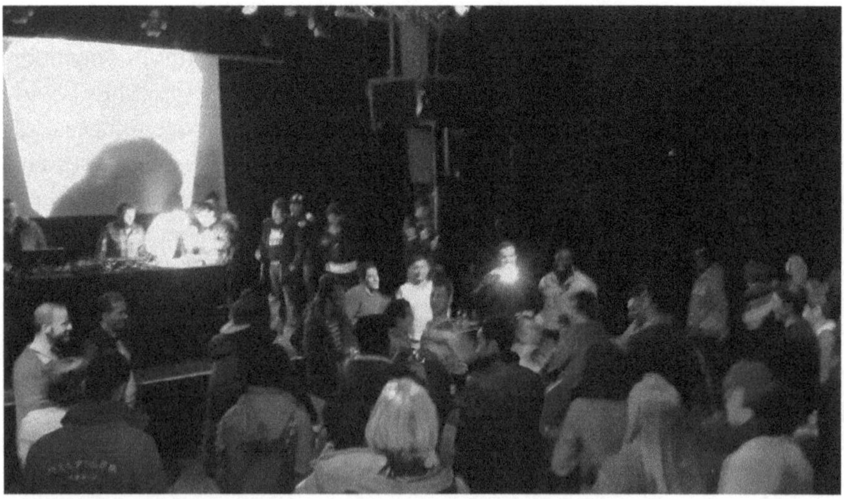

Figure 6.2 Dancers and the DJ booth at Plug in Beats in 2016

Source: Thomas Lechner.

sharing something of themselves or their culture because together they had a stake in the culture of Feierwerk.

Feedback loops

For migrant attendees, dancing together and sharing music was a way to make friends, practice new languages and learn German cultural norms. "The people at the party all come from different corners," one Afghan migrant explained, "we hardly meet elsewhere, but we always meet there ... [At Plug in Beats]. I feel really good, I see people, I have lots of friends around, we dance. Once a month we dance together." The familiar space of Feierwerk facilitates a monthly musical togetherness, an "inoperative community" strung together through the communication of songs and beats (Nancy 1991). People assembled on a Friday night, they briefly held the space together, then dispersed to different locales and social realities, often with new appreciations.

For many German-born attendees the party provided the first social occasion to meet a "newcomer". Many said that the experience of meeting migrant people shifted their way of thinking about who migrants were and what should be "done" about the newly arrived people. Participants of all nationalities explained that the embodied act of dancing and chatting together at the party had strengthened their sense of solidarity. As one German participant explained:

> When we meet in this frame of dancing, then you automatically have something in common. So, it's very easy to talk to this person and to get to know each other [...]. It is very necessary for Germany now to find peace in this whole debate, and not to produce more hate, where there is already ... a very, very difficult relationship with migrants right now.
>
> (interview, 20 August 2018)

He was correct. Hate was rampant in the streets as much as in the state. A 2018 report by Müller and Schwarz (2018) detailed 3,335 instances of hate crimes against refugees in Germany between 2015 and 2018 incited by the efforts of the far-right party Alternative für Deutschland.

In July 2018, Horst Seehofer, then prime minister of Bavaria joked about the deportation of 69 Afghans to Afghanistan on his 69th birthday. The same day, Seehofer unveiled his approved "Migration Master Plan", which advocated for social control and cultural preservation through harsh anti-migrant legislation. Although migration numbers had already fallen to pre-2015 levels, the plan proposed solving the "problem" of asylum through the establishment of more migrant detention centres, increased and faster deportations, increased EU border securitization and other deterrence methods all in the name of "cohesion within".

Feierwerk's programming itself could not address exclusion or inequity at their roots, but it could provide a place for where people could meet and platforms for practising new forms of social negotiation. This was an awareness-building process that could potentially provide a foundation for a broader political struggle by building an increased sense of solidarity between migrants and locals. For many Feierwerk attendees, it motivated them to question the status quo of migration policy in Germany and to increase their activist participation outside of the cultural space.

Transformation (or containment?)

In the words of Anand, Gupta and Appel (2018: 2), "infrastructure is a terrain of power and contestation". It may be built with specific kinds of social and cultural reproduction in mind, but how resources are used and who is ultimately provisioned is not fully controlled by infrastructure's architects.

In July, a few weeks after Seehofer's plan was launched, 50,000 people marched in Munich against the politics of fear and attacks on human rights promulgated by the surveillance state. Under the banner *#Ausgehetzt* (which loosely translates as "shocked", "outraged" or "been incited"), the demonstration was organized by an alliance of groups working on issues of migration, anti-racism, peace, LGBTI+, feminism and social issues. The march stopped at various sites around the city and culminated in Königsplatz. Local bands of all genres and citizenship statuses played their songs to the waiting crowd. The captain of a Mediterranean rescue ship gave a wrenching speech about the cruelty of EU deterrence tactics and a migrant and German dance group that often participated at Plug in Beats led the crowd through a *dabke*. Among those who organized the alliance and this spectacular event – one of the largest protests in Munich's history – was Thomas Lechner of Feierwerk, offering a key site from which to organize.

No direct line can be drawn from the siphoning of cultural funds, or the consciousness building work done in Feierwerk's intercultural programming to the larger project of legitimizing migrants claims to political belonging. Nor can it be inferred that Plug in Beats' initial popular effort to expand urban belonging necessarily stood the test of time. For Lechner, the limits of Feierwerk's and other civil-society organizations' advocacy became quickly apparent. At first it "felt like a revolution", Lechner stated. After two years it "felt like there were some doors opening about how a society could be, how you could deal with even strangers, people living in the city, how you could deal with a moment of crisis. There were so many moments of solidarity, so many beautiful things". By the time of his interview in 2018 he felt this possibility had "completely gone. Now we're really fighting", he lamented, "like even with friends getting racist and former supporters saying 'yeah, we do all for them, but we can't expect [anything]'" (interview, 5 July 2018).

Events like Plug in Beats are important for contesting more restricted cultural values, but if the overall vision of national culture is restrictionist, the work of such nodes in the larger cultural infrastructure are limited in their reach. At the best of times cultural inclusion can be a bitter liberal balm against the burn of political exclusion. Ultimately, even *#Ausgehetzt* did not change the political order nor result in any mass naturalization of newcomers. Although Seehofer and his cronies were embarrassed, his power was not significantly diminished, and clearly the anti-migrant lobby was not silenced by this action. The cultural infrastructure accommodated mass protest without compromising the power structure it exists, in part, to protect.

CONCLUSION: CONTINGENT CULTURAL INFRASTRUCTURE

Despite the genuine wish to treat migrants as "new citizens", urban cultural infrastructure, like the cultural funds that support Feierwerk, are ambivalent structures. They can simultaneously mark the border between a society's members and non-members while, at the same time, accommodating difference. From time-to-time when cultural workers manoeuvre their resources toward expanded publics, cultural activity may shift the normative definitions of belonging in state cultural space, which may in aggregate and reshape cultural infrastructure itself over time. Any one institution's siphoning effort, however, is unlikely to lead to fundamentally new and fully inclusive approaches to funding, partly because the infrastructure is not contingent on any one of its nodes. Although attitudes can change in cultural institutions – expanding cultural space and contributing to shifts in its structure of feeling – the feedback loops that might disturb the status quo would have to become dominant ideals for the whole infrastructure to change. Cultural infrastructure, then, has its limits: even a revolutionary transformation in the ideology of belonging in an urban or national culture would have to extend beyond inclusion; it would also have to abandon and reorder the existing terms of *political* membership for such a shift to have lasting power.

Nevertheless, the task of developing and scaling up the work of expanding belonging in the cultural sphere remains a crucial one, and efforts to advocate for the transformation of cultural infrastructure are vital and cannot wait on radical transformation in the state institutions of political belonging, borders or citizenship. Migrant justice advocates and cultural workers must continually fight for space and resources by siphoning wherever possible – from cultural infrastructure and otherwise – towards more capacious concepts of membership and belonging. It remains crucial that resources and spaces be used for the consciousness-building work that destabilizes the legitimacy of "blood and soil" cultural politics and ethno-nationalism whether cloaked or explicit. Scholars too – as key nodes in institutional culture-making – can partner and form coalitions with political organizers to fight for changes in alignment with what is assumed to be possible, even if it is done from the margins or the marginal spaces eked out in cultural institutions. Much is at stake since the acts of siphoning and feeding back to transform cultural infrastructure have no *a priori* political valence; they can be attempted by liberals, conservatives, white nationalists, or anti-racist and no-borders activists.

Ultimately, institutional culture is profoundly shaped by cultural infrastructure. It relies upon it as a point of contact with an intended public and acts as a safety valve for managing the definition of cultural belonging while preserving power. In large measure, therefore, cultural infrastructure's promise is the preservation of cultural hegemony with just enough elasticity to negate challenges to the fundamental structure of who is in power and what cultural formations are commensurate with political belonging. Still, cultural infrastructure's institutional nodes are sites where a contest over cultural and national belonging might be fought. In the cultural institutions where urban cultural infrastructure is sometimes reappropriated to provision generally excluded people or cultures, culture must not be sequestered from its political entanglements. Movements for cultural space and support for migrant life must fight together, avoiding recourse to liberal sentimentality, by unsettling the infrastructure that designs belonging and building the political capacity to shake the very foundations of racist nationalism.

CHAPTER 7

EMBODYING CULTURAL INFRASTRUCTURE IN CARNIVAL

Martha Radice

INTRODUCTION

All cultures enact rituals to mark or celebrate significant events. Some are rites of passage marking life stages, like initiations, weddings or funerals, while others follow an annual ritual calendar. Carnival in the Christian calendar is one of these: a period of revelry and overindulgence that culminates in Shrove Tuesday – Mardi Gras, "Fat Tuesday", a last day of fun and feasting before the fasting period of Lent, which begins the following day, Ash Wednesday, and continues until Easter Sunday, 47 days later. The earliest written records of Carnival festivities date to the twelfth century, and it is still celebrated in many places around the world.

What Carnivals share is a cultural infrastructure that allows certain kinds of things to happen: forms of sociability and exchange, performances of parody or pageantry and affectively charged sensory and aesthetic experiences of music, movement, spectacle, food and other stimulants. This chapter argues that Carnival as cultural infrastructure is a product of the encounter and negotiation between three other kinds of infrastructure: (1) an overall temporal and organizational infrastructure; (2) the embodied infrastructure of the people who create and enjoy Carnival; and (3) the regulatory infrastructure that permits, monitors, categorizes and accepts or rejects elements of Carnival. This argument is illustrated using a case study from New Orleans, Louisiana, the largest Carnival in North America. The rest of this introduction sketches out Carnival as a global phenomenon. The first section situates Carnival in New Orleans, tracing its history and the specific temporal and organizational infrastructure on which it currently depends. Second, Carnival is discussed as embodied infrastructure, bound up in the physical, sensory joys and pains of the people who make it happen. The body is central to Carnival, since costume, movement, exuberance and sensory excess are what demarcate the festivities from the everyday. The third section reflects on Carnival's encounter with the regulatory infrastructure of the city, specifically the processes for securing permits and policing. The discussion centres on a particular subset of Carnival practices, drawing on ethnographic research conducted since 2016 through participant observation in Carnival, semi-structured interviews with its practitioners, and analysis of social media, news media and municipal documentation.

Carnival is a shapeshifter: it takes on qualities and practices from other festivities and lends its own to them. It can be hard to distinguish pre-Lenten Carnival (with a capital C, following Kinser 1990), from (small-c) carnivals of other types or times. Bakhtin's (1968) classic theorization of the carnivalesque as a totalizing, rebellious and potentially emancipatory force is based on his study of feast days in medieval Europe, when people would stop working to eat, drink and play, subverting the social order through parody, ribaldry, masquerade and inversion (men dressing as women, paupers dressing as kings and so on). Pre-Lenten Carnival celebrations endure mostly in regions that came under strong Catholic influence. European Carnivals include Nice and Mulhouse (France), Cádiz and Sitges (Spain), Venice (Italy), Cologne and Nuremberg (Germany) and Maastricht (Netherlands). Carnival diffused to the Americas with colonization, where it is celebrated most famously in cities all over Brazil as well as Port of Spain (Trinidad), New Orleans (USA), Montevideo (Uruguay), Oruro (Bolivia), Quebec City (Canada) and elsewhere. Caribbean Carnival has followed diasporas to cities like London, Leeds and Toronto, where it shifts out of chilly February to the summer months.

Each local Carnival is complex and distinctive, a product of its own time, place and society, yet all Carnivals share certain themes. First, Carnival is a public ritual, taking place mostly in the streets. Even private events like balls encourage mingling with (masked) strangers and are publicly visible to a degree (the earliest Carnival "parades" were processions of guests to balls; Kinser 1990). Carnival thus depends on urban material infrastructure: "Carnival may be seen as a huge play in which the main streets and squares became stages, the city became a theatre without walls and the inhabitants, the actors and spectators" (Burke 1978: 182). Second, the play of Carnival typically dramatizes power relations and conflict between different social groups. In Europe in the seventeenth and eighteenth centuries, "the double needs of centralizing states and reforming churches led to attempts at repression of Carnival's sinful pleasures and vulgar disorder" (Kinser 1990: 7). In the Americas, Carnival not only amalgamated festive practices from African, Indigenous, Asian and European cultures, but also "acted as a ritual site for sociocultural contestations and esthetic resistance, between a hegemonic European group and subordinate indigenous, creole, mestizo and African peoples" (Nurse 1999: 667). London's Notting Hill Carnival began in 1966 as an expression of multi-ethnic unity, drawing on the diverse traditions of the working-class neighbourhood's residents. In the 1970s, it became more Trinidadian, then Pan-Caribbean, communicating black resistance to the rise of overtly racist politics and policing (Cohen 1993). Third, Carnivals often hold in tension bottom-up, vernacular, disorderly participation versus top-down, spectacular, orderly pageantry. Relatedly, scholars have debated whether Carnival functions as a "safety-valve" allowing people to "let off steam" so that order can be maintained the rest of the year, or a site of resistance, empowerment and transformation (Godet 2020). Lastly, no matter how much they invoke tradition, Carnivals do not represent an unbroken line of annual celebration from time immemorial to the present; many have been revived from dormancy or wholly or partly invented, often as a place-marketing, tourism-boosting strategy. Claims to authenticity are thus pitted against charges of commodification (Kinser 1990). Carnival is, above all, polysemous and protean.

SITUATING CARNIVAL IN NEW ORLEANS

Carnival features in the founding myths of New Orleans. In 1699, four French navy ships led by Jean-Baptiste and Pierre Le Moyne, Sieurs de Bienville and d'Iberville, administrators of Nouvelle-France, made landfall at the mouth of the Mississippi River. Realizing it was the eve of Shrove Tuesday, the crews celebrated at a place that would be called Pointe du Mardi Gras, 60 miles south of where Bienville would found New Orleans as a French colony in 1718. The city became Spanish in 1763, then French again for three years before Napoleon sold Louisiana to the USA in 1803. By then, the culture of New Orleans was distinctively shaped by Afro-descendant enslaved and free people of colour and by people from Caribbean islands, especially Haiti and Cuba, as well as Catholic European settlers (Sublette 2008). Collectively, they kept, adopted or adapted Carnival as a holiday. A young Parisian clerk recorded his Mardi Gras experience in New Orleans in 1730 for which he dressed as a woman (Caillot 2013). By the 1790s, Carnival was the pretext for a season of private and public balls held between Christmas and Lent, some of them masked, which "allowed for kinds of contact between blacks and whites, male and female, which were unthinkable in the streets" (Kinser 1990: 24). By the 1830s, Carnival festivities also included loosely organized street parades with masked and costumed figures, ornate carriages and musicians, as well as boisterous, sometimes violent merrymaking.

The rising Anglo-American business elite used Carnival to assert their claim to the city just before and after the American Civil War, impressing order, in their view, on the revelry. In 1857, a select group of white men founded a secret society, the Mistick Krewe of Comus, which held the first formal parade of "two small but exquisite floats" (Gill 1997: 45). This divided spectators from performers, and introduced the social infrastructure of the "krewe", a social club that organizes Carnival events. The Krewes of Rex and Momus formed in 1872 and Proteus in 1882. The members of these elite, white krewes were deeply invested in upholding white supremacy and dismantling the civil rights gains of the post-war Reconstruction era; both this new form of Carnival and laws regulating it were designed to reinforce prevailing racial and class hierarchies (Gill 1997). Nonetheless, the idea of the krewe caught on: over the twentieth century, Carnival krewes multiplied, and there are now hundreds. No exhaustive list or taxonomy exists, but they vary by degree of formality, gender and racial composition, size, social class, politics, aesthetics, cost and exclusivity. Reflecting New Orleanian society, Carnival krewes tend toward social stratification, and most are overwhelmingly white, although some are primarily African American, and others explicitly strive for diversity. Black New Orleanians maintain distinct Carnival traditions, including the Black Masking Indians and the Baby Dolls, that are separate from parading krewes. The original "old-line" upper-class white men's krewes still exist, although Comus and Momus stopped parading in 1992 to protest a municipal ordinance obliging krewes to desegregate if they wanted to use public infrastructure (Gill 1997). Most krewes organize a public parade (with floats and costumes matching their chosen annual theme), and a private ball, although some hold just one or the other. Crucially, they are self-sustaining, with activities supported by members' dues and fundraising rather than sponsorship or civic grants (bylaws expressly prohibit advertising in Carnival parades). Of course, some krewes can leverage more resources than others.

New Orleans' Carnival is still framed by the temporal infrastructure of the annual ritual cycle. Between January 6, Epiphany or Twelfth Night, when Carnival season opens, and its final day, Mardi Gras, over 45 parades roll in New Orleans Parish and dozens more in the suburbs. Each parade has its allotted date and time, some during daylight, others at night. The season has a distinct rhythm. Four krewes parade on Twelfth Night, then there is a lull, when krewes may hold balls, reveal their "royalty" or officers for the year, or otherwise prepare for parades. These pick up again the fourth and third weekends before Mardi Gras. Busiest are the 12 days from the second Friday before Mardi Gras to Mardi Gras day, during which several krewes parade one after the other most days, followed by a huge City-run clean-up operation. For administrative reasons, the City of New Orleans' municipal code designates this period as "Carnival parade season" (§34–1), but in popular understanding, the season is much longer. As well as its actual events, Carnival also generates much public discussion and media commentary – arguably, itself a kind of discursive infrastructure.

A key distinction between krewes is whether they ride on floats or walk. Each float-riding krewe's parade consists of 14–45 floats pulled by tractors, usually "uptown" (upriver of Canal Street), along a route centred on broad St Charles Avenue. Masked krewe members ride on the floats, tossing "throws" – trinkets like beads, plush toys and go-cups – to spectators. High school and college marching bands and dance or other performance troupes appear between the floats. These large-scale mainstream parades contrast with smaller-scale krewes' parades in which most members walk alongside floats pulled by mules, bicycles or humans, usually along the smaller streets of neighbourhoods downriver of Canal Street, so they are sometimes called "downtown" Carnival krewes (Wade *et al.* 2019). I call them "new-wave" krewes, in contrast to "old-line" and mainstream krewes, and they are the focus of my ethnographic research.

New-wave krewes emerged from the counter-cultural movements of the 1960s and 1970s and have proliferated since Hurricane Katrina in 2005, yet their small scale and carnivalesque ethos hark back to the free-form Carnival of the eighteenth and early nineteenth century. Their politics tend to be progressive and satirical, and they make their costumes, throws and floats by hand, rather than outsourcing them to New Orleans' professional Carnival design industry. They are cheaper to join than mainstream krewes (up to $200 rather than over $500), so their membership can be diverse in terms of class. New-wave krewes are mostly white, although a few Latinx and black krewes have emerged. Being on foot and propelled by smaller brass bands than the mainstream parades, they have an affinity with the other major parading tradition of New Orleans' public culture: the participatory annual "second line" parades of the city's African American Social Aid and Pleasure Clubs, which take place every Sunday during the cooler months (Breunlin & Regis 2006). Some new-wave krewe leaders learned the art of parading from great figures in Social Aid and Pleasure Clubs (Breunlin *et al.* 2009); some krewes even call themselves Social Aid and Pleasure Clubs.

The organization of new-wave krewes varies. Unlike mainstream krewes, most new-wave krewes are small and form part of an "umbrella" krewe by which the parade is known. Krewe du Vieux, one of the oldest new-wave krewes, has 17 sub-krewes; the huge sci-fi and fantasy themed Intergalactic Krewe of Chewbacchus has more than 100. Some krewes parade independently, among them the looser "societies" that hold beautifully costumed rambles on Mardi Gras day. As in many volunteer organizations, personalities and opinions can clash, leading to splits between sub-krewes and the umbrella krewe or the formation of new krewes and parades. Leaders emerge or leave and krewes form or disband according to members' energies and affinities. Individuals may be members of several krewes (new-wave or mainstream). People join new-wave Carnival krewes to have fun, to play, to exorcize their everyday frustrations through satire, to rise to creative challenges, to "give something back" to the city and to belong – to a friend group, a community and New Orleans.

Throughout the city's three centuries of colonial existence, New Orleanians have thus elaborated a set of cultural practices that constitute Carnival, underpinned by the temporal infrastructure of the annual ritual calendar and the organizational infrastructure – often unwritten – of mainstream and new-wave krewes and other social groups (like musicians). The celebration of Carnival takes a great deal of labour, as the next section explores.

EMBODYING CARNIVAL

> When I woke up the morning after the day after the parade, Janine was screaming. "It hurts so bad! It feels worse than anything I've ever had," she managed to tell us. I felt helpless watching my friend writhe in pain, knowing nothing about what her condition might be, nor how to navigate American privatized healthcare. Janine knew where to go, though, and another friend staying at the house was a nurse who knew how to soothe a person terrified by her body's sudden betrayal. Janine's husband took her to an urgent care unit, where she was diagnosed with acute sciatica and dehydration. She came home with hefty painkillers and instructions to drink water and set about sourcing physiotherapy and advice on other things that might help from friends on social media. The goal: recover in time for the next parade.
>
> (Fieldnotes, 5 February 2018)

This scene took place during my fieldwork in 2018, two days after the 'tit Rəx parade. The Krewe of 'tit Rəx ("'tit" being short for "petit", so, "little Rex") was founded in 2009 by a group of friends who took the local childhood tradition of making carnival floats from shoeboxes out of the schoolyard and onto the streets, soon claiming an official spot on the annual parade calendar. Janine is one of the two co-captains of 'tit Rəx, and I was staying with her and her husband, Brett, along with two other out-of-town krewe members. I had met Janine and Brett in January 2016 at a panel discussion on "Making Mardi Gras" held at the Main Library. They invited me to a "tiny throw meet", a gathering to make throws at someone's house, where I met other krewe members and began really learning about new-wave Carnival. In 2017, Janine invited me to join her float team (each can have up to four people), and I have helped make our throws and float and rolled in every 'tit Rəx parade since.

When you pull a float made from a shoebox on a leash in a parade, your body twists: you have to keep one eye on where you are going and one eye on your float behind you. You must keep the right distance from the float in front and keep your float rolling smoothly around the potholes and bumps in the road. This keeps your body in tension and your attention divided. You absorb the jolts through the little wheels of the float, the music from the nearest of 'tit Rəx's four brass bands and the clamour of the crowds delighting in the parade and begging for throws. Janine had pulled the float for most of the three-hour long parade. In her day job, she works on her feet as a waiter and bartender at a popular burger restaurant on the edge of the French Quarter. At the parade, she was wearing the black kitten-heel boots she loves, but those low heels put strain on her back as the twisting inflamed her sciatic nerve. What with drinking at the party after the parade and a Superbowl watch party the next day, Janine was dehydrated – and a thirsty nerve is a tight nerve. The crisis of pain forced Janine to stop and take care of herself: imperative if she wanted to participate the following Sunday in Box of Wine, a rowdy, rogue kind of a parade that – rare for a walking krewe – rolls on the uptown, mainstream float parade route, just ahead of the super-krewe Bacchus, pouring wine into spectators' mouths in homage to the big parade's namesake, the god of wine. Somehow, the Mardi Gras magic that people so often evoke worked a spell on Janine's back, and she rolled pain-free and ecstatic in Box of Wine.

Janine's travails of 2018 show how deeply the cultural infrastructure of new-wave Carnival is embodied – and how fragile it can be. New-wave Carnival, I argue, depends on the soft, personal infrastructure of muscles, joints and neural pathways, which must navigate the hard infrastructure of New Orleans' streets, notoriously poorly maintained. All krewe members parade with the body they have, shaped by their occupations and their age, health and dis/ability. Carnival bodies are often vivid, exuberant, funny or gorgeous, but they also work hard, parading, performing, pushing or pulling floats, connecting with throngs of spectators. New-wave Carnival is not a young person's game, because it requires the resources and stability that people acquire in their late-twenties or thirties. Most of 'tit Rəx's members are Generation X, now in their forties or fifties, some starting to experience age-related physical vulnerability. Krewe du Vieux has an especially broad age range, since it includes original members from the first parade in 1987, as well as new members. In 2020, I watched their parade twice, from different points along the route, and noticed how tired they looked the second time.

Distributing throws is another embodied task of Carnival in New Orleans. Paraders engage with spectators to give throws out, and spectators engage with paraders in the hope of receiving them. These verbal and non-verbal interactions can be joyful but also wearing. A parader must manage their supply of throws to last the whole route and fend off rude spectators who try

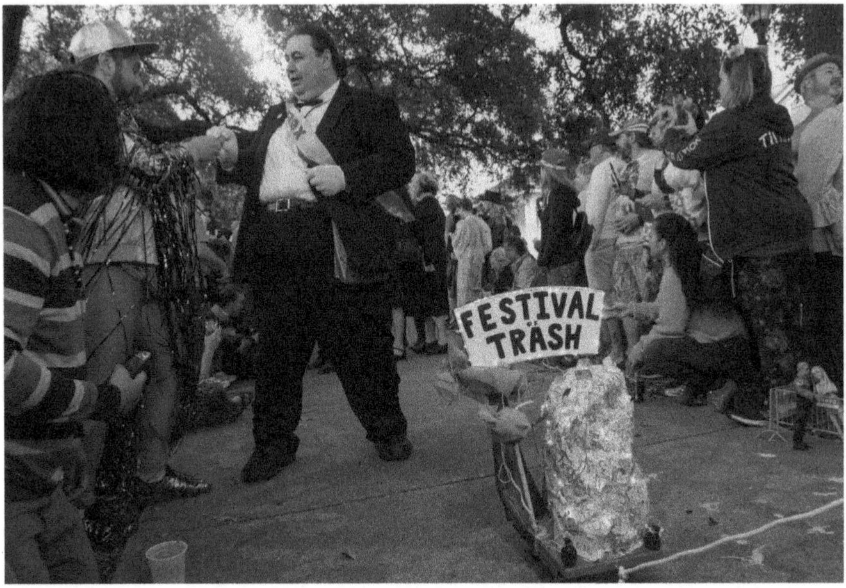

Figure 7.1 The 'tit Rəx parade in New Orleans in 2020. Caesar Meadows is handing a throw to a spectator while a teammate pulls his float

Source: Ryan Hodgson-Rigsbee.

to snatch them up before they are offered. Sometimes, men in the audience feel entitled to get up close to parading women. One women's krewe left the new-wave krewedelusion parade because people – presumed to be tourists – were too "grabby", as the captain put it, in the narrow streets of the French Quarter. Their group now walks only between the floats of uptown parades, where the broader avenue makes it easier to control proximity to the audience. Indeed, most krewes have marshals whose job it is to keep crowds back and make space for the parade – an embodied art in itself, since marshals must protect both the krewe and the ambiance, often performing their role in character and costume.

Carnival is also embodied because it is costumed and adorned. Each year's costumes must be creative, expressing parade or group themes if applicable, and can be a way to transform one's character or tell a good story. Yet they should ideally be comfortable for long periods of walking and dancing, suitable for the weather and manageable in dubious public bathrooms. Conversations about Carnival include the instruction to "pace yourself", as people acknowledge the need to take care of themselves as they participate. New-wave Carnival can be both gruelling and ecstatic. It takes a toll on the body, yet the body is also the site where the intense joy of Carnival is generated, where extraordinary sensations and emotions are felt. In these ways, the human body is the foundational infrastructure of Carnival.

NEGOTIATING CARNIVAL

At one scale, the cultural infrastructure of new-wave carnival involves every body's encounter with the concrete infrastructure of the streets, in a context of ecstatic sensory saturation. At a larger scale, it implicates krewes in negotiations with the municipal agencies that regulate carnival. Historically, Carnival laws and norms have often been used to uphold – and occasionally challenge – New Orleans' social and racial hierarchies (Gill 1997). Today, the City prides itself on its capacity to manage special events, putting the ordinary infrastructure of the city – public space, policing, sanitation – to use in the service of extraordinary celebration. However, tensions about whose Carnival matters and why play out in the permitting and policing process, a contemporary dimension of the dialectic between revelry and regulation.

The City of New Orleans treats mainstream Carnival parades very differently from new-wave and all other parades. A 29-page chapter of the municipal code (adopted in 1999) is devoted to Carnival and Mardi Gras, regulating matters like traffic and parking, use of pavements, float safety codes, prohibited throws, itinerant vendors, minimum number of marching bands and more. However, it covers only the 34 float parades that roll in official "Carnival parade season" – its final 12 days. These krewes pay a modest parade permit fee of $750–1,500, depending on number of floats, and submit paperwork on their route and line-up to the New Orleans Police Department (NOPD), which assigns officers to police the parade as part of their regular duties. The roster is conservative, only guaranteeing timeslots to krewes that paraded the previous year; a new krewe can only be introduced on the recommendation of the current parading krewes whose representatives form the Mayor's Mardi Gras Advisory Council.

All other parades, Carnival-related or not, must obtain a special event permit and, crucially, request and pay for their own policing (though the anarchist krewe Eris does not on principle and endured police violence in 2011). This means that among their other tasks – recruiting and renewing memberships, accounting, organizing marshals, booking bands and venues – new-wave Carnival krewe captains must navigate a bureaucratic process that is transparent in theory, but opaque and anxiogenic in practice. First, the krewe captains submit application forms with their parade route and clean-up plans to the City's "One Stop" permitting office. Then, they are (or were, pre-pandemic) summoned to a meeting at City Hall. At the meeting of January 2020, when leaders from Chewbacchus, 'tit Rəx, and Krewe du Vieux presented their plans, I noticed that none of the officials present – some wearing uniforms of the emergency services, others in business clothes – introduced themselves. This seemed to amplify the imbalance of power that positions new-wave krewe captains as supplicants. Still, captains say that special event permits are rarely denied. Securing policing is less certain.

Special event policing is managed by the city's Office of Police Secondary Employment (OPSE), established in 2013 to relieve the NOPD of this task. As the name suggests, the policing duties the OPSE covers are classed as optional overtime which means that police officers choose to work the shifts that appeal to them. If not enough officers sign up, the NOPD can decide to shorten the parade route, or even cancel it. In 2022, Chewbacchus – with over 2,200 members in 107 sub-krewes – was told less than 48 hours before its parade starting time to cut its route in half because not enough officers had signed up for the duty (Golden 2022). This caused logistical headaches for organizers, paraders and spectators who had to reroute, which was possible only because krewes communicate mostly via social media and email, and significant losses for the bars and restaurants along the route that had been counting on the custom. Captains of other new-wave krewes anxiously awaited news of their own police details while the City "warned that a lack of law enforcement could lead to shortened routes at the last minute" (Ravits 2022: n.p.). Krewe du

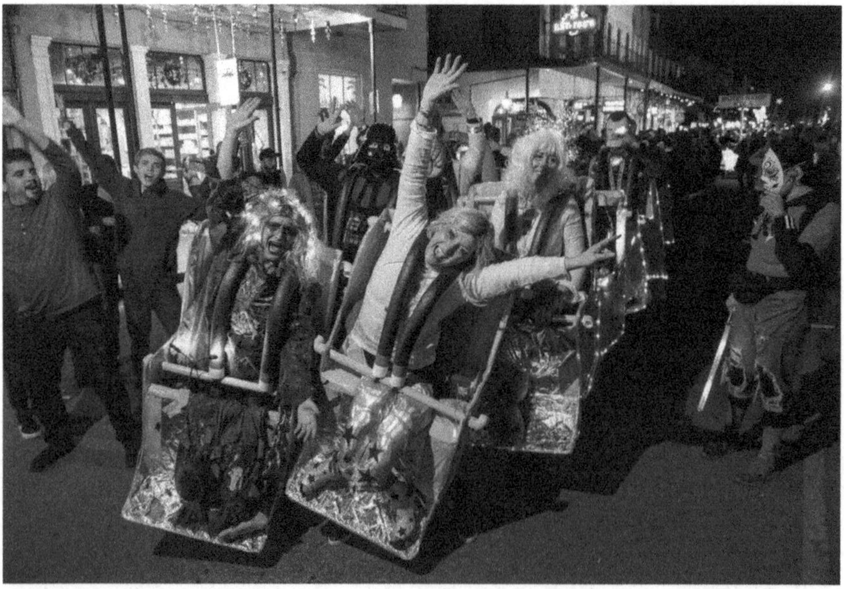

Figure 7.2 Mothership-NOLA, a sub-krewe of the Intergalactic Krewe of Chewbacchus, parades through the French Quarter in 2020 in costume as the Zephyr, a rollercoaster from the local amusement park Pontchartrain Beach, which closed in 1983

Source: Ryan Hodgson-Rigsbee.

Vieux's route had already been cut. Even the mainstream krewes had their parades shortened in 2022 – although as members of the Mayor's Mardi Gras Advisory Council, they knew months in advance, rather than hours. The Krewe of 'tit Rəx hoped their little parade of 100 people and 33 tiny floats was too small to be shortened. They recalled the year when no police escort showed up at all, and their marshals and friends had to stop traffic as the parade crossed St Claude Avenue.

Such uncertainty is hard for new-wave krewes to accommodate, but more frustrating is the lack of transparency and accountability. Krewes do not know what formula the OPSE uses to calculate police details, nor what might entice officers to sign up for them. The OPSE specifies that parade organizers can offer higher rates of pay to attract officers, but organizers do not know what the magic number might be, nor whether police sergeants will enforce or override the maximum hours their officers can work. Some krewes historically relied on good relationships with particular sergeants, but those relationships last only as long as the officer is in post, and the OPSE has centralized and depersonalized the process. In the absence of accountability, rumours about NOPD morale and the Mayor's ulterior motives thrived on social media, and questions were raised about why NOPD serves some Carnival-making citizens and not others.

New-wave krewes do not uniquely suffer from the City's lack of accountability in issuing permits and policing. Just after Hurricane Katrina, the Social Aid and Pleasure Clubs saw policing costs for their second lines rise exponentially – ostensibly due to increased violence at the parades – and fought the price hike (Barrios 2010). They partnered with the American Civil Liberties Union to sue the city on first amendment grounds, and a federal judge argued the permitting process was discriminatory. However, they still pay more than other special event parades and much more than mainstream Mardi Gras krewes (Times-Picayune & NOLA.com 2017). Recently, the City pledged to crack down on the size of second lines, citing NOPD staff shortages due to the pandemic and post-Carnival fatigue (Sledge 2022).

What the 2022 NOPD staffing crisis makes plain is that the urban regulatory infrastructure sets up a hierarchy of parades with mainstream krewes at the top, who are guaranteed taxpayer-funded policing. This is justified in at least one krewe captain's view by the millions of dollars in tourism revenue that big parades help attract (Times-Picayune & NOLA.com 2017). The City has long valued the place-marketing function of mainstream parades, while overcharging, over-policing and undermining African American parading traditions that are centred on community and neighbourhood (Barrios 2010). New-wave Carnival krewes are largely invisible in these urban cultural politics, and unlike mainstream krewes, do not yet have a channel for collective representation. The City effectively treats them as optional extras at best, irritants at worst, despite the devotion that their thousands of members and tens of thousands of spectators show in making them happen each year.

New-wave krewes feel that their parades also contribute to Carnival. They draw fewer out-of-towners than the big parades, but they matter materially and symbolically to their participants and spectators and the downtown neighbourhoods where they typically roll. Materially, they generate much local tourism, as New Orleanians and suburbanites come to see them and spend money along their routes. Symbolically, they signify a participatory, "do-it-yourself" ethos and a sense of belonging to the city (the place) that matter little to the City (the government). Navigating the regulatory infrastructure that polices bodies, movement and property on city streets is supposed to secure new-wave krewes a place in Carnival. Yet the unpredictable process reveals that in some quarters, their embodied Carnival practices do not count as "real" Carnival.

CONCLUSION

A Carnival in any place is a cultural infrastructure that enables certain kinds of activities, events, sensations and representations. While Carnivals are always exuberant and may seem to foster spontaneity, they do not just happen. Whoever puts them on and whatever form they take, they require meticulous planning, coordination and negotiation in cities whose infrastructure is not given over to celebration for most of the year, but instead supports the humdrum relations of production, consumption and reproduction.

This chapter has argued that, as urban cultural infrastructure, Carnival is the product of three other kinds of infrastructure. Each Carnival is framed by an overarching temporal/organizational infrastructure, which specifies the locally specific social formations and types and times of events that make it happen. At the scale of the person, Carnival is created through the embodied infrastructure of the people who make it happen. It is a site where the labouring body, which works at its everyday occupation and toward Carnival events, coincides with the festive body, which revels in the gorgeous, sometimes gruelling glory of the season's rituals. At the scale of the urban collective, the makers of Carnival must negotiate with the urban regulatory infrastructure that makes Carnival events possible by managing streets, security and sanitation, among other things. This negotiation between the three kinds of infrastructures always refracts questions of privilege and marginalization, power and contestation, and material and symbolic value. In the case of New Orleans, the intersection of the regulatory infrastructure (the policing and permitting processes) and the temporal/organizational infrastructure (mainstream versus new-wave krewes) reveals the implicit (sometimes not so implicit) hierarchy of whose Carnival matters most to the City, and thus whose embodied practices of Carnival are guaranteed a protected place on city streets.

CHAPTER 8

YOUTHFUL CITY-MAKING THROUGH PERIPHERAL CULTURAL INFRASTRUCTURE

Antonio Moya-Latorre

INTRODUCTION

Cultural production is assumed to be led by professional artists and cultural workers residing in urban centres (Scott 2008). Conversely, urban peripheries across the globe – low-density suburbs, working-class neighbourhoods flooded with cookie-cutter public housing, self-built settlements – are often mischaracterized as uncreative and culturally dependent on centralized artistic niches (Bain 2013; Jones *et al.* 2019). Yet the often self-taught creative youth from these same peripheries have been recurrently inundating cities and digital platforms with their artistic creations (Mullings & Habib 2022; Sitas 2020), demonstrating how they also act as active producers of their cities' cultural infrastructure.

Latin American youth are no exception. Over the past few decades, young artists born and raised in self-built urban peripheries across the region have propagated self-managed cultural spaces and practices in their neighbourhoods that differ significantly from what can be conventionally found in consolidated urban centres. Often raised amid long-lasting patterns of stigma and infrastructural violence (Baumann & Yacobi 2022; Lemanski 2018, 2020, 2022; Malmström 2022; Mosselson 2021), the youth in these peripheral neighbourhoods are performing city-making processes that satisfy their basic material needs while advancing self-defined cultural rights beyond established understandings of civic, political and social rights, which still manifest extremely unevenly within Latin American cities (Heil 2021).

Studying this widespread youth-led infrastructure-building process across urban peripheries in Latin America holds significant potential for further globalizing urban theory (Ren 2022; Robinson 2022). Building on the so-called infrastructural turn in urban theory – focused on the material and political consequences for underserved citizens of the (insufficient) infrastructural provision by the state and other development agents (see Baumann &

Yacobi 2022; Kanai & Schindler 2022; Lemanski 2018, 2020) – this chapter evaluates the urban, cultural and political implications of peripheral cultural spaces and practices in Latin American cities when these are studied as a form of city-making. Departing from frameworks portraying peripheral citizens as infrastructure consumers or claimants (Lemanski 2022; Malmström 2022; Mosselson 2021), it analyses how the youth from the peripheries also proactively *produce* new infrastructure. Thus, the concept of *peripheral cultural infrastructure* is used to theorize these "repeated instances" (Montero & Baiocchi 2022) of urban creativity embodied in peripheral communities' everyday city-making processes.

To undertake this analysis, first, the chapter provides evidence of burgeoning culture-centred initiatives across Latin American urban peripheries. Second, it establishes the "genetic comparative ground" (Robinson 2016, 2022), arguing that this widespread cultural explosion derives from analogous environments of inequality and diversity following massive migration processes. Third, it introduces the concept *peripheral cultural infrastructure* to conceptualize youth-led pedagogic spaces and practices that mobilize communities around issues of urban social justice. Fourth, after reformulating the notion of cultural rights, it suggests that such infrastructure both derives from and expands *insurgent citizenship* (Holston 2008) through creative and artistic performances of citizenship that challenge stigmas and preconceptions of these communities while creating tangible opportunities for them to thrive. The chapter concludes by explaining how peripheral cultural infrastructure enables a new relationship between culture and spatial politics within and beyond Latin American cities through everyday acts of city-making with the potential to forge trans-local alliances among young creative leaders. Throughout, the discussion is sustained by ongoing community-engaged action-research that began in 2016 with cultural initiatives in the peripheries of Medellín, Oaxaca and São Paulo.

PERIPHERAL CULTURAL EXPLOSION

A 35-year-old theatre company in the north-eastern periphery of Medellín; a music school near Oaxaca's biggest landfill that recently celebrated its tenth anniversary; and a cultural organization born in 2018 after an art festival on a dumping site in a favela in São Paulo (Figure 8.1) – self-managed cultural initiatives across Latin American urban peripheries are driving city-making processes within the neighbourhoods where they are located and beyond, shaping the built environment and influencing the lives of residents touched by their reach (see Moya-Latorre 2022).

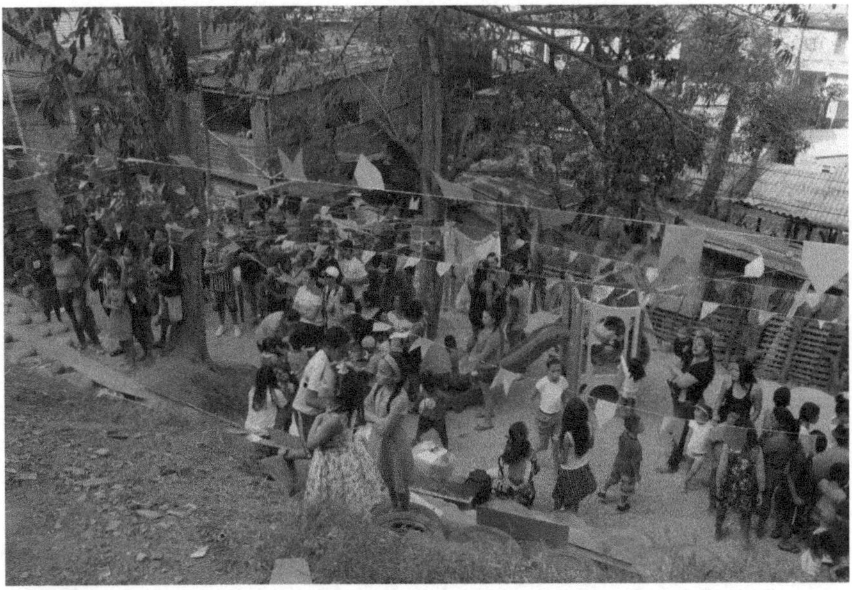

Figure 8.1 Second edition of the art festival in Jardim Colombo, São Paulo

Source: Ester Carro.

While the literature on suburban cultural production and creativity and its relevance for the making of cities in global North countries is well-established (Bain 2013; Jones *et al.* 2019), scholarship on the Latin American context is just beginning. Hence, there is still little theorizing about what this phenomenon occurring in self-built peripheries entails for southern and global urban theory. Nevertheless, a search on scholarly databases with the words *culture* and *periphery* (in Spanish, Portuguese and English) confirms the growing interest among scholars in peripheral urban art in Latin America.

The range of peripheral cultural initiatives across the region covered by recent literature is wide and diverse. In Colombian cities, self-organized theatre groups today derive from the *Nuevo Teatro* tradition, which, since the 1950s has been giving voice to subaltern people in the country (Ballesteros Cubillos 2021). Neighbourhood-scale theatre spaces in smaller cities across the state of Cundinamarca become settings for citizens from the peripheries to engage proactively in theatre and art. Mexico's urban cultural scene has staged a proliferation of rap groups in Spanish and indigenous languages, promoting what Josep Cru (2017) calls a *linguistic bricolage*. Rap performances and contests in Mexico City take place in emblematic public spaces in the city, gathering hundreds to watch groups of rappers from the peripheries improvise lyrics on contemporary issues of social and cultural discrimination (Santos Cid 2022). In Lima, the juxtaposition of multiple urban identities with a tradition of resistance against Fujimori's recent dictatorial regime converged into new forms of collective art in the peripheries of the Andean capital. Reclaiming a derogatory word to refer to non-white and poor migrants in the city, the art collective CHOLO united dozens of urban artists in the first Encuentro de la Cultura Emergente de Lima in 2009 (Ramos Ochoa 2018), becoming a public performance of mestizo identities and cultural production whose spirit has been kept alive by recent urban collectives from the peripheries – typically led by fine arts students – exploring new forms of participatory and community art (Guevara 2019).

Not specific to any country, urban street art has filled the streets across Latin American cities with colourful cultural motifs. Coordinated initiatives like Ola Urbana in La Paz bring attention to the need to protect the cultural diversity of Bolivia, which plays out in very uneven forms of urban development (Cesio 2017). Urban art festivals in Mexican, Brazilian and Colombian cities attract the attention of citizens and visitors, who get exposed to social realities hidden behind the formal city (LA Network 2017). In Chile's Valparaíso, a degraded urban heritage is recuperating its value through the work of street muralists disputing the idea that graffiti is equal to danger (Aragón 2017). Overall, many of these initiatives deal with a creative tension with local authorities, who ultimately decide what forms of street art are legitimate and which ones must be erased (Morrison 2020).

Peripheral communities in Brazilian cities are staging a particularly pervasive wave of urban art. Funk music, dance, poetry and literature created in favelas and other peripheral neighbourhoods in São Paulo and Rio de Janeiro show how stigmatized communities, recurrently portrayed as problematic and poor, can be the source of inspiring art that gets appreciated by audiences from within and beyond their own communities (Bertelli 2017). Self-organized cultural events in urban peripheries are behind the growing interest of young people in becoming writers and making a living out of their literary productions (da Silva 2016). The bestselling sensation *O sol na cabeça* (*The Sun on my Head*), by Geovani Martins, born and raised in Rio's favela Vidigal, reflects this shift in public opinion about what counts as valuable literature (Martins 2018). Through 13 short stories, the young writer invites readers to see the city from the perspective of a *favelado* and embody the stigma experienced by peripheral citizens.

MIGRATION, REMOTENESS AND DIVERSITY

This short overview of some of the peripheral artistic movements that have captured scholarly interest is just a glimpse of a vast array of cultural spaces and practices emerging in Latin American cities – an "explosion of cultural production" (Caldeira 2015: S131). Despite the variety of peripheral contexts and the diversity of artistic creations, there are shared causes that justify its study at a regional – even global – scale. This section lays out five of these underlying factors to establish a "genetic comparative ground" (Robinson 2016) for the wider conceptualization of culture-based city-making.

First, most large and mega-cities in Latin America are the result of massive migration processes from rural areas and small towns. The movement of millions of individuals, families and even entire communities looking for economic security caused unprecedented demographic growth in the main cities in a span of two to three decades during the second half of the twentieth century (Caldeira 2015; Davis 1999; Holston 2008). Forced to build their own shelters, migrants have gradually replaced their temporary constructions with brick-and-mortar dwellings, resulting in larger self-built neighbourhoods, most of which are still relatively young – even consolidated massive informal settlements like Ciudad Neza in Mexico City are not even 60 years old. The descendants of these first settlers – the first generation of residents born and raised in these settlements – are the ones engaging in self-expression practices and creative acts of citizenship (Caldeira 2015; Holston 2008).

Second, the reach of the neoliberal project in Latin America between the 1980s and early 2000s aggravated the division between urban centres and peripheries at the very time that these peripheries were consolidating (Holston 2008; Wolseth & Babb 2008). On the one hand, the spatial expression of market reforms magnified the geographic injustice that already characterized the largest urban agglomerations in Latin America, which manifested in extremely uneven contiguous urban spaces – a salient case being the Brazilian favelas. On the other hand, neoliberal reforms also spurred economic opportunities for young settlers looking to increase their income through easily accessible jobs as construction workers, cleaning women, janitors and other (so-called) low-skilled jobs in the adjacent wealthy neighbourhoods (Davis 1999). Combined, neoliberal urbanization processes ended up influencing both settlers' self-awareness of urban injustice and their (economic) capacity to act upon it, stimulating insurgent forms of citizenship among neighbours in the peripheries ready to fight for their right to have rights (Holston 2008).

Third, the remoteness of the state experienced by residents in Latin American urban peripheries resulted in ubiquitous self-organizing processes in response to the deficient state-sponsored infrastructure provision (Davis 1999). The geographic distance from the state of most of these self-built settlements – which in the largest metropoles keep growing in rings towards the outskirts – is paralleled by social, political and cultural forms of estrangement between their residents and the governing political and economic bodies. Notoriously, the state – understood both as an overarching institution representing citizens' interests and the socio-material infrastructure

(Mosselson 2021; Ramesh 2022) spanning national territory in the form of certain facilities (from police to schools and hospitals, to public administration facilities with bureaucratic functions) – does not play a significant role in the everyday life of peripheral citizens in Latin America (the main exception being public schools). Hence, as Holston (2008: 247) argues, "remoteness [from the state] enabled a certain off-work and out-of-sight freedom to invent new modes of association, at the same time that illegality motivated residents to demand inclusion in the property, infrastructure, and services of the legal city". That is, distance from the state worked as a breeding ground for creative expressions of peripheral city-making.

The notion of *cultural distance* from the state is particularly important when studying this culture-based infrastructure-building phenomenon. As Davis (1999: 616–17) elaborates,

> when combined with other forms of estrangement, cultural distancing may be a key factor in explaining the nature of social movement organization, especially why ethnic and linguistic movements in Latin America may be more likely to reject any effort to connect with the state and instead struggle for autonomy.

In other words, not being part of mainstream cultural circuits opens the door for a self-provision of culture – a factor that resonates with peripheral cultural processes in other world regions' cities (Bain 2013; Mullings & Habib 2022; Sitas 2020). Perhaps counterintuitively, the constant stigmatization and stereotyped representation of the culture of peripheral citizens – both their way of living and the artistic creations and performances that reflect and shape their lifestyles – ended up nurturing the youth's willingness to produce a self-image contesting such stigmas (Moura *et al.* 2020).

Fourth, nearly universal schooling seems to have played a crucial role in the capacity of the youngest generation to fight for their rights (da Silva 2016). The virtually full literacy rates across Latin American cities today are undeniably one of the greatest achievements attributable to state investment in public education. With schools often being the primary point of contact with the state during childhood, the youth in the peripheries have also cultivated over the past three decades their capacity to navigate the system while defining and pursuing their cultural rights outside of it.

Lastly, most of these settlements are composed of highly diverse populations, with migrants coming from varied cultural origins, even when moving from within the same national territory (Allen 2022). This cultural diversity is not necessarily a source of social strength – rather, it often implies an initial lack of cohesion and undefined collective identity among neighbours who will share the same territory for years or decades to come. Over time, this same disaggregated sense of identity triggered by people's forced displacement motivates the (re)making of migrants' places of arrival (Heil 2021), materialized through the production of new forms of urban culture in which the youngest generations feel represented.

To summarize, the most recent waves of peripheral art are a product of (at least) five material processes: (1) massive in-country migration processes; (2) the dual influence of neoliberal urbanization on the self-awareness and the economic capacity of residents; (3) communities' geographic and cultural distance from the state; (4) widespread schooling and literacy rates; and (5) the drive to co-create new collective identities out of diverse cultures of origin. To study such shared causes underpinning the "repeated instances" (Montero & Baiocchi 2022) of cultural production in Latin American urban peripheries paves the way for its conceptualization beyond the local relevance of each artistic initiative.

CULTURAL INFRASTRUCTURE FOR SOCIAL MOBILIZATION

Theorizing the role of peripheral cultural initiatives in city-making requires framing them in terms of the urban, cultural and political changes they contribute to accomplishing. This chapter proposes the term *peripheral cultural infrastructure* to push urban theories to consider what this art-based city-making phenomenon across the continent aspires to realize. In line with the so-called infrastructural turn within urban studies, this notion of cultural infrastructure is grounded in a socio-material understanding of infrastructure (see Allen 2022; Bain 2013; Heil 2021; Lemanski 2018, 2020, 2022; Mosselson 2021; Simone 2004, 2021). As Lemanski (2018: 352) defends:

> Within this contemporary perspective, infrastructure is conceptualized as more than just the physical manifestation of the city or the material means through which the urban is able to function. Certainly cities and urban dwellers need roads, electricity, water, sanitation and housing for example [...]; but infrastructure is also inherently social in the way it is both produced and used.

Equally, cultural infrastructure is composed of physical and social elements. On the one hand, it grows around a physical neighbourhood anchor – a *hard* infrastructure – where the youth gather to engage in their cultural production and related daily social practices. This material side of cultural infrastructure depends heavily on the aesthetic value of the spaces where community leaders and other residents perform art. Not surprisingly, in most of these locations – be they closed buildings or open spaces – one can often contemplate street art, listen to music or attend public performances, all of which contribute to sparking an emotional response among neighbours and visitors. On the other hand, cultural infrastructure depends on a *soft* or social infrastructure, and as such is contingent on relational processes and social networks weaved over time (Star 1999). Hence, cultural infrastructure is an account of mobilizing structures – social, intangible community-based networks that bring residents together to claim unattended rights seeking to improve their living conditions (Davis 1999) – that also encompasses more fluid and less politically explicit forms of mobilization pervading the daily lives of people in peripheral communities.

Cultural infrastructure plays two critical pedagogical functions. First, it shapes a collective identity among neighbours of relatively young settlements – indeed, the search for shared identities and cultural projects is what often drives mobilizing processes (Polletta & Gardner 2015). Not surprisingly, cultural infrastructure often grows organically as more community members feel attracted to, represented by and pulled to become part of it. Second, by touching upon social and cultural issues, cultural infrastructure sparks dialogic and awareness-raising processes that can themselves become the breeding ground for social mobilizations. The collective artistic performances and creations that take place in self-created cultural spaces enable artists' self-awareness and capacity to experiment with feasible alternative futures as they engage in artistic experiences of radical imagination with others (Kallianos & Fumanti 2021).

Such peripheral cultural infrastructure in Latin America and elsewhere constitutes mainly a youth-led phenomenon resonating with the region's historical social mobilizations. That students behave as instigators of change and cultural innovators during tipping points in modern history is partly a result of their "[struggling] to manage their local everyday realities [while imagining] global possibilities for change" (Wolseth & Babb 2008: 3). Peripheral youth are "less frequently involved at the state level" and "often in the vanguard of new social movements and in the literary, arts, and cultural scenes of urban centres" (Wolseth & Babb 2008: 10). It is precisely the latter that concerns cultural infrastructure: the combination of a withdrawal from formal politics, an ongoing struggle to live dignified lives, and the increasing contact – through the variegated digital media – with communities regionwide and worldwide equally struggling for their rights. Together this is all collapsing into an unprecedented youth-led cultural cocktail in the urban peripheries of Latin America.

Cultural infrastructure catalyses a community's "repertoire of communication", as defined by Alice Mattoni (in Treré 2012) who has conceptually tweaked Sidney Tarrow's (1998) well-known framework of "repertoires of contention" – namely, the varied organizing strategies that social movements engage with to pursue their political goals. Young artists from the peripheries are exploring individual and collective artistic avenues to raise their voices and share their experiences with the world. This engagement with arts-based forms of communication – music, theatre, poetry, photography – appears as a refreshing mobilization strategy that captures the attention of people from within and beyond the community.

Lastly, the artistic nature of cultural infrastructure also infuses it with the emotional momentum that makes social mobilization an enjoyable, even pleasurable endeavour, sometimes even "independently of the ultimate goals and outcomes" (Goodwin *et al.* 2001: 9). This pleasurable feeling gets magnified when individuals engage "not just in *any* intentional activity but in the course of making history, and not just any history but a history they perceive as more *just*" (Wood 2003: 235, emphasis in original). Young artists are convinced that a fairer world is desirable and possible, and such conviction drives their motivation to create art and, through it, shape their urban lives.

In short, peripheral cultural infrastructure consists of *youth-led artistic pedagogic spaces and practices that mobilize peripheral communities around issues of identity and urban social justice.* Building on a history of "*barrio* movements" (Friedmann 1989) and a legacy of neighbourhood-based organizations such as homeowners associations or churches, these cultural spaces and practices are nourishing community capacities to keep on mobilizing around self-defined objectives.

PERFORMING NEW URBAN CITIZENSHIP

Cultural infrastructure enables new forms of what Lemanski has called infrastructural citizenship in reference to how the access (or lack thereof) to state-provisioned infrastructure determines citizens' livelihoods (Lemanski 2018, 2020, 2022). This section discusses how cultural infrastructure contributes, first, to advancing the rights of peripheral communities to be treated with full-citizen dignity (Holston 2008), and second, to inventing (Moura *et al.* 2020) and *performing* new urban citizenship, destabilizing in the process existing understandings of cultural rights and democracy.

Marshall's mid-twentieth-century conceptualization of rights in terms of a *social* citizenship is helpful for this discussion (Marshall & Bottomore 1992). As he argued, albeit in an essentializing manner, the idea of social rights only took off in the twentieth century, following the consolidation of civil rights and political rights in the previous two centuries. Civil and political rights by themselves did not generate just societies, understood as social agreements where most people are *de facto* able to fully participate in a democracy. Much to the contrary, it was not until the formalization of social rights across democratic countries that the majorities of the world – from women to excluded races, ethnicities, castes and non-normative sexualities and genders – would begin being treated as fully participatory citizens:

> [Social rights comprise] the whole range from the right to a modicum of economic welfare and security to the right to share to the full in the social heritage and to live the life of a civilized being according to the standards prevailing in the society. The institutions most closely connected with it are the educational system and the social services. (Marshall & Bottomore 1992: 8)

Two elements of this definition establish the base for the (re)definition of cultural rights. The first one is the assumption that social rights are mainly the responsibility of state-sanctioned institutions. As discussed, access to basic education in Latin America has undoubtedly been a significant milestone for all individuals and communities to be treated more fairly. However, attributing the fulfilment of social rights exclusively to the state across Latin American countries (through educational institutions and other infrastructures) poses serious limitations to the expansion of citizenship, given how the state in this region is usually perceived as remote by peripheral communities (Davis 1999).

The second element of Marshall's definition (Marshall & Bottomore 1992) that reveals the limits of social rights frameworks becomes clear when testing the concept of full citizenship against the preconception of *existing* social systems – "the standards prevailing in the society". Even if the state is assumed capable of fully delivering social rights, peripheral communities have historically *not* played significant roles in the very definition of those social systems and standards. Consequently, state-sanctioned social rights, at best, would allow these communities (the majorities of the world) to develop a *limited* kind of citizenship within the constraints of those predefined and deeply uneven systems. Therefore, pursuing *full* urban citizenship that would give historically excluded communities the actual possibility of changing the social systems they are part of requires transcending the traditional concept of social rights and reframing them in terms of *cultural* rights.

The concept of cultural rights was recognized internationally in the Universal Declaration of Human Rights in 1948, enumerated along with economic and social rights, which, combined, are "indispensable for [everyone's] dignity and the free development of his [*sic*] personality" (United Nations 1948, Article 22). The concept has developed, resulting in the creation of institutions like UNESCO committed to spreading the fulfilment of cultural rights across the globe. However, profound limitations in widespread understandings of cultural rights derive from their framing in *reactive* terms – either as the "right to participate in the cultural life of the community" (United Nations 1948, Article 27), as an egalitarian "spread of culture" following "international conventions", or as a protection of the "cultural identity of minorities" (Symonides 1998: 563–4). All these definitions denote a previously accepted hegemonic cultural system which all communities aspire to enjoy, or in which underrepresented cultures can only claim a minor space hoping to receive recognition.

By contrast, cultural infrastructure constructed from the urban peripheries in Latin America approaches the development of cultural rights in a *proactive*, even insurgent, manner. James Holston's (2008) powerful articulation of "insurgent citizenship" in his study of peripheral urban identities in Brazil provides an understanding of culture-based forms of citizenship that can destabilize social systems and democracies built upon centuries of social exclusion and inegalitarian social conventions. When "entrenched regimes of legalized inequality" (Holston 2008: 33) are put in dialogue with debates on urban infrastructure, peripheral citizens can be read not just as "infrastructure claimants, consumers and complainers" (Lemanski 2022: 668) but as infrastructural *producers* in their own right. Cultural infrastructure, then, becomes a socio-material institution for performing multiple forms of citizenship and reimagining democracies in new, self-defined cultural terms. Young artists from the peripheries are no longer claiming to join society and be recognized within existing social parameters – rather, they are expressing, through their individual and collective creations, their dissatisfaction with existing societies and democratic systems alongside proposals for their reconfiguration.

In sum, peripheral cultural infrastructure in Latin America goes beyond defiance and critique to the enunciation, through tangible, space-based performances, of alternative urban scenarios. Impregnated with a *celebratory insurgency* (Moya-Latorre 2022), this cultural infrastructure infuses the creations and performances of young artists with a tactically festive character that becomes the hallmark of a renewed form of city-making. Cultural movements tell stories of celebrated social realities that counter the widespread representation of "peri-urban precariousness" (Kanai & Schindler 2022) that keeps stigmatizing peripheral communities. Through self-constructed cultural infrastructure, young peripheral artists experiment with creative mobilization practices around social issues, expanding on twentieth-century repertoires of participatory and democratic processes.

PERIPHERAL CITY-MAKING

Some of the tangible effects of cultural infrastructure are often self-evident. In the youth-led arts-based movement in the favela Jardim Colombo, the collective capacity built after the first art festival became crucial in preventing a devastating health outcome during the first wave of the Covid-19 pandemic. Among other initiatives launched after the festival, the Fazendeiras project stands out: as a training programme for women learning to become proficient construction workers – a profession historically associated with men – this initiative is both contributing to women's economic and professional self-sufficiency and to the physical improvement of dwellings in and outside of the favela (Moya-Latorre 2022). Similarly, the music school in the periphery of Oaxaca has allowed dozens of young people to pursue professional musical careers and has been essential in imprinting a new collective identity on the neighbourhood, which is now recognized locally, nationally and even internationally as a community of musicians (Lakhani 2016). The music school building has notably grown over the years, and the recently expanded concert hall (Figure 8.2), along with the new classrooms and embellished landscape architecture around it, strengthen its image as a "shelter" for the youth in the

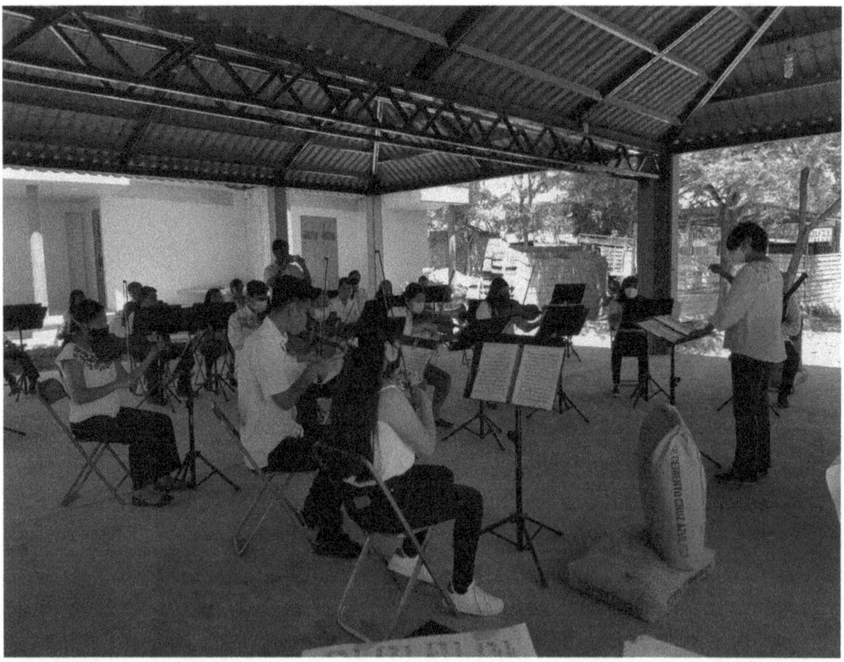

Figure 8.2 Concert at the Santa Cecilia Music School in Oaxaca for one of its sponsors

Source: Antonio Moya-Latorre.

community. As for the theatre company in Medellín, it has become an essential cultural asset for residents in the north-eastern area of Medellín, with weekly activities and events that people of all ages attend. Along with other peripheral cultural infrastructure, this theatre-centred organization became one of the key urban stakeholders involved in the thorough transformation of the city during its well-studied process of social urbanism in the early 2000s (McGuirk 2014). If cultural infrastructure's material effects on their urban surroundings is what counts, why engage in a discussion of the spatial politics associated with this phenomenon?

It could be argued that the tension between culture and spatial politics underlies any discussion of peripheral city-making in Latin America, even when not explicitly addressed. Apparently apolitical, preconceptions of urban and cultural standards reflect a hegemonic way of being in the world that obscures many others, raising political questions for those who do not recognize themselves in such conventions. Conversely, as Arturo Escobar (1992: 76) states, "to live differently, to assert one's difference, is to practice cultural innovation and to engage in some sort of political practice". That is, living differently inevitably becomes political in the eyes of those comfortably inhabiting existing systems. Succinctly put, within urban peripheries in Latin America, everyday politics and everyday cultures are mutually constitutive.

Therefore, ordinary city-making practices (Robinson 2002) can be proactively leveraged as a counter-hegemonic political practice with wider implications beyond localized urban contexts. The space-based notion of cultural infrastructure offers a promising anchoring point between systems-change aspirations and everyday acts of citizenship and politics. This chapter has argued that peripheral cultural infrastructure grows out of a balanced remoteness from the state that enables the radical imagination and *performance* of alternative forms of city-making, destabilizing in the process unchallenged urban standards and conceptions of society and democracy. Through these everyday artistic performances, young peripheral artists in Latin American cities are steadily escaping from the stigma traps (Allen 2022) that keep reproducing their suffocating material and social realities. At the same time, they are also subtly defining new political repertoires (Bertelli 2017) through which they may aspire to slowly take over "hegemonic and institutional infrastructures" (Kallianos & Fumanti 2021: 1110).

Given that peripheral cultural infrastructure does not refer to isolated instances of subversive art but to a growing phenomenon of cultural spaces and practices across Latin American cities, such a possibility is not unthinkable. Taking advantage of available digital tools and networks, young creative leaders of the urban peripheries are already forging trans-local synergies among peripheral cultural initiatives and increasingly reaching civic leaders, signalling that their claim for full citizenship is simultaneously a local/urban and a global/transnational phenomenon. If this becomes a pattern in the countries' biggest cities, where decisions of national impact are made, peripheral citizens will have the opportunity to leverage their cultural infrastructure to bolster networks of action that operate concurrently from the bottom and from the top – or quite literally, from the peripheries to the centres.

CONCLUSION

Regardless of whether such scenarios become reality, the notion of peripheral cultural infrastructure can be a helpful heuristic device to advance global urban theories that learn from city-making practices steered by peripheral urban actors. As the evidence provided here and many other stories of urban creativity could also illustrate, artistic spaces, creations and performances in Latin American peripheries suggest urban, cultural and political realities that scholarly debates on urban infrastructure and citizenship should engage with more substantially. The performance of multiple iterations of urban citizenship taking place in self-built spaces in the peripheries over the past decades is, this chapter has shown, a source of cultural production and creativity that can inform new ways of being in contemporary cities and organizing fairer and more diverse urban systems.

Paying close attention to the advent and consolidation of peripheral cultural infrastructure in Latin American cities and elsewhere will evidence how, in the immediate term, these are already producing tangible opportunities for youth prosperity even though their possibilities to flourish have been greatly inhibited by (infra)structural violence from the moment they were born on the edges of city-regions. It is not a coincidence that it is the youth in the urban peripheries who are overwhelmingly driving this culture-based pattern of city-making. All across the globe's variegated urban peripheries – suburbs (Bain 2013), slums (Sitas 2020), working-class neighbourhoods (Jones *et al.* 2019) – increasingly connected and informed peripheral urban youth are striving to be heard on their own terms and establish new social and democratic standards. In the longer term, the materialization of these creative peripheral youths' structure-changing aspirations will largely depend on wider social recognition and acceptance that these forms of city-making are indeed (part of) the path forward.

III
CONSUMING CULTURE

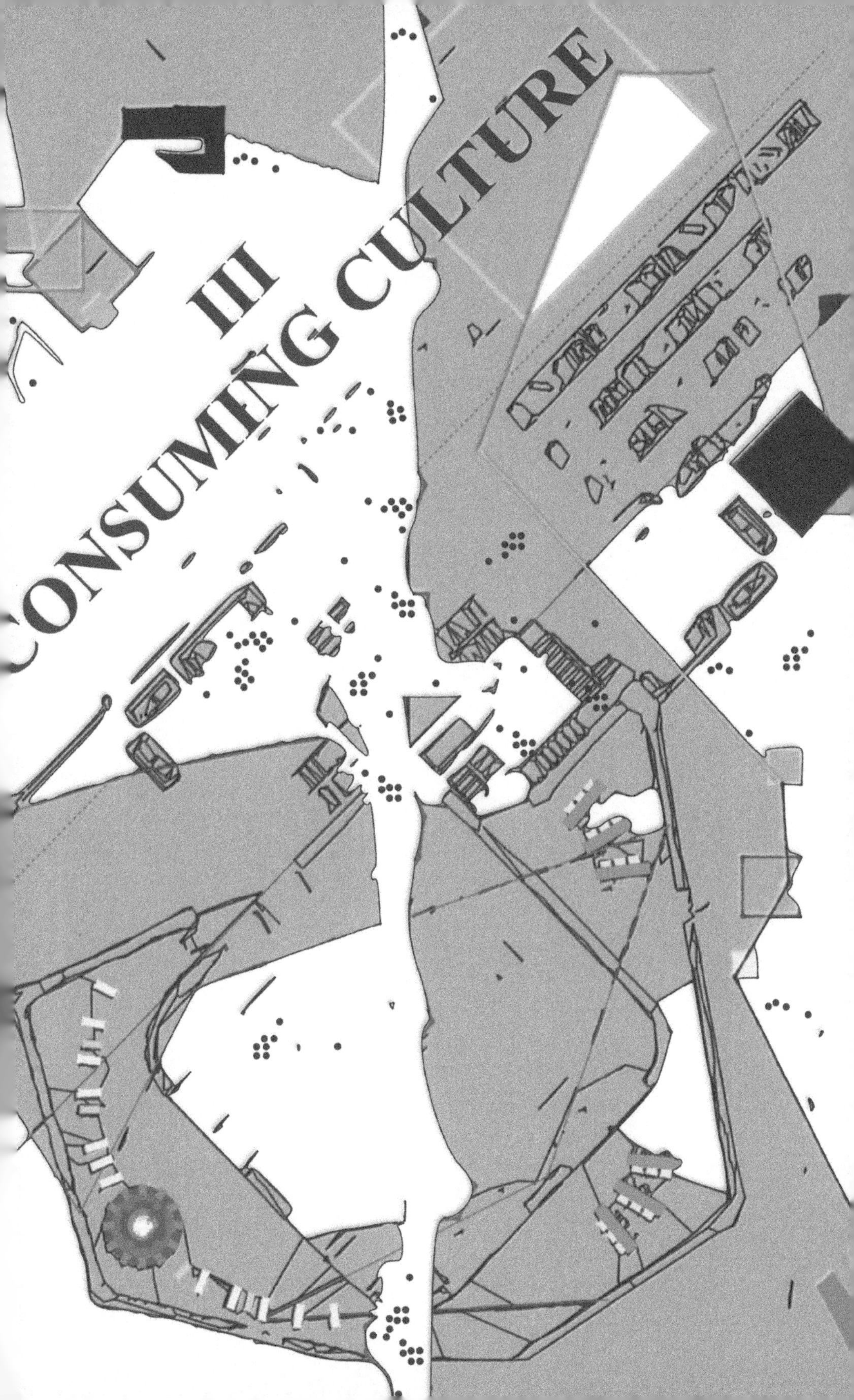

PART III

CONSUMING CULTURE

Around the world, urbanism in the twenty-first century is marked by contradictory trends in consumption. In high-income countries, a seemingly unending drive towards mass production and centralized global distribution in large warehouses and big-box stores sits in tension with a middle-class quest for novelty within niche markets of consumption and commodification (Zukin 2010). In a competitive world of late neoliberalism where cities have only themselves to sell, the hyper-drive to ground global capital in place and retain creatives and "culturepreneurs" leads to pockets of urban homogeneity in tension with a search for difference and particularity (Lange 2011). Informal street hawkers and traders juxtapose with a global drive to homogenize the retail landscape through shopping malls, while DIY subcultures in wealthy cities appropriate the ancient informality and localism of pop-up trade. In mid- and higher-income countries, some neighbourhoods are branded as districts of art and entertainment, while gentrification is encouraged by introducing hipster bars, cafes, galleries, studios and farmers' markets into low-income communities and public spaces (Hubbard 2016). This palette of middle-class cultural amenities fosters consumptive opportunities to build cultural capital and distinction.

Civic leaders and real estate developers seeking to normalize neoliberal urban rule also deploy cultural capital in the marketing of lifestyles, identities and urban spaces (Novy & Colomb 2013), such that neighbourhoods, or specific spaces within them, might be experienced as "cultural" by visitors. The expressly symbolic leveraging of urban cultural infrastructure and the affective atmospheres of creativity, ethno-cultural "diversity" and heritage to change the perception of a place – culture-led urban placemaking – is inevitably linked to the destructive dimensions of urban regeneration. It builds the products of culture into places often at the expense of local communities. Civic leaders also deploy technocratic spatial rationalities in the planning of streetscapes, demonstrating hostility towards disorderly and informal appropriation of urban space by hawkers, panhandlers and the homeless for the discordance they present to a modernist aesthetic of cityness (Watson 2003). In contradistinction to the emphasis on physical and technical infrastructure as modes by which cities are made productive, street trading emphasizes "people as infrastructure" to facilitate economic and social opportunities for poor urbanites (Simone 2004). This highly flexible and mobile urban social infrastructure provides access to urban economic niches that can reduce vulnerability to poverty and form the basis of what a city has always been, a meeting place for trade (Pieterse 2013).

This section explores the cultural infrastructure of urban consumption through the themes of hawking street food, hipster retail, fashion districts and arts festivals. Street trading is an ancient occupation. It is a globally pervasive survivalist livelihood for the urban poor that depends upon the lifestyles and consumptive practices of the middle class as well as transnational networks of migrants (Rogerson 2016). Embedded within the urban public infrastructure of streets, parks, squares and gardens, street trading redefines the meaning and limits of public space through innovative and unplanned infrastructural uses that variously confront and evade municipal authorities (Schindler 2014). Commercial streetscapes have also been financialized, dampening their potential for creative reinvention and innovation as bars, restaurants and chain stores require high revenues to pay commercial rents. The British "high street", for example, has been the subject of scholarly debates about changing consumption patterns where the digitization of consumption due to internet shopping and door-dashing and the globalization and suburbanization of retailing often renders local shopping and its social life obsolete. As the "heart of many communities", the "death of the high street" promises social disarray and the erasure of local identity (Hubbard 2017). Idealized as democratic and adaptable, local commercial infrastructure is further being displaced by the rise of "hipster" consumption practices – third-wave coffee shops, micro-brewery bars, vintage clothing boutiques, organic and wellness health food stores, and specialized home decor outlets – that purposefully and ironically "invade" traditional ethno-cultural districts to capitalize on the "authenticity" of streetscapes (Hubbard 2017). Hipster hawkers sell pulled-pork, ham bao bao and yakitori in Singaporean markets, while hipster tea houses, cafes and waffle shops in Mumbai and Delhi sell pinsas, cheese teas and Liège waffles, and bubble tea shops, poké take-aways and charcuteries line the streets of Montreal's former working-class districts.

Urban foodscapes are intensely local cultural experiences, but they implicate a global cultural infrastructure of food producers, cooks and chefs, food markets and retailers, street vendors and high-end restaurants as well as cultural intermediaries such as food bloggers, recipe writers and critics who promote and circulate ideas about a city's food cultures, including its street food (Kong 2015). Municipal governments also promote their urban foodscapes as culture, a form of "culinary soft power" to attract tourism and investment and enhance global city status. In Chapter 9, Lily Kong and Aidan Wong examine the many infrastructural dimensions of Singaporean hawker cultures, highlighting the juxtaposition between its historic itinerance and the purpose-built embedding of hawker centres in the urban fabric. Hawker centres are locally-based, taken-for-granted sites of consumer culture shaped by creativity and innovation that continually reproduce street food culture. Yet the physical, social, economic and digital infrastructure that supports them simultaneously exposes a complex socio-spatial cultural politics at the intersections of local and global food cultures, the reproduction of authenticity and mimicry, and social inclusions and exclusions, all of which are mediated through a tension between physical and virtual urban life.

The micro-enterprising practices of hawker culture and their trade in the tension between global/local and authenticity/simulacra has parallels in hipster retailing, including the social infrastructures of labour markets, the production of consumer niches and the placement of consumption within the city and its urban plans. Hipster retailers, whose businesses of restaurants, boutiques, art galleries and coffee shops form visible spaces of lifestyle and cultural consumption, are central to global urban revitalization toolkits. As vendors of symbolic goods and services who create spaces of selective sociability, these "culturepreneurs" (Lange 2006) produce the conditions for consumers to realize their "good taste" in curated trans-local products that reinforce their social distinction through global networks (Bain & Mark 2020). In Chapter 10, Bryan Mark draws from retail ethnography, Instagram netnography and semi-structured interviews to trace the contemporary marketplace of hipster retailing as a middle-class mode of urban cultural infrastructure. Examining the material and digital dynamics of an ice cream boutique in Toronto, Canada, he argues that the hipster aestheticization of ice cream is mediated by proprietary control over "backstage" processes of culinary experimentation and "dessert innovation" and "frontstage" strategies of "creative" atmosphering and visual food merchandising. An aspirational, networked public forms around a digital urban cultural infrastructure of mobile social media users and entrepreneurial Instagram "influencers" who geotag the site-specific location of the ice cream boutique and hype its spatial aesthetics as an informational good that contributes to the visualization of the "urban middle-class good life".

The online marketplace has also greatly impacted the fashion industry and urban fashion districts. While London, Paris, Milan and New York City are the superstar cities of the fashion industry, these creative industry capitals are crowded and competitive marketplaces with a costly built infrastructure for emerging independent fashion designers (Brydges & Hracs 2019).

Circumventing the costs of such alpha fashion cities and confronting the fast fashion of global brands, independent fashion designers in conjunction with personal style fashion bloggers strategically use social media and digital technology to change where, when and how they live and work in cities, redrawing the urban cultural infrastructure map on a global scale (Brydges & Sjöholm 2019). Such online aesthetic labour also has cultural infrastructural implications for the bricks-and-mortar storefronts of commercial urban arteries, the economic backbones of neighbourhoods. In Chapter 11, Taylor Brydges, Deborah Leslie and Norma Rantisi focus on the crafting of urban fashion worlds in response to the "perfect storm" brought by the rise of online digital retailing and the shuttering of stores due to Covid-19 pandemic lockdowns. While large "ultra-fast" fashion retailers took this opportunity to divest of bricks-and-mortar retail spaces, many small independent fashion designers and retailers pivoted by innovatively adapting their physical and digital infrastructure. Through case studies of independent fashion retailers in Toronto, Montreal, Sydney and Melbourne, the chapter examines how the creation of soft online infrastructure (affective atmospheres, in-store sensory experiences and a commitment to local communities and sustainability) rework but also maintain local urban fashion districts.

Around the world in cities of all sizes, the embodied labour of creative entrepreneurs enhances the "authenticity" of locales, creating economic development place-promotion opportunities for residents and tourists alike to celebrate local urban cultures and ways of life in the guise of spectators as well as consumers (Duxbury & Richards 2019). Urban arts festivals, as Bernadette Quinn demonstrates in Chapter 12 with respect to Dublin, Ireland, showcase local culture and creativity, yet as infrastructure, they are often dismissed as ephemeral, transient, unstable and unimportant. Her chapter argues that these very characteristics lend arts festivals, especially those staged in public space, the fluid, flexible and somewhat subversive qualities that enable them to offer "out of the ordinary", participative and immersive experiences (O'Grady 2015) that are not only affective but also multi-sensorial in nature (Jordan 2016). Festivals encourage different ways of being in, belonging to and engaging with local places that do not necessarily involve making purchases. By breaking down some of the barriers that limit everyday engagement with places, arts festivals unsettle prevailing notions about who and what city spaces are for, temporarily transforming them into sites of cross-cultural and class encounter. While the limited personal mobility and curtailment of social interaction brought by the Covid-19 pandemic produced crises for arts festivals, it also produced experimentation with digitally enhanced infrastructure and ultimately a new appreciation of their value.

At their core, cities were founded as sites of trade and points of consumptive convergence. The chapters in this section all treat the city as a marketplace, demonstrating the diverse ways that urban cultural infrastructure is consumptive. Specializing in fashion, entertainment, food, night life and sex, a range of consumer districts animate cities along with vibrant night markets, traditional souks and identity-based ethnic shopping streets and bazaars. But far from disrupting regimes of power, the cultural infrastructure of consumption involves an image-conscious stage-management of streetscape veneers, belying the multiple realities and conflicting meanings hidden beneath them. Perhaps more than other components of urban cultural infrastructure, consumption is a key glocalizing and place-making force within cities. While it operates through networks that can be both exclusive and excluding, it is also definitive of individual and collective place-based identities that offer each city a unique yet recognizable consumerscape.

CHAPTER 9

HAWKER CULTURE AND ITS INFRASTRUCTURE: EXPERIENCES AND CONTESTATIONS IN EVERYDAY LIFE

Lily Kong and Aidan Wong

INTRODUCTION

Hawker foods characterize urban Asia, with similarities and differences across cities that forge both cultural commonalities and distinctions. From the itinerant to the fixed location, from the temporary sites to the purpose-built, hawker foods are served in informal settings, with varying degrees of tradition and innovation, hygiene and squalidness, local authenticity and globalized influence. In the side-streets of Beijing where local delicacies such as scorpion are served, to the abundant food cart vendors on Bangkok streets, to the *warung* (small, typically family-owned eateries) in Surabaya, and the carefully planned and designed hawker centres in Singapore, hawker culture is a distinctive characteristic of Asian urban culture. This usually low-priced food option feeds a consumption culture that is casual, relaxed and pervasive.

The nature of this consumption culture is forged from multi-layers of infrastructure that enable the (re)production of hawker or street food culture. This infrastructure includes physical, social, economic and digital dimensions, with the relative interplay of the various dimensions resulting in distinctive characteristics of hawker culture in different urban contexts. This chapter refers to *physical infrastructure* as the sites and locations, architectures, physical structures and systems that enable the production and consumption of hawker foods. These could be purpose-built hawker centres or makeshift street-side stalls. The latter is intuitive, and indeed, embedded in the very meaning of "hawking", but as this chapter will illustrate, itinerance need not be a requisite physical manifestation, and relative permanence and fixity can also characterize hawkers. *Social infrastructure* refers to the person of the hawker, the quintessential cook, micro-businessperson, purchaser, marketing and sales personnel, often all rolled in one. *Economic infrastructure* takes the form of economic policies and business models that enable hawker culture, and *digital infrastructure* refers to new models of transaction, including e-payments, online ordering and other practices enabled by digital technologies, which have empowered some hawkers while leaving others behind. These four dimensions of infrastructure are common across cultures and jurisdictions, but the precise expression and manifestation, particularly in relation to hawkers, may differ, in some cases revealing the creativity and innovation that support the continuance of hawker culture, but often also exposing the underlying spatial and cultural politics, including issues of inclusion/exclusion, physicality/virtuality, authenticity/mimicry and locality/globality.

An infrastructural lens is an important means through which to examine the social, cultural and economic practices surrounding hawker foods. Whereas infrastructure and its systems have been typically understood in the global North as material networks that facilitate "flows of people, goods, energy, water, waste and information" (Addie *et al.* 2020: 10) and are held up as the fix for better urban futures, the reality is often quite the opposite: urban decline is real, and it has both physical and social dimensions (Kinder 2016). In contrast, scholarship on the global South contextualizes infrastructure within discussions of political economy, social networks, access, culture, geopolitics, ecologies and affect (Addie *et al.* 2020), detailing how infrastructure encompasses not just the hard/technical, material artefacts and systems, but also the soft social and cultural networks that enable business and urban life to flourish. Irrespective of whether it is understood in material or non-physical terms, scholars agree that infrastructure enables the urban.

Focusing on the city-state of Singapore, this chapter examines the infrastructure of its iconic hawker centres. Revisiting Kong's (2007) investigation of Singapore's hawker centres, it illustrates how street food culture is (re)produced, and how this sometimes taken-for-granted aspect of urban culture is enabled but also simultaneously challenged by physical, social, economic and digital infrastructure. What follows is, first, an introduction to street food and hawker culture in Singapore, and second, a discussion about the infrastructural (re)production of hawker centres.

STREET FOOD, HAWKER CULTURE: CONSUMPTION IN SINGAPORE

Singapore is a city, island and state all at the same time. It obtained independence from Malaysia in 1965, becoming a sovereign state. Little more than 700 square kilometres, it is entirely urban. Out of necessity, its urban fabric is composed predominantly of high-rise buildings, the majority of which consists of public housing. State-led urban planning is central to optimizing the use of limited land in this hyper-urban and dense context where hawker centres are located.

Hawker centres are an iconic feature of Singapore's cityscape. Deeply embedded in the popular imagination and rhythms of everyday life, they provide a distinctive attraction to curious tourists and a locus of memories for Singaporeans. Hawker centres pulsate with a life and dynamism that was taken for granted until Covid-19 struck in 2020 and they had to close down for public safety reasons. At no point in time in their history have they been more missed by consumers.

What constitutes this familiar, sometimes taken for granted everyday hawker culture in Singapore? It is that melange of hawker centre, hawker food, "uncle" and "aunty" and hipster hawker stallholder, the multitudinous and varied customers, and the cleaning crew. A hawker centre refers to a collection of stalls selling different types of inexpensive cooked food, predominantly, but not exclusively, local fare (essentially Chinese, Malay, Indian), with drinks and desserts. The hawker stalls are housed in covered, non-air-conditioned, open complexes where there are common seating areas for customers (Figures 9.1 and 9.2). Although sometimes hot and

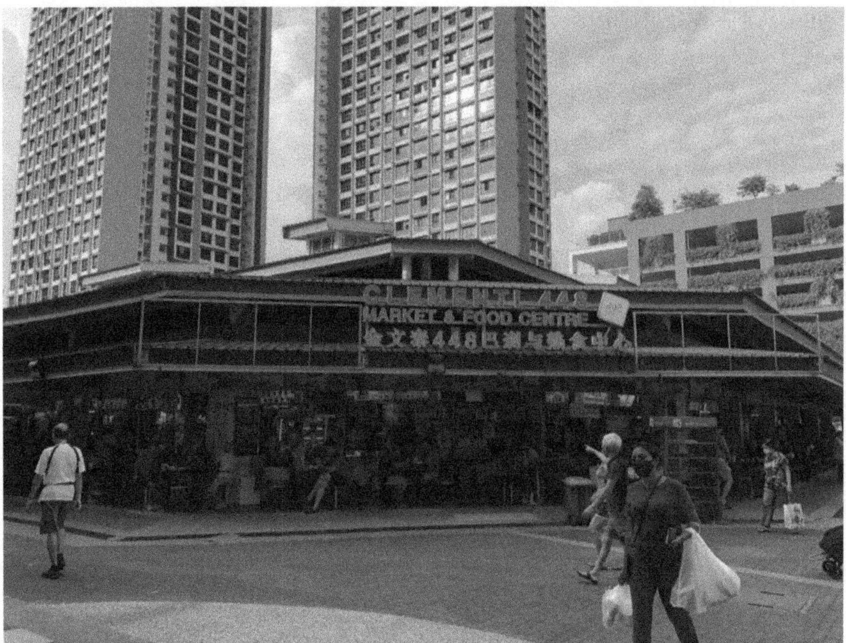

Figure 9.1 A hawker centre located in a public housing estate in Clementi, Singapore: in the background are two tall public housing blocks, and in the foreground, a small open plaza where temporary bazaars are occasionally held

Source: Aidan Wong.

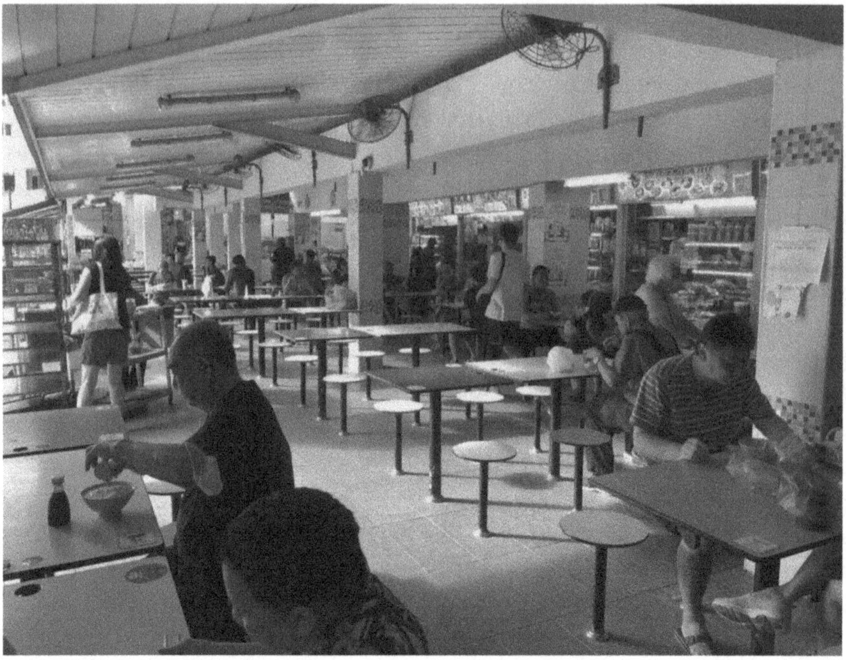

Figure 9.2 Tables in hawker centres are arranged to facilitate interaction and sharing, designed to accommodate four to eight diners together, with only a small handful of tables for two diners

Source: Aidan Wong.

noisy, the quality and affordability of hawker food draws crowds of locals and tourists. Whereas their antecedents were itinerant street traders, hawkers in Singapore now have proper amenities and facilities, including potable water, electricity, sewerage and drainage systems, toilets, lighting and garbage bin centres for waste disposal. Today, many hawker centres have Wi-Fi and barrier-free access. The name "hawker centre" is so familiar in Singapore that its irony is not always apparent. A hawker, according to the Oxford English Dictionary, is someone who travels about selling goods. But Singapore's hawkers have permanent stalls; they are no longer itinerant.

Hawker centres serve affordable food for executives with demanding schedules as much as they cater to families with busy routines. They are community places where neighbours meet, and casual places where all social types gather – the CEO and the office cleaner, grandparents and juniors, different races and genders, nationalities and cultures (Figure 9.2). Hawker centres are a microcosm of Singapore society and have mirrored the changing Singapore life and urban landscape over time. They are a window into consumer culture in Singapore – more than consumption *per se*, they reflect and reproduce particular values and express Singaporean identity while responding to, reproducing and simultaneously challenging the physical, social, economic and digital infrastructure that enable their production. In this sense, they illustrate how infrastructure reproduces consumer culture and consumer society.

HAWKER CENTRES AS PHYSICAL INFRASTRUCTURE

The *physical infrastructure* that enables the continued existence of street food is a fundamental component of hawker culture. Singaporean hawker centres are products of urban planning and policy initiatives in the 1960s and 1970s to clear the streets of itinerant, unlicensed hawkers operating in barely regulated and less than hygienic conditions, and frequently obstructing traffic. In an effort to further order and regulate the built environment, the state relocated hawkers to purpose-built structures with clean water supply, electricity, gas, seating areas for customers, ventilation, fans, crockery collection points and, in some cases, interesting architecture with culturally inflected decorative features.

Singapore's hawker centres are part of a larger urban planning paradigm in this city-state, anchored in public housing estates and woven into tightly regulated planning parameters and regimes. Public housing estates are planned, organized and designed to provide easy access to amenities, from schools and clinics to hawker centres and retail shops. For every designated number of public housing blocks and households, requisite amenities are planned, assigned and built, including hawker centres. In other words, hawker centres are deliberately planned into the making of new towns and public housing estates. After three decades of careful planning and dedicated inclusion of hawker centres into town planning regimes, in the 2000s, as fast food took root and air-conditioned comfort in the equatorial heat enticed customers into the food courts of shopping malls, the government halted construction of new hawker centres. In response to local resident requests for proximate and affordable food, it reversed this policy position in the 2010s, again building new hawker centres in housing estates.

When the Covid-19 pandemic struck, the enabling physical infrastructure of hawker centres became a barrier and challenge. The openness and porosity of the hawker centre made it difficult to regulate the flow of visitors. Makeshift barriers were erected so that single points of entry and exit would be enabled, and digital records kept of the identity of those entering and exiting for tracing purposes, if and when necessary. The cosy settings with proximate seating could not be fully utilized as safe physical distancing between diners became a necessity. Hawkers also found it difficult to operate their businesses all day wearing masks. Delivery personnel had few suitable pick-up points. All these physical design challenges – notably ventilation and spacing – are now taken into consideration when new hawker centres are built.

SOCIAL INFRASTRUCTURE: CONTESTATIONS OVER AUTHENTICITY, LOOKING BEYOND HAWKERS

The success of Singapore's hawker centres also hinges on a robust *social infrastructure* anchored in the person of the hawker (in interaction with policymakers, planners, cleaners, food bloggers, hawker association chiefs and delivery service providers). The hawker is the quintessential micro-entrepreneur – the purchaser, marketing and sales representative, cashier and cook all combined into one person. In colonial and early post-independence years, the barriers to entry into this occupation were low. Considered a socially respectable trade, hawking was a means of making a living (not just for the urban poor) that required relatively little start-up capital. Overheads were also affordable, and there were no constraints on what hawkers sold or the hours they worked. Hawkers were, by and large, their own bosses and made independent decisions. Originally an informal trade, hawking gradually became licensed in the 1930s (with only partial success) and in a more concerted way from the 1960s onwards, with island-wide exercises conducted to bring the large number into the formal sector economy.

As Singaporean society has matured and globalization has shaped every facet of life in the city-state, both the character of hawking and the profile of the hawker have changed. The variety of foods sold has expanded dramatically. Mexican chicken skewers, German bratwurst and wiener sausages, Vietnamese beef noodles and rolls, Italian pasta and Japanese don sets are increasingly common along with more traditional Chinese, Malay and Indian fare. With new food offerings has come a savvy breed of younger hawkers, more educated and cosmopolitan. There are also hawkers who have dropped out of school and use their entrepreneurialism and hard work to establish their businesses. Together, these "hipster hawkers", or "hawkerpreneurs", reflect the changing character of the hawker.

As competition for customers increases, hawkers have become ever-savvier with promotion. The battle for customers has extended to online promotions with food bloggers building loyal online followings. Social media platforms have also provided opportunities for many hawkers to post reviews and images of their food offerings, or their friends and children have done so on their behalf, especially during Covid-19. Young and new hawkers also often undertake their own social media marketing and even work with influencers to help promote their food. The social infrastructure supporting hawker culture has thus extended beyond the hawker as a lone operator with a menial helper or two at best, to an infrastructure that extends to the digital world.

Hawkers and their occupational skills form part of the country's intangible cultural heritage, that is valorized and celebrated, but also contested and debated. The key sites of contention centre on who constitutes the legitimate socio-cultural bearer of this urban culture, and the imagined authenticity of their edible cultural products. Government policy dictates that only Singaporeans and permanent residents (PRs) are permitted to operate hawker stalls managed by the National Environment Agency (NEA). Stallholders may operate their stalls with the assistance of their spouses, some of whom may be foreigners, subject to NEA's approval. This is largely because some of the stalls pay subsidized rentals as a means of keeping food costs manageable, with the subsidies directed towards Singaporeans and PRs rather than foreigners. Quite apart from the policy objectives, however, the public imagination is one that excludes foreign nationals, even naturalized ones, from assuming an "authentic" location, whatever their skills may be. Critics have argued that non-Singaporeans who serve local fare have somehow adulterated the original taste with their labour. Constructions of authenticity, then, are tied up with questions of citizenship rather than, necessarily, culinary skill.

Just as food bloggers and influencers are now part of the social infrastructure in Singapore's hawker culture, delivery riders have become important partners. As customers begin to use online order platforms, riders and walkers are hired to undertake local deliveries. Again, migrant opportunities are largely locked out, as hiring is based on nationality (only Singaporeans and PRs are accepted). Riders must be aged 18 and above, have a valid licence and a mobile device that can access their computer application. Those who choose to be walkers are based at home, and their radius is small, unlike those with cars or bikes. Cyclists and motorcyclists make up the majority of delivery crews. Just as traditional hawkers found the entry barriers to the trade to be low, the new business operations have offered employment to many people as riders who deliver food. These delivery personnel serve as intermediaries between hawkers and customers, and now form part of the social infrastructure that enable the consumption of hawker fare.

In many cities, public hygiene concerns surrounding street food are common. In Singapore, policymakers have introduced cleanliness regimes and grading systems to ensure that a basic level of hygiene is kept, and indeed, cultivates a culture that aims for exemplary performance. Cleaning regimes are regular and monitored, even while hawker centre cleaning and maintenance provides many senior citizens and migrants in Singapore a source of livelihood. Hawker centre associations, led and populated by volunteers and emergent, grassroots leaders among hawkers in each location, are a means by which hawkers can provide feedback to authorities, and work to promote, enliven and otherwise improve their hawker centres.

Clearly, the social infrastructure that enables hawker culture to continue, if not thrive, has expanded well beyond the lone itinerant hawker. The profile of hawkers is more varied now, a source of simultaneous lament and hope – lament for the imagined or real loss of authenticity and hope for the continuance of a cherished urban culture. Beyond the hawker, the additional social infrastructure – food bloggers, influencers, delivery riders and walkers, cleaners, hawker association chiefs and policymakers are essential ecosystem actors that enable the continuation of hawker culture.

ECONOMIC INFRASTRUCTURE: EVOLVING MODELS

The third aspect of enabling infrastructure is *economic* in nature, referencing the economic policies and business models that provide the framework for hawkers to make their living, enabling access to livelihoods and moderating costs of living. The shift from low subsidized rentals to ownership to market rentals to experiments with social enterprise models and the contested politics around each shift demonstrate the simultaneous enabling and constraining effects of economic infrastructure.

Historically, when hawkers were itinerant, licensing was the main way of managing the number of hawkers. When a policy decision was made to relocate hawker stalls from the streets to hawker centres, hawkers needed encouragement to make the shift, and those who did, enjoyed cheap rentals as "first-generation hawkers". The rental subsidy policy was also important because hawker centres played, and continue to play, an important role in moderating increases in food prices, thereby performing an important social service. Hawkers needed only to pay for utilities, service and conservancy charges, and licence fees. The subsidies were in place until 1993 when a stall tender scheme was introduced, which allowed the public to tender for vacant stalls and pay tendered rent. Today, all hawker stalls are rented, and about one-third are subsidized. The early economic incentive has been an important factor in the infrastructural equation, enabling hawkers to make a viable living.

While subsidized rental schemes enabled some hawkers, others found it constraining. Where stalls were subsidized, strict restrictions were in place to govern their use. For instance, the hawkers could not be employed in other occupations, nor could they sublet their stall. They must also personally operate their stall and cannot assign it to others to run on their behalf. In the past, stallholders have had their licences revoked for being continuously absent from their stalls and relying on assistants to maintain them.

Reflecting perhaps the changing economic conditions, the mid-1990s was when a Stall Ownership Scheme was introduced for selected hawker centres across the island. It allowed incumbent stallholders in selected hawker centres to purchase the stall they were operating. Stall owners could enjoy the freedom that came with ownership – they could sell their stall or rent or sublet it. If they wished, family members could also be made co-owners. In 2013, however, it was announced that the scheme would be discontinued once the ownership term for existing owned stalls was over because of a wider economic slowdown.

As the subsidized rental scheme works its way out of the system, the tender scheme, where rental of hawker stalls is based on market rates, will become the dominant mode of leasing. Hawkers will increasingly need to have the business know-how to run their stalls, in addition to developing culinary skills. At the Institute of Technical Education, a vocational college, for example, courses like "Introduction to Managing a Hawker Business" have been introduced, as they offer training on establishing and managing a food stall.

In addition to ownership and rental models, in 2012, a Hawker Centres Public Consultation Panel recommended that to better meet changing demographic needs hawker centres should offer all-day dining options so that they can more effectively function as vibrant cultural hubs. In response, alternative management models for hawker centres were proposed and subsequently piloted. This entailed a social enterprise or cooperative model, with stalls set aside for the lower-income and special needs persons to enter the trade, in effect giving them a chance of earning a livelihood in a relatively low-cost business. The model was introduced with the aim of ensuring food prices were kept low, thus making the hawker trade sustainable.

Over the years, across a range of different management models, hawker culture and infrastructure has persisted as an elemental part of Singapore's urban fabric. Most hawkers have remained small businesspeople, whether their stalls are rented or owned, subsidized or not. A few have expanded the number of stalls they manage (up to a maximum of two, by policy), franchising their business, entering the restaurant (or other) business, or even going international.

Franchising has also been encouraged and facilitated by the government. Other entrepreneurial hawkers have sought to bottle their condiments (e.g., chili sauces) as an alternative way to bring a selection of their products to market. Still other especially well-known stalls have sold their recipes, generating sufficient profit to retire. The ambition and vision of the entrepreneurs, and the growth of the original hawker stalls illustrate the economic infrastructure that supports, enables, encourages and facilitates their growth and success.

DIGITAL INFRASTRUCTURE: DIGITAL HAWKERS, NEW BUSINESS MODELS, MODERN BUSINESS OPERATIONS

Given how digitalization is transforming many industries and businesses, it would be a surprise if hawkers have been left totally untouched. From e-payment to online ordering and the use of delivery platforms, the world of traditional hawking is changing rapidly, although the change has been uneven, with older hawkers especially resisting digitalization shifts.

Electronic payments may well be the lowest hanging fruit when it comes to going digital. As part of a larger Smart Nation drive by the Singapore government, cashless payment methods have been enabled and encouraged. While some hawkers still prefer the certainty of cash in hand, digital payment seems more readily welcome than other forms of digitalization, such as online ordering and the use of delivery platforms. The government has sought to incentivize hawkers to adopt a unified e-payment system, allowing different contactless payment options by renting payment terminals for free for the first three years and covering the cost of transactions fees during this period. Clearly, providing digital infrastructure is necessary if a successful and widespread transition is to be possible.

As modern operational practices take root, business models also evolve with digitalization. Expedited by Covid-19, the restrictions on mobility and the requirement for physical distancing pushed hawkers and their customers to use online ordering and delivery platforms. For those who eschewed online platforms for ordering and delivery, either the challenge of entering the digital world was too much or they valued the personal relationship with their customers that comes with in-person interactions. It was also questionable whether there was sufficient business sense in incurring hefty commission charges when the food prices were low to start with. For customers, similar concerns arose when a significant proportion of the total cost of a meal goes to delivery charges. Further, some hawkers felt that their food would not taste good by the time it was delivered, especially if the delivery person picked up food from several stalls.

Such "soft" infrastructural adjustments do not just involve hawkers. Platform providers, which include major players such as Grab but also a myriad of smaller ones, are also experimenting with new business models and revising business operations as circumstances change, and particularly as the Covid-19 pandemic transitions into an endemic. They have sought to respond to customer needs and facilitate hawkers, finding ways to recreate some of the relationships based on in-person transactions (e.g., emulating physical layouts on digital platforms to help customers to identify their preferred stalls). As the platform matures, opportunities may become available through messaging tools to facilitate the building of relationships between hawkers and customers. Grab is considering the extension of delivery services to wet market stalls together with hawker centre items, thus increasing efficiency for delivery riders, increasing hawkers' business and of course, increasing earnings for Grab itself.

The life of the digital hawker is rapidly changing, just as the customer, the online order and delivery platform, the delivery crew and others are evolving. An entire new ecosystem has emerged, and various actors continue to innovate, leveraging digital infrastructure and its capabilities, but also reliant on traditional material infrastructure – such as good road systems and effective public and private transportation, without which digital ordering alone is ineffective. The urban cultural ecosystem of hawking is made possible by the interweaving of digital and material infrastructure.

CONCLUSION

This chapter has illustrated through the case of Singapore hawker centres how infrastructure enables and constrains the hawker trade – an occupation that is central to the cultural and social life of the city. It has demonstrated that infrastructure has physical, material dimensions, but also social, organizational, economic and digital components; the time when infrastructure is recognized only for its materiality is past (Melosi 2020). More than mere "technical sinews of the modern metropolitan area", infrastructure has a social history in terms of how its systems and networks were constructed, operated, and used by different groups in society – "with variation not only from country to country but also from time period to time period within nations" (Tarr & Dupuy as cited in Melosi 2020: 145).

Given that multiple layers of infrastructure make and remake hawker culture in Singapore, undergirding the consumption of street food across the city, this chapter has argued that infrastructure is a mode of intervention in cultural reproduction. Beyond the urban planning and social history specificities of hawking in this Southeast Asian city, the cultural perspective on urban infrastructure that this chapter affords underscores how infrastructure – as an intersectional concept and tool – links the physical to the digital, the global to the local, the economic to the social, the authentic to the mimicked.

CHAPTER 10

AESTHETICIZING HIPSTER RETAIL INFRASTRUCTURE: FROM NEAPOLITAN TO COSMOPOLITAN

Bryan Mark

INTRODUCTION

Local shopping streets and neighbourhood retailing are universal urban forms of commerce that produce and maintain the lifeblood of the cultural infrastructure of cities as a marketplace of public cultures (Zukin *et al.* 2016). Forming the public face of local identity and sites where social identities emerge, the socio-spatial assemblage of brick-and-mortar stores and buildings, business owners, workers and shoppers comprise the consumption infrastructure of urban retailing. This infrastructure organizes encounters between different publics in cities, producing street-level sites of exchange and dignified livelihoods for marginalized actors and international newcomers (Hall 2012). Into the twenty-first century, however, local shopping streets – everyday sites of retail diversity – face extreme competition from online retail shopping (Zukin *et al.* 2016), while the concentration and internationalization of financial retail capital displaces and replaces low-capital independent shops with brand-name global chain stores (Mermet 2017). Moreover, the aestheticization of production and consumption represents an additional force of homogenization, blitzing the social, cultural and economic heterogeneity of neighbourhood retail shopping streets with new consumer cultural forms of lifestyle-centred, upscale market values of distinctiveness, individuality and authenticity (Ley 2003; Zukin 2010). This homogenization standardizes urban retail infrastructure into specialist bubbles of cultural commerce that maintain and validate the social networks and aesthetic preferences of the new urban middle class. It also signals the roll out of new local micro-retail actors who embody an emerging occupational type and consumption pattern that feeds the postmodern marketplace of post-industrial cities: hipster retailing.

Exploring the aestheticization of urban retail infrastructure, this chapter begins by tracing paradoxical class identity formation processes of "the hipster" within aestheticized spheres of consumption and production in the city, highlighting how in the twenty-first century the hipster embodies a distinct form of entrepreneurial retail. It then offers a case-study analysis of an independent ice cream boutique in downtown Toronto, Canada as a microcosm of the dynamics of hipster retailing. The chapter argues that hipster retail infrastructure is both physical and virtual, materializing from culinary and image processes of making and selling that are structured by an "aesthetic disposition" of the self-employed proprietor and amplified by digital self-branding imperatives of mobile social media users.

IF YOU'RE READING THIS, IT IS TOO LATE: THE IDENTITY PRACTICES OF HIPSTER COOL

The etymological roots of the modern hipster are found in the American jazz avant-garde and the musical artistic practices of the male black Bebop player in the 1930s and 1940s. The "hip" jazz player was then fetishized by "rebellious" white American youth subcultures who co-opted the "offbeat moniker" of the black hipster transforming it into angsty fashion with an individualized theme of "underground" consumption (Hill 2017). In the contemporary zeitgeist, the "look" of the hipster remains gendered and raced, identified in normative media discourse as a "rugged" yet groomed white male lumbersexual whose "shabby chic" image incorporates "sleeve" tattoos, "man bun" haircuts, skinny jeans, "Buddy Holly" glasses and rustic facial hair (le Grand 2020). More complex sociological analyses complicate this stereotypical cluster of symbols noting that the embodied subjectivity of the hipster is a chaotic identity construct that is ambiguous, contested and paradoxical, rooted in processes of class distinction and appropriation (Maly & Varis 2016). The ambiguity of the hipster lies in the interplay between aesthetic tropes of authenticity and individuality, wherein hipster "legitimacy" is found in binary distinctions between insider/outsider, fake/real and trend follower/trendsetter (Michael 2015). Through a specific set of consumption practices, the "real" hipster engages in the casual but perpetual competitive struggle to stay on top of the trendsetting field of cultural cool "by discovering and appreciating new cultural items quickly", which translates as a form of symbolic capital rendering social power and aesthetic prestige in the realm of consumer culture (Michael 2015: 164). Such modernist style regimes of cool committed to the fetishization of the new sits in tension with hipster aesthetics appreciating and appropriating "old-fashioned" forms of traditional objects and sentimental styles that recontextualize the taste of kitsch into a scheme of distinction (Schiermer 2014). In both cases, the high cultural capital of hipster cool relies upon the charismatic authority of nonchalance, wherein ease with a diversity of cultural goods *appears* unstudied and therefore socially legitimate (Michael 2015).

Yet the hipster's hunger for the next trend cannibalizes the mystique of cool, as consumers overtly strive towards markers of hipster identity by studying established indexes of taste and lifestyle. This cultural contradiction internalizes "the conflict between individualization and imitation" (Schiermer 2014: 169), in which "being a hipster comes with very strong and reoccurring identity discourses that all focus on authenticity, yet paradoxically form the basis of a very collective style" (Maly & Varis 2016: 644). Such paradoxical dynamics of the twenty-first-century hipster play out at multiple scales, from the local to the global, rendering hipsters a "trans-local population" (Maly & Varis 2016). The local embeddedness of global hipster culture is "polycentric", materializing a "number of centres of normativity", wherein "what is labelled as 'hipster' differs contextually depending on who uses the concept and in which part of the world" (Maly & Varis 2016: 638). While hipster identity embodies the local vernacular, the consumption spaces of global hipster culture rely on a standardized material infrastructure of "cool authenticity" that makes "offbeat" cultural venues into the niche cultural preferences of the "hipperati" (Zukin 2010). The "alternative consumption practices" of hipsters gentrify neighbourhoods and "become a means of excluding poorer, 'ethnic' shoppers" (Zukin 2008: 725).

Geographies of hipster infrastructure maintain, and are based in, mythic associations of bohemian urban life (Lloyd 2010). As the unity of capital reinvestment, media attention and historical state neglect recycle visual images of industrial economic decay and the spatial stigma of street crime into branded simulations of gritty urban authenticity, so the "crunchy chic" of the hipster is made (Kern 2015). This glamourization and aestheticization of urban grit, with its "drama of living on the edge" is a ruinous quest (Lloyd 2010: 80). The *emplacement* of concentrations of new urban consumption spaces and services privileging the economic and cultural capital of a young, educated and "alternative" clientele drives the *displacement* of long-time social bonds and established everyday geographical routines of traditional working-class neighbourhood life (Valli 2015).

Urban hipster infrastructure not only introduces new consumption spaces into gentrifying urban built environments but also reflects new micro-entrepreneurial retail patterns of aesthetic production within the contemporary cultural economy of cities (Scott 2001). For Scott (2017: 62), the hipster has undergone an occupational migration "deploying culture to create self-employment opportunities", shifting from the realm of consumption into the sphere of production as an economic strategy of neoliberal self-survival. The hipster enters the work force as a new micro-entrepreneurial vendor of high-end neo-artisanal and fashion-oriented goods and services, re-aestheticizing mundane products with authenticity and individuality. Such *hipster retailing* includes a catalogue of niche products for purchase that proliferate across forms of commerce, including third-wave coffee shops, vinyl record shops, tattoo studios, eyewear boutiques, "vintage" second-hand clothing stores, vegan restaurants, gluten-free bakeries, lifestyle wellness clinics, grooming salons and barber shops, micro-craft beer breweries and nose-to-tail butcher shops. The socio-spatial character of hipster entrepreneurship signals the rise of new "cool" jobs of high-status manual work within the elite urban retail economy (Ocejo 2017). The "expert knowledge" practices of hipster retail entrepreneurs with respect to objects and styles serves to legitimize the placement of new niche products within older inner-city neighbourhoods (Ley 2003). New youth micro-enterprises transmit the visual aesthetics and material artefacts of hipster culture as markers of distinction into less economically advantaged regions of the world. In Kabul, Afghanistan, a new barbershop displays a "[g]iant photo of tattooed and bearded hipsters" while in Nairobi, Kenya, craft-beer companies brew "Mexican pineapple sour" beers for the middle class, and in Goma, Congo, a cafe serves "quinoa protein bowls as well as 'latte macchiatos'" (*Economist* 2020: 59–60). Following Harvey (2012), such transnational hipster retailing can be seen as a manifestation of "collective symbolic capital" in which market-shaped claims to authenticity, uniqueness and individuality connect with extracting and standardizing global flows of capital.

In this way, the cultural transmuting of "old" occupations and their sites of production cannot be analytically divorced from geographies of global inter-urban competition. The aesthetic business models of hipster retailers lend the hype of "cool" to the marketable imagery of newly post-industrial cities, adding to the global toolkit of cultural redevelopment strategies that seeks "to encourage entrepreneurial innovation and creativity, cleanse public spaces of visible signs of moral decay, and compete with other capitals of the symbolic economy of finance, media, and tourism" (Zukin 2010: 234). The next section of the chapter empirically grounds this theoretical discussion in the material and digital infrastructure of a hipster ice cream boutique.

THE SCOPE OF THE SCOOP: THE SHOP FLOOR OF HIPSTER ICE CREAM RETAILING

Situated within a larger socio-historical context of urban redevelopment that aestheticizes and commodifies old manufacturing built-forms across inner-city Toronto (Bain 2003; Bain & Mark 2020), the micro-geographies of boutique ice cream synthesize complex links between spatial retail change, cultural micro-entrepreneurship and hipster consumption practices on and within Ossington Avenue. The commercial space of the ice cream boutique is located in a former automobile repair shop. The installation of a new shop floor of light craft manufacturing and gourmet food production reinforces the distance between new trendy businesses and the original culture of the ethnic neighbourhood Little Portugal. Except for the water-based gluten-free flavours vegan chocolate and raspberry sorbet that are sourced from outside suppliers, each product of small-batch ice cream sold over the counter at this Ossington Avenue retailer is made on-site, processed one tub at a time through a single industrial ice cream machine and stored in a walk-in freezer. The ice cream is paired with "house-made" non-vegan and vegan cookies, hand-piped French choux pastries, cream-cheese frosted cinnamon buns and Hong-Kong-style waffles, as well as seasonal speciality goods including macarons, mochi, pie, doughnuts, bread pudding, butter tarts and chiffon cake. Food production depends on a team of full-time bakers and makers, while the selling of these specialized products depends on front-of-house service worker to not only manually scoop the product but also legitimize notions of "authenticity". The on-site production of local ice cream and baked goods corresponds to expensive prices that ranged pre-pandemic from CDN$4.15 for a single scoop (four ounces) of ice cream, to CDN$4.95 for a half ice cream sandwich, to CDN$7.96 for a Hong-Kong ice cream waffle with four ounces of ice cream.

Instrumental to the making process is the conceptual labour of the proprietor as a "culturepreneur" (Lange 2011). In "seeking to legitimate the intellectualization of new areas of expertise" (Featherstone 1991: 91), she folds the object of ice cream into the milieu of urban hipster retailing by deploying the "economic valorisation of the aesthetic disposition" (Ley 2003: 2540). With a fine arts degree in illustration and previous employment as an ornamental sugar worker who sculpted cakes, the proprietor transposes and imposes the symbolic power of "cultural competency" onto ice cream goods, designing "interesting" flavours to tempt foodie palettes (Johnston & Baumann 2015). Her ice cream inspiration "comes from *anything* I eat ... it's often from a savoury meal and *I'll take that and turn it into* something sweet" (interview, 1 February 2019). The "interesting" flavours she has created replace classic vanilla, strawberry and chocolate. They reference food forms such as craft beer, avocado, black sesame, fig and goat cheese, cream of corn, taro, raspberry lychee and rosewater, ginger milk, mango coconut with warm sticky rice, matcha tiramisu, chamomile and salted honey. This ice cream boutique privileges consumers with omnivorous tastes who have the cultural capital and competency to appreciate food fashion.

Such aestheticized dynamics not only reflect backstage processes of making but also frontstage forms of selling (Figure 10.1). Theatrically staging

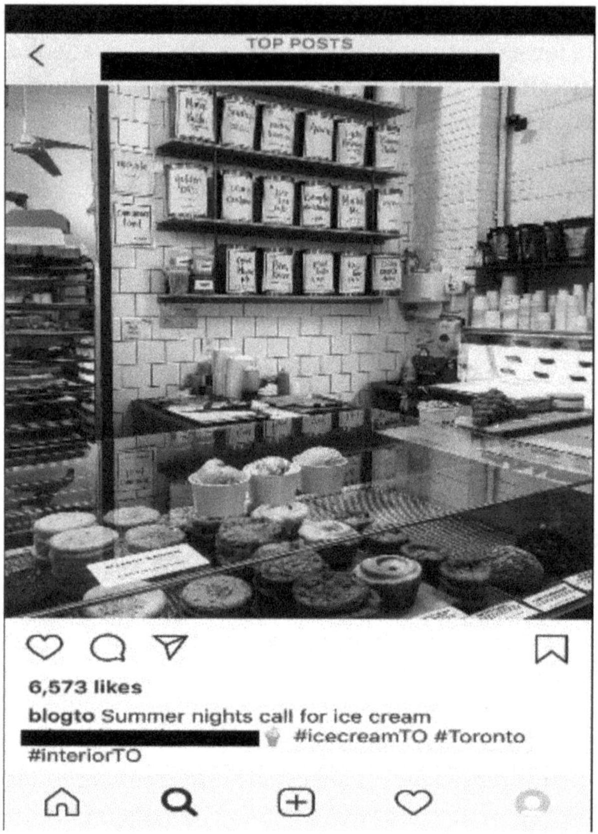

Figure 10.1 The carefully designed commercial interior of the ice cream boutique, minus working bodies, as featured by a lifestyle blog on Instagram with more than 5,000 likes

the *mise-en-scene* of merchandising, the proprietor highlights how her artistic training informs the imaging of the products' aesthetics:

> I mean illustration *turned into* cake decorating, which is *very particular* and *very aesthetic*. It was very much about the way something looked. It was very much a visual thing. In terms of ice cream … there are products that we have that people like to Instagram [and] put out on social media [which reflects] the detail to aesthetic and the way something looks.
>
> (Interview, 2 January 2019)

In contrast to a mainstream ice cream shop where the variety of ice cream is conventionally displayed upfront for the customer to see and identify, the hipster orientation of ice cream merchandising abstracts the method of ordering by invisibilizing the ice cream dipping cabinets and forcing the customer to order from a stylized menu of text. Showcased across five standardized rows of symmetrical stainless-steel buckets, the metallic menu interfaces the product and the customer through the cold glamour of industrial chic, symbolizing neo-artisanal small-batch production processes. Moreover, individual flavours are manually *illustrated* on sheets of white paper, designed with a thick slanted-edge black Sharpie, calligraphed by the proprietor. The business owner's controlling and discerning gaze curates the food on display in uniform rows behind a custom-built wooden case shielded with transparent glass. Minimalist whitewashed materialities of white paint, tile, and cylindrical pendant lights appropriate the art world's "white cube" aesthetic, to frame the food (O'Doherty 1999). In this way, the interior visual environment seeks to focus and seduce the gaze of the middle-class consumers, capitalizing on their aesthetic disposition and desire for creativity and authenticity, even in their food.

In addition to curating and designing the interior and exterior spaces of the ice cream boutique, the food itself is displayed to be "Instagramable", that is, aesthetically "worthy" of posting and disseminating on the global mobile photo-sharing social media platform Instagram. Such "Instagramability" of hipster ice cream retailing demonstrates the mobile cameraphone practices and social media production of entrepreneurial "influencers" territorializing urban fabrics and geotagging site-specific locations as informational locales "compatible" with the self-branding of "authenticity" in the promotional pursuit of visibility, attention and "likes" (Marwick 2013). In this way, the ice cream boutique's Instagram geotags aggregate an aspirational networked public of "in-the-know" middle-class consumers. These consumers exploit the spatial aesthetics of hipster for self-promotion. They visualize the aspirational lifestyle of the "urban middle-class good life" by depicting site-specific ice cream commodities as "priceless", "obligatory" and "justified" and locationally frame the site in Instagram photographic posts against an "edgy" and "gritty" backdrop of alleyway graffiti and a streetscape that treats "'the street' not merely as a location or space, but as an idea, an aesthetic, and a potential" (Cronin 2008: 75).

Moreover, as the high visibility of influencer imaging amplifies the publicity of the ice cream boutique within the digital public realm, the store has been forced to deal with unprecedented retail queues (Figure 10.2). The queues manifest as a local form of trendy knowledgeability that is a variant of hipster retail infrastructure itself. Indeed, passers-by often have one of three auditory reactions that speak to their resources of cultural capital: outsiders who do not know what the line-up signifies assume that the wait "must be worth it"; some insiders who recognize the queue is for "the ice cream place" praise the product and/or brag about having waited longer while others scorn, often with profanity, the conspicuousness of queuing as "uncool" and refuse to do it. In this way, the line-up acts as a spatial form of local hipster vernacular, demonstrating the multi-layered and contradictory meanings of hipster cool, while at the same time amplifying the entitlement of middle-class consumer cultural claims over urban retail landscapes.

In the context of the Covid-19 pandemic, and following the global enforcement of public health measures by governments to control its spread, virtual infrastructure, including information technology software, digital devices and social media platforms, have been institutionalized as the primary means of enabling human communication and social connectedness. As screen-based attachment to social media platforms becomes entrenched as paradigmatic pandemic behaviour, "Instaproof" hipster urban streetscapes may disproportionately benefit from the institutionalization of virtual infrastructure in everyday cultural life. The aesthetic image of products and places in the hipster marketplace folds into the aesthetic norms of social media proprietorship that are always seeking to publicize curated information and maintain branded appearances on digital platforms (Khamis *et al.* 2017). In this way, the pandemic-fuelled digital transformation of everyday life may intensify and amplify the unevenness of urban visibility, as "Instaesthetic" gentrified neighbourhoods and "social media ready" urban retail products of global

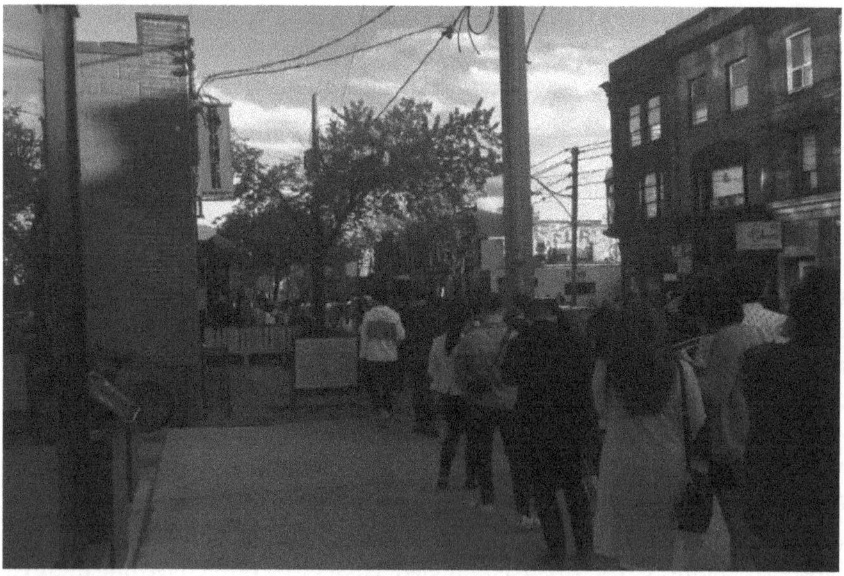

Figure 10.2 The retail line-up extends north on Ossington Avenue, governing urban pavement space

Source: Bryan Mark.

hipster infrastructure appeal to visual economic practices of "glancing" in the global capitalist attention economy, while less economically advantaged locales and livelihoods in the same city are unrepresented and invisibilized (Zulli 2018).

CONCLUSION

The aesthetic marketplace of hipster retailing increasingly personifies the cultural infrastructure of urban shopping streets in metropolitan areas around the world. This case study of one ice cream boutique on a street in downtown Toronto has highlighted some of the material and digital dimensions constituting the hard and soft infrastructure of hipster retail, namely how the proprietary imposition of aesthetic food tastes and the circulation of highly visible social media images inform, maintain and animate the production and consumption of "culinary cool". But it is important to remain critical of how the social media savviness of hipster retailing deepens forms of physical and virtual infrastructural exclusion. The digital divide exacerbates the visibility of "have" and the invisibility of "have-not" businesses on local shopping streets (Zukin *et al.* 2016). With the market expansion of hipster retailing aestheticizing both products and places, the social potential of retail infrastructure to materialize encounters across difference that can foster a shared sense of local belonging through the buying and selling of goods risks diminishment. In contemporary cities, the collective identity of many retail shopping streets is diverging from a public culture of ordinary services and everyday necessities and moving towards a private culture of extraordinary middle-class desires and social media popularity contests.

CHAPTER 11

CRAFTING ALTERNATIVE URBAN FASHION INFRASTRUCTURE IN A DIGITAL AND PANDEMIC AGE?

Taylor Brydges, Deborah Leslie and Norma M. Rantisi

INTRODUCTION

Recent years have witnessed a "perfect storm" in the fashion industry. The rise of ultra-fast, online-only fashion (Camargo *et al.* 2020), the growing influence of platforms such as Amazon (Stewart 2022) and the ongoing pandemic (Brydges *et al.* 2021) have caused havoc for many fashion retailers. These developments have major implications for high streets and shopping malls in the world's fashion cities (i.e., centres with a concentration of leading fashion districts, designers and media, such as New York City, London, Milan and Shanghai). Recent media attention has focused on a number of major brands shuttering stores and filing for bankruptcy protection (Chitrakorn 2020). All of these challenges raise questions about the future of the fashion industry and its urban cultural infrastructure.

This chapter focuses on one segment of the industry – small independent fashion retailers – examining their responses to the crisis. It explores the ways that these retailers forge alternative urban infrastructure and affective atmospheres, interweaving in-store sensory experiences with digital and social media technologies. Through a hybrid use of old factories and warehouses, independent fashion retailers engage different spaces and materials. They cultivate closer relationships between producers, consumers and designers, advancing a "politics of reconnection" (Hartwick 1998) that seeks to address the social and environmental costs of fashion. As the crisis in the fashion industry intensifies, these small urban retailers maintain diverse linkages with their surrounding neighbourhoods, and, during the pandemic, became key sites of economic and social resilience in the face of global supply chain disruptions. In the process, they foster alternative realms of fashion, illustrating how urban infrastructure is at once cultural and political, as well as material (Alam & Houston 2020).

Utilizing a mixed methods approach, this chapter draws upon international trade reports, newspaper articles, websites and other social media, as well as open-ended interviews with alternative fashion retailers in Canadian and Australian cities. Organized into three main sections, it begins by providing an overview of global fashion infrastructure associated with major fashion centres. The second section discusses the crisis confronting the industry today and the third section examines how small, independent fashion retailers are responding to this crisis, utilizing physical, digital and cultural infrastructure to craft alternative urban fashion spaces.

GLOBAL FASHION INFRASTRUCTURE

In a context of globalization, marked by financialization, the dominance of communication technologies and increased trade liberalization, fashion brands are now global corporate players. Major brands in both the luxury and mass market segments, including Louis Vuitton and Chanel, as well as H&M and Zara, can be found in cities across the world and accessed virtually from nearly any place (Crewe 2017). Despite the rise of a global fashionscape, fashion remains intricately connected to place and sedimented in the world's major metropolises. Both established "global cities" (e.g., London, Milan, New York City, Paris, Tokyo) and relatively newer, "not-so-global cities" (e.g., Dakar, Mumbai, Toronto, Auckland, Shanghai, Seoul, Sydney) count among the world's major fashion capitals (Breward & Gilbert 2006). These cities are home to the major fashion labels, as well as other key elements in the field of fashion, including major retailers, textile and trim suppliers, fashion design schools and trade associations. The world's fashion cities are also the site of associated marketing functions (e.g., the head offices of fashion and trade magazines), modelling agencies (Rantisi 2004) and international fashion weeks (Weller 2008). While a lot of manufacturing has been outsourced overseas over several decades, some critical infrastructure remains (particularly in the inner suburbs) and continues to support the sector, oriented toward smaller batch production and the use of more advanced technology (Rantisi 2002).

The status of "global" and "not-so-global" cities is attributed in large part to a concentration of high-end designers and fast fashion brands and the cultural capital associated with these labels (Crewe 2016). Within these cities, major retailers tend to concentrate in upscale and gentrified neighbourhoods, including high streets and fashionable downtown locations (e.g., Fifth Avenue in New York City, Oxford Street in London or Bloor Street in Toronto), although they also anchor themselves in large regional shopping malls.

Within such districts, major labels seek to build their brand by fixing their presence spatially, which is especially significant in an era of global off-shoring (Crewe 2017). This "spatial fix" is manifest in the selection of trendy locations populated by other consumer and cultural institutions, ranging from high-end boutiques to upscale restaurants and art galleries, from which the major labels draw – and contribute – "symbolic capital" (Evans 2003). Their presence is further fixed through the hard infrastructure of their flagship stores, often designed by star architects (Crewe 2010). Prominent cases such as the Prada "Epicenter" in Soho, New York City, designed by Rem Koolhaas' OMA or Christian Dior's flagship store in Tokyo, designed by SANAA, present a fusion of architecture and fashion. They foreground divergent, yet potentially complementary elements. As Crewe (2010: 2093) contends, while fashion is often perceived as ephemeral and delicate, architecture is commonly associated with sturdy and durable materials, signifying "longevity, permanence and solidity". Such stores also highlight commonalities across the fields – shared understandings of shape, style, composition and space (Crewe 2010). The spectacular and innovative designs of flagship stores therefore offer distinctive platforms through which to (re)model fashion. These stores represent exclusive spaces of consumption that use similar aesthetics around the world to exude an aura of wealth and power that appeals to a transnational elite (Crewe 2017).

Logos are generally imprinted on storefront windows and awnings and at times projected onto pavements, anchoring major fashion players to the physical space of the city (Crewe 2017). The extension of fashion retail into the public realm thus becomes a means of extending their brand presence, both geographically and symbolically (Crewe 2016). And the prominence of fashion retail landscapes within global cities ensures that place is connected to product (Molotch 1996; Scott 1999, 2001). This interconnection between fashion and place is reinforced through the marketing of high-end areas as "fashion districts" in tourist brochures, maps and street banners (Williams & Currid-Halkett 2011) (Figure 11.1). The infusion of fashion into the landscape is also manifest in street and mall design – replete with smoothly paved walkways, colourful signage, decorative light fixtures and public benches that facilitate pedestrian access and promote the leisure of shopping, allowing consumers and passers-by to more easily buy into the dominant fashion culture and individually experience it as a flaneuse.

The same techniques of commodity branding are applied more generally to a hard-branding of the city (Evans 2003), with these methods contributing to an entanglement between people, the material and the visual culture of a place (Amin 2008). A space's "functional and symbolic interpretation, its material arrangement" furnishes a field of "action and orientation" (Amin 2008: 11). For Billie and Simonsen (2021), the material is a key element in the

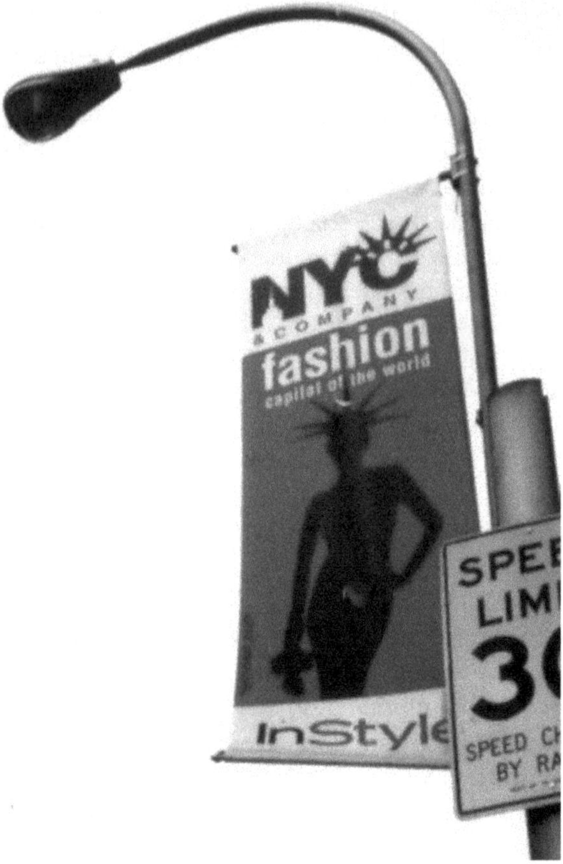

Figure 11.1 Lamp post banner in New York City's fashion district
Source: Norma M. Rantisi.

creation of "affective atmospheres", a set of sensations and experiences. And the social encounters, networks and scenes that transpire in these spaces – the soft, cultural infrastructure – in turn bolster the symbolic associations. As Scott (1996) asserts, through these branding processes, places become known for specific forms of culture (such as fashion), developing a reputation that yields a monopoly rent. Producers draw upon the cultural assets of place to imbue their products with a certain look and the products' images feedback into the region's basin of cultural assets (Williams & Currid-Halkett 2011).

Within the world's fashion centres, the up-scale neighbourhoods where major brands cluster tend to be elite, exclusionary and sanitized spaces (Zukin *et al.* 2009). However, beyond these neighbourhoods, there are a range of smaller independent designers and retail shops, oriented to locally made slow fashion, second-hand retail and clothing rental/sharing. These shops benefit from a concentration of alternative infrastructure, including small-scale manufacturing facilities, avant-garde designers, local art scenes and community organizations (as well as more traditional fashion education, production and marketing infrastructure). This alternative segment tends to be situated in more affordable and bohemian neighbourhoods of the city, which are home to different relations, aesthetics and identities (Leslie *et al.* 2014, 2015; Rantisi & Leslie 2010). Lower rents allow retailers and designers to maintain independence and experiment with cutting-edge designs, while also enabling access to larger warehouse or loft spaces that can be configured as design studios, production facilities *and* retail venues. Significantly, independents are also drawn to the distinct aesthetics and materiality of these neighbourhoods, often former industrial settings characterized by high ceilings, exposed brick and large, bright windows (Bain 2003; Podmore 1998). Creative products take shape and acquire distinct attributes through interactions with the material and social infrastructures of these sites (Rantisi & Leslie 2010). These interactions assume greater prominence in periods of crisis. The next section elaborates on one such moment – the contemporary crisis in fashion.

FASHION'S PERFECT STORM

Despite being fixed in time and place, fashion is an industry in constant flux. Scott (1999), for example, discusses how, within cultural industries such as music and film, there is a "see sawing" between periods where major companies dominate and times where smaller independents flourish. Within this broader trajectory, there are points of rupture and system branching where shifts in a cultural industry can emerge. One could argue that the 2020s represent a point of crisis for the global fashion sector (Brydges *et al.* 2021), leading to the destabilization of industrial practices and the creation of new paths (Rantisi 2004).

In the current period, fashion confronts a perfect storm, created in part by rising concerns on the part of consumers related to the social and environmental costs of fashion (Niinimäki *et al.* 2020). Over the past several decades, consumers have begun boycotting major fashion retailers, and in the aftermath of the Rana Plaza collapse, pressure has been rising on major fashion brands to transform their labour relations and supply chains (Leslie *et al.* 2014). Concern is also growing over the environmental consequences of fashion, including the increasing disposability of clothing, the carbon footprint of global sourcing and toxic chemicals utilized in manufacturing (Brydges & Hanlon 2020). As a response, there has been a growth of small independent boutiques offering slow fashion (i.e., high quality products that are locally and more sustainably produced in terms of materials and processes). There has also been a rise of second-hand clothing stores (Gregson & Crewe 2003).

In addition to this ethical crisis, another transformation impacting the sector is the rise of new digital infrastructure. In the past decade, online sales of clothing have been expanding, a trend that has greatly accelerated since the pandemic (Monroe 2021). Many retailers have seen digital revenues increase at the expense of on-site sales and have been closing stores to account for this trend, while other retailers have seen business migrate to players more focused on the online market.

As one example of this phenomenon, there has been a rise of online-only, ultra-fast fashion retailers, such as the multi-brand platforms of Zalando, Boohoo and ASOS or the single brand platform Shein (Monroe 2021). These ultra-fast fashion digital retailers have several advantages over traditional fast fashion retailers, including the fact that they do not have expensive physical storefront infrastructure to maintain, which keeps overhead costs low (Monroe 2021). Another advantage is their speed to market. While fast fashion retailers such as Zara can get a product to market in two weeks, Boohoo has reduced this down to a few days. Once consumers get used to the ease and speed of these online retail outlets, it will be difficult to encourage them to return to a bricks-and-mortar environment. Moreover, the range of products introduced in digital space far exceeds that of physical space. While Zara adds hundreds of new products every week, ASOS introduces approximately 7,000 new items (Monroe 2021). Ultra-fast fashion retailers have a more flexible and agile inventory management infrastructure which reduces their stock. In 2018, for example, it was estimated that H&M had $4.3 billion in unsold inventory, while Boohoo and Shein can order a few hundred items at a time and wait and see if they sell (Monroe 2021). Digital retailers also harvest a wealth of data on customer purchases organized by geographic area, demographic and type of buyer (first-time versus repeat). This consumer data is fed back into the supply chain, leading to a highly responsive framework.

Other non-specialized online digital platforms (e.g., Amazon) have also been gaining ground. In 2019, Amazon became the largest retailer of apparel in the US, selling more clothes than Target or Walmart (Danziger 2020). The company uses the massive amount of data they collect to produce their own-branded merchandise. While Amazon has had difficulties attracting higher-end brands to its site because of fears that the site would cheapen their image, Amazon now has plans to launch its own luxury fashion platform (Danziger 2020).

Another way digital technologies are transforming the fashion sector is through the growing influence of social media platforms. New online ultra-fast fashion retailers rely heavily on social media influencers to promote their brands, diminishing the role played by fashion editors, marketers and advertisers (Monroe 2021). Social media platforms are also transforming dominant patterns of clothing consumption, as more clothing is purchased to be worn online. Young consumers post images of themselves wearing different outfits and are reluctant to be seen in the same garment twice. This social media landscape strengthens the trend toward inexpensive, ultra-fast fashion.

The pandemic has exacerbated the crisis of the industry, intersecting with its digital transformation. The lack of access to physical stores – as well as initial concerns over the safety of in-person shopping – dealt a severe blow to the industry and its physical spaces (Brydges *et al.* 2021). Stores concentrated in tourist districts were especially hard hit due to travel restrictions, but all outlets were dramatically affected, including major international mainstream brands. Some American retailers, such as Neiman Marcus, JCPenney, J. Crew and Brooks Brothers, went out of business altogether, while others, including Burberry, Levi Strauss & Co. and Ann Taylor, have been closing physical locations and laying off employees. The loss of this storefront infrastructure in the downtowns of major cities has significant consequences for urban economic development and the future viability of urban high streets and shopping districts (see, for example, Toronto's Yorkville District in Figure 11.2, where almost half of the luxury fashion retailers closed their doors in 2020). In general, retailers are increasingly reliant on digital retail spaces.

Within this broader context, however, other fashion retail paths are emerging. This chapter focuses on one segment of the industry, small independent

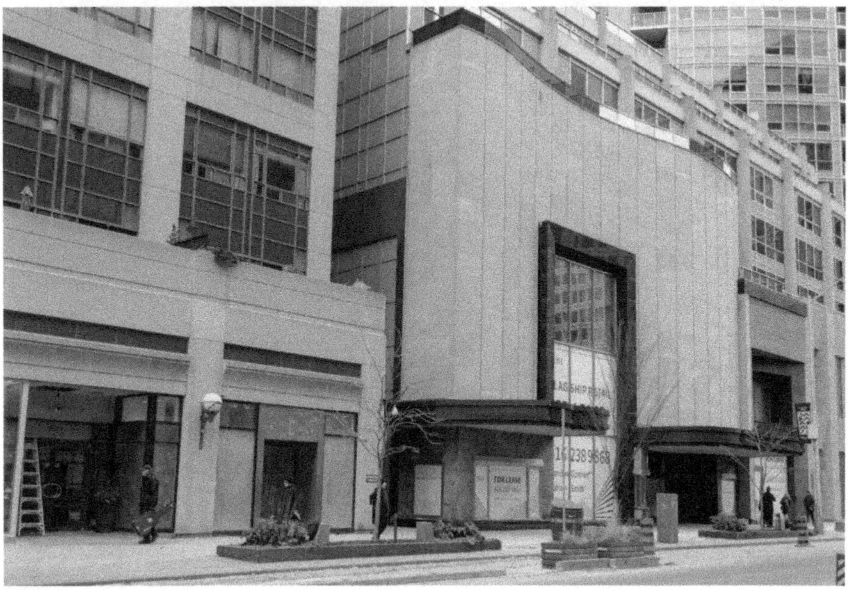

Figure 11.2 Store closures in Toronto's Yorkville district

Source: Andrew Stevenson.

fashion boutiques, foregrounding their use of physical, cultural and digital infrastructure to create an alternative to fast and ultra-fast fashion. Many are forging closer ties to consumers, producers, neighbourhoods and the environment to contribute to a local ethics of care.

INDEPENDENT BOUTIQUES AS ALTERNATIVE INFRASTRUCTURE IN THE WORLD'S FASHION CITIES

In this uncertain urban retail landscape, independent fashion boutiques employ a range of strategies, utilizing both digital and physical spaces, and promoting alternative aesthetics. Independent fashion businesses often choose to occupy more bohemian districts of the city, such as Mile End in Montreal, a former centre for apparel manufacturing in the mid-twentieth century. In the case of Mile End, retailers are attracted to proximate subcultural art scenes (independent music studios, performance venues, art galleries), more affordable rents, cultural infrastructure and access to distinct industrial architecture, which allows them to create distinctive mixed-use spaces (Figure 11.3).

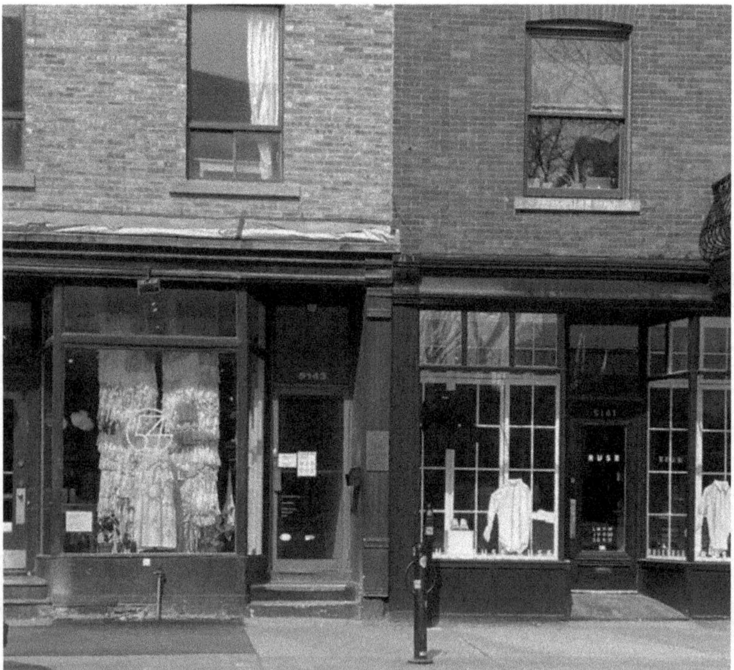

Figure 11.3 Fashion boutique in Mile End, Montreal

Source: Norma M. Rantisi.

Similar features attract retailers to districts such as the Brunswick neighbourhood in Melbourne, which is a multi-cultural, inner-suburb that is accessible by public transit and replete with former industrial spaces that have been converted into live-work spaces, makerspaces or combined production/retail facilities. Like Mile End, it also faces development pressures and gentrification associated with new consumption offerings, including retail and restaurants, that challenge the authenticity and grittiness that made this area so desirable in the first place. Drawing upon the alternative aesthetics and infrastructures associated with these neighbourhoods, independent fashion boutiques contribute to the immediate and changing needs of local communities.

Forging connections in-person and online

Independent fashion boutiques have carved out alternative urban infrastructure by engaging with consumers and communities online and in-person. Since the onset of the pandemic, it has become important to offer customers a range of shopping experiences to accommodate personal preferences and changing public health guidelines. Some independent shops have redesigned the layout of the store and/or increased the size of the change rooms. Others added new ventilation systems. Some independent boutiques limited the number of shoppers or offered private shopping, which allowed customer(s) to access physical retail space without being in the presence of others. Retailers providing this option emphasize the range of precautions they have taken to keep customers safe (e.g., vaccination and temperature checks, sanitation between appointments). Many business owners were also reminded that they still have a customer-base looking for an in-store experience where they can see, feel and try on clothing, while also connecting with designers and/or employees. Despite access to new digital technologies, these are still features that are incredibly difficult, if not impossible, to replicate online.

Stores have also had to respond to the fact that some consumers are no longer in the habit of shopping, while others have moved out of cities altogether. With a growing number of consumers turning to online shopping during the pandemic, independent fashion boutiques have further expanded their online presence, such as through increasing the number of photographs and amount of detail provided on garments, offering live-chat services to provide information on sizing, styling and shipping. They are also providing try-on videos on social media. It remains questionable, however, whether independent fashion design boutiques will abandon their retail locations altogether and make the transition to online-only businesses, or if there are still benefits to a retail location.

Making new products, including personal protective equipment

Around the world, independent fashion boutiques have contributed to local efforts to produce personal protective equipment (PPE), including many ethical, slow and sustainable fashion labels. This was especially prominent in the early days of the pandemic, when, due to growing demand and supply chain shortages, access to equipment was limited. In cities around the world, many independent (and global) fashion brands pivoted toward the production of masks and other medical garments (such as hair nets and gowns) for local healthcare workers. Retailers also shifted to filling local markets for more fashionable PPE. Often these activities made use of left-over materials to reduce waste and up-cycle and/or were made by local contractors. Access to local garment manufacturing facilities and infrastructures (including combined studio-retail spaces) therefore supports the ability of independent designers to produce equipment locally, as well as providing an important source of revenue for businesses during a time when sales have collapsed (Brydges *et al.* 2021). The forging of these connections strengthens the social and economic infrastructures of the neighbourhood.

Many independent designers and retailers have also donated some of the proceeds from the production of face masks to healthcare workers, laid-off service workers, homeless shelters, LGBTQ2S centres and other local non-profit organizations. Others have become more politically engaged in their local communities, raising awareness of the importance of public health measures. Very different affects and emotions are tied to these local expressions of care than are typically associated with the dominant cultural infrastructure of fashion; this is further exemplified in the greater orientation of independent boutiques toward ethical and environmental objectives.

Remaining attuned to social and environmental sustainability concerns

While adapting their businesses to ever-evolving circumstances, independent fashion businesses remain committed to social and environmental concerns. These forms of retail seek to disrupt the conventional practices of the mainstream fashion industry. Despite the growth of online shopping platforms, physical retail spaces continue to play an important role for consumers to learn about where and how their clothing is made. These spaces promote a "politics of reconnection" between producers and consumers (Hartwick 1998). Alternative fashion spaces also provide an opportunity for sustainable fashion communities to be formed around these in-person experiences, which may support the transition towards new patterns of consumption

(Taylor 2019). For example, several independent fashion designers in Toronto and Melbourne host a range of events, including clothing swaps, pop-up shops and tours of studios and maker-workshops (Leslie *et al.* 2015). More intimate encounters between retail staff, customers and materials foster alternative affective connections with the product.

Apart from these local ties, infrastructure such as collective manufacturing spaces are needed to support mandates of ethical and sustainable fashion. The Fashion Exchange in Toronto is an example of one such space. Created by George Brown College, it is a local production facility that supports small independent designers that require a local facility to produce small batches (Gallant 2016). The Fashion Exchange forges connections with the neighbourhood of Regent Park where it is located, running a series of training programmes for low-income youth. The facility also engages in cutting-edge research into recycled and sustainable textiles and has invested in high-tech equipment to support these initiatives.

Efforts to reorient fashion retail (i.e., offering new in-person experiences, new products and new connections to community) draw upon and foster new urban infrastructure. Not only are independent boutiques reworking the internal architecture and design of stores, and creating hybrid mixed-use spaces, they are reimagining the boundaries between the digital and physical in ways that enhance, but do not replace, face-to-face interaction. Independent fashion retailers are also drawing new lines of connection and care between an array of actors, including local producers, consumers and communities.

CONCLUSION

The infrastructure of "new fashion architectures ... make it possible to resist, escape, or offer alternatives to the dominant consumer culture" (Crewe 2010: 2094). Locating in a range of alternative spaces and neighbourhoods, independent fashion boutiques work through an urban cultural infrastructure of care and reconnection to foster new retail atmospheres, relations and aesthetics. Within these spaces and during the pandemic, they have crafted alternative ways of doing business that are tethered to physical and digital spaces in ever-more complex ways.

Independent fashion scenes, while still promoting a distinct aesthetic, are also forging hybrid spaces of production/consumption and building new alliances with local communities, healthcare workers and non-profits. In the context of mounting critiques of (ultra) fast fashion, they are creating new engagements with the materials they work with, fostering lively, ethical and sustainable fashion connections. These shifts rework the temporality and spatiality of fashion, creating new landscapes in the world's fashion cities, as well as new affects and engagements.

In order to support these shifts in fashion (and in creative industries more broadly), there is a critical need to nurture and sustain an alternative infrastructure of affordable retail and studio space. Like artists, alternative fashion designers and entrepreneurs are drawn to more improvisational spaces in cities that are not strongly classified, homogenized or gentrified (Bain 2003). While this has always been important to independent designers, it is even more crucial given the context of declining sales related to the pandemic and the rise of online retail. The bricks and mortar stores that do survive require lower rents and a location in diverse and mixed-use neighbourhoods. But there is a danger that by building new forms of community and engaging in efforts to ensure social reproduction in the neighbourhood, these small business owners will contribute to the very gentrification to which they – and others – are then subject (Kern 2013). Continued increases to commercial and residential central-city real estate suggest the need for holistic, coordinated rent regulation across the work–live divide and new collective models of ownership.

In addition to having the presence of nearby production facilities, many independent designers – like other craft and cultural industries – benefit from combined studio/production and retail spaces. As such, there is a need to preserve lands zoned as industrial in the central city, preventing their conversion to residential and commercial-only spaces and also allowing the co-location of retail and manufacturing uses on some sites (contingent upon preserving a percentage of the floor space as industrial). The pandemic has also illuminated the problems associated with dependence on global supply chains and the need to develop more localized and resilient economies through the formation of hybrid and local workspaces.

A consideration of the experiences of independent fashion retailers thus lends insight into the kinds of infrastructure that support alternative spaces of fashion in the city. Independent fashion retail shops draw upon socially and economically diverse, mixed-use urban settings, interweaving them with digital spaces to promote distinct aesthetics and nurture "more than commercial" relations. An examination of these hybrid geographies of independent retailers, particularly in the context of the pandemic, also sheds light on the associated affects and infrastructure of reconnection that can model more socially and environmentally sustainable forms of urban fashion.

CHAPTER 12

EMBODYING ARTS FESTIVALS AS INFRASTRUCTURAL TRANSFORMATION OF PLACES

Bernadette Quinn

INTRODUCTION

Arts festivals are important forms of cultural production and consumption (Négrier 2015). Irrespective of genre (e.g., visual arts, music or film) and whether single or multi-disciplinary, their primary endeavour is to engage people in the making, showcasing and performance of art. Yet arts festivals do not necessarily receive recognition or attention based on their cultural attributes alone. Festivals and events have become "central to entrepreneurial cities' efforts to generate commerce, regenerate place and stand out on the highly competitive global stage" (Quinn *et al.* 2020: 1875). Along with arts and cultural activities more generally, recent decades have seen cities use them to "lure ... consumption, property development, and knowledge industries" (Grodach 2017: 89) as a means of addressing social and economic urban problems. Inspired by neoliberal, creative-city style thinking, arts festivals now commonly feature on urban policy agendas the world over, with several researchers highlighting the prevalence of festivalization processes as "entire cities have transformed themselves into major stages for a continual stream of events" (Richards & Palmer 2010: 2).

Amid all the economic ambition, with its attendant commercial hype and spectacle, the role that arts festivals play in the cultural life and wider cultural systems of cities is often ill understood. Their ephemeral, intangible and immaterial nature lends them something of a chameleon quality which can be interpreted to mean that festivals do not matter as much as the other forms of creative practice that programme year-round activities and/or have a physical building to call their own. The invisibility that attaches to their immateriality, in contrast to the hard fixity of other cultural forms, is a particular problem when it comes to understanding how they form part of a city's cultural infrastructure. Researchers tend to focus on what Allen and

McCreary (2021: 51) call "enduring material landscapes rather than temporary enactments such as festivals and parades". City planners, when conceiving of cultural infrastructure tend to invest mostly in hard, material elements like art galleries, museums, theatres and performance spaces. Yet while arts festivals are commonly defined by their short duration, in reality, they are always connected into wider, year-round arts activities in complex ways that defy their apparent temporally bounded nature. As such, they represent "a local articulation within a wider whole" (Massey 1994: 4), with Hjalager (2009: 267) discussing how festivals "contribute to, and establish links in, rather complex value chains and innovation systems" in the wider musical economy. Quinn and Wilks' (2013: 26) study of traditional music festivals in the UK and Ireland supports this argument. They point to "the highly mobile, fluid and internationally connected circuit of flows that make up the world of festivals", finding festivals to be materially and immaterially linked to different traditional music spheres involving, for example, performers, media professionals, artistic directors and audiences, all embodying diverse resources, knowledge, expertise and practices.

In light of the above, this chapter asks how arts festivals can be understood in terms of cultural infrastructure. Posing this question is timely because the idea of social gatherings for cultural purposes, especially in conventional, indoor venues like theatres and concert halls has become inordinately problematic because of pandemic-related public health and safety concerns. There is a sense that we must find new ways of socializing without fear, and of reconfiguring social spaces to alleviate health risks and anxieties about being in proximity with others. The temporal and spatial flexibility and agility of arts festivals make them well placed to experiment with different ways of bringing people together to encounter art and culture. For this reason alone, the infrastructure of urban arts festivals needs to be better understood.

ARTS FESTIVALS AS MATERIAL AND FIXED

As several researchers note (Dodson 2017; Howe *et al.* 2016), there has been an infrastructural turn in several areas of study, but few researchers have tried to understand whether or how this might have relevance for arts festivals. The term infrastructure has a strong association with fields such as engineering and with material artefacts and elements like pipes, cables and tunnels. Even when the focus is on cultural infrastructure the tendency to think in terms of built structures and tangible entities seems strong. References to cultural infrastructure in practice and in academia usually refers to physical buildings like theatres, museums, cinemas and libraries (Getzner 2020) and overall, the impression created is that cultural infrastructure is physical, tangible and material in nature. Such an understanding accommodates those arts festivals which have dedicated venues, but a great many festivals do not fall into this category. Accordingly, they can all too easily be dismissed for being transient, critiqued for being unstable, and overlooked as being unimportant, relative to other cultural infrastructure components.

Certainly, many festivals are known to have been established with few resources and very shaky material underpinnings. However, recent scholarship reminds us that infrastructure is never static (Korn *et al.* 2019), but rather is dynamic, open to negotiation and alteration, and constantly evolving. Silver (2014a) similarly explains that infrastructure is incremental in nature, and this often applies to festival infrastructure. Some very well-established arts festivals now have a fixed material presence, often achieved after many years of successful festival activity, campaigning, and activism. This is borne out in the histories of festivals like the Shaw Festival, which began in Niagara on the Lake in Canada in 1962. Conolly (2011) describes how it was first housed in very rudimentary conditions in the assembly hall of the local courthouse. Over time, the festival has become deeply embedded into the place such that it now stages 10 or more productions, in three theatres, for audiences that can exceed 250,000. The Salzburg festival in Austria is another example. First staged in 1920, the period immediately prior to its founding, as well as its early years, were characterized by the repurposing of pre-existing buildings and the development of new buildings to house festival activities. The Wexford Festival Opera is a further example. It was established in Ireland in 1951, and its sustained success over time led to the development of Ireland's first arts centre outside of the capital city in 1974, and to the development of the country's first custom built opera house in 2008. Internationally, there are numerous other examples of how festivals have a catalytic effect, developing venues and serving to stimulate the development of further festivals and cultural activities in ways that expand, deepen and/or diversify the cultural offering of a place. Very importantly, examples like these point to the vital role that local activism involving artists, arts enthusiasts and other social and cultural actors campaigning and taking risks to establish festival activities, can play in cultivating cultural demand that gradually attracts resourcing and support from public agencies. Such supports can fund the establishment of resource centres, professional networks, and venues to accommodate creative production and performance. Upon deeper investigation, they further illustrate not only the inherently dynamic quality of infrastructure but also the contestation and negotiation that shapes their constant evolution as politically charged endeavours.

Sometimes, as argued above, softer arts festival structures develop into material forms as people mobilize, campaign and secure fixed infrastructural elements in the process. However, often, they do not become fixed;

yet this does not detract from their vitality or vibrancy in shaping cultural life. In rural areas, for example, where permanent venues are scarce or possibly non-existent, festivals are vital. Even in metropolitan areas where recognizable cultural infrastructure is often plentiful and possibly magnificent, festivals matter precisely because they can act as counterpoints or even as sites of opposition to the cultural activities associated with more permanent infrastructural elements. Frey (1994) makes this point, arguing that festivals enable a freedom of expression that is denied to cultural institutions bound by government regulations and weighed down by tradition and societal expectations. Obvious examples of this are the fringe festivals found in many cities, like the Edinburgh Fringe Festival in Scotland. According to Jamieson (2004: 67), its "initial unauthorized status added to its rebellious and provocatively playful character and pitted it against the legitimate and civilizing International Festival". Fringe festivals whether in Edinburgh, Montreal, Sydney or Dublin frequently repurpose vacant or underused premises (e.g., empty shops, factories, warehouses) and reimagine small public squares, green spaces and plots of underused land as festival venues. Over time, claiming space and creating cultural infrastructure in this way unsettles and challenges established ideas about how urban space should be used and equally about what constitutes an appropriate cultural venue. It can also lead to the creation of new relationships between cultural actors/venues and actors operating in all kinds of commercial, social and political arenas, which in turn can lead to new collaborative opportunities.

In a variety of more mainstream and more tangible ways, urban planners and designers are now taking increasing account of how cities can be transformed into stages for festivals and events and how urban physical space can be programmed with activities (Smith *et al.* 2021). Public spaces are being upgraded with a view to making the task of staging festivals and events easier, less disruptive and more environmentally friendly. The development of a new civic office complex in Dublin City in 1994, for example, incorporated an outdoor amphitheatre for concerts and events. Such amphitheatres are now to be found in many cities and towns. In the theatre district in Montreal, the Daoust Lestage-designed *La Place des Festivals* project (2012), repurposed surface car parks into outdoor theatres for both everyday urban life as well as for large-scale festivals (Daoust Lestage 2018). Much more modestly, city spaces are now increasingly being fitted and upgraded with in-built power and water supplies, fixtures that can be used to anchor temporary structures like tents and awnings, and storage facilities to store materials needed to stage festivals and events as the need arises (Sendra 2015). These developments demonstrate the prevalence of arts festivals and other events in urban cultural life, their elevated standing in urban political agendas and their influence on urban cultural and recreational infrastructure more generally.

The wider literature on infrastructure frequently distinguishes between "hard" and "soft" infrastructural elements, and this dichotomous thinking is helpful to a point in understanding the arts festival phenomenon. However, it fails to fully capture the complexities at issue. To fully understand how arts festivals contribute to cultural life and shape infrastructure, it is vital to realize that festival-making is a creative practice that extends far beyond the spectacle showcased during the timebound staging of the festival programme itself. Festivals can manifest in hard, fixed infrastructural form, as explained earlier, but they always exist as flows and networks of people, ideas, creative impulses and resources of all kinds, all of which are contextualized in dynamic time-space. During festival periods, festival organizations programme events that animate and fill the spaces of the permanent cultural venue infrastructure (e.g., theatres, concert halls, libraries, etc.) available to them. Outside of the festival window, engaging in collaborative practices like co-commissioning and co-production, as well as other activities like creative workshops and rehearsals, are further examples of how arts festivals extend and develop their own creative practice and reach, as well as that of other cultural infrastructure entities with which they collaborate. According to Portmann (2020), the linkages between festivals and other cultural institutions are becoming harder to disaggregate as festivals increasingly collaborate as co-commissioners and co-producers with other cultural organizations, as opposed to working alone. She argues that it is no longer possible to separate festival work from that of other cultural institutions like theatres, especially not when the production and consumption of culture is now so heavily mediated by digital technology.

ARTS FESTIVALS AS EMBODIED, SENSUOUS AND AFFECTIVE

To fully appreciate how arts festivals function as cultural infrastructure, it is necessary to emphasize their human characteristics. Arts festivals flourish everywhere in the guise of people, individually and collectively, developing and utilizing varied resource networks to create and perform culture. Arguably, they exemplify the role of networks in infrastructuring cities and perfectly illustrate Simone's (2004) argument that people are the means through which culture flows in cities. For researchers like Pløger (2010), festivals are full of potential, always a force in the "becoming" of cities (Sheller & Urry 2004), serving as "ongoing mechanisms for investing and replenishing economic, spatial, socio-cultural, and symbolic resources" (Wynn 2015: 12). While arts festivals are ever-present, they are perhaps not very obvious all of the time. They function year-round, engaging in networks of activity, performing culture in a variety of ways as earlier discussed, as they prepare to bring their spectacle to the public for the days/weeks of the staged festival programme. Then they emerge to energize, animate and transform the sights, sounds, atmosphere and possibilities of city spaces. Meyboom (2009) has written about the need for infrastructure to design lively public space and arts festivals have this ability in abundance.

Through the spectacles they create, arts festivals demonstrate why festivalization holds such appeal for the entrepreneurial city. However, arts festivals mean much more than spectating. They offer out of the ordinary (O'Grady 2015), participative and immersive experiences that are not only affective but multi-sensorial in nature. Being fluid, flexible and somewhat subversive – particularly those staged in public spaces – they have the potential to transform space in ways that are "multi scalar and varied, involving the human and the non-human, the social and the material" (Sweeney *et al.* 2018: 573). Public space is never neutral or fixed. It is always open to change and influence and, as Merx (2011) notes, it matters a great deal how social engagement is performed there. Staging festivals holds the potential of churning places into motion (Falconi 2014) and of encouraging different ways of being in, belonging to and engaging with place. Increasingly, researchers understand festivals as performative sites that "spatially concentrate and vigorously mobilize a wide range of artistic practices, sensory experiences, and embodied practices" (Kingsbury 2016: 223). Studying the material and corporeal transformations through which festivals are produced and consumed is now of growing scholarly interest. Distinctive sensory notes encompassing noises, smells, sights and tastes accompany all these transformations and come together to produce very distinctive festival atmospheres. These affective dimensions alone make festival activities especially important for delivering and consuming cultural experiences because they enable affects to "infuse and circulate among bodies and across spaces, all the while constructing the social worlds through which they flow" (Carter 2019: 201). For Jiang and Yu (2020), place must be felt if it is to make sense, and festivals have the ability to make a place come alive. Increasingly we understand festivals as opportunities for embodied experiences: people watch and listen, but they also move, sing, laugh, taste and engage viscerally. Furthermore, festival audiences often do so in community with others, with Dickson's (2015: 718) study of Glasgow Film Festival arguing that festivalgoers may actively develop "commonalities with strangers through modes of appreciation (e.g., laughing at the same parts, synchronised clapping)". Studies like this promote the suggestion that the performativity involved in festivals offers possibilities for different cohorts of people to find common ground. As such, it is argued that they can help to foster dialogue between diverse groups by creating alternative structures of identification and social configuration, disrupting the symbolic boundaries that impede people's ability to engage (Rapošová 2019). Finding common ground in festival settings is not, however, inevitable. In communities characterized by entrenched divisions, as in the Northern Irish city of Derry/Londonderry, it can prove too difficult to be the case (Devine & Quinn 2019).

Nevertheless, researchers have been noting how in festival settings, sensuous bodies, rhythms and movements between different actors, create "dynamic, ... varying and emerging relations to each other" (Giovanardi *et al.* 2014: 113). The bodies in question may include visitors, perhaps attracted by festival city branding, as well as cohorts of residents, workers and other regular city users. All of these presences, gathered together through the festival, change the dynamics of the place, disrupting regular routines, creating encounters with others and offering what Zukin (1995) calls the transformative co-presence of strangers. Even in a context where powerful tourism stakeholders lobby cities to support arts festival infrastructures in ways that privilege tourism interests, "envisage only spectating roles for local residents" (Quinn 2005: 940) and erase local communities from their tourism vision, it is possible for diverse cohorts of the public (e.g., recent immigrants, longstanding residents, city-centre and suburban dwellers) to simultaneously derive meaningful festival experiences.

In essence, arts festivals create infrastructure – networks of people and resources, places and moments – that support the production and consumption of cultural experiences. All arts festivals hold the potential to occupy and transform space in ways that surprise, disrupt, renew and unsettle the status quo. By creating engaging emotional atmospheres, and encouraging embodied social interactivity, they have the effect of turning everyday space into convivial spaces. Accordingly, festival space offers opportunities for individuals and groups to negotiate and contest the everyday cultural politics of race, sexuality, gender and class, as well as normative ideas about who/what belongs in particular spaces. Consistently, researchers, including Waitt (2008), emphasize how festivals and other events have the ability to confront and challenge established geographies of all kinds because of how they can temporarily suspend social relations and sustain playful practice. Fringe and community grassroots festivals can be seen to be investing energies in creating infrastructure by, for example, innovatively and transformatively using public, communal and private space (e.g., staging dance workshops in playgrounds, programming concerts in churches, displaying art work in shopping centres, etc.) as a means of performing their own, alternative interpretations not only of culture but of urbanism more broadly (Zilberstein 2019).

PANDEMIC RESTRICTIONS, INFRASTRUCTURAL ADAPTATIONS AND THE EMBODIED EXPERIENCE OF FESTIVALS

The global onset of the Covid-19 pandemic in March 2020 and the subsequent introduction of public health guidelines restricting personal mobility and advocating social distancing severely disrupted cultural activities. The public spaces of towns and cities normally bustling with life fell silent. Somewhat ironically, the fundamental importance of arts festivals, so often appreciated by city managers mainly for their tourism and associated values, was suddenly laid bare as the public spaces of cities lay silent, empty and still. The images shown in Figures 12.1 and 12.2 show contrasting images of Dublin's Smithfield Square: in fully festive mode in July 2019 on the one hand, and devoid of activity during the pandemic in 2020 on the other. Never was it so apparent that festivals bring places to life, and that urban public space is nothing if not socially produced through the energetic, interactive and expressive activities of endeavours like festivals.

In the depths of city lockdowns when governments decreed that public space and communal socializing was off limits, the profound need that people have for social connectivity came through in multiple examples of grassroots,

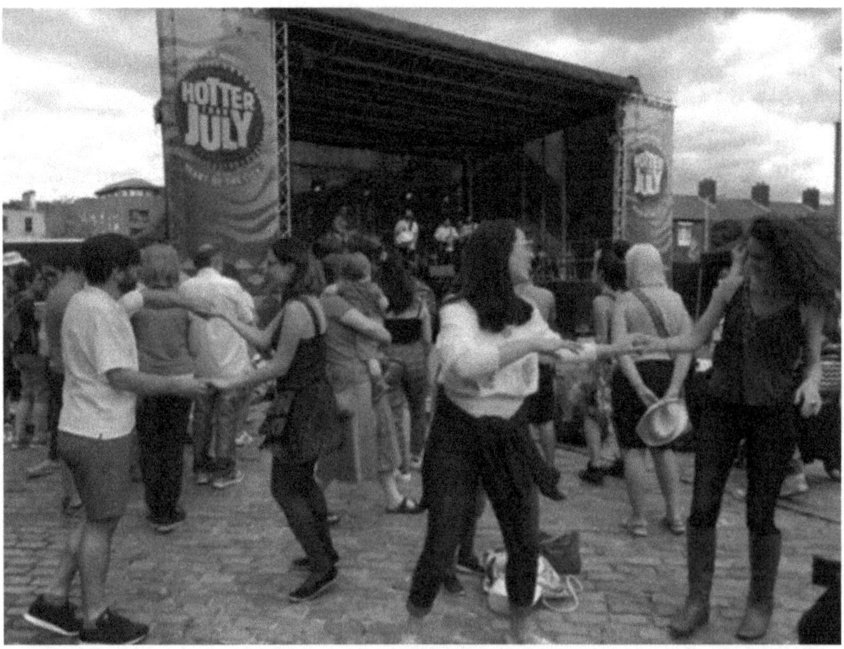

Figure 12.1 Smithfield Square, Dublin, in festive mode during the Hotter than July festival in 2019

Source: Bernadette Quinn.

spontaneous social activism countering the new regulations. From a New York neighbourhood diner playing the iconic "New York, New York" song over loudspeakers as "cheering residents in the surrounding block leaned out of their doors and windows to sing along" (Tett 2022: n.p.) to dancing on balconies in Menorca (Villalonga-Olives *et al.* 2021) and displaying artwork signalling thanks to frontline workers on windows and garden railings in Dublin (Quinn 2021), people instinctively and ingeniously created their own cultural infrastructure to keep them socially connected and to sustain them through the crisis. A marked feature of the pandemic period has been a shift to digital space, and it is here that many arts festivals quickly reinvented themselves to keep creating, programming and engaging with audiences. The digitization of cultural infrastructure has been ongoing for some 20 years but remains a work in progress. For many aspects of social, cultural and economic life, the pandemic meant an accelerated transition to digital space (Florida *et al.* 2021).

For most arts festivals, performing in digital space is a relatively new endeavour that poses challenges in terms of delivering quality experiences in the absence of live, in-person staging. During the pandemic, many festivals lacked the resources to avail of the potential offered by rapidly developing digital technologies and were unable to sustain engagement with their audiences. However, others, like the National Arts Festival in Grahamstown, South Africa, found that mapping their activities onto digital infrastructure

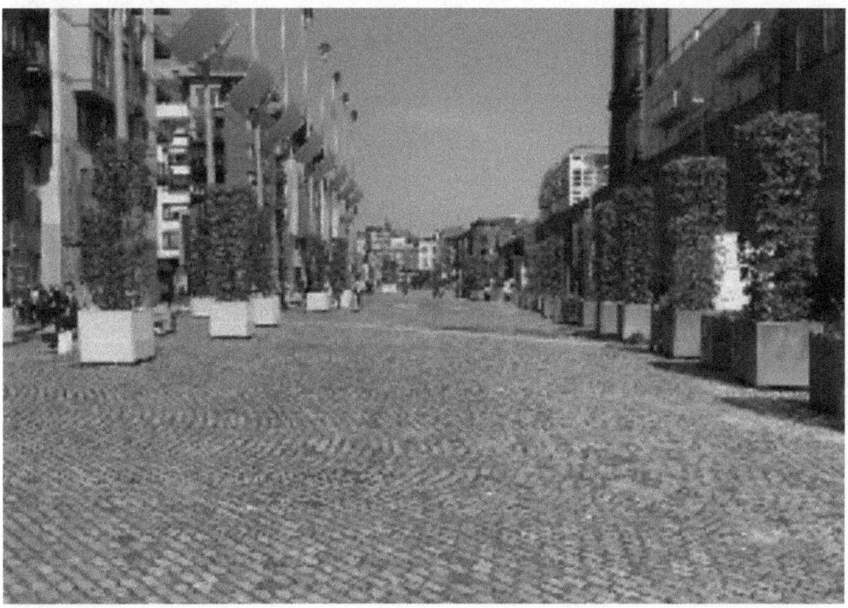

Figure 12.2 Smithfield Square, Dublin, festival time, July 2020 during the pandemic

Source: Bernadette Quinn.

significantly increased their audience reach (https://nationalartsfestival.co.za/about-us/). Everywhere possible, festivals creatively performed their cultural activities in digital space in ways that continued to encourage highly affective and embodied engagements. Illustrative examples from Dublin are the St Patrick's Festival and Culture Night, which encouraged people to record themselves creating content (e.g., dressing up and performing a parade), using private spaces (e.g., homes and back gardens) and local public spaces (e.g., parks and streets) as stages. This material was then curated and widely shared digitally. Dublin Fringe Festival developed activities that involved mailing audiences contextual material and asking them to download an app with instructions to engage with their local environment (e.g., by walking in the rain or by being in a green space while experiencing a soundscape as in the *1000 Miniature Meadows* project pictured in Figure 12.3). John Gerrard's *Mirror Pavilion*, a digital art installation, created in response to the escalating climate crisis and commissioned by the Galway International Arts Festival

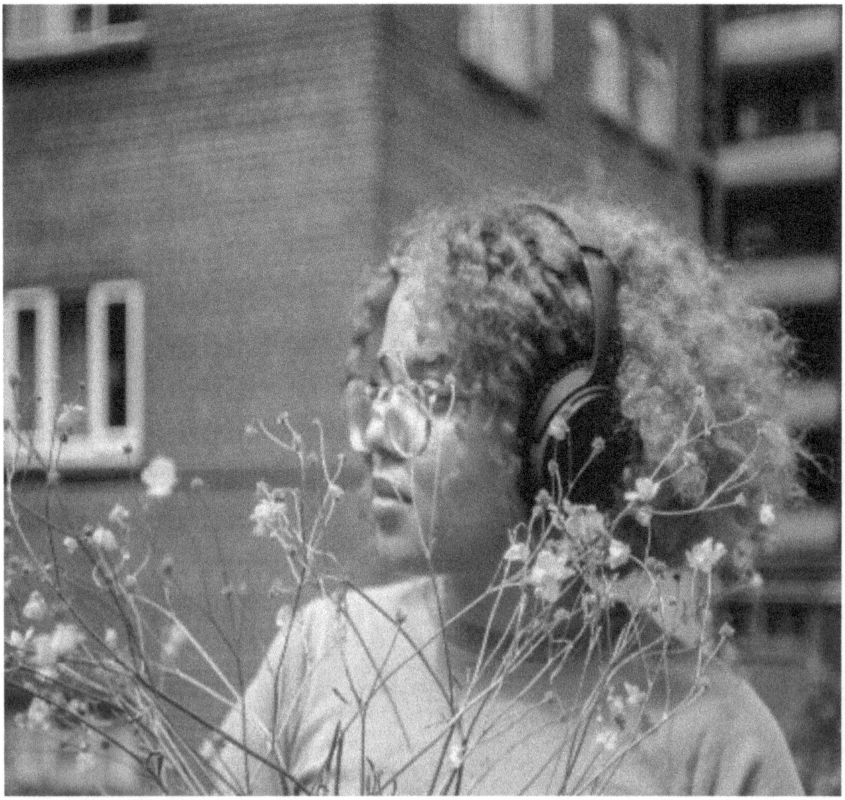

Figure 12.3 Dublin Fringe Festival 2021, *1000 Miniature Meadows*

Source: Fergal Styles.

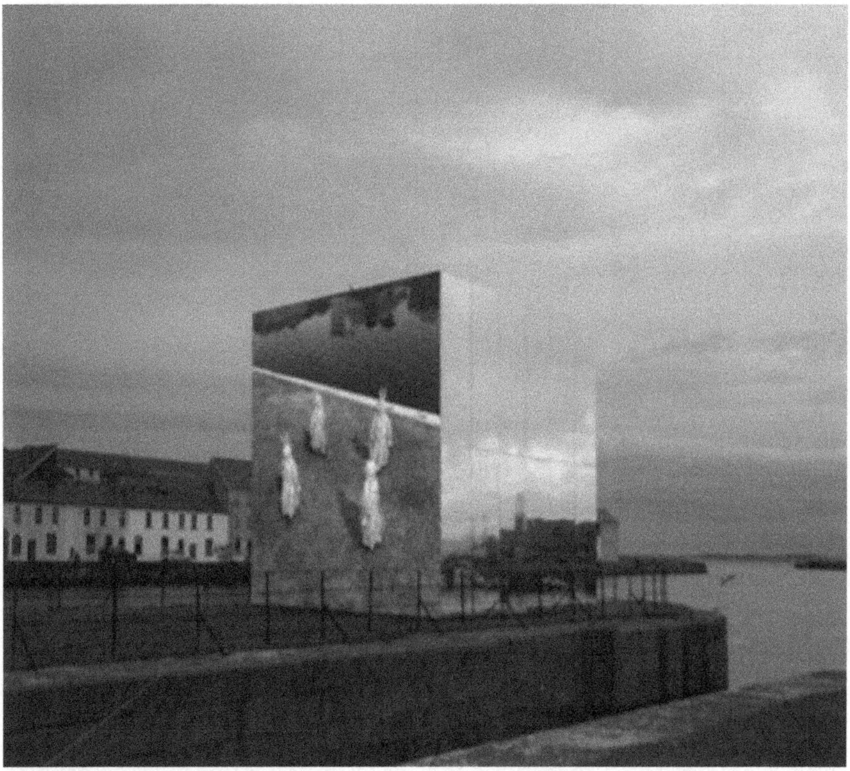

Figure 12.4 *Mirror Pavilion*, Galway International Arts Festival, 2021

Source: Bernadette Quinn.

(GIAF) (pictured in Figure 12.4), invited deep reflection on nature, the past and the future.

Many festivals mixed elements of physical and virtual creation and delivery, experimenting with ways of stimulating creativity and capturing festivalgoers' imaginations. These are but a few examples of the ways that many festivals continued during the pandemic to urge people to actively interpret and engage afresh with the material realities and traditions of their cities and to creatively encourage affective embodied experiences. These creative endeavours signal an aptitude for continuously reinventing immersive and highly affective engagement with place. However, they also demonstrate how resilient, flexible and agile festivals can be when they need to adapt and innovate to maintain their creative practices and maintain audience engagement. In the highly restrictive conditions associated with the Covid-19 pandemic when normal cultural venue networks were unavailable, festivals proposed new ways of engaging with art and turned a variety of everyday spaces into art galleries and performance spaces. Sometimes this meant that

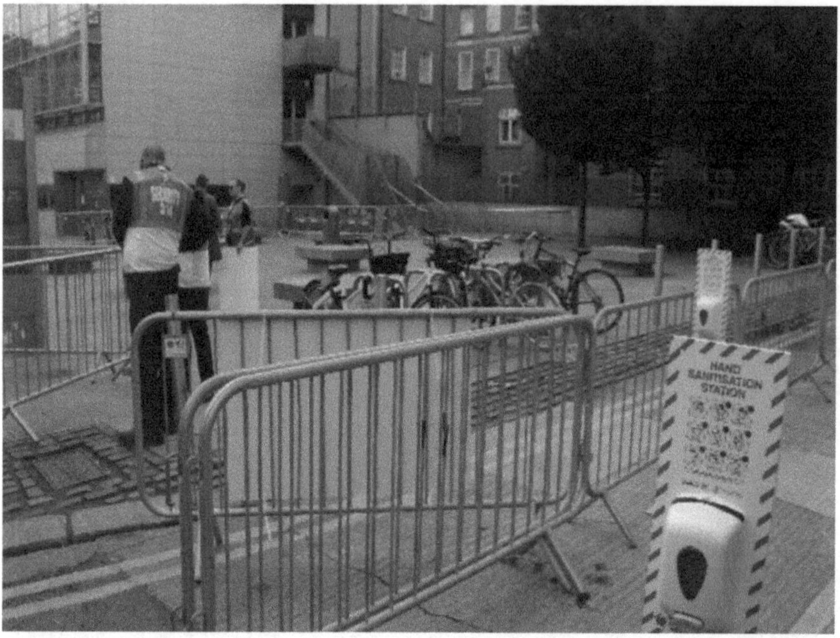

Figure 12.5 Temporary infrastructure, Culture Night 2022 Barnardo Square, Dublin
Source: Bernadette Quinn.

the harder infrastructure required to stage festivals became more obvious, as organizers were obliged to comply with public guidance on social distancing and health and safety. Often this resulted in festivalscapes looking like the one pictured in Figure 12.5, which shows Dublin's Barnardo Square during Culture Night 2022. In some jurisdictions, public health measures continue to regulate personal mobility, social contact, hygiene practices and behaviour more generally, and in the operational setting, these requirements are manifest in hard infrastructure like barriers, cordons, security presence, signage and sanitation stations. All of these highly visible structures, in addition to possible limitations on audience size, undoubtedly disrupt the usual ambiance and atmosphere effected by festival performances. They also increase the cost of producing and maintaining arts festival infrastructure, a factor that may widen divergences and inequalities in arts festival production and consumption.

A HYBRID FUTURE?

Undoubtedly, the pandemic accelerated festival infrastructure's intersection with digital technologies and networks. The evidence emerging shows that

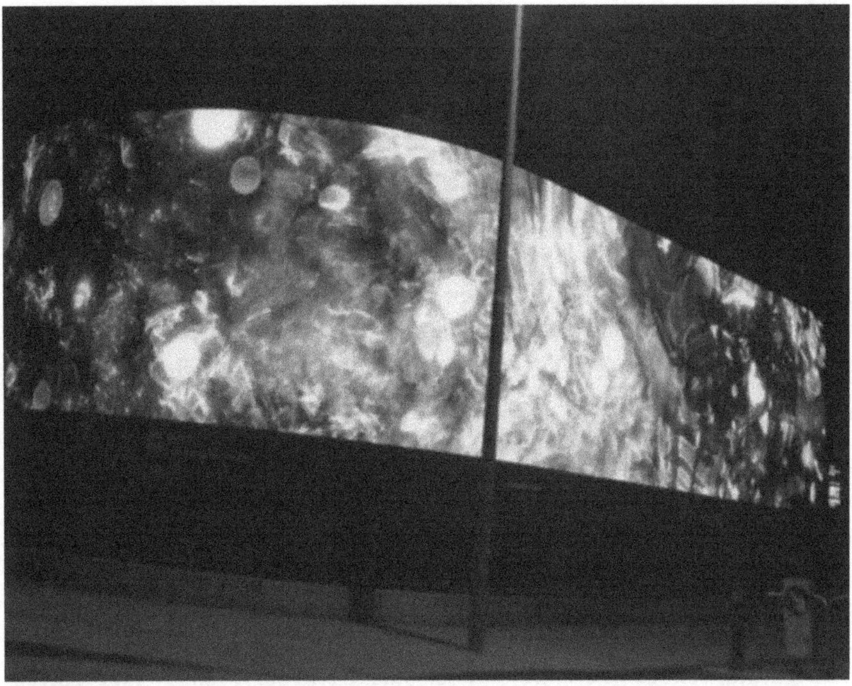

Figure 12.6 LED screen, Wilton Place, Dublin

in digital space arts festivals perform differently. As the potential to extend audience reach increases, there is tremendous opportunity to create immersive experiences in new directions with technology enabling social connectivity. Accordingly, cities are increasingly investing in adapting their spaces to enable digital events. Figure 12.6 shows an image of a LED screen, funded through a public–private arrangement, in Wilton Place, Dublin. However, research on infrastructures highlights its power to "disclose differentiation within cities" (McFarlane *et al.* 2017: 1396) and there is a concern that arts festivals will now become a more uneven social practice. Operating in digital space demands resourcing, upskilling and capacity-building with some cities better able than others to invest and support the development of arts festival infrastructure in this direction. Accordingly, the ability to produce and sustain festival infrastructure may become more variable across cultural sectors and across cities in different jurisdictions. It also seems likely that arts festivals will become more contested terrain in that the extended audience reach that the broadcasting and livestreaming of arts festivals engender will likely heighten their commodification and appeal for corporate and tourism interests. This may intensify tensions between a festival's cultural vision and the commercial demands placed upon it by sponsors or municipalities. In a context where public finances stretched by the costs associated with the burdens of the pandemic make economic recovery a top urban policy priority, digitally enhanced events seem very well placed to advance the entrepreneurial city's array of city branding, economic development and urban regeneration objectives. Already, physical spaces festivalized by arts events are useful assets widely employed for city branding. Once digitized, the urban imaginaries created in festivalized settings have the potential to extend much further through virtual and social media channels. Finally, while researchers argue that festivals have long created spaces of encounter that forge belonging and foster cultural exchange (McClinchey 2008), there is now uncertainty about what digitally enhanced arts festival infrastructure will mean for the unpredictability and inclusiveness that public space represents (Low & Smart 2020).

There is also uncertainty about the extent to which arts festivals will embrace digital infrastructure into the future. In the summer of 2022, in cities where the pandemic has eased, indications are that the urge to perform and to experience culture in physical space is very strong. While the move to digitize infrastructure is likely to continue, the delivery of arts festivals in physical space will certainly not disappear. The earlier discussion of the explosion of spontaneous, localized, grassroots efforts to create public space and improvise cultural venues where art could be staged and communally experienced (e.g., on apartment balconies, the gable ends of buildings and garden railings) attests to this. However, physical delivery in terms of production and consumption will change. Digitization will become a stronger feature as cities with available resources invest in reconfiguring physical space to facilitate the installation of broadband connections and LED screens, enabling arts festivals, and live performances more generally, to straddle the physical/virtual divide with blended, hybrid events.

CONCLUSION

This chapter began with a rarely asked question: how can arts festivals be understood as cultural infrastructure? This question is seldom posed largely because, as a support structure for cultural activity, festivals only publicly materialize at certain points in time. Over the course of any given time period, they act to gather people and generate activities with varying degrees of intensity. However, they exist as flows and networks of people, ideas, creative impulses, materialities and resources of all kinds, all of the time. As with all infrastructure, a key feature of arts festivals is their mobile, fluid and flexible quality. Their particularly human nature is also very striking. Indeed, at first glance it is tempting to see them as oppositional to the hard fixity usually associated with the term infrastructure. However, categorizing arts festivals as soft is mistaken. Indeed, the "hard"/"soft" dichotomy that tends to characterize discussions on infrastructure is not necessarily helpful given the multi-faceted roles that arts festivals play in creating, performing and consuming culture. None of these roles are easily identifiable, visible or even measurable. Furthermore, festivals perfectly illustrate what it means to say that infrastructure is incremental in nature (Silver 2014a) and dynamic. As festivals become more embedded into place, their infrastructural form morphs accordingly. The fact remains, however, that the infrastructural turn in festival studies is only beginning. Empirical evidence supporting many of the assertions made in this chapter are scant and numerous unanswered questions remain. Viewing festivals through an infrastructural lens can help develop understanding of a complex phenomenon that is sometimes viewed in rather simplistic terms. Hopefully, this chapter will stimulate further enquiry into how urban arts festivals change in form and character over time as they continuously reinvent their role in the ongoing reproduction and consumption of artistic activities and experiences in cities around the world.

IV
COLLECTING CULTURE

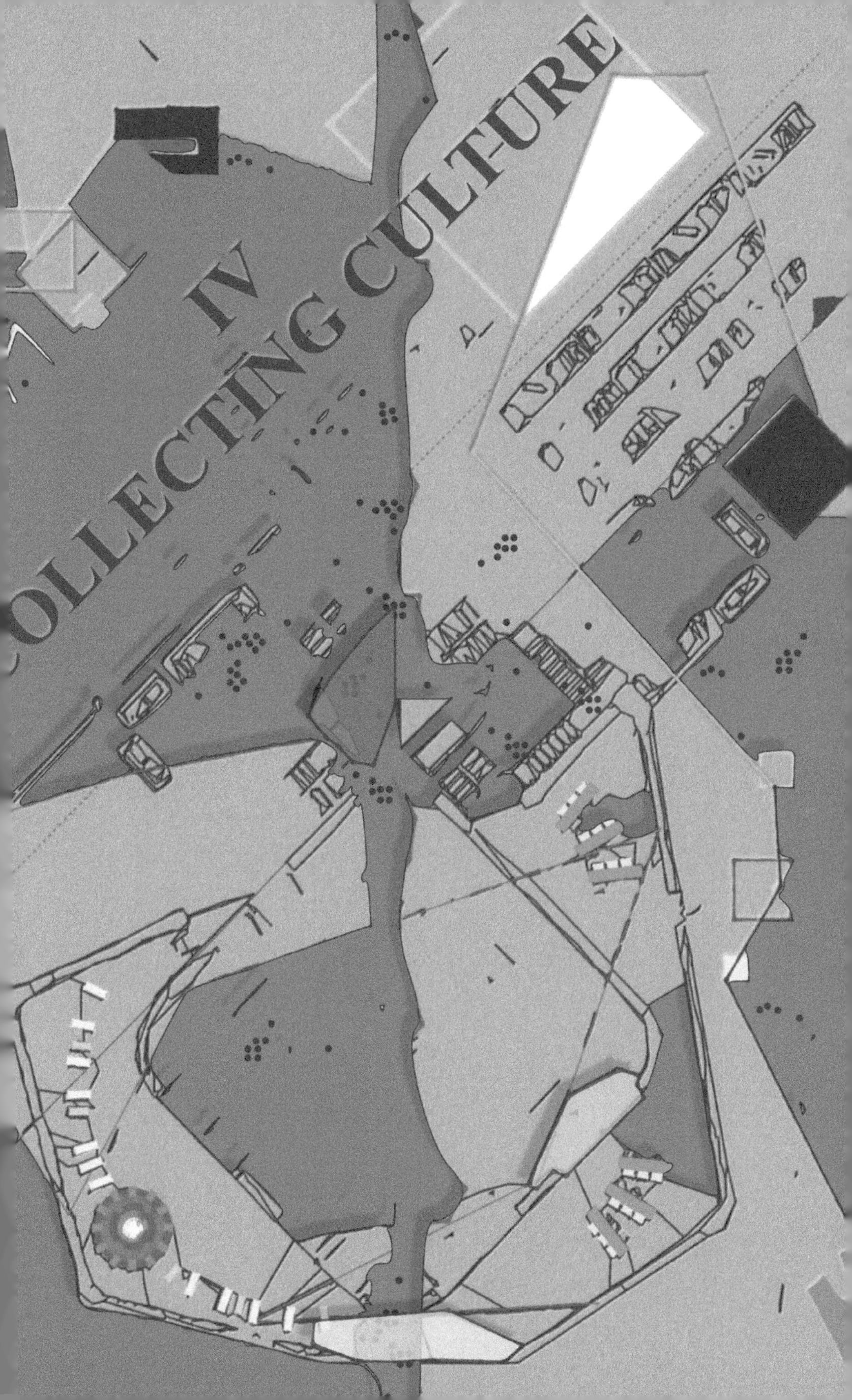

PART IV

COLLECTING CULTURE

Cities themselves are living archives. Their built form and streetscapes are at once prosaic and visually spectacular, messy and ordered, permeable and bounded. As complex, incomplete and ever-changing entities, cities and their cultural infrastructure are the repositories of urban life (Rao 2009). Nevertheless, there are cultural institutions within cities that have explicit mandates to collect, store and exhibit memories, histories and knowledge that become the foundations of state-sanctioned culture. These range in practice from small personal collections to the activist reading rooms and archives of oppositional groups, to state-sanctioned municipal libraries, national archives and metropolitan museums. Within these collections are images, texts and material culture from the past through to the present that are catalogued, indexed and stored for selective display and reinterpretation. In cities, these repositories provide the cultural infrastructure through which to recuperate the past and reimagine urban futures.

The collection of culture – the possession and assembly of rare and valuable objects – "is consumption writ large" (Belk 1995: 1). Whether compiled for archival activism or to nostalgically represent the past by refashioning new spaces and subcultures, collections make new relationships between objects, spaces, communities and their histories (Sellie *et al.* 2015). Collecting invariably brings objects together and, in the case of hierarchical structures like libraries, museums and archives, gives them an order in relation to one another based on classification systems (Derrida 1996). As Elsner and Cardinal (1994: 2) assert: "[i]f the peoples and the things of the world are the collected, and if the social categories into which they are assigned confirm the precious knowledge of culture handed down through generations, then our rulers sit atop a hierarchy of collections." Collecting is a process of social display that distinguishes between things. It aspires to be distinctive and sometimes disruptive of norms while also reinforcing what constitutes taste and culture.

This section focuses on the socially admissible collecting of museums, libraries and archives, attending to how this cultural infrastructure of collection serves the public good (Bain & Podmore 2020). More than just tangible institutional repositories of written, visual, sonic and material culture, they are also spaces of urban encounter across socio-cultural, ethnic and generational divides that are embedded in locales (Amin 2008). In the face of shrinking subsidies, changing demographics, decreasing membership and the rise of digital technologies, these institutions have reinvented themselves to confirm their societal relevancy as variously: community centres, intergenerational social hubs, innovation labs, learning commons, meeting places and, increasingly, makerspaces (Van Melik 2020). From preservationists, information providers and narrators, the expertise of curators, librarians and archivists has been reframed, assigning them new roles as community facilitators, educators, animators and matchmakers who bring people and ideas together. In this reframing, cultural institution staff and volunteers increasingly perform social, communal and emotional labour that transforms such sites of collection and exhibition into places of care and community (Ang 2015, 2019). Such role reversals are more difficult to enumerate than membership, collection size, number of visitors or books, artefacts and exhibits borrowed. Engulfed in questions of equity, access, mediation and representation, these cultural institutions are contested infrastructure (Clapperton 2010). Many marginalized communities, therefore, establish their own counter-cultural informational infrastructure to combat the societal exclusions shaping disinformation, denial and erasure (McKinney 2020). The chapters explore through examples from Berlin, Ahmedabad, Nijmegen and Montreal, how museums, libraries and archives function infrastructurally within cities as sites of encounter that are located within wider conflicts over colonial knowledge production, religious and ethno-cultural differences, societal and artefactual reparations, and the chrononormativities that marginalize sexual and gender minority histories.

For hundreds of years, museums have sought to inspire and interest select publics. Some of the earliest Western museums were cabinets of curiosity that contained miscellaneous artefacts belonging to royalty and wealthy families (Geoghegan 2010). In the contemporary period, museums – as buildings and institutions that preserve, store, classify and exhibit objects of scientific, historical, cultural and artistic significance in climate- and theft-controlled environments – have been leveraged by civic leaders to enhance a city's reputation for civility and culture, yet they have also been critiqued as elitist for the ways in which they represent and reinforce the powerful. In their adherence to "principles of taxonomic classification in the acquisition, organisation and display of their collections, an intellectual and spatial division" is often "drawn between the expert knowledge of the curator at work behind-the-scenes and the public space occupied by the museum visitor" (Geoghegan 2010: 1462–3). The elitism of this spatial division is also challenged by questions about the often-extractive providence of objects, what is present and absent within collections and which material narratives are communicated to the general public by them (Becker 2009).

The primary function of museums is curatorial and archival exhibition, but collections are constantly being built through philanthropy by leveraging donations, endowments and gifts from wealthy donors to enhance holdings and loan offerings while also mounting exhibitions, often at significant expense (Becker 2009). With educational mandates, museums teach the public through their catalogues, programmes and labels that narrate intention and significance (Brault & Kaplansky 2010). Yet access to, social understanding of and conflicting ethno-cultural and colonial dynamics inevitably shape how visitors interpret and experience museums because their objects and exhibitions make cultural references that are not universally interpreted. Since museum attendance has been widely perceived as a middle-class activity (Phillips *et al.* 2015), many administrators and curators are actively addressing cultural democratization in response to profound questions about access and inclusion within the plurality of contemporary society (Zukin 1995). Under urban neoliberalism, museum boards have faced this longstanding challenge using vehicles such as "free entrance" days and times, which themselves are underwritten by the same corporate sponsors who finance the spectacle of "blockbuster" exhibitions that financially maintain their infrastructure. The urban cultural infrastructure of museums, then, is part of what Bishop and Green (2008) described as "philanthrocapitalism", a new paradigm of urban development through which philanthropic donors replace the social function of the state. With municipal austerity-driven measures intensifying inequities and exclusions in access to housing, education, public spaces and culture, new waves of philanthrocapitalism are shaping urban cultural infrastructure around the world, raising fundamental questions about who and what is funded and through which strategies.

Deploying a practice-based and conflict-oriented approach to museums, in Chapter 13 Friederike Landau-Donnelly explores spatially and socially engaged ways of doing museums differently. She proposes an analytic of "infrastructuring" to describe what museums do as urban cultural infrastructure. Through case studies of the Conflictorium in Ahmedabad, India and the artistic intervention of the "Women's Walking Museum" in the Schwules Museum (Gay Museum) in Berlin, she demonstrates how institutional vulnerability can accommodate contingency and contemporary cultural critique. These examples of museums as urban cultural infrastructure offer insight into activist museum forms that negotiate complicated histories of absence and presence, conflict and political difference. They raise profound questions about what future-oriented museums can look like if they are to become infrastructural spaces of care and solidarity.

Care is a practice of offering emotional support and material assistance that transcends the private realm of familial and household social reproductive practices, occurring every day in a range of different institutions and sites, from healthcare settings to community drop-in and childcare centres, to museums and public libraries (Bain 2022). As urban cultural infrastructure within liberal democracies, municipal public libraries are "adaptable" civic institutional artefacts at the interface of multiple publics (Leorke *et al.* 2018). More than middle-class havens of quiet contemplation (Freeman & Blomley 2019), repositories of material and virtual cultural artefacts (Bingham-Hall & Kaasa 2018) or innovation hubs that circulate knowledge and skills in support of smart city techno-urban agendas, historically, public libraries have had social and educational mandates to serve the "public good" in multiple ways. Through their operationalization of social inclusion and justice logics (Pateman & Vincent 2016), public libraries exemplify civic identity, but in so doing, inculcate the middle-class behaviours that inform modern urban civility (Burgum 2019). Public libraries also provide a cultural infrastructure of low-intensity encounter that function like community centres and educational repositories. Embedded within the social tectonics of neighbourhoods, public libraries usually have the responsibility to represent diverse social groups without discrimination through their materials, displays, programmes, information, hosting of writers and poets and collaborations with schools, community and artistic organizations (Brault & Kaplansky 2010); but so too do they have the potential to reinforce social norms by redistributing public resources to already privileged social groups (Bain & Podmore 2020). Fraying social service nets and austerity budgeting further serve to constrain the material, programming and spatial resources of public libraries, increasing the difficulty of effectively redistributing resources to all patrons regardless of income or social status (e.g., homeless, mentally ill, elderly, refugee and asylum seekers, newcomers and youth). However, at their core, libraries are a cultural infrastructure that functions as a reparative urban commons. When libraries are treated as shared "people's property" they can become a "city's living room" – where people can sleep, eat, read, converse, socialize and work (Freeman & Blomley 2019: 204). When not privatized through annual membership fees or corporate sponsorship, public libraries play a key infrastructural role in the democratization of knowledge, digital technology and culture. They are perhaps the most widely used of all cultural infrastructure, offering engagement, participation and entryways into cultural worlds.

The socio-cultural infrastructure of public libraries and their contribution to the everyday life of cities is the focus of Chapter 14 by Rianne van Melik. She interrogates Dutch municipal "librarizing" practices with particular attention to the role of volunteers in the performance and reception of care in one small city's library system. As some libraries transform into spaces of encounter, what is constructed as the daily work of librarians is shifting away from cataloguing, lending, programming and ordering collections and towards practices of social service care. It is therefore important not to merely focus on what the library as cultural infrastructure is, but also how it comes into being through informal and embodied sayings and doings. In tandem with Landau-Donnelly's focus on museum infrastructuring in Chapter 13, van Melik accentuates how public libraries are "constantly becoming" infrastructure, where staff, visitors and artefacts continuously intertwine, readjust and rearrange in response to systemic challenges such as austerity measures, illiteracy and socio-cultural exclusion.

Like libraries, archives are cultural institutions constantly in process, becoming infrastructure through the collecting labour of archivists, volunteers and users. Generally understood as repositories of historical artefacts, archives are places to which objects, images and documents from the past are consigned and given order within unifying systems (Derrida 1996). Through systematization, Foucault (1966) argued, government archives become tools of state biopolitics, sorting out which subjectivities are represented or silenced and those that are celebrated versus those that are pathologized. The powerful ordering of archival temporalities is critiqued by post-colonial scholars who assert that they have been "both sites of the imaginary *and* institutions that fashioned histories as they concealed, revealed, and reproduced the power of the state" (Stoler 2002: 96, emphasis in original). Archives, therefore, serve as cultural infrastructure in support of claims to historical "fact" through their ordering authority and what they set aside to be remembered, the power of which are also reinforced by their architectural gravitas and central civic location (Mbembe 2002). But as Appadurai argues (2003: 16), the current "archive fever" (Derrida 1996) is "more frequently the product of the anticipation of collective memory", a view of archives as sites of aspiration rather than recollection. Whether on- or off-line, individuals and communities intervene in the urban historical record by creating activist archives that disrupt the order of the mainstream with alternate (re)collections. Alternate archives are not just repositories of subcultural information; they are places of affect where people go to "feel differently, but [also] to know differently" (Buchanan & Bastien 2015: 435). As local, autonomous free spaces, activist archives afford spaces for different historical narratives and identities to be forged and commemorated while reconfiguring and reinterpreting the archive itself (Sellie *et al.* 2015).

In Chapter 15, Julie Podmore examines how local, community-based archival activists collect and organize knowledge to disrupt the instituting imaginaries of official archives that frequently pathologize and erase their collective histories. The chapter uses the concept of "chrononormativity" (Freeman 2010) to address the significance of LGBTQ+ archival movements in queering urban cultural infrastructure. Through their collections, LGBTQ+ community-based archives provide the space for the collection, preservation and exhibition of affective memories of queer urban sites, enhancing societal visibility and community empowerment. Drawing on the conceptual frameworks of "counter-topography" (Katz 2004) and "city-as-archive" (Rao 2009), the chapter provides a case study of Montreal's LGBTQ+ archival infrastructure and two digital mapping projects that were initiated during the Covid-19 pandemic to bring communities, spaces and pasts together and build social connection for sexual and gender minorities. Digital infrastructure created opportunities to view the city-as-queer-archive and generate a sense of visibility and empowerment, while also potentially reinforcing chronormativities of their own making by selectively documenting and reconstructing queer pasts.

Taken together, the chapters in this final section on collecting culture discuss a selection of civic and community-based institutions – libraries, museums and community archives – to demonstrate the hard and soft synergies that support their adaptation as repositories of culture and memory into sites of care in the service of public good. Inevitably, dynamics of philanthrocapitalism and austerity inform the collection practices of these institutions. However, with examples drawn from cities in the Netherlands, Germany, India and Canada, the section illustrates the persistence and durability of cultural infrastructure reinforced by the power of historical memory and the social justice programming that emerges from it. Furthermore, they demonstrate that although the "official culture" dominating hard urban cultural infrastructure is rarely completely reconfigured, its softer elements can be leveraged in the service of care and social inclusion within cities.

CHAPTER 13

INFRASTRUCTURING MUSEUMS

Friederike Landau-Donnelly

INTRODUCTION: REFRAMING MUSEUMS AS INFRASTRUCTURE

This chapter uses the analytic of *infrastructuring* to conceptualize museums along the lines of what they *do*, rather than by what they *are* or are supposed to *be*. With a practice-oriented and activist approach to museums, this chapter challenges existing, conventional museum definitions. It thus engages infrastructure as a verb rather than as a noun. Infrastructure as a noun predominantly grasps concrete and tangible human, organic, technological and material facilities. In contrast, Matthias Korn *et al.* (2019: 12) describe infrastructuring as a verb that initiates a shift "from single artefacts and sites to the connectedness and entanglement between them". Accordingly, infrastructuring is understood as an embodied process and practice, that shapes, and is shaped by, socio-spatial encounters between different actors – including people, places, objects, feelings, discourses, histories, herstories and memories. Hence, the chapter deploys the lens of infrastructuring as a malleable and mobile conceptual frame to understand and practices of collecting culture.

This chapter argues that if museums are thought of as fluctuating formations that are articulated via practices of infrastructuring, we can better attend to different people and places, as well as the symbolical and material absences and presences of voices, narratives, traumatic and joyful memories, hopes and dreams, that together constitute cultural infrastructure. With the encompassing notion of *infrastructuring the museum*, existing definitions of museums can be radically challenged. When museums are approached via a lens of infrastructuring, it not only allows for more versatile and less spatially fixed imaginaries of museums, but importantly, also makes room for more socially diverse and intersectional practices of museum-making. The objective of this chapter, then, is to chart novel socially and spatially engaged museum practices as exemplary approaches of *doing* museums differently.

For this purpose, the chapter discusses two projects of infrastructuring the museum, one from Ahmedabad, India, and the second from Berlin, Germany.

To approach museums as activist exercises of infrastructuring, this chapter is situated in theories of political difference and conflict (Landau *et al.* 2021). Political difference, in a nutshell, distinguishes between the realm and practices of "politics" (which aim to create order and control with the goal to maintain and institutionalize power) and "the political" which extends beyond formalized and routinized institutions where the logic of politics resides. The political is more excessive, untameable and ever-present, embodying an irreducible dimension of conflict that cannot be contained or settled. Both overlap in real life, thus cross-contaminating each other. "The political" amplifies the analytical trajectory of *infrastructuring* to draw attention to the fact that any position of power, be it spatial or symbolical, is always conflictually and contingently put together, namely, *infrastructured*. In the context of reframing museums and practices of collecting and exhibiting culture, "the political" lens assists with moving *beyond* narrow and institution-centric understandings of museums. Interlaced with the infrastructuring of museums, a more conflict-attuned, and thus political understanding of museums seeks to push museum scholarship and practice into a more activist practice.

Inspired by cultural mediator and museum scholar Nora Sternfeld's (2018) work on the "radical democratic museum", such a conflictual understanding of infrastructuring museums foregrounds their contingent character, but also their potentially critical role in processes uprooting systemic injustices in the cultural field, and the urban cultural fabric more broadly (e.g., showing solidarity with refugees and migrants, gentrification-induced displacement, homo- and transphobia and institutional racism). Thus this chapter aligns with literatures that consider the museum as activist actor (Janes & Sandell 2019) or disobedient place (Message 2018). To ground such a conceptual proposition, the chapter introduces two examples of what infrastructuring museums can look like. First, the Conflictorium – Museum of Conflict in Ahmedabad, India, founded by artist, curator and dancer Avni Sethi. Located for nearly a decade in the vibrant urban neighbourhood of Mirzapur, the Conflictorium's infrastructuring museal activities also take place in many other spatial settings. Second, the Women's Walking Museum (WWM), which notably has *not* taken place somewhere *yet*, but as imagined by artist Yishay Garbasz and writer Maike Stein, has been growing as a counter-proposition and queer alternative in comparison to the already existing Schwules Museum (Gay Museum) in Berlin. The chapter concludes with a poetic outlook on how future-oriented, infrastructured museums might contribute to intersectional and embodied practices of doing the museum.

TOWARDS A CONFLICT-ORIENTED UNDERSTANDING OF MUSEUMS

Museums have historically maintained and continue to shape hegemonic representations of history as well as social values and norms about what is normal, civil or morally good (see Hetherington 1997). These charged processes of inclusion and exclusion – determining, in short, who and what *matters* in museums – undeniably point to the conflictuality of museums previously touched upon via the frameworks of political difference and conflict. In the quest for a conflictual conceptualization of the museum, Sternfeld (2018) has assembled a rich collection of essays challenging what a museum "is" according to the standards of the International Council of Museums (ICOM). The latter's formally acknowledged definition, instituted in 2007, defines the museum as follows: "a museum is a non-profit, permanent institution in the service of society and its development, open to the public, which acquires, conserves, researches, communicates and exhibits the tangible and intangible heritage of humanity and its environment for the purposes of education, study and enjoyment" (ICOM 2007: n.p.). Sternfeld (2018: 37) extracts five definitional parameters of the museum (i.e., acquisition, conservation, research, communication and exhibition) and inverts them into the following five parameters to advance understanding of the counter-hegemonic, or radical democratic, museum:

1. Challenge the archive.
2. Appropriate (exhibition) space.
3. Organize counter-publics.
4. Produce alternative knowledge(s).
5. Radicalize (cultural) education.

With this reversal, Sternfeld turns the definition of a museum on its head, stretching it beyond common parameters of collecting culture, or agreed-upon conventions of what counts as a museum. This approach contributes to existing critiques of the standing museum definition, which (after undergoing transformation for a number of years), was redefined by the ICOM in 2022 as:

> a not-for-profit, permanent institution in the service of society that researches, collects, conserves, interprets and exhibits tangible and intangible heritage. Open to the public, accessible and inclusive, museums foster diversity and sustainability. They operate and communicate ethically, professionally and with the participation of communities, offering varied experiences for education, enjoyment, reflection and knowledge sharing.
>
> (ICOM 2022: n.p.)

The ICOM Standing Committee for Museum Definition, Prospects and Potentials (ICOM 2018) had initiated a global, participatory process to develop a new and arguably more inclusive definition already in 2018, but many of the suggestions were critiqued as being "too political" and "too vague". Others found the museum charged with too many social, environmental and humanitarian tasks. While the 2022 definition incorporates some of these aspects (e.g., by explicitly naming diversity and sustainability as values museums "should" embrace), it does not, however, radically redefine what a museum "is". In terms of infrastructuring, a singular definition – regardless how broad – might appear essentializing, controlling and constricting, reining in the logic of "politics". In contrast, the logic of "the political" aligns with infrastructuring because it leaves room for ambivalence and difference in an effort to envision museums differently.

At this critical junction of the future of museums, Sternfeld (2018) proposes the term "para-museum" which posits the Greek prefix παρά (besides/against) as a precondition for critical, counter-hegemonic museum formations. The para-museum does not merely reject the museum, but wrestles with the complicated continuous existence of museums. The para-museum can be a real or imagined institution "in which fugitivity and continuity do not exclude each other, which enables us to think singularity and collectivity together, which simultaneously insists on criticality and pushes forms of reappropriation" (Sternfeld 2018: 64, translation by author). The para-museum thus both reproduces and contests conventional museum logics, logistics, spaces and institutions. In this sense, it seeks to intervene *besides and between* institutional museum practices and places without wanting to tear them down for good. It is here that the conceptual synergy with the logic of infrastructuring comes to the fore. In the para-museum, the place, presence and absence of objects and stories to be exhibited can be challenged, reconfigured and, ultimately, *infrastructured*. The para-museum forages new answers to the question of what museums could *do* for very diverse people, places and objects.

The proposition of the para-museum resonates with conceptualizations of micro-museums (Gregory & Robertson 2018), post-museums (Watermeyer 2012) or placeless museums (Rojas-Pick 2014). Albeit differently imagined, these museal formations share a political trajectory to challenge hegemonic and oft-exclusive practices of collection, education and leadership. However, these accounts do not conceptually tackle the crucially conflictual dimension of museum space that a conflict-oriented approach emphasizes. Yet it crucially matters *whether* and *how* conflicts are embraced in museums (Landau 2021). In sum, the conceptual leverage of the para-museum pushes museum scholarship and practice to unsettle hegemonic notions, places and practices of museums. While it is an intriguing abstract proposition, the para-museum's biggest challenge is that it remains difficult to grasp empirically. In a quest to provide more concrete empirical footing for a conflict-attuned or para-museum, infrastructuring is deployed as analytical lens to shed light on two projects that exhibit, embody and *do* museums differently.

INFRASTRUCTURING MUSEUMS

Beyond conventional associations of infrastructure with technological set-ups (e.g., sedate and bulky buildings, concrete jungles, autobahns, tracks, trails, arrows, as well as cables, data, flows of bits and bytes as information infrastructure), the "infrastructural turn" (Amin 2014) directs attention to the manifold socio-material, affective and more-than-human usages of infrastructures in urban and political life. Social and cultural theoretical accounts qualify infrastructure as matter of "promise" (Anand *et al.* 2018) or as matter of "politics" (McFarlane & Rutherford 2008). With regards to the potential of infrastructure to reimagine spaces of and for the commons, Lauren Berlant (2016) emphasizes the potential of infrastructure to develop new approaches to difference. This resonates with the analytic of political difference discussed above, to situate the infrastructuring of the museum as a political practice. Furthermore, it aligns with Michael Glass, Jean-Paul Addie and Jen Nelles' (2019: 1634) observation of a renewed interest in the politics of infrastructure that positions it as "a setting and stake of social struggle". Accordingly, this chapter extrapolates the political, poetic and activist understanding of infrastructure into the realm of critical museum scholarship and practice through the concept of *para-infrastructuring*.

Extending Sternfeld's suggestion of the para-museum, para-infrastructuring points to the diverse potentials for relation-building and place-making practices by different agents (including subjects, objects and things) in museums that exist *besides* or *beyond* their institutions or spaces. In that sense, the concept of para-infrastructuring adds to critical and counter-hegemonic approach to museums in its embrace of conflict, contingency and radical versatility. On the one hand, para-infrastructuring offers a decidedly *spatial* focus on museums because it is concerned with *where* and *how* infrastructured museums could materialize. The spatial politics of infrastructured museums unfold the museum not only as a contact zone (Clifford 1997), but also as a place where different meanings and actors meet, and mutually constitute their social positions and identities. More politically, the museum also comes to the fore as *conflict* zone (Løgstrup 2021; Mouffe 2016). In sum, para-infrastructuring the museum as a conflict zone creates an arena where culture is produced through tensions about presences, absences, voices and meanings.

Para-infrastructuring suggests that museums do not have to "be" permanent to become (infrastructured as) museums. With such an open-ended, permeable approach, the infrastructuring – and queering – of museums can begin to unravel possibilities to envision and enact museums as places of activism, care and ever-present possibility for change and transformation in the spirit of the political (Sullivan & Middleton 2020). To see how queering as a verb interlinks with (para)infrastructuring in a conflict-laden museum landscape, the chapter now turns to two museums that differently infrastructure conflicts, activisms and care.

INFRASTRUCTURING A MUSEUM FROM NOTHINGNESS: CONFLICTORIUM – MUSEUM OF CONFLICT

The Conflictorium was founded in 2013 in Ahmedabad, India's fifth-largest city, with over five million inhabitants. Located in the western province of Gujarat, Ahmedabad has experienced droughts and earthquakes in conjunction with historical and ongoing violent political and religious upheaval between Hindus (82 per cent of the local population) and Muslims (14 per cent) (Bobbio 2015). The Conflictorium is located on the east side of the Sabarmati River in the historic Old Town, designated India's first World Heritage Site in 2017. It sits amid a Hindu Temple, a mosque and a Christian church in a two-storey building that once housed a hair salon and NGO storage space.

As the Conflictorium name suggests, it does not only understand conflict as the opposite of peace, or as married to war, but rather conveys a significantly broader understanding of conflict as integral to life. With 30 exhibitions – including temporary and more permanent ones such as *Moral Compass*, *Empathy Alley*, *Conflict Timeline*, *Gallery of Disputes* or *Sorry Tree* – the museum educates not only about historical lines of conflict and the struggle for democracy in India, but also by appealing to visitors as the primary co-producers of the space (Figure 13.1). The museum relies heavily on participation and the co-design of museum objects, experiences and encounter. It challenges the archive by not collecting artefacts in the conventional sense of a museum definition (#1) and radicalizing the exhibition space by leaving it to participants to temporarily "fill" (#2). While the Conflictorium can be *experienced* as a lively and joyful space, it is also a space for mourning, reflection and the marking of absence and erasure in museums (Landau-Donnelly & Sethi 2022). The Conflictorium is nothing but what visitor-produced everyday objects, narratives, memories and feelings bring to the space. Furthermore, this (para-)museum invites counter-publics that may use the museum space for non-museum usages such as sleeping, playing hide and seek, chatting and

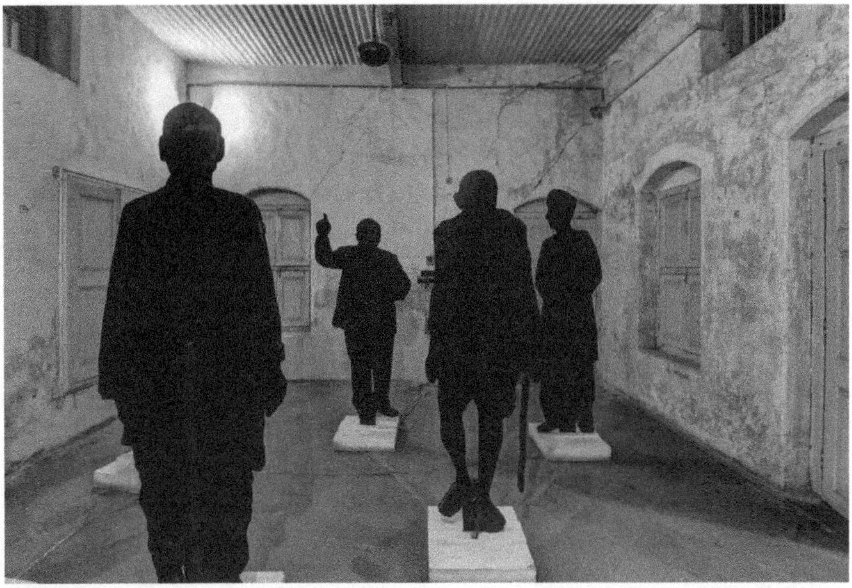

Figure 13.1 View of the permanent exhibition *Empathy Alley* at the Conflictorium

Source: Conflictorium.

phone charging (#3). Using diverse modes of communication and finding ways to invite atypical museum audiences into their space, the Conflictorium both seeks to produce alternative knowledge about what a museum can do for its local context (#4) and implicitly offers an alternative approach to cultural education (#5). In sum, this place enacts para-infrastructuring by expanding its activity to various urban (and rural) places, both local and international, concurrently a neighbourhood drop-in space and a location on social media, thus existing *besides* or *beyond* museum institutions or spaces.

EMBODYING A MUSEUM WITHOUT WALLS: WOMEN'S WALKING MUSEUM

The second case study of infrastructuring museums is the Women's Walking Museum (WWM), initially envisioned by Berlin-based, British-Israeli trans artist Yishay Garbasz (2021), together with Berlin-based writer Maike Stein. In dialogue, Yishay and I have imagined how new/other/different museums can actively fight against ongoing systemic exclusion, erasure and exoticization of trans women artists in contemporary gallery and museum contexts (Landau-Donnelly & Garbasz forthcoming). We acknowledge that hierarchies of sexual desire and (in)visibility, in museums and elsewhere, are complex and sometimes create mutually aggressive forms of gender-related exclusion, oppression, objectification and vilification. Hence, we share the desire and dream to envision and embody cultural infrastructures otherwise, making space for vulnerability, individuality and care.

It is important to note that the WWM project has not yet received cultural funding and in that sense has never claimed space in Berlin or elsewhere. Hence, the following descriptions of such embodied museum practice – which is neither reliant on, nor constricted by physical museum space – stem from personal thoughts, ideas and sketches by Yishay and Maike, and their continued imagining about the futures of museums. Yet the WWM will never be *one* discrete or fixed place; rather, it would act as a moving formation, a para-infrastructure *par excellence*. In contrast to conventional forms of museum display such as walls, cabinets, pedestals and screens, WWM aims to mobilize museum display onto the micro-political unit of the body. Imagined to first take place in Berlin, WWM sets out to intervene in an existing museum landscape of more than 170 museums in Berlin ranging from prestigious historical collections, national galleries to world-renown contemporary art museums such as Gropius Bau or Hamburger Bahnhof. Within Berlin's rich urban cultural landscape, which remains attractive to tourists and locals alike, WWM seeks to address a heterogenous set of haphazard spectators or passers-by.

The drive to critique existing museums in para-museal activity, comes from Yishay and some of her colleagues' disappointing experiences with established institutions such as the Berlin-based Schwules Museum, which has long privileged cis-gender and gay male positionalities in museum exhibitions and management. This discontent with the Schwules Museum has, in part, crystallized in the WWM as a response to this insufficiently queer museum institution. WWM is intended to publicly mark that Schwules Museum is not a safe and welcoming place for *every* member of the inherently multiple queer community. With regards to the lens of para-museums, WWM acts in critical relation with an established museum, but simultaneously aims to work *beyond* the existing institution of Schwules Museum to request another, more inclusive gay museum – a *queer* museum – that also exhibits trans positionalities, is open to elderly and disabled artists, and artists without academic degrees, to name a few different social groups that are often marginalized within art scenes and art communities. With this leap, WWM envisions an intersectional museum space and practice, infrastructured by differently abled artist-agents.

The WWM's DIY, low-tech and low-cost easily replicable approach to mobile museum display proposes the body as a place and plane for exhibition. Makers of the WWM can choose to wear a harness, similar to a backpack, over their shoulders (Figure 13.2). After temporary exhibition walks, lasting different amounts of time, the harnesses are returned to the museum

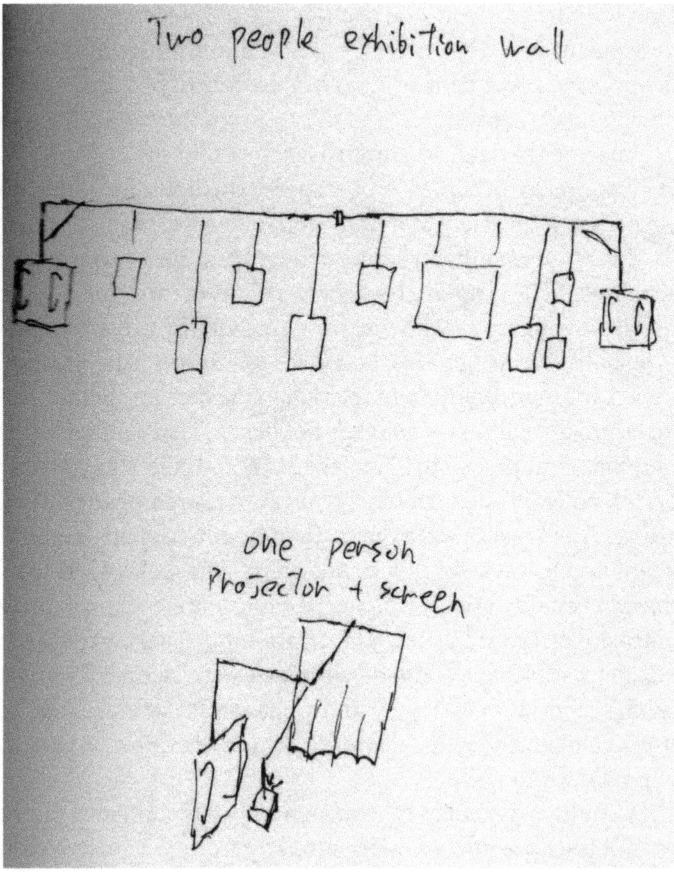

Figure 13.2 Sketch of WWM exhibition views and harness

Source: Drawn by Yishay Garbasz.

organizers, and reused in the next iterations of WWM. The WWM can be an individual body's exploration into public space, or a collective exercise of a million mini-museums walking into urban space (relating to the para-museum's aim #2). This infrastructured museum can appear in countless different forms and it is different every time it takes place (and can also take place in different places across the globe). Touching this embodied museum may be allowed – of course, only if the museum carriers are consenting. Panels with objects, texts and other artefacts can be carried and displayed; small objects, replica or informational materials might be available for take-away in the harnesses; perhaps spectators can write on it, maybe it speaks, maybe there are sounds, smells or tastes. WWM can be walked, wheelchaired, danced, crawled, painted, projected or Instagram-storied. This museum creates an ingeniously multi-dimensional, immersive museum experience: you can see the museum walking past you, you can see its back, its front, its face and you see it in movement. With this inventive intervention, museum space does not necessarily become redundant or wholly abandoned, but appears as a constantly moving object, dependent and in service of the carrier's physical and emotional capacities and micro-curatorial choices. In sum, WWM variously takes and temporarily occupies urban space; this museum does not need walls. Its pieces can be safely stored at home, in accessible deposits spread over town, this museum infrastructure can be open 24/7 (para-museum #2).

The harnesses themselves are bodily extensions of their volunteer carriers who can flexibly switch roles with visitors or passers-by to become part of the WWM. Arguably, "everybody" can become a museum-maker and everybody can experience museum content. In relation to the para-museum framework, WWM then broadly addresses counter-publics or "non-audiences" (#3) and offers an alternative approach to knowledge (#4) and education (#5). This radically experimental and open approach, however, also comes at various costs. The harness-carriers invest and exhaust their bodily capacity (and this might have different implications for different harness-carriers), which enables and invites some and could possibly (further) exclude others who do not feel welcome in museum settings. In sum, WWM attempts the para-museal critique against existing institutions, and radically expands the scope of who and what is to be exhibited in museums, who and what can make museums, who and what *matters*. It might add to the democratization of exhibition arrangement, build-up and dismantling.

With these multiple practices of extension and embodiment of the museum, WWM resembles a practice of queer infrastructuring, which is committed to the interconnected struggles against sexism, racism and oppressive heteronormativity (Brochu-Ingram 2015). In the museum context, queer para-infrastructuring then actively works towards the decolonization of the museum beyond its Western-centric, hetero- and/or cis-normative and/or and masculinist historical baggage. Moreover, museum initiatives such as WWM attend to the much-neglected role of bodies and embodiment in the museum (Leahy 2016). Hence, if we take seriously Tiwari's (2010: 18) claim that "it is the body that inscribes its thoughts, emotions, meanings, and memories onto the space, and in the process is transformed", museum space is an embodied place that cultivates learning and understanding, gaining traction in efforts to critique, decolonize and queer museums. In sum, WWM proposes an alternative to disembodied or "cold" museum halls. By means of personalizing opportunities for display, and drastically multiplying choices of what, when, where and whom to exhibit, WWM de-mystifies the making and unmaking of museums, which all too often appear as immutable, majestic decisions that no mortal being could ever reverse. Aligned with the para-infrastructuring of the museum, WWM's movements grow into and out of museums – to intervene and uproot existing structures, privileges and places of exhibition, but also to create wholly new ones.

OUTLOOK: MUSEALIZING YOUR SKIN

In lieu of a conclusion, I have written a poem that shares a dream about museums of the future, conveying a sense of what visiting, dwelling and being in infrastructured museums might feel like:

> you wear this museum on your skin
> spotty museum display
> dark pores, a hair here and there
> the body (as) museum
> sometimes, this museum is tired, it might need to rest
> this museum is human, after all
> the infrastructured museum literally visits your limbs
> oh, *this* is what they meant by "access"
> they don't need walls anymore, boxes fall flat
> this museum is a hosting body
> chosen family of people, places and things – infra-dance

This chapter has outlined how the lens of infrastructuring can unravel new ways of projecting, presenting, and carrying culture into urban space. By interconnecting conceptual threads of conflict and political difference with existing accounts of activist and para-museums, the chapter has sharpened the notion of para-infrastructuring, those malleable museum formations between human and more-than-human agents, places and dreams that jointly *critique* existing hegemonic, and therefore exclusionary museums, but at the same time also *do* museums differently. The chapter has problematized the desire to define museums, which might reproduce power asymmetries. Instead, it has opened space for conflict, difference and queer practices, articulating museums as counter-hegemonic, activist spaces that engage in the fight against systemic marginalization, inequity and exclusion. With this provocation, the chapter extends discussions about museums not only as urban cultural infrastructure (Landau 2020b), but as para-infrastructuring entities that advance an intersectional understanding of care in and for museums. For museums to be infrastructured as spaces of care and solidarity, it is necessary to make space, time and resources available to accommodate vulnerability in all of its unevenly distributed forms (Butler *et al.* 2016). At last, these exercises of dreaming might help to rethink museums of the future as queer infrastructure from which 'the political' can *take* place.

CHAPTER 14

BECOMING SOCIO-CULTURAL INFRASTRUCTURE: LIBRARIZING PRACTICES IN PUBLIC LIBRARIES

Rianne van Melik

INTRODUCTION

Over the past decade, research on the role of infrastructure in societal transformation has blossomed, labelled as the "infrastructural turn" in social sciences (Amin 2014). Increasingly, the focus is not limited to large technical systems that facilitate resource and energy flows such as (rail) roads, ports and power lines, but also encompasses cultural institutions such as public libraries and museums. Libraries are long-acknowledged places for information provision and knowledge transmission, but they increasingly also function as important socio-cultural infrastructure that contributes to the everyday life of cities (Klinenberg 2018; Latham & Layton 2019). Arguably, this transition of libraries from information to socio-cultural infrastructure is generative to society, but it is also what is necessary for libraries as a public institution to avoid extinction (Van Melik & Merry 2021). Shrinking subsidies, changing demographics, decreasing membership and the rise of digital technologies force libraries to reinvent themselves: as community centres, innovation labs and makerspaces.

This transition has changed the "hardware" of libraries, which now offer fewer physical books and more mobile usages of library space. A library's furniture needs to be flexible to allow for rapid spatial reorganization to accommodate a wide range of non-book-based services, including art classes, homework, social service assistance, language instruction, crafts and yoga classes. But more fundamentally, this transition also requires a change in libraries' "software", reframing the librarian's role from "information experts to community advocates, teachers, and as match-makers for people to meet one another and new ideas" (Barniskis 2016: 114). Community librarian courses are organized to equip staff for these new duties, like arranging lunch meetings for elderly patrons. Turning the library into socio-cultural infrastructure not only requires staff to increasingly perform "emotional labour" (Julien & Genuis 2009), but also to demonstrate and legitimize the library's social values beyond its role as information provider (Van Melik & Merry 2021).

To understand the practices behind these transformations, this chapter focuses on how the library as socio-cultural infrastructure comes *into being* through (in)formal practices. Rivano Eckerdal (2018) coined the term "librarizing" versus "library", to highlight that these cultural institutions are constantly becoming organizations, where staff, visitors and artefacts continuously intertwine, collect and are rearranged in response to systemic challenges like austerity measures, illiteracy and social exclusion. Building upon this terminology, this chapter explores librarizing practices performed in public libraries and how they contribute to the library becoming socio-cultural infrastructure (Klinenberg 2018). Alongside its collections of books and information, the "collection of care" is an increasingly important function of the library. Schloffel-Armstrong *et al.* (2021) claim that this care responsibility of libraries needs to be problematized and interrogated to illustrate the restructuring of care practices across urban spaces more generally.

The chapter is empirically situated in the Netherlands and builds upon my (auto)ethnographic experiences as a volunteer since 2004 in a small-town public library on the outskirts of the country's fourth largest city, Utrecht. Library landscapes are far from uniform, with large differences in library policies and budgets between but also within countries. Although there are notable exceptions – for example, Pyati and Kamal (2012) on community libraries in Bangalore's slums, or Chen and Ke (2017) on Singang Library in Taiwan – there is still an Anglo-Scandinavian hegemony in academic literature on libraries as public sphere institutions (Vårheim *et al.* 2019). It is important to also include other spatial contexts, as some trends described in this body of literature do not necessary apply worldwide. For example, although the Netherlands certainly also experiences budget cuts and closures of libraries (Corble & Van Melik 2021), austerity measures are much more severe in countries such as the United Kingdom and United States (e.g., Forkert 2016; Klinenberg 2018). However, differences may also be observed between libraries within the same country (e.g., between wealthier metropolitan libraries and rural libraries) or within the same city (e.g., between central libraries and community libraries in lower-income neighbourhoods or informal settlements). This chapter focuses on one library and its contingent, place-specific version of socio-cultural infrastructure. However, although the found practices might be place-specific, the insights that socio-cultural infrastructure does not evolve on its own but rather unfolds through continuous librarizing practices by staff and volunteers is applicable in many different spatial contexts, including less economically advantaged regions of the world.

The chapter first outlines the concept of librarizing, after which it briefly sketches the Dutch urban public library landscape. It then proceeds to discuss two different librarizing practices: caring by community librarians and caring for/by volunteers. It ends with a conclusion that puts this collection of care in perspective.

LIBRARIZING PRACTICES

This chapter explores the set of (in)formal practices library staff and volunteers carry out while performing their labour in the library in order to provide, maintain and safeguard them as important socio-cultural infrastructure. Rather than looking at object-centric notions of what a library as a socio-cultural infrastructure *is* (i.e., buildings, collections), this chapter examines how it comes *into being* through (in)formal practices. A practice-oriented framework departs from the idea "that in order to understand higher-order ... economic and social outcomes ... it is necessary to first closely observe and understand the micro-social activities (i.e., practices) carried out and performed by people living, labouring, and creating in the everyday economy" (Jones & Murphy 2010: 376). Reckwitz (2002: 249) defines practices as routinized behaviours consisting of "forms of bodily activities, forms of mental activities, 'things' and their use, a background knowledge in the form of understanding, know-how, states of emotion and motivational knowledge". Thus, a practice is an action that enrols a number of heterogeneous elements into the creation of a social phenomenon. In this conception, a single person can carry a multitude or practices, and each practice can contain many discrete actions.

Rivano Eckerdal (2018: 1409) coined a new term to describe the proactive role that both the institution and the profession can have in society: "instead of talking about the library as a noun, we speak of it as a verb, *to librarize*". Comparable to the analytic of "infrastructuring" (Korn *et al.* 2019), Rivano Eckerdal (2018) regards the library as an "ongoing performance", a fluid and constantly becoming organization, in which staff and patrons continuously perform maintenance work on artefacts, collections and infrastructure. The spaces and functions of libraries, then, are malleable; they can be transformed to support lending, rentals, social service assistance, workshops and food provision. Libraries change not just defensively in response to (financial) threats, but with aspirations to produce urban innovations in their own right. This chapter borrows Rivano Eckerdal's (2018) terminology and uses the term librarizing to discuss the active practices performed to turn libraries in the Netherlands into socio-cultural infrastructure.

THE DUTCH LIBRARY LANDSCAPE

The Dutch library landscape is changing quickly, among other factors, in response to the library law of 2015 (*Wet stelsel openbare bibliotheekvoorziening*). The law stipulated that everyone should have the right to have access to a library, as they play a vital role in the personal development of people. It specified five functions a library should fulfil: (1) providing knowledge and information; (2) offering possibilities for personal development and education; (3) stimulating reading and acquaintance with literature; (4) organizing encounter and debate; and (5) becoming acquainted with art and culture. The last two functions were specifically added to this list to highlight that libraries ought to be more than collections of books, providing opportunities for encounter, debate, art and culture. This trend of public libraries housing all sorts of activities can also observed in many other countries, such as Sweden, New Zealand and the UK (Latham & Layton 2019; Schloffel-Armstrong *et al.* 2021).

The evaluation of this Dutch law – required after five years – was generally positive (Van Mil *et al.* 2019), but nevertheless the advisory Council of Culture (*Raad voor Cultuur*) concluded that the ambition to have a library for everyone is far from achieved. Although the national law dictates that all communities must have a library, it cannot enforce this, as the actual financing and management is organized on a municipal level. Consequently, 16 out of 352 Dutch municipalities do not offer any library services. Moreover, some municipalities allocate larger budgets than others.

The empirical insights discussed below are drawn from ethnographic research in a small public library in a fairly homogenous (white, middle-class) town. The studied library is open four days/25.5 hours per week, when at least one paid staff member and one or two volunteers run the library. It managed by a regional cultural body along with five other library branches, a theatre and an arts centre, among other functions. The six libraries share collections, staff and activities, but are each subsidized separately via their respective municipalities. The case-study library is located in a community centre, which also includes two primary schools, a day care centre and a music school. For this chapter, I repeatedly interviewed staff and fellow volunteers. I also made elaborate fieldnotes of my volunteering experiences and participant observations of socio-cultural activities. To respect the anonymity of the library and its staff and visitors, its precise location is not revealed and all names in this chapter are pseudonyms.

The following two sections reveal several commonly observed practices from the case study related to the notion of librarizing: caring by community librarians and caring for/by volunteers. This overview of practices is not comprehensive as it is always possible to identify more, nor does each individual librarian or volunteer carry all these practices.

CARING FOR THE COMMUNITY

Library managers Anne and Linda started working at the library in 2017 as "public service employees" (*medewerker publieksservice*), which implies they manage the library during opening hours together with a team of volunteers. As the library is part of a regional library network that shares its collection, Anne and Linda have limited say regarding the collection of books, newspapers and other material artefacts. In contrast, they have more freedom to organize the collection of care by organizing social activities as they see fit. This includes a weekly lunch meeting called "Guest at the table" (GATT). On average 6–14 people visit these lunch meetings to discuss a chosen theme, such as the hobby, expertise or journey of the invited guest, while enjoying their home-brought food together. Anne invites the guest, moderates the discussion and provides free coffee and tea. At first glance, GATT resembles *Tischgesellschaften* (table societies), such as coffee houses where people meet to discuss issues of common interest (Vårheim *et al.* 2019). However, GATT's primary aim is not to educate its visitors, but rather to reduce loneliness – although the meetings are purposely not framed and advertised as such. Visitors are mainly older and/or disabled people, often single or widowed and suffering from chronic loneliness (for more information see Van Melik & Merry 2021). With such vulnerable patrons, Anne and Linda act as social workers, although they are not trained as such, and officially, do not offer care.

Nevertheless, Dutch libraries are increasingly aware that they need to equip their staff with formal training on how to run a more socially oriented library. Anne was offered the opportunity to follow a one-year postgraduate programme to become a so-called "community librarian". Community-led librarianship (CLL) is "an integrated approach in which librarians seek to work *with*, not *for*, community members to better meet what they need and want from their public library" (Freeman & Blomley 2019: 206, emphasis in original). Developed in 2017, the Dutch postgraduate programme provides students with tools and theories on how to improve society by facilitating knowledge creation in their communities that now annually attracts between five and 15 librarians (Huysmans & Palliser 2017).

Anne recently graduated with a research project on mini-libraries, also known as micro-libraries, community bookshelves or book boxes, where people can take and leave books. Although these mini-libraries could be seen as competitors of the library, both serve the purpose of reading-by-sharing.

Anne started her own mini-library at home, mapped all other micro-libraries in town, and interviewed the initiators about their love for books and the community. She developed a walking tour of the mini-libraries and offered library patrons the opportunity to walk this tour together with a volunteer. As such, the tour offered access to books, but also moments of exercise and encounter. Anne's practices illustrate how she aims to attract new communities into the library and how organized activities are extended beyond the physical contours of the library.

Other recent activities organized in the library include a cartoon workshop for children, a monthly "Repair Cafe" – during which people gather to (learn how to) restore items such as electronic devices, computers and clothing – and weekly storytelling sessions for toddlers and their caregivers, the so-called "Play-and-Share (*speel-en-deel*) Cafe". Posters in the library (Figure 14.1) also aim to attract older youth: "Studying for school? Come to the library! Studying for tests and exams in a quiet, inspiring environment. Free Wi-Fi, attention ☺ and a first cup of coffee/tea." With this range of different activities, the library aims to attract and create its own communities, but it also offers existing communities the opportunity to host their activities for free in the library, such as meetings of the knitting club and expositions of the drawing club.

However, being a community librarian for these different populations is challenging. First, who actually *is* the community? With limited budgets and opening hours, they have to prioritize whom to accommodate first. Linda expressed some frustration that the library is only financed to host activities for "lost souls" (*zielenpoten*), such as the lonely elderly, and believes it should organize more than lunch meetings to truly function as a socio-cultural infrastructure for the entire community (Van Melik & Merry 2021). Second, some users and activities are potentially conflicting, such as social activities that make the library more vibrant like storytelling or cartoon workshops, but less suitable for quiet contemplation. In a more extreme example, Freeman and Blomley (2019) illustrate tensions between different communities using the Edmonton Public Library, especially those generated when homeless people use the library as a warm place to sleep. Third, some community groups are harder to connect with using outreach strategies, such as older youth and migrants. This raises questions about where the responsibility of the library stops, or as Mattern (2014, n.p.) asks: "is it too much to expect our libraries to serve as soup kitchens and recovery centres when they have so many other responsibilities?" The reality is that those who would benefit most from the library's services are often also those that are most difficult to attract and serve.

Moreover, successfully reaching out to the community and organizing valuable social activities is one thing but demonstrating and legitimizing the value

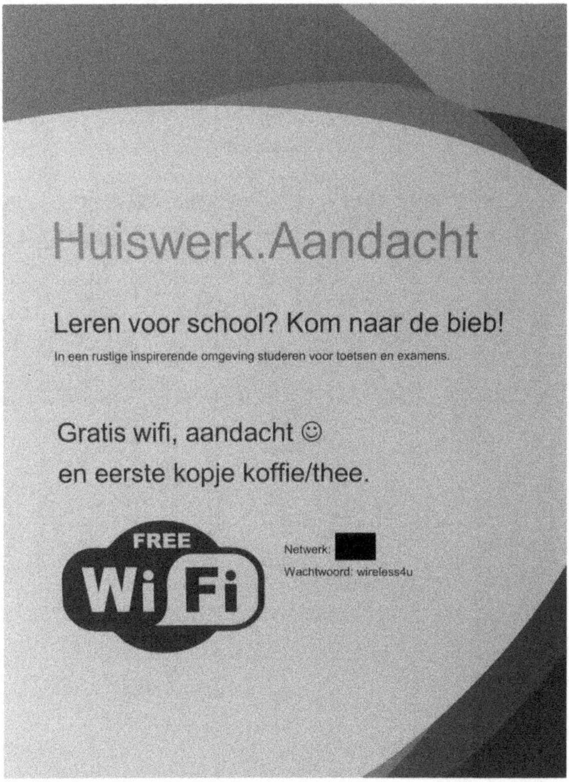

Figure 14.1 Offering more than a quiet place to study: poster in library announcing "Free WiFi, attention ☺ and a first cup of coffee/tea"

Source: Poster designed by Anne, photo by Rianne van Melik.

of these practices is another. Worldwide, public libraries are heavily reliant on government subsidies, forcing them "to demonstrate their value to the public to earn … financial and intellectual support" (Chen & Ke 2017: 45–6). Yet the impact that care provision and a sense of community can offer is certainly more difficult to quantify than membership or books borrowed. In the case study library, a guestbook circulated at the end of each lunch meeting to collect information on visitor experiences. Linda also developed an infographic in which she combines quotations from the guestbook with quantitative data to visualize the added value of this activity (Figure 14.2). Similarly, the library's Annual Report lists a diverse set of performance measures to show that the library is more than an information infrastructure only used by members, listing statistics on membership and item check-outs, but also the number of visitors and activities. Being a community librarian therefore entails the organization of all kinds of (social) activities, but also "social bookkeeping" (Van Melik & Merry 2021).

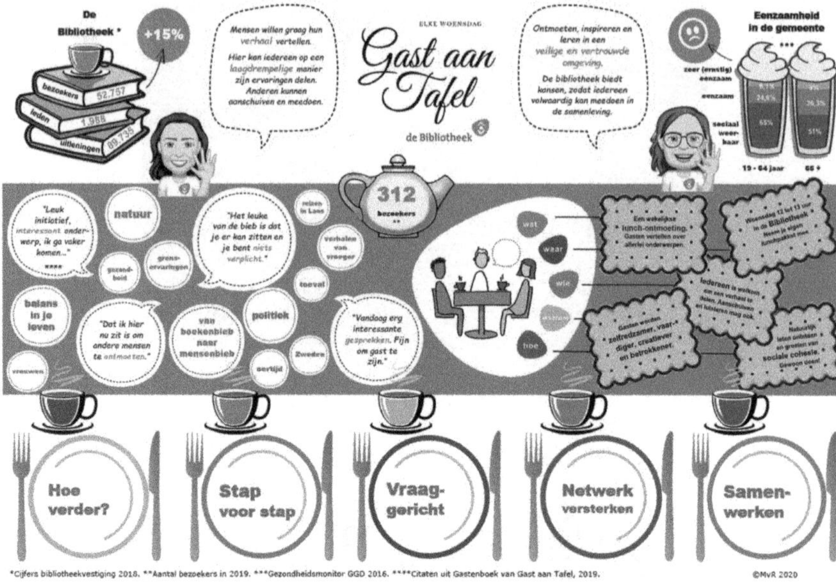

Figure 14.2 "Social bookkeeping": infographic for Guest at the Table (GATT)

Source: Designed by Linda.

CARING BY/FOR VOLUNTEERS

Worldwide, the role of the volunteer in the public library is viewed differently. In countries with strong trade unions like Canada, volunteer labour is often objected to and seen as a way to substitute skilled library workers with unpaid work (Forkert 2016). In the UK and Australia, there are examples of libraries that are completely run by volunteers (Williams 2018), often in response to austerity and budget cuts by local governments. Such volunteer-run libraries are rare in the Netherlands, but nevertheless the role of the volunteer is large. According to the Association of Public Libraries of the Netherlands, more than 22,600 people volunteered in Dutch libraries in 2021, a tripling compared to the number of active volunteers in 2011. One out of three library organizations depends on volunteer labour for more than 150 hours per week.

Volunteers also play an important role in the case study library. During opening hours, at least one paid staff member looks after the library, always supported by one or two volunteers. The pool of volunteers consists of 13 people, mostly older females, who contribute to the library's daily management, including shelving books and other materials, which allows the paid staff to focus on other tasks, including the organization of social activities. This support is also acknowledged in the Annual Report: "the volunteers are very important for our staff, because they [staff] can realise all the projects that we try to initiate. That would not be possible if you have to hire professionals!" Although this quotation could be interpreted as evidence that neoliberalizing pressures result in volunteers replacing qualified librarians, this is not the case in the studied library. Both the numbers of paid staff and volunteers have remained fairly constant over the past decades, showing that the volunteers have not recently replaced staff. Instead, volunteers alleviate some of the work pressures, enabling paid staff to focus on caring practices. Moreover, the volunteers are from the local community: they know the residents and neighbourhood issues.

In turn, the pool of volunteers is one of the most important communities the library supports. Volunteering is hardly ever purely altruistic; volunteers do not just give their time and skills, but also gain something in return such as interesting conversations (Williams 2018). For myself, the opportunity to meet new people and become part of the local community I just moved into was an important reason to sign up to volunteer. Moments of sociality are important for other volunteers as well. The library also provides volunteers with opportunities for individual empowerment (Norcup 2017) by developing skills and self-esteem. Volunteers, thus, provide but also receive care through their volunteering activities as librarians on staff continuously invest in recruiting, training and organizing fieldtrips and feedback sessions for the volunteers.

Of course, it is important not to romanticize the role of the volunteer and the importance of the volunteering community. Rimes *et al.* (2017) have explored the dynamics of volunteer and staff interactions and found that conflicts often arise due to communication problems, lack of trust, divergent expectations and perceptions of job vulnerability. Such tensions have not been observed or experienced in the case study library. It is arguably easier to work with volunteers in a relatively small, not too busy library branch in a homogenous spatial context, where tensions and austerity pressures are limited. Within the same library network, other larger libraries prefer to pay students to shelve books instead of using volunteers. This raises questions on the relationship between volunteering practices and their spatial context: where and when does volunteering enable the social functions of libraries, and under which conditions does it not?

CONCLUSION

This chapter has uncovered some of the "software" of public libraries by focusing on how their function as socio-cultural infrastructure comes into being through practices by library staff and volunteers. This narrativized practice-oriented perspective illustrates that the cultural infrastructure of public libraries is certainly not static but requires constant readjustment. Several librarizing practices were revealed, such as social bookkeeping, outreach to different communities and caring for/by volunteers. This collection of care is not exhaustive, nor does every staff member or volunteer carry out all of these practices. Instead, each librarian and volunteer brings together a unique assortment of expertise and (caring) practices.

Consequently, there is no fixed formula of what a socially engaged library is or should do. The act of librarizing should be considered inherently situated in specific urban geographies; circumscribed within the context in which it takes place and entangled with a diverse array of elements including the library's "hardware" (design, collection), institutions and policies, as well as the minds and bodies of those who carry the practices themselves. A successful practice such as organizing lunch meetings or building a loyal team of volunteers might work in certain (spatial, financial and regional) contexts, but not in others. Similarly, a successful practice in the past can fail in the future or during a pandemic.

Hence, librarizing consists of a constantly evolving set of practices and the library as socio-cultural infrastructure is very dependent on context. This chapter has only investigated one single library and its contingent, place-specific version of a socio-cultural infrastructure. The found practices are not only place-specific, but also based on who is performing the labour. But perhaps more important than staff composition or expertise, the success of librarizing practices seems to be the freedom librarians and their volunteers receive to arrange whatever (low-cost) activity they see fit in their library, despite being part of a bigger library network. With their enthusiasm and energy, they embody what Barniskis (2016: 118–19) calls "a sense of diving in" and a culture of "trying things out" which she finds to be more common among librarians without lengthy careers in library administration. New library practices are being developed on the spot. They are tested, amended and sometimes stopped again. Librarizing is never finished.

Therefore, librarizing public libraries does not come with a fixed toolbox of practices that can be performed anywhere by anyone. Ignatow (2011) already described how the provision of public library services is highly unequal, both within and between countries. Such variation is inevitable and not necessarily negative, as libraries are embedded in very different social and spatial fabrics, requiring place-specific activities and collaborations with particular local stakeholders (e.g., social workers). However, if the role of public libraries as important socio-cultural infrastructure is to be taken seriously, the dedication and creativity performed by community librarians and volunteers needs to be matched with at least minimum levels of funds and training.

CHAPTER 15

QUEER COUNTER-TOPOGRAPHIES: LGBTQ+ COMMUNITY-BASED ARCHIVES AS URBAN CULTURAL INFRASTRUCTURE

Julie A. Podmore

INTRODUCTION

An archive is understood to be a repository of historical artefacts, a place to which objects, images and documents from the past are consigned in anticipation of the collective will to remember (Appadurai 2003). In contrast with modernist state archives (the Archive), community-based archives are collections of materials that originate from, are collected by, and preserved for a "grassroots" community of interest to document and maintain control over community heritage (Caswell 2014). Since the rise of the LGBTQ+ social movement in urban North American and Europe in the 1960s, activists have been generating and collecting the materials that provide the basis for their own community-based counter-archives (Sheffield 2020). LGBTQ+ community-based archives are sites where "evidence of non-normative sexualities and gender non-conformity has been preserved", repositories of queer knowledge that can potentially challenge "heteronormative and homocentric ways of being and knowing" (Sheffield 2020: 11). Such "activist archives" provide an infrastructure to "forge new relationships between parallel histories, reshape and reinterpret dominant narratives, and challenge conceptions of the archive itself" (Sellie *et al.* 2015: 454). Binding together material, digital and imagined spaces, these sites of "memory-in-action" provide community support networks, capacity building and skill-sharing both through their references to the past and practices in the present (Sizemore-Barber 2017: 127).

This chapter reflects on such sites of "memory-in-action" as urban cultural infrastructure. While LGBTQ+ community-based archival collections are geographically variable, due to the historic metropolitan materialities of their communities, their informational and physical infrastructure is primarily urban. Unlike the "hard", large, official and durable urban infrastructure that underpins modernity and materially manifests biopolitical social norms (Gandy 2011), the infrastructure of LGBTQ+ community-based counter-archiving is oppositional, relational and place-based having been co-constructed and maintained through soft networks of people (Amin 2014). As social movement archives, their collections – or information infrastructure (McKinney 2020) – provide some of the only documentation of the queer "city-as-archive" (Rao 2009). Thus, they are intimately bound to the project of tracing local "queer infrastructure" described by Campkin (2021: 82) as the "dispersed, interconnected, heterogeneous" LGBTQ+ urban community spaces that traverse time through memory and stretch across metropolitan areas. Like the city-as-archive, archival counter-mapping projects that seek to recuperate urban queer infrastructure disrupt normative processes of urbanization by contesting erasure and bolstering claims to a lost urban heritage by mapping past spaces to interrupt the present and open-up alternative urban futures (Hetherington 2013). Through historical counter-mapping projects that link documents, memories and urban spaces, LGBTQ+ archival activism undermines heteronormative urbanization processes by reconnecting the disparate sites of queer infrastructure that create new spaces for hope and action (Katz 2004).

The chapter begins with a critical examination of the infrastructural temporality of the public archive, demonstrating how its instituting imaginaries – chronormativity and queer erasure – can be undone by reconsidering the city-as-archive. Drawing on examples from queer urban archival movements globally, it then explores the asynchronous infrastructure and infrapolitics of LGBTQ+ community-based archives as counter-topographical sites of action. The chapter then describes the relationship between Montreal's queer urban and LGBTQ+ archival infrastructure and details two archival counter-mapping exhibition projects that provided alternate outreach strategies during the Covid-19 pandemic. It concludes by reflecting on the potential of LGBTQ+ community-based archives to imagine alternate queer urban futures.

INSTITUTING IMAGINARIES: THE INFRASTRUCTURAL TEMPORALITY OF THE PUBLIC ARCHIVE

Like libraries and museums, public archives provide an official infrastructure for collective memories by setting aside fragmentary artefacts and incorporating them into a single corpus through identification, selection and classification (Derrida 1996). From this privileged location, the archive's selective and often accidental traces are at once domesticated by its "archontic unity" and then instrumentalized as they shift from private fragments into public goods (Derrida 1996: 10). For Foucault (1966), state archives give these public goods the "order" necessary to augment its biopolitical function: as "repositories for selective national memories", archival narratives reproduce hegemonic societal norms, silences and violent erasures. Embedded in this infrastructural order are antiquated and hierarchical notions about which pasts count, producing "systemic erasures" that result in what Caswell *et al.* (2016: 5) call "symbolic annihilation" since a lack of archival materials limits which pasts can be reconstructed and whose histories can be represented. But the Archive is more than "an authoritarian ivory tower relic" or an "oppressive document space" (Sizemore-Barber 2017: 118). For Appadurai (2003: 16), national archives are "accessories in the state's policing, surveillance and governmentality" because they preserve the case study documentation that pathologizes society's "others" in police, prison and public health records, reinforcing the regulation of non-normative bodies while evacuating their subjectivities. As history's informational infrastructure, the public archive underpins its contested truths by enabling authoritative claims that are "based upon a unique access to, and interpretation of, primary traces and evidence" while deeming other traces "unworthy, insignificant, or unimportant to the dominant normative narrative being constructed" (Burgum 2020: 507).

By providing the documentary infrastructure for authoritative historical narratives, the public archive also upholds heteronormative temporalities, a chronopolitics that, as Freeman (2010) argues, reflects and reinforces the timelines and benchmarks that give order to heterosexual reproductive life. Such "chrononormativity" – the use of time to "organize individual human bodies toward maximum productivity" – gives order to "historically specific regimes of asymmetrical power" which change "the value and meaning of time" by binding it to norms that alter "seemingly ordinary bodily tempos and routines" (Freeman 2010: 3). Chrononormativity has the power to disorder colonized societies or induce labour to the rhythms of capitalism, but also to discipline queer bodies for being out-of-step with the temporality of heterosexual reproduction. As Halberstam (2003: 313) has argued, queer "uses of time and space develop in opposition to the institutions of family, heterosexuality, and reproduction, and queer subcultures develop as alternatives to kinship-based notions of community". Queer subjectivities, affects, traumas and energies are traced through the alternative, subcultural temporalities of queer creative practices that permit "their participants to believe that their futures can be imagined according to logics that lie outside of the conventional forward-moving narratives of birth, marriage, reproduction, and death" (Halberstam 2003: 313). Asynchronous with chrononormativity, the transient archival traces that queer subcultures generate are what in the hierarchy of record types is considered ephemera

(Muñoz 1996) – archival materials that were created for short-term use (e.g., ticket stubs, flyers, brochures, stickers, banners, theatre programmes, matchbooks or posters) but have nevertheless been preserved for the longer term – a category of documents that are often considered by traditional archivists as "unclassifiable objects" (Kumbier 2014). If, as Muñoz (1996) argues, it is the circulation of these objects through and across historical time that reveals queer world-making, their second lives become an impossibility when they are discarded from the public record.

Beyond upholding chronormativity by valorizing "more substantive" records, the public archive's hierarchical information infrastructure reinforces the authority of knowledge through its built infrastructure (Burgum 2020). Knowledge produced using the Archive's primary source materials as evidence derive authority from the melding of fragmentary traces with the hard infrastructure of buildings. State archives accumulate authority through the fusion of "colonial era architecture and documentation practices with post-colonial desires and agendas" (Sizemore-Barber 2017: 118). As Mbembe (2002: 19) argues, the built and informational components of the Archive's infrastructure are therefore mutually constitutive:

> The archive has neither status nor power without an architectural dimension, which encompasses the physical space of the site of the building, its motifs and columns, the arrangement of the rooms, the organisation of the "files", the labyrinth of corridors, and that degree of discipline, half-light and austerity that gives the place something of the nature of a temple and a cemetery.

Akin to a religious space where relics are stored and tombs enshrined, the authoritative power of the public archive lies in both the monumentality of its building and the authentic, protected, tangibility of the material records that it preserves. Those who have a stake in maintaining the archive as a coherent relic view it as a talisman of posterity and embrace its "instituting imaginary" while subaltern and subcultural critics interrogate its coherence by reading its fragmentary traces for disconnections and silences (Mbembe 2002: 19). Undermining this infrastructure by reassembling its fragments and reimagining stories in its silences, the Archive can move from a "tomb of the accidental trace" or a site of dead recollections to a place of aspiration (Appadurai 2003: 17).

One means of deinstituting archival imaginaries is to move them elsewhere, whether by creating alternative archives or reconsidering objects, bodies, performances, representations as well as spaces, buildings or cities, as archives in and of themselves. In their analysis of the infrastructure of

Australia's Wangi Power Station as archive, Chapman and Matthews (2021) argue that an archive is both an epistemological and an architectural enterprise because knowledge of the past is inherently linked to the spatiality of its presentation. The built infrastructure and urban centrality of municipal libraries in the United Kingdom are an archive of the attempt to "modernize" or "urbanize" the public by offering a site exemplifying civic identity and inculcating proper civic behaviour (Burgum 2020). With its architectural order of cells, yards, blocks, showers and walls, the prison is an archive of the gender binary judicial system and the carceral violence experienced by incarcerated trans bodies (Sanders *et al.* 2022). In the absence that it creates, the demolition of Johannesburg's Ponte City residential high-rise becomes a melancholy archive of a trashed apartheid city (Charlton 2020). And cities may themselves be viewed as archives of the lived experiences and materialities that shape and are shaped by their spatial organization (Sheringham 2010). From the most ordinary building to the overall street layout or the specific set of place names, the city is a palimpsest of fragmentary traces embedded in the built environment that resonate in the present (Hetherington 2013).

The "city-as-archive" has become a method for interrogating the reification of urban spatial constructs and its reinforcement through the erasures of the Archive's instituting imaginary. The fragmentary narratives of built urban infrastructure, undone by the passing of time and invaded by disorderly everyday processes, reveal counter-narratives that unravel more authoritative imaginings. Echoing Simone's (2004) "people as infrastructure", Rao (2009) adopts the "city-as-archive" as a tool to undermine the city's authority over its own territory by refocusing on the contestations, aspirations and possibilities generated by people through their everyday practices. Such an agentic view is also central to more performative interpretations of the city-as-archive where discarded objects offer material traces of social practices or evidence of ephemeral events documented through media after-images of contests over the meaning of urban spaces that are later brought into the present through exhibitions (Charlton 2020), creative performances (Beswick *et al.* 2016), or walking tours (Burgum 2020). Instead of a quilt or a palimpsest, the city-as-archive can be a methodological intervention for "navigating the voids of the present" and reading "the urban fabrics created by these voids" by drawing on living memories of urban experiences (Rao 2009: 381). Thus, the city-as-archive queerly capitulates to the impossibility of "accurate" and authoritative representations of the past while emphasizing the asynchronous and ephemeral living memory of subcultural urban experiences that can potentially refashion urban futures.

QUEER ASYNCRONICITIES: THE URBAN INFRAPOLITICS OF LGBTQ+ COMMUNITY-BASED ARCHIVES

To counter the instituting imaginary of the archive, social groups create their own community-based archives where they collect and store materials that are rarely retained anywhere else. This category includes a wide range of independent archives with community identifications based on "locality, ethnicity, faith, sexuality, occupation, shared interest or a combination of one or more of these" (Flinn 2007: 153). It includes very disparate types of "communities" ranging in political intensity from more nostalgic leisure-based documentation of local histories to the more politically charged gathering and preservation of knowledge by and for historically marginalized groups (Caswell 2014). Community-based archives are collections created and maintained by minority ethnic communities, political movements, workers' or heritage groups and their content may include "collections of material objects, paper and digital records, audio-visual materials and personal testimonies" (Flinn 2007: 153). What distinguishes them from private and state archives is that they are "created and held by the community" for whom "control and ownership of the project is essential" as part of a broader social movement for justice (Flinn 2007: 153). Like those maintained by other marginalized groups, LGBTQ+ community-based archives are more than just repositories of collective memories: they play affective and social roles within their communities with their politics and practices often crossing over into activism.

Community archives are, therefore, important venues of activist labour to promote "community empowerment and broader social change" through "public history-making processes" (Cifor *et al.* 2018: 69). Posing a challenge to established archives through their collections and outreach, the archival activism of marginalized cultures brings communities together around their histories, collecting and preserving records that affirm their existence, and promoting community empowerment by enacting "a form of memory justice for those who would otherwise be forgotten" (Caswell *et al.* 2016: 11). Such quiet labour is unlike the more public demonstrations and occupations associated with social movement activism; it is more "infrapolitical" in the sense that it involves a set of unobtrusive practices of resistance "that are not quite political enough to be perceived as such" (Marche 2012: 3). Many such community-based archives – London's Black Cultural Archives, Eastside Community Heritage or Moroccan Memories archives (Flinn 2007) – function as empowerment tools that contribute to the social reproduction of a pre-existing community by creating a free space to build cohesion (Sellie *et al.* 2015). Others, such as Brooklyn's Interference Archive (a collection of local ephemera from art, activist, punk and DIY cultures) are transmovement archives that strive to forge connections between communities by creating networks of solidarity through the archival process (Sellie *et al.* 2015). Community-based archives, therefore, serve a dual infrastructural function: they are scenes of infrapolitical practices to combat societal erasure through the preservation of alternate histories; and they are themselves an infrastructure that facilitates community empowerment, solidarity, identity and posterity.

LGBTQ+ community-based archival activism depends on and is shaped by the materiality of cultural infrastructure in multiple ways. Most North American LGBTQ+ community-based archives (from the Los Angeles' One Archives, to the Brooklyn-based Lesbian Herstory Archives to Vancouver's BC Gay and Lesbian Archives or Montreal's Archives gaies du Québec) began as the "empowerment archives" of pre-existing communities. Their impetus was to collect and protect cultural materials generated by mid-twentieth-century homophile, gay liberation and rights and autonomous lesbian and trans movements that were unwanted by government, university and public archives at the time (Sheffield 2020). These materials and their management constitute a form of "informational infrastructure" that while full of content, is also contingent upon classification systems and the technologies used to "parse large amounts of information that would make marginal lives visible" (McKinney 2020: 3). The storage and processing of this informational infrastructure is also deeply implicated in access to material urban spaces and queer infrastructure. While some autonomous LGBTQ+ community-based archives maintain their own premises in houses or rented office spaces, many remain contained within spatially challenged LGBTQ+ organization spaces and community centres in gentrifying inner-city areas. Others have been donated to municipal archives and university collections involving many risks as they are taken out of the community and placed in the public institutional realm. Still others straddle a semi-public location, kept in homes but having a virtual presence on the internet and digital platforms.

Public accessibility and community visibility is therefore a question of available urban and cultural infrastructure. Most LGBTQ+ community-based archives were originally the collections of a few people and were retained in the domestic infrastructure of their homes. The informal infrastructure of such semi-public, home-based forms of LGBTQ+ archival activism queerly challenged "the divide between personal and institutional archives" while simultaneously creating issues of archival access, visibility and sustainability (Cooper 2016: 261). The Lesbian Herstory Archives and the Arquives: Canada's LGBTQ2+ Archives in Toronto maintained autonomy and acquired their own semi-public premises within the domestic infrastructure of historic inner-city neighbourhoods. The material amassed by the Lesbian Herstory Archives in the 1970s first found a home in the Manhattan apartment of activists Joan Nestle and Deborah Edel, but through a fundraising campaign, a house was purchased in Brooklyn to permanently house this archive in 1992 (Nestle 2015).

Tasked with the challenge of transmovement work across the LGBTQ+ acronym and its generations, LGBTQ+ community-based archives must maintain their collections, physical spaces and digital presence while upholding public visibility and community relevance. Archives lacking in space find it challenging to work on existing collections, accept new materials and support research. Archives lacking community infrastructure have few volunteers and struggle with organizational renewal leading to invisibility and irrelevance and, ultimately to questions of community utility. Sizemore-Barber (2017: 117) describes how Johannesburg's GALA (Gay and Lesbian Memory in Action), the only queer community archive on the African continent, combats (in)visibility and (ir)relevance by taking "on a number of roles unusual for an archive, becoming a community center, art therapy facilitator, and publisher". Here, the archive has an activist relationship with outreach that only starts with archiving, proceeding to research and action, that can take the form of workshops with LGBTQI youth in schools, running the Queer Jo'burg Walking Tour, or organizing Art for Activism workshops in neighbouring countries where sexuality is heavily policed. By embracing the interplay between the stability of the archive as a collection and its action-based repertoire GALA "restructures our understanding of what an archive can be and should do, as well as its relationship to history, memory, and political movements" (Sizemore-Barber 2017: 117).

Like many community-based archives, GALA has adopted counter-mapping projects as a central tool for increasing archival visibility. Through exhibitions, walking tours and counter-mapping workshops these interventions re-enact the city-as-queer-archive by using memories of past spaces to reanimate the voids of the present brought by urban processes such as gentrification and displacement. As Sizemore-Barber (2017: 123) argues, queer counter-mapping undermines chrononormativities that privilege "certain genealogies, chronologies, narratives, and bodies" by rescripting past spaces in present voices. Such projects can be powerful tools of empowerment because they recuperate the "lost" LGBTQ+ spaces that testify to their existence (Ketchum 2020). Like the media's "scène du visible", counter-mapping projects are tools for transgressing social invisibility in the city's archive and material landscape where historic queer places are rendered and their community claims to space become visible, sayable and hearable (Pidduck 2020). By reconnecting the disconnected nodes of queer urban infrastructure, they potentially offer urban counter-topographies that denaturalize "that which appears given" and exposes "the enormous work involved in making the world of appearances seem permanent and natural" (Katz 2004: 257). By drawing lines between the "fragmented and fleeting" queer urban spatial experiences, queer counter-mapping produces sets of "overlapping, embodied paths and stories" forming "constellations" that bind queer memories across generations and differences in space (Gieseking 2020: 941).

LGBTQ+ COUNTER-TOPOGRAPHIES: REMAPPING MONTREAL'S QUEER URBAN INFRASTRUCTURE

Montreal is a city with a long history of LGBTQ+ activism and a dense and historic queer infrastructure built through the latter half of the twentieth century in its downtown and eastern inner-city neighbourhoods (Podmore 2006). While defined as regional, its LGBTQ+ archival communities primarily collect and preserve the memories of queer lives lived within Québec's largest metropolis. Two community-based archives lie at its centre, the Archives gaies du Québec (AGQ) and the Archives lesbiennes du Québec (ALQ), both founded in 1983 to retain the records of lesbian and gay activism of the 1970s. The AGQ was founded to preserve "ephemera" (initially the records of activist organizations and independent bookstores, physique photography and AIDS posters) unavailable in state archives (Higgins 2018) and to ensure its availability locally after the Toronto archival movement requested its donation to their Canadian "national" archives (Prince 2009). Paralleling the city's gay village where it rents office space, today the AGQ has become a transmovement archive supported by more than 500 member-donors that has gay history at its heart but strives to represent and forge connections between all LGBTQ+ communities. The ALQ, in contrast, was originally part of a vibrant, autonomous lesbian arts and community centre, but it became inaccessible after the centre closed in 1994 and remained so even after 2001 when it was deemed "for lesbians only" and deposited in a small office space in the city's LGBTQ+ Community Centre (CCLGBTQ+). It was not until 2016 that a new collective with a mission to "acquire, process, preserve and disseminate" materials "relating to lesbianism, lesbians, gay and queer-identified women and homosexuality in general" relaunched the ALQ and began seeking a community to support its archival activism (ALQ 2022). Today, it operates from an office at CCLGBTQ+ and is supported by grants rather than member donations. Like the city's disappeared "golden age" of lesbian urban infrastructure of the 1980s and 1990s (Podmore 2006), the ALQ is primarily a lesbian empowerment archive of a bygone era that struggles with its own anachronism as it reanimates its collections and builds space to create cohesion across the generations.

During the lockdowns for the Covid-19 pandemic in 2020, both archives were asked by the city's pride organization and national library to create virtual exhibitions to help overcome the loss of visibility and community created by social distancing, the shuttering of community spaces and cancelling of annual celebratory events and activism. The loss of commercial infrastructure with the closing of gay villages and other LGBTQ+ spaces, the temporary digitization of LGBTQ+ mutual aid and social service agencies, and confinement to unsupportive domestic environments unevenly impacted the health and well-being of many LGBTQ+ populations resulting in social isolation, economic instability and forced re-closeting, especially for youth and elders and transgender and gender diverse communities (Miles *et al.* 2021). During the pandemic, collecting information about and remapping shifting LGBTQ+ resource landscapes in accessible digital formats became a key method to address the lack of queer infrastructure (Sevelius *et al.* 2020). For LGBTQ+ archival activists, archival counter-mapping seemed intuitively like an ideal tool for outreach at a time of re-closeting and confinement. Since both archives now had their own websites, were in the process of digitizing their materials and more geolocation tools were now available, a project that focused on remapping Montreal's queer urban infrastructure would be an opportunity to increase archival visibility and renew community relevance.

Creating an archival counter-mapping project requires the consideration of the type of platform, the participants and the types of media to be included. Crowdsourced, geolocated projects like Gregor Mattson's (2016) "Mapping lost lesbian bars, 2006–2016" or Lucas LaRochelle's (2017) "Queering the map" constitute their own archive, generated by individuals who mark meaningful places on a digital online platform with personal memories. By directly locating individual queer moments anywhere from park benches and street corners to schools and libraries to hotels and trains, "Queering the map" supplants the hierarchical infrastructure of the LGBTQ+ community-based archives by valuing all entries and extending queer memory everywhere on the world map. Such projects are more participatory and recuperative, but they are highly individualized and lack temporality. In contrast, historical counter-mapping projects that focus on "documenting the location of more formalized geographies with fixed dates does something different" (Ketchum 2020, para. 8). The collective archival mapping of queer infrastructure (i.e., bars, bathhouses, bookstores, cruising grounds or cultural spaces), has a more reparative function because it provides "a sense of space, situated in specific historical moments, which future generations can situate themselves in relation to and build upon" (Ketchum 2020, para. 8).

The ALQ took this opportunity to create a map of "historic lesbian places" (ALQ 2020) by using the online archival mapping tool Historypin.org (Historypin 2010–20). Historypin is a tool for digital storytelling that provides an interface between geocoded locations and digitized archival materials. It is intended to "bring people together around local history" by "bringing their resources to life" (Historypin 2010–20). "Lieux lesbiens à Montréal (Montreal Lesbian Places)" was an opportunity to relaunch the archives after a period of dormancy and rebuild an archival community by starting a conversation about the archive through the exhibition of its analogue materials. A team of three archivists selected 10 initial sites that were seen as foundational to Montreal's late twentieth-century lesbian movement describing them as "significant places in Montreal lesbian history". The collection included bookstores, bars and community spaces as well as more ephemeral events such as demonstrations, picnics and dances that took place between 1972 and 1998, each of which was geolocated and situated in time and space. The collection can be navigated through space by clicking on pins or as a tour over time by moving the timeline. Each "pin" juxtaposed past and present using archival images, descriptions and in some cases contemporary images of the building sites. Figure 15.1, for example, geolocates Bar Lilith (1983–92), but it also includes a written description, an advertisement scanned from a periodical from the ALQ's collection, and a contemporary photograph of its entrance on St-Denis Street, once the heart of one of the city's most fashionable shopping districts. Periodicals from the ALQ's collection were used to locate the bar within Montreal's urban infrastructure and provide context

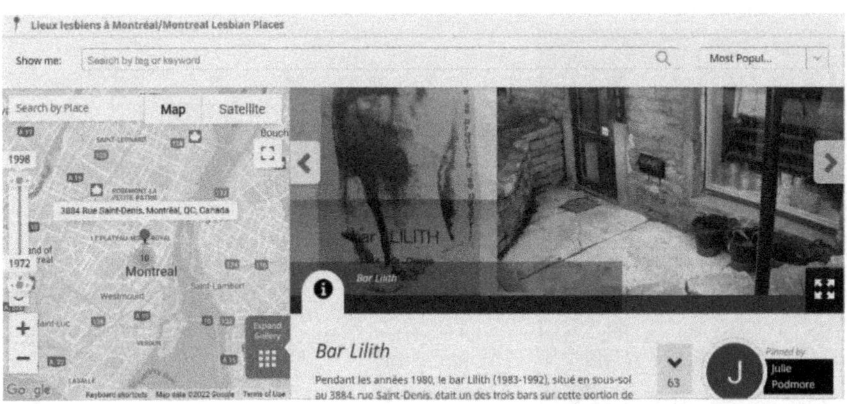

Figure 15.1 Montreal lesbian places on Historypin: sponsored by Les Archives lesbiennes du Québec, curated by Laure Neuville and Julie Podmore with added material by Julianne Pidduck

Source: Historypin.org (www.historypin.org/en/lieux-lesbiens-a-montreal-montreal-lesbian-pl/geo/45.501689,-73.567256,11).

for the description (an interview with the owner was published in 1991). Since there are no photographs of this space available in the archives, an image of the current site embeds the collective memory of this space in palimpsest of Montreal's urban landscape. The digital infrastructure provided by the Historypin platform not only makes Bar Lilith visible once again; it also supports an intervention into the city-as-archive by bringing together ephemera from multiple time-periods to document the temporary use of this fragment of the city's urban cultural infrastructure for lesbian communality and solidarity.

The AGQ's project, "Walls have Ears: The Stories of Montreal's LGBTQ2S+ Spaces" (Figure 15.2), operated at a different scale and was exhibited both within the city's urban infrastructure and more relationally on the archives' own website. The outdoor exhibit was developed as a pilot project supported by Victor Samoylenko's student internship and drew on primary source materials from archives, archival networks to people for oral history interviews, and historical LGBTQ+ secondary source materials to map the historic districts of queer life. It sought "to not only put the diverse experiences of LGBTQ2S+ people on a map, but also to render them audible and combine different types of media" (AGQ 2021: n.p.). It used seven oral histories and secondary sources to create an "atlas-like" collection of past and present LGBTQ+ spaces, with one map outlining this queer infrastructure across the central area over the past 70 years and panels that zoomed in on specific areas (such as the city's red-light district) that asynchronously juxtaposed past and present spaces within one district. A complementary

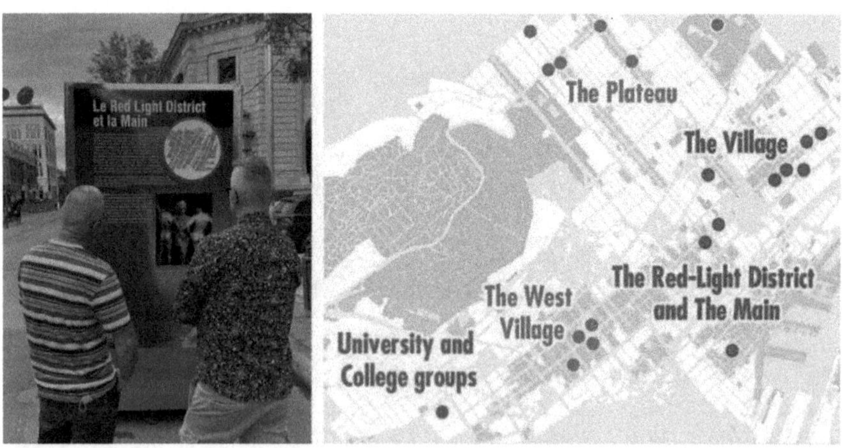

Figure 15.2 "Walls Have Ears: The Stories of Montreal's LGBTQ2S+ Spaces": curated by Victor Samoylenko with added material by Marion Daigle

Source: Archives gaies du Québec (http://agq.qc.ca/en/wallshaveears/); photo by Jonathan Proulx Guimond.

exhibition was later mounted on the organization's website (AGQ 2021) that combined the maps with archival materials (photographs, newspaper clippings, hand-drawn maps, advertisements and posters), audio recordings and descriptive text. By bringing archival materials into the physical space of a gay village experiencing decline and desolation during pandemic lockdowns, the project reanimated emerging voids in the city's queer infrastructure. By organizing the exhibit around portraits of different districts within the city's queer infrastructure, the project reconnected previously dispersed, fragmentary and fleeting venues, reconfiguring the "constellations" that bind queer memories across generations and differences to create counter-topographies for hope and action.

CONCLUSION

The objective of this chapter was to investigate the relationship between archives and urban cultural infrastructure through their convergence in the city-as-archive concept. Paralleling arguments about the political power of mapping queer infrastructure to transform urban policy by making visible the network of venues and actors who connect them (Campkin 2021), it pointed to the vital role of LGBTQ+ community-based archives in providing the resources for such projects, especially in this era of community displacement from central city areas. It began by demonstrating the extent to which the authority of the public Archive is infrastructural since it depends on the melding of its own temporal order with its urban built infrastructure to assign authority to chrononormative histories in which queers are relegated to the realm of the ephemeral and deviant, or are erased. By moving outside of the Archive's walls and interpreting the city itself as an archive of ordinary, everyday life, the city's parallel chrononormative social order is further exposed (Rao 2009).

LGBTQ+ community-based archives sit in this asynchronous place, built through a quiet infrapolitics of collecting and preserving the rejected ephemera that provides evidence of their social movements, collective memories and urban heritage. To retain these memories, archival activists have struggled to maintain empowering community spaces where they can store, catalogue, collect and share these materials. Many have experienced displacement and dormancy when relegated to private and inaccessible sites due to constrained entry into commercial land markets and a lack of available space in LGBTQ+ community sites. Efforts to preserve their rare documents, maintain their information infrastructure and ensure their relevance as a community resource requires dedicated archival activism but also queer infrastructure in terms of physical spaces, community visibility and digital worlds. Archival counter-mapping projects that bring the archives back into the city – physically and digitally – offer important opportunities to demonstrate this relevance, especially during the lack of access to queer infrastructure during the recent Covid-19 pandemic. By reconnecting the nodes of past queer urban infrastructure, queer counter-topographies such as these interrupt the chrononormativities present in urban cultural infrastructure, bringing with them hope for different queer urban futures.

CHAPTER 16

CONCLUSION: RECONFIGURING URBAN CULTURAL INFRASTRUCTURE

Alison L. Bain, Julie A. Podmore and Chan Arun-Pina

INTRODUCTION

Infrastructure is definitive of cities, intimately embedded in their constant change – their expansion and densification, their sprawl and contraction, their construction and decline (Melosi 2020). In addition to reconfiguring energy, water, sewage, solid waste, transportation and communication systems to persistently address complex societal issues (e.g., climate crisis, environmental pollution, deepening inequalities and exclusions, economic decline and privatization) and reshaping urban futures, infrastructure is also cultural. Over a decade of interdisciplinary scholarship has investigated the centrality of urban infrastructure to the transformation of cities demonstrating how "direct user involvement" in its malleable networks (Furlong 2010: 47) actively shape the extent to which residents can participate in urban life (Baumann & Yacobi 2022). Despite offering technology- and actor-focused explanations of infrastructural capacities and entanglements (Rutherford 2020; Rutherford & Coutard 2014; Silver 2014b), such research has largely neglected the cultural sector. Even as more recent scholarship attends to the palimpsest of socio-technical layers that rhythmically persist across time and space within systems (Monstadt 2022) – the "heterogenous configurations" of "different coverage, technologies, operations, logics and ownerships" (Lawhon *et al.* 2018: 723) that reinforce the *longue durée* of infrastructure choices (Moss 2020) – culture remains underexamined.

By focusing on the cultural infrastructure that supports practices of producing, performing, consuming and collecting culture, this book affirms the centrality of culture to the imagination, mediation and constitution of cities in the present and into the future. It has illustrated how cultural infrastructure is multi-faceted and relationally embedded in different material and socio-economic structures and social practices that undergird cities and city-making around the world. As cultural institution and artefact, this infrastructure might appear inert and fixed within local geographies and histories, but it is in the often-uncomfortable tension between obduracy and change where artistic and prosaic cultural practices unfold, creating urban imaginaries of living otherwise. Following Escobar (1992), embodied practices and imaginaries of living otherwise produce alternate political practices leading to forms of cultural innovation that chart different infrastructural futures. Subaltern and countercultural politics and practices of difference emerge in cities everywhere whether from their spatial, economic, cultural or sexual margins. As Giuseppe Campuzano's poster mounted outside Jean Nouvel's starchitectural extension to the Reina Sofia Art Centre in Madrid succinctly states: "Queer futures are being shaped every time we create imaginaries of living otherwise" (Figure 16.1). Even spectacular and state-funded institutional cultural infrastructure has a role to play, then, in reimaging, representing and reconfiguring urban futures by offering a central and authoritative site for public dialogue about what it is to live differently in cities.

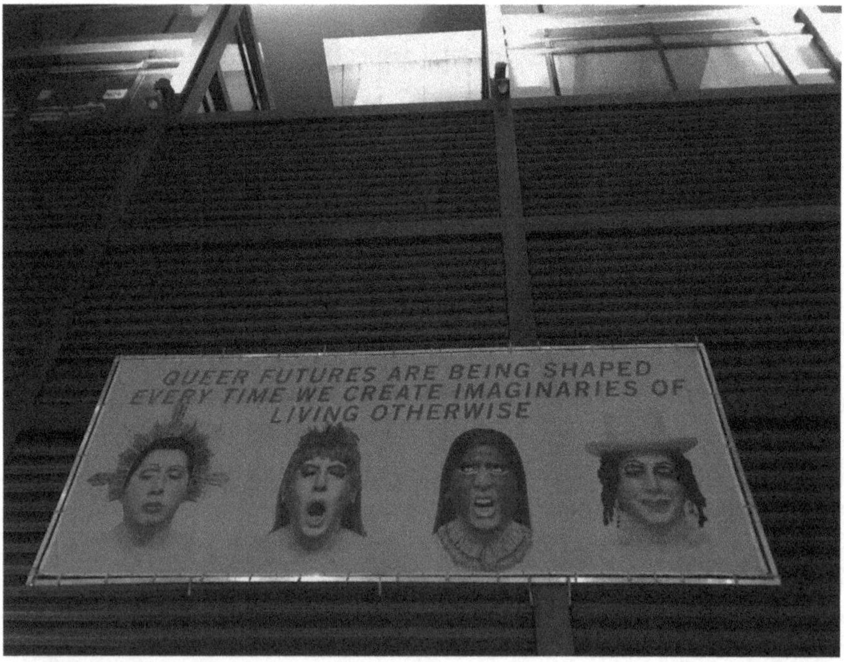

Figure 16.1 Representation of "Queer futures ... of living otherwise" by Giuseppe Campuzano and Miguel Ángel López (2014) outside the Reina Sofia Art Centre in Madrid, Spain

Source: Alison L. Bain.

URBAN FUTURES OF CULTURAL INFRASTRUCTURE

In this collection, urban futures of cultural infrastructure are imagined through four specific dimensions: production, performance, consumption and collection. Each thematic section opens with an artistic representation of its respective facet of urban cultural infrastructure, serving as a representation of urban futurity based in the experience of difference and alternate imaginaries. The Canadian-based and Indian-born architect, visual artist and geographer, Chan Arun-Pina, describes the process of developing the original artwork for the collection, entitled *Reconfiguring urban cultural infrastructure: a polyptych in flux* (2022) (Figure 16.2):

> Across the book's polyptych, each of the four sections opens with a representation of infrastructure in flux. Conceptualized as a cyclical progression, the cover images engage latent urban algorithms that aspire to unlock the potentialities of spaces within spaces, cultural worlds within cultural worlds, and new pathways within entrenched pathways. These algorithms connect bodies to urban cultural infrastructure through a sense of mutual inhabitation, their latency signalling the pieces of cities that we (once) live(d) in that are still living inside of each of us. This commissioned artwork represents traces of infrastructural transformation over time wherein cultural infrastructure fluctuates between (in)complete realization and (ir)retrievable loss. As a continuum, my polyptych is inspired by and works in tandem with the structure of this edited collection that considers the concept of "infrastructuring" as an ongoing urban-social process of producing, performing, consuming and collecting cultures.

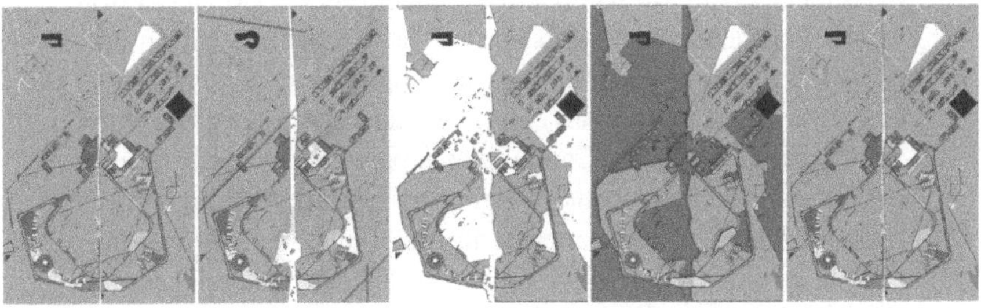

Figure 16.2 *Reconfiguring urban cultural infrastructure: a polyptych in flux* (2022): from producing to performing to consuming to collecting to (re)producing culture

Source: Original digital artwork by Chan Arun-Pina, 2022.

I chose semi-realism as the genre to express these ideas, rendering the scene only partially comprehensible while conveying a sense of scale and institutional setting. The plan view that is deployed draws from and is deeply embedded in real-world urban spaces and cultural infrastructure. The base drawing, however, is not a specific library or a museum building; rather, it is derived from pieces of libraries, museums, art galleries, and other cultural institutions that I may have inhabited. It is a composite of the institutional spaces from my life as a queer trans person of colour with roots in Indian cities, excursions into Southeast Asia, and residence in Toronto who has studied architecture and urban form from around the world. The fragments from my shifting memory that are integrated into this composite drawing include: an octagonal, high-ceilinged reading space with a full-length glass window meeting the dome above, that overlooked the pond area from the library of my school in Rajkot, Gujarat; a free-floating wall with eccentric geometry inclined at sharp angles to create an engaging dark exhibition space at a design institute in Ahmedabad; an outdoor plaza that offers a semi-informal extension to institutional spaces exemplified by the designs of starchitects Renzo Piano (Centre Pompidou, Paris), Daniel Libeskind (Jewish Museum, Berlin) and Maya Lin (Vietnam Veterans Memorial, Washington, DC) that I studied as an architecture student. The Centre Pompidou is the archetype of inside-out spatial design in which the interior infrastructure becomes the building's exterior, while the Jewish Museum exemplifies designing voids and empty spaces, and the Vietnam Veterans Memorial is grounded in a freestanding wall that juxtaposes present and past through memory and reflection.

The polyptych's amalgamated and seemingly static technical base layer is activated across the sections in a series of shifts that dynamically respond to imaginary encounters between cultural infrastructure and the events and publics that animate it. In Part I, the image sets the scene for Producing Culture. Several differently-sized and interlinked clusters of spaces merge around the institutional base layer. Concurrently, part of the "hard" ground of the semi-real institution begins to rupture. Through these ruptures, pieces of grey concrete are lost, but their voids are gradually filled with underlying layers of "soft" life whose colours (and shades of grey) peek through. To introduce Part II, Performing Culture, the sharp forms, edges and connecting links begin to momentarily disappear into more transient and organic forms.

> Porous boundaries emerge, animated by the props of carnivalesque performance (e.g., ribbons, rings and ladder rungs). The rupture deepens and people appear as clustered dots in plan view. A river of street life now passes right through the previously landlocked space. Such ruptures offer openings that create new points of access and orientation for experiencing embodied cultures and transforming the circulation of knowledge and power. In Part III, Consuming Culture, the voracious appetite of capitalist consumption eats away at the cultural landscape, digesting its spectacle. In the detritus of neoliberal urbanism, half-eaten and dispersed elements of culture are now primed for (re-)collection. In Part IV, Collecting Culture, therefore, pieces of cultural infrastructure are reassembled in new combinations. The ruptures become new pathways of production, performance, consumption and collection. The concluding frame, then, subverts a linear progression, initiating once again another cultural cycle.

In its contribution to infrastructure studies, this book's thematic attention to the role of cultural infrastructure in the cyclical progression of producing, performing, consuming and collecting culture is both pragmatic and philosophical. On the one hand, it practically counters the instrumentalization of culture as capital and urban entrepreneurial asset (Courage & McKeown 2018; Hesmondhalgh & Pratt 2005). On the other hand, it inserts culture into the scholarly infrastructural turn where it has been treated primarily as a synonym for people and their networks (Simone 2004) or as a source of struggle over the materialization of competing urban imaginaries (Gandy 2011). As Melosi (2020: 147) has underscored, a cultural perspective on infrastructure is valuable because it poses key questions about meaning, ideals and "abstract implications", namely, "the intent of infrastructure and its influences on societal change". But the materiality of cultural infrastructure, its form and function, is also crucial. The relationships between the material and non-material, between the hard and soft dimensions of infrastructure's urban cultural elements, therefore, have played a central role in the collection with contributors reflecting on the social reverberations of cultural infrastructure and the fundamental work in society that culture does to provoke, critique, find meaning and inspire change. The book's cultural vantage point on urban infrastructure has addressed four interrelated questions used to create dialogue between its primary themes and individual chapters. This conclusion selectively summarizes those commonalities and continuities while de-emphasizing their geographical differences.

THE SPATIAL POLITICS OF CULTURAL PRODUCTION

First, *how is urban culture produced in particular physical and virtual venues and with what dynamics of creativity, innovation and ensuing spatial politics?* The range of physical venues examined in this collection include cultural districts, open creative labs, studio buildings, theatres, arts centres, carnivalesque streets, peripheral self-managed cultural spaces, hawker centres, storefronts, cultural districts, fashion districts, museums, public libraries and community archives. Across the chapters emerged a persistent theme in the literature on urban culture, which has repeatedly highlighted a socio-spatial politics of displacement. New-wave Carnival krewes, community-based archives, international migrants, peripheral youth and even independent fashion designers and small theatre companies are but some examples of actors embedded in this precarious urban spatial politics, but it was artists (and their studio buildings, housing, rehearsal, exhibition and performance spaces) – simultaneously displaced by property relations and exploited for their urban value in a world of competing cities – who exemplified the ongoing story about culture and cities.

Employed in one of the lowest paid sectors of urban economies, professional artists across different mediums, and the artistic communities they form, are embedded in capitalist urban land markets but are often dependent on philanthrocapitalism and state funding systems to survive and create their work. This tension raises fundamental questions for civic leaders about how to preserve, protect and expand the spatial repertoire of venues where culture is produced, performed, consumed and collected. Modernity's equation of artistic production with urbanity is not just representational: the gathering of artists and cultural infrastructure in cities is an occupational, sectoral and creative imperative that has been inadequately addressed to date in urban planning and policy. The creation of urban spaces that foster collective concentration and sociability is foundational to artistic practice, but it also determines who can come together to take up space, shape the conversation and propose new urban imaginaries. The production of urban culture is, therefore, embedded in a tense spatial politics driven by a continual quest to create forms of proximity that nurture creativity while navigating processes of repeated and constant displacement wrought by sector-wide funding instability and economic precarity.

The question of affordability hounds cultural production, especially in large, super-gentrifying cities of the global North. Here, the economies of culture through creative city policy agendas have sought to revalorize inner-city industrial districts and neighbourhoods by myopically replacing, rather than protecting, this productive space with residential and commercial land uses. Cultural communities and the art scenes they generate require low-cost, secure and sustainable spaces in proximity to affordable housing where culture is more than an interim land use within a borrowed infrastructural model and can be created sociably over the long-term away from the prying eyes of publics and critics. But the cultural sector has seemingly become dependent upon the property market to produce under-utilized space that can, over the short-term, create temporary access for cultural production until market conditions change again and urban developers want to take advantage of increasing land values.

A vibrant and viable cultural sector cannot be sustained in contemporary cities in the face of super-gentrification and the limited availability and spatial fixity of the post-industrial built heritage that once sustained the experimental dynamics of inner-city artistic communities with proximity, spatial largess and affordability (Lees 2003). Moreover, urban cultural policies and the infrastructure and creative economy ecosystems they support cannot be sustained in a competitive, individualizing funding framework that pits artists and cultural organizations against one another without adequately taking its infrastructure into account. In terms of urban cultural investments, artistic communities not only need funding for artists; they also need the infrastructural support of spaces and commitment to their seemingly mundane maintenance that goes beyond questions of profitability. Big ticket and spectacular cultural investments in starchitecture and flagship venues (e.g., opera houses, theatres, museums, art galleries, libraries and luxury fashion retailers) as well as cultural districts are infinitely more attractive to investors and brandable for cities than the high-maintenance, adaptively reused buildings that support community-based artistic networks and their communities. Such a fragile cultural infrastructure will only be able to provide a liveable creative urban commons if property markets are fundamentally reworked.

The fragility of the urban creative commons was revealed by the Covid-19 pandemic, raising the question of what "a livable provisional life" could be in cities (Berlant 2016: 395). As material cultural infrastructure venues closed, information communications technologies offered the internet as an "infrastructure of continuity" (Berlant 2016: 402) for some creatives and their audiences, differently connecting people and places both locally and at greater geographical distances. Although digital tools, services, skills and training are unevenly shared, they draw attention to the extent that cultural infrastructure has a referent in the virtual realm while some exists there in its entirety. Ultimately, however, urban cultural infrastructure does not function without the materialities that make proximity and relationality, virtual or otherwise, possible. Composed of the diverse and loose networks of artists with non-profit organizations and cultural organizations, digital and material urban cultural infrastructure derives its creativity from complementarity, participation and diverse networks (Borrup 2011). If these networks are not supported, the physical and virtual venues of cultural infrastructure will have nothing to showcase.

DIGITAL FLOWS AND HUMAN NETWORKS

Second, *how is the cultural infrastructure of cities animated by "soft" networked and digital flows and relations that create tensions for governance, design, and usage?* In the twenty-first century, digital flows and networks have reshaped urban social relations (Castells 2004). In cities – particularly in economically developed, industrialized countries – such networks contribute to an increase in micro- and digital entrepreneurship, which, in turn, necessitates not only new ways of working collectively but also producing, performing, consuming and collecting culture. Digital flows and networks have transformed social interactions, making them less dependent on face-to-face relations while simultaneously deepening the connections between heretofore disparate people and places. A new social order and forms of sociality have emerged, re-creating norms of behaviour in public spaces such that third party conversations from elsewhere are co-present in real time physical spaces and digital interfaces are more likely to guide wayfinding assistance than kind strangers (Van Melik & van de Schraaf 2020). The broader drive for cities to become technologically "smarter" in their management of urban spaces, infrastructural assets, people and data has deepened practices and capacities for surveillance and biopolitical control as well as opportunities for users to generate content and collaboratively problem-solve.

When leveraged by cultural workers and community actors, the soft networked and digital flows of urban cultural infrastructure can animate the materiality of buildings and neighbourhoods. Digital platforms can be used to hype hipster retail landscapes, rate, review and order from food hawkers, communicate "care" to local fashion boutique customers or produce queer counter-topographies of the heteronormative city. It is through such networks and flows that information and skills diffuse, that knowledge is shared, communities of practice are built, events are organized, products and experiences are sold, and, ultimately, urban spaces are reconfigured. While the great range of open creative labs (e.g., fab labs, open workshops, repair cafes, hackerspaces, living labs, creative hubs and makerspaces) epitomize the reconfiguration of built materiality and social networks through digital flows, there are numerous examples of such reconfigurations of cultural infrastructure from across this collection that include ice cream vending, virtual theatre performances and arts festivals, and archives.

Through the social networks it coalesces and the digital flows that increasingly mediate it, the governance of urban cultural infrastructure compels participation by those interested in being part of a networked society (Hillier & Abbruzzese 2022). Such participation, however, requires access to information communication technologies and training, both to create with and disseminate cultural products and to connect with audiences, as well as the capacity and interest to consume culture. While digital networks can transform social relations by reducing dependence on face-to-face interactions and in-person gatherings, they can also disrupt confinement and create connection when community spaces are closed. Not only does digital cultural infrastructure deepen connections between disparate people and places, it extends the reach of cultural producers and artists and circumvents pre-existing hierarchies that determine what cultural products are visible and available to audiences. At the same time, digital cultural infrastructure shapes identity-based consumption niches that are implicitly tied to the imagery of specific urban places. Hipster urbanism and its specific consumptive ideals of "authenticity" and "originality" are writ large on social media sites such as Facebook, Instagram and TikTok that depend on place-imagery to support advertisers in building exclusive consumer markets. Such unjust urban consumptive landscapes are nevertheless reworked through other forms of digital cultural infrastructure such as community-based activist and archive networks that digitally critique gentrification and post historic images of past streetscapes. Through these reworkings, alternative spaces of community care can emerge, with the potential to articulate alternate stories and inscribe counter-topographies in urban space that challenge systemic exclusions and inequalities.

INFRASTRUCTURING ADAPTATIONS AND RESPONSES TO EXCLUSIONS AND INEQUALITIES

Third, *what adaptations and responses to systemic challenges of austerity, exclusion and inequality have occurred in urban cultural infrastructure to articulate forms of solidarity, care and community within and beyond crises like Covid-19?* The verb infrastructuring invites a reframing of infrastructure along the lines of what it *does* rather than what it *is* supposed *to be.* Infrastructuring is necessarily an embodied process and practice that permits an opportunity to explicitly challenge the systemic exclusions and inequities of infrastructure, its spatial fixities in institutional structures, investment and access.

Many modern civic cultural institutions are the sites of historical injustices and upper-middle-class "civilizing" missions, but so too are they more than their built forms and collections. As weighty socio-cultural infrastructural formations, museums, libraries, theatres and archives all often have mandates that extend beyond representation and knowledge sharing. They have staff and volunteers who serve the "public good" in numerous interventionist and caring capacities, acting as interfaces of encounter with urban publics and embodying performances of infrastructure. The "para-museum", for example, wrestles with the museum's instituting imaginary, contesting its conventional spaces and logics and proposing alternate forms of encounter with its artefacts. Libraries amplify their social role through "librarizing", a reorientation of the interface between staff, visitors and collections that provides a cultural infrastructure to combat social exclusion. In many cases, reduced public funding and shifting demographics has necessitated such reimaginings. De-emphasizing the collecting role of such urban cultural infrastructure, they are now reconfigured as community hubs, adding to an ever-changing toolbox of practices and local outreach programming. Similarly, the cultural infrastructure afforded by arts festivals is appreciated for its convivial modes of commonality with strangers, reconfiguring such temporary events into moments of community interaction and care.

How care manifests through cultural infrastructure changed during the pandemic as pivoting entered common parlance. The capacity "to pivot" became an urban neoliberal celebration of the creativity, ingenuity, adaptability and resilience of people to withstand constant change and uncertainty. Theatre producers pivoted by offering outdoor and digital performances while independent fashion designers produced "caring" PPE masks for local communities and food hawkers developed a delivery and take-out infrastructure. Pivoting has involved individual, institutional and industry-wide cultural infrastructural reckoning about responsibilities to artists, audiences, buildings, neighbourhoods and cities. It has necessitated constant trade-offs between the fixity of hard infrastructure with its rooted accountability to local communities and the malleability of soft infrastructure with its capacities to connect to geographically extensive new audiences and artistic collaborators. Across the cultural sector in the visual and performing arts and the arts organizations, institutions and para-public institutions that support them (from museums to libraries to studio buildings to archives to performance venues), infrastructure-based decision-making continues to be made about spatial needs and digital competencies, administrative values and governance mandates, audience outreach and community engagement, and programme planning and employment contracts.

The flexible infrastructural systems that the pandemic necessitated are perhaps here to remain as they neatly align with urban neoliberalism's entrepreneurial reliance upon ever-flexible individualized labour and consumption of temporary spectacles. However, such systems were also costly to accelerate in terms of investments in digital technologies as well as with respect to training and human resources. It remains questionable whether moving forward, cultural institutions and individuals can maintain hybrid digital and in-person delivery of arts and culture products and programming, especially in the face of audience screen-time fatigue and the challenge of recuperating costs through online ticket sales for virtual as opposed to in-person events.

The larger question of how arts and culture workers – many of whom were rendered even more vulnerable by the pandemic – can be better cared for and supported by the state through the adoption of cultural policies of solidarity remains. What would our cities look like if artists were treated as an essential service in society, not just during moments of crisis, but indefinitely?

THE FUTURES OF URBAN CULTURAL INFRASTRUCTURE

The fourth question that this collection has reflected upon is: *what capacities does the cultural infrastructure of cities have to foster more resilient and hopeful urban futures?* And, perhaps more importantly, for whom? When urban cultural infrastructure is made malleable, supporting mixed uses and playful and embodied encounters across social differences by multiple publics it holds potential to nurture resilience and hope for a greater range of people, especially those who are disenfranchised. At the heart of urban cultural infrastructure and its maintenance is professional practice, but also the DIY and making do of volunteerism, the production of culture for culture's sake in celebration of identity and solidarity, and the desire to have lives that are richer and more connected. Cultural infrastructure is as much about creating social life that devotes energy to supporting community-based organizations as it is about mobilizing a cultural response to social issues facing local communities (e.g., lack of resources, community invisibility and fragmentation or loss of space and heritage). Yet the futurity of urban cultural infrastructure is about playful experimentation, invention, exploration and transformation.

Play underscores the liminality and multi-sensory experiences of cultural infrastructure, offering a distinctive yet often neglected way in which to engage with people, spaces, built forms and imaginaries of cities. With its repertoire of spontaneous, improvisatory and sometimes irrational and risky behaviours (Stevens 2007), play moves through urban cultural infrastructure, loosening cities and pushing the envelope of urban possibility by disrupting the instrumental efficiencies of everyday life. Whether it involves playful individual encounter or building affective networks of solidarity, urban cultural infrastructure offers the potential of resiliency through relationality, connecting and motivating efforts to imagine urban alternatives.

Carnival exemplifies what play can do to cities *par excellence*. It transforms the public infrastructure of streets, squares and plazas along with negotiating the norms of policing and sanitation while striving to include everyone in its revelatory embrace. Like other urban cultural infrastructure, Carnival sets the stage for creative possibilities, inviting opportunities for sociability, information and knowledge exchange, performance, sensory and aesthetic experiences, consumption and collection. Carnivals, like arts festivals, never "just happen"; they are meticulously planned events that leverage and transform public infrastructure into sites of celebration. In so doing, carnivals, through their temporal, organizational, and embodied infrastructure reimagine the urban – its spaces and sociabilities – offering resistant and resilient energy suggestive of different futures.

The human body and its playful imagination underpin and animate all urban cultural infrastructure from the centres to the peripheries of city-regions, from middle-class neighbourhoods to working-class self-built communities. In the face of multiple adultist disenfranchisements, young people are not just infrastructural users and claimants, but are themselves city-builders. When confronted with the inequalities, exclusions, spatial stigma and infrastructural violence of inhabiting the urban periphery, many have reimagined alternative urban futures for themselves by producing cultural infrastructure to meet their creative needs locally. From within their own neighbourhoods and leveraging public spaces beyond them to connect with wider audiences, young people proactively engage in theatre, music, dance, poetry, literature and new forms of participatory and community arts to represent their lived experiences. They repurpose neighbourhood-based hard cultural infrastructure and, through their creative experimentations, digital connections and radical imaginations mould the soft infrastructure of collective identities, awareness-raising and social mobilization from which alternative urban futures can be realized. Cultural infrastructure, then, offers great potential to insurgently make claims to inclusion within hegemonic socio-cultural systems, and, in so doing, destabilizing and reworking them along with the cities they have made.

If a key feature of cultural infrastructure is that it has the potential to expand the collective imaginary around urban citizenship and belonging, to generate openings where counter-cultural and intercultural life can be nurtured in cities, what happens when it is funded through philanthrocapitalism or the state? Does cultural infrastructure, then, lose its promise of transgression because its investors treat it as little more than a "safety valve" for maintaining existing social relations? When majority interests are funded through state subsidies, culture is reproduced as middle-class, to the exclusion of many youth, migrants, refugees and undocumented residents. When held in a state-funded Munich cultural centre, the infrastructure supporting an intercultural dance party such as Plug in Beats, may only promise temporary and atomized inclusion through brief encounter. Although funding, institutional spaces and administrative and material resources can all, to some extent, be reconfigured, there remains an ambivalence to cultural infrastructure. Built to make space for political and social difference in the cultural sphere and to do important consciousness-raising work about social justice and structural challenges, cultural infrastructure may serve to simultaneously contain those same differences and buffer the state from having to make larger infrastructural changes.

The capacity of urban cultural infrastructure to foster more resilient and hopeful urban futures lies in "infrastructural citizenship" (Lemanski 2018), an analytical framework that explores state–society relations through the material, social and legal registers of citizenship within everyday urban life. For Lemanski (2022: 668), infrastructural citizenship refers to "how the state conceives of and plans for citizens as infrastructure claimants, consumers and complainers; as well as how urban dwellers' citizenship perceptions and practices (in relation to the state and other citizens) are materialised through infrastructure". Cultural centres, city streets and peripheral public spaces are produced through normative ideals of good citizenship, but their infrastructure is a physical mediator of social exclusion and contestation, permitting select citizens to articulate their visions of the city and participate in shaping its future. Given that the state has long subsidized culture, cultural production and the creation and maintenance of cultural infrastructure, culture should be foregrounded in any understanding of infrastructural citizenship. Culture encapsulates the "ceaseless human endeavour to change the world" (Harvey 2000: 195), while cultural infrastructure becomes the socio-spatial mediator that can offer hope for more socially just and politically progressive urban futures.

CONCLUDING REMARKS

Across a wide range of metropolitan areas (e.g., Ahmedabad, Berlin, Dublin, Hamilton, Leipzig, London, Medellín, Montreal, Munich, New Orleans, Oaxaca, San Francisco, São Paulo, Singapore, Sydney, Toronto and Utrecht), from their centres to peripheries, this book has centred culture in the infrastructural imagination, mediation and making of cities around the world. Cultural infrastructure has been presented as the relational and multi-faceted socio-material cultural ecosystems within cities that supersede the spaces, buildings and networks that are commonly the focus of urban studies scholarship after the infrastructural turn. Most importantly, the collection demonstrates the persistence of artistic lives, livelihoods and practices as being at the core of urban cultural infrastructure. Within the hard infrastructure of the built environment, professional and amateur actors, painters, writers, poets, musicians, dancers, performance and community artists all make creative spaces that nurture complex and networked cultural ecosystems that constantly cycle through processes of creation, dissemination, exhibition, consumption and participation. From this creative core and extending across a diverse cultural sector is a loose network of differently sized non-profit organizations and facilities whose infrastructure supports "decentralized, nonhierarchical, participatory, and culturally diverse" individual and collective (sub)cultural expression through volunteer participation in and consumption of activities and programming (Borrup 2011: 21).

Given the centrality of artistic labour to the existence and maintenance of urban cultural infrastructure, this collection commissioned and showcased original artwork representing the cyclical and infrastructural generation of culture. Its imaginaries of urban futurity fluctuate between (in)complete realization and (ir)retrievable loss in a polyptych that treats "infrastructuring" as an ongoing urban-social process of producing, performing, consuming and collecting cultures. By approaching infrastructure through the gerund of infrastructuring, its analytical priority became the more expansive embodied practices of reconfiguring infrastructure rather than the foreclosed expectations that accompany institutional spatial fixity. Across a continuum of doing culture, the supporting cultural infrastructure is understood as more malleable, relational and adaptable to local urban contexts, inviting opportunities to directly challenge systemic urban exclusions and inequities that manifest in differential access, programming and spatial investments.

By understanding cultural infrastructure across a continuum of actions, it became clear that "producing" culture is an ecosystem-wide nurturing practice that demands spatial and economic security for artists in cities. "Producing" culture situates the fixed studios and rehearsal spaces of individual creatives and arts organizations within wider, more heterogeneous networks inhabited by communities and generations that constantly regenerate the cultural ecosystem. Thus, any productive future for urban cultural infrastructure, and one could also argue for cities more broadly, is inconceivable without basic improvements to the status of artists in society and how their creative work is remunerated and sustained through access to affordable and centrally located working and living spaces (Brault & Kaplansky 2010). The future of producing urban cultural infrastructure lies in dedicating space in cities for creativity that is economically sustainable enough to encourage experimentation, build proximity within studio buildings or cultural districts, and encourage improvisational sociality rather than marginalization and dispersal. Whether this necessitates state-led designation of artists as "essential workers" who provide social care through their creative service to society or the preservation of lands zoned as industrial in central cities through creative land trusts to prevent their conversion into gentrifying residential and commercial-only spaces, is debatable, but it needs to be an urban planning and policy priority.

To view cultural infrastructure through the prism of "performing" is to render visible embodied artistic and creative labour in all of its repetitious and ordinary or more carnivalesque and spectacular forms. Through the mobile and ephemeral events that come to life on the city's formal and informal theatrical stages – adaptively reusing its streets, public spaces, bars, community centres, schools and religious institutions, for example – performing culture is the livedness of cultural infrastructure, a visceral expression of urban citizenship. Theatre troupes, dance and opera companies and orchestras use designated cultural infrastructure in the entertainment and cultural districts of cities that appear to have permanence in the urban landscape, but when they are forced to close or digitize, embodied experience becomes highly mediated, challenging the soft networked relationships between performers and audiences. Fundamental questions have been raised about how flexible such cultural infrastructure can be, and how many times it is possible for individuals and organizations to pivot without unravelling and completely destabilizing the cultural sector altogether. State-sanctioned cultural infrastructure produces the confinement of performances and limits their audiences making the only recourse for marginalized performers the deployment of their own personal infrastructure in self-made cultural venues in ways that challenge urban citizenship claims and recreate the city itself.

Given that the marketplace has long defined the economic trading role of cities, consumption is a crucial element of urban cultural infrastructure. Beyond the society of the spectacle and the performance of distinction through urban symbolic economies, the cultural infrastructure of consumption is multi-faceted, place-based and glocal, grounded in neighbourhood street life with its high streets, strip malls, retail storefronts, public markets and street vendors. Located in the everyday spaces where people live, even mass consumption acquires the patina of local social reproduction. Beyond the niche-market branding of neighbourhoods and cities and the homogenizing force of global franchises on streetscapes, there remains a sociality to practices of consumption that requires a more culturally sensitive approach to the planning, construction and maintenance of its infrastructure to slow the forces of gentrification and prevent the desertification of local retail landscapes. In the absence of a diverse cultural infrastructure of consumption that supports a vibrant public life of eating, drinking, shopping and socializing, cities will cease to be themselves.

To include collecting as part of urban cultural infrastructure is to enlarge the remit of consumption and to be aware of the temporality and cyclical progression of cities. Civic and community-based cultural institutions of libraries, museums and archives have for centuries been the repositories of the cultural ideals and memories of collective urban life. Valued for their informational infrastructure, the staff and volunteers who labour in these collecting institutions gather, store, organize and display culture, reproducing them for their users as more than oppressive, selective and exclusive repositories of knowledge and memory. Through innovative programming and countercultural and intercultural interventions, these cultural institutions become infrastructure and can be reconfigured as sites of sociality, care and political activism beyond the status quo needs of the middle class. To support the urban cultural infrastructure of collecting, a broader view of what constitutes infrastructure beyond state sponsorship is needed, revitalizing ongoing debates about the social role and responsibilities of knowledge institutions, who is doing the acquisition, interpretation and narration, how and where collections are shared, and who has access.

In all of its empirical diversity, this book is an invitation to urban studies scholars to rethink generalized claims about the relationship between infrastructure and cities by reconsidering the place and role of culture (McFarlane & Rutherford 2008). Like roads, sewers, water pipes, electricity grids, fibre optic cables and public transit, urban cultural infrastructure is manifest materially in the built environment, is heavily subsidized and can be reconfigured. Yet rarely prioritized as essential and often the first to be cut when urban austerity measures are implemented, cultural infrastructure is fragile and readily aestheticized as part of the symbolic economies that give cities their global competitive edge. For these reasons, the cultural sector tends "to close in on itself to protect the few resources" it has (Brault & Kaplansky 2010: 56), reinforcing internal hierarchies, bounding professions and communities of practice and excluding culturally diverse and emerging cultural actors. To foster and sustain the creative resources of cities and their residents, urban planners and civic decision-makers must do more to explicitly cultivate cultural leadership that emphasizes the construction, maintenance and diverse use of cultural infrastructure. The lives, livelihoods and spaces of people involved in conveying culture and reinventing urban communities for and with local residents should be at the core of any discussion of what an affordable, accessible and sustainable future can be for urban cultural infrastructure.

REFERENCES

Addie, J.-P. *et al.* 2020. "Regionalizing the infrastructure turn: a research agenda". *Regional Studies, Regional Science* 7(1): 10–26.

Adorno, T. & M. Horkheimer 1979 [1947]. *Dialectic of Enlightenment*. London: Verso.

Alam, A. & D. Houston 2020. "Rethinking care as alternative infrastructure". *Cities* 100: 1–10.

Allen, A. 2022. "Navigating stigma through everyday city-making: gendered trajectories, politics and outcomes in the periphery of Lima". *Urban Studies* 59(3): 490–508.

Allen, D. & T. McCreary 2021. "Performing black life: the FAMU marching 100 and the black aesthetic politics of disruption, presence and affirmation". *Cultural Geographies* 28(1): 41–55.

Amin, A. 2008. "Collective culture and urban public space". *City* 12(1): 5–24.

Amin, A. 2014. "Lively infrastructure". *Theory, Culture & Society* 31(7/8): 137–61.

Amin, A. & N. Thrift 2017. *Seeing Like a City*. Cambridge: Polity.

Anand, N. 2017. *Hydraulic City: Water and the Infrastructures of Citizenship in Mumbai*. Durham, NC: Duke University Press.

Anand, N. *et al.* 2018. *The Promise of Infrastructure*. Durham, NC: Duke University Press.

Anderson, B. 2016. *Imagined Communities: Reflections on the Origin and Spread of Nationalism*. London: Verso.

Andres, L. & O. Golubchicov 2016. "The limits to artist-led regeneration: creative brownfields in cities of high culture". *International Journal of Urban and Regional Research* 40(4): 757–75.

Ang, I. 2015. "Change and continuity: art museums and the reproduction of art-museumness". In A. Witcomb & K. Message (eds), *The International Handbook of Museum Studies, Volume 1: Museum Theory*, 211–31. Hoboken: John Wiley.

Ang, I. 2019. "Museums and cultural diversity: a persistent challenge". In K. Drotner *et al.* (eds), *The Routledge Handbook of Museums, Media and Communication*, 315–27. New York: Routledge.

Ang, I. *et al.* 2016. *Mapping Culture: Venues and Infrastructures in the City of Sydney LGA*. Institute for Culture and Society Report. https://apo.org.au/node/74213

Angelo, H. & C. Hentschel 2015. "Interactions with infrastructure as windows into social worlds: a method for critical urban studies". *City* 19(2/3): 306–12.

Anheier, H. *et al.* 2021. *Culture, the Arts, and the Covid-19 Pandemic: Five Cultural Capitals in Search of Solutions*. Berlin: Hertie School.

Appadurai, A. 2003. "Archive and aspiration". In *Information is Alive: Art and Theory on Archiving and Retrieving Data*, 14–25. Rotterdam: V2_NAi Publishers.

Aragón, R. 2017. "Identidad urbana en América Latina a través del grafiti". *Ciudades Sostenibles*. https://blogs.iadb.org/ciudades-sostenibles/es/identidad-urbana-grafiti/

Archives Gaies du Québec (AGQ) n.d. "History: the Quebec Gay Archives, yesterday and today". http://agq.qc.ca/en/history/

Archives Gaies du Québec (AGQ) 2021. "Walls have ears: the stories of Montreal's LGBTQ2S+ spaces". http://agq.qc.ca/en/wallshaveears/

Archives Lesbiennes du Québec (ALQ) 2022. "Our story". www.archiveslesbiennesduquebec.ca/en/our-story/

Archives Lesbiennes du Québec (ALQ) *et al.* 2020. "Montreal lesbian places". www.historypin.org/en/lieux-lesbiens-a-montreal-montreal-lesbian-pl/geo/45.501689,-73.567256,11/bounds/45.400051,-73.705615,45.603144,-73.428897/paging/1

Arts Council England 2019. "Creative Land Trust". www.artscouncil.org.uk/creative-land-trust

Bain, A. 2003. "Constructing contemporary artistic identities in Toronto neighbourhoods". *The Canadian Geographer* 47(3): 303–17.

Bain, A. 2004. "Female artistic identity in place: the studio". *Social & Cultural Geography* 5(2): 171–93.

Bain, A. 2005. "Constructing an artistic identity". *Work, Employment, and Society* 19(1): 25–46.

Bain, A. 2007. "Claiming space: fatherhood and artistic practice". *Gender, Place & Culture* 14(3): 249–65

Bain, A. 2010. "Creativ* suburbs: cultural 'popcorn' pioneering in Etobicoke". In T. Edensor *et al.* (eds), *Spaces of Vernacular Creativity: Rethinking the Cultural Economy*, 63–74. London: Routledge.

Bain, A. 2013. *Creative Margins: Cultural Production in Canadian Suburbs.* Toronto: University of Toronto Press.

Bain, A. 2018. "Artists as property owners and small-scale developers". *Urban Geography* 39(6): 844–67.

Bain, A. 2022. "Queer affordances of care in suburban public libraries". *Emotion, Space, and Society* 45. https://doi.org/10.1016/j.emospa.2022.100923

Bain, A. & F. Landau 2018. "Artist intermediaries in Berlin: cultural intermediation as an interscalar strategy of self-organizational survival". *Urban Research & Practice* 11(3): 247–62.

Bain, A. & F. Landau 2019a. "Artists, temporality, and the governance of collaborative place-making". *Urban Affairs Review* 55(2): 405–27.

Bain, A. & F. Landau 2019b. "Assessing the embeddedness dynamics of the Baumwollspinnerei cultural quarter in Leipzig: introducing the POSES Star Framework". *European Planning Studies* 27(8): 1564–86.

Bain, A. & F. Landau 2022. "Generationing cultural quarters: the temporal embeddedness of relational places". *Urban Geography* 43(10): 1610–37.

Bain, A. & L. March 2019. "Urban redevelopment, cultural philanthropy, and the commodification of artistic authenticity in Toronto". *City & Community* 18(1): 173–94.

Bain, A. & B. Mark 2020. "Re-imaging, re-elevating, re-placing the urban". In M. Moos (eds), *Canadian Cities in Transition: Understanding Contemporary Urbanism*, 6th edition. Oxford: Oxford University Press.

Bain, A. & H. McLean 2013. "The artistic precariat". *Cambridge Journal of Regions, Economy, and Society* 6(1): 93–111.

Bain, A. & L. Peake 2022. *Urbanization in a Global Context.* Oxford: Oxford University Press.

Bain, A. & J. Podmore 2020. "Scavenging for LGBTQ2S public library visibility on Vancouver's periphery". *Tijdschrift voor economische en sociale geografie* 111(4): 601–15.

Bain, A. & N. Rallis 2017. "Crawling with art: public art installations on James Street North in Hamilton, Ontario". In M. Radice & A. Boudreault-Fournier (eds), *Urban Encounters: Art and the Public*, 134–60. Montreal and Kingston: McGill-Queen's University Press.

Bakhtin, M. 1968. *Rabelais and His World.* Cambridge, MA: MIT Press.

Ballesteros Cubillos, L. 2021. *Colectivos teatrales en periferia: dinámicas de acceso cultural en Cundinamarca.* Master's thesis, Universidad Nacional de Colombia.

Banks, M. & J. O'Connor 2021. "'A plague upon your howling': art and culture in the viral emergency". *Cultural Trends* 30(1): 3–18.

Barniskis, S. 2016. "Access and express: professional perspectives on public library makerspaces and intellectual freedom". *Public Library Quarterly* 35(2): 103–25.

Barrios, R. 2010. "'You found us doing this, this is our way': criminalizing second lines, super Sunday, and habitus in post-Katrina New Orleans". *Identities* 17(6): 586–612.

Baumann, H. & H. Yacobi 2022. "Introduction: infrastructural stigma and urban vulnerability". *Urban Studies* 59(3): 475–89.

Beall, J. *et al.* 2019. "Understanding infrastructure interfaces: common ground for interdisciplinary urban research?" *Journal of the British Academy* 7(s2): 11–43.

Becker, C. 2009. *Thinking in Place: Art, Action and Cultural Production*. Boulder, CO: Paradigm.

Becker, H. 1982. *Art Worlds*. Berkeley, CA: University of California Press.

Bedford, W. 2015. "'Montreal might eat its young, but Montreal won't break us down': the co-production of place, space, and independent music in Mile End, 1995–2015". *Journal of Urban Cultural Studies* 2(3): 335–45.

Belk, R. 1995. *Collecting in a Consumer Society*. London: Routledge.

Berlant, L. 2016. "The commons: infrastructures for troubling times". *Environment and Planning D: Society and Space* 34(3): 393–19.

Bertelli, G.-B. 2017. "Introdução". In *Vozes à Margem: Periferias, Estética e Política*. São Paulo: Editora da Universidade Federal de São Carlos.

Beswick, K. *et al.* 2016. "The road to Epidaurus is like the road to creation: tapping the urban archive". *Cultural Geographies* 23(3): 545–52.

Bethel, N. 2022. "A song of ourselves: playing out the pandemic in the Bahamas". *HowlRound Theatre Commons*. https://howlround.com/song-ourselves-playing-out-pandemic-bahamas

Bhattacharyya, S. 2021. "The pandemic and the play: Indian theatre's survival strategies in the 'new normal'". *Cenacle* 1(11): 40–7.

Billie, M. & K. Simonsen 2021. "Atmospheric practices on affecting and being affected". *Space and Culture* 24(2): 295–309.

Bingham-Hall, J. & A. Kaasa 2018. "New cultural infrastructure: can we design the conditions for culture?" Working paper of Theatrum Mundi. https://theatrum-mundi.org/library/can-we-design-the-conditions-for-culture/

Bingel, K. 2019. *Dritte Orte kreativ-urbaner Milieus: Eine gendersensible Betrachtung am Beispiel Braunschweig*. Bielefeld: Transcript.

Bishop, M. & M. Green 2008. *Philanthrocapitalism: How the Rich Can Save the World*. New York: Bloomsbury.

Bliemel, M. *et al.* 2019. "Accelerators as start-up infrastructure for entrepreneurial clusters". *Entrepreneurship & Regional Development* 31(1/2): 133–49.

Blum, A. 2003. *The Imaginative Structure of the City*. Montreal and Kingston: McGill-Queen's University Press.

Bobbio, T. 2015. *Urbanisation, Citizenship and Conflict in India: Ahmedabad 1900–2000*. New York: Routledge.

Borin, E. & F. Donato 2015. "Unlocking the potential of IC in Italian cultural ecosystems". *Journal of Intellectual Capital* 16(2): 285–304.

Borrup, T. 2011. "The emergence of a new cultural infrastructure: lessons from Silicon Valley". *Journal of Urban Culture Research* 2: 16–29.

Bourdieu, P. 1993. *The Field of Cultural Production: Essays on Art and Literature*. Trans. L. Kritzman. New York: Columbia University Press.

Bowker, G. & S. Star 2000. *Sorting Things Out: Classification and Its Consequences*. Cambridge, MA: MIT Press.

Brault, S. & J. Kaplansky 2010. *No Culture, No Future*. Trans. J. Kaplansky. Toronto: Cormorant.

Breunlin, R. & H. Regis 2006. "Putting the Ninth Ward on the map: race, place, and transformation in Desire, New Orleans". *American Anthropologist* 108(4): 744–64.

Breunlin, R. *et al.* 2009. *The House of Dance and Feathers: A Museum by Ronald W. Lewis*. New Orleans: UNO Press/Neighborhood Story Project.

Breward, C. & D. Gilbert 2006. *Fashion's World Cities*. London: Bloomsbury.

Brinks, V. 2019. "'And since I knew about the possibilities there ...': the role of open creative labs in user innovations processes". *Tijdschrift voor Economische en Sociale Geografie* 110(4): 381–94.

Brochu-Ingram, G. 2015. "Building queer infrastructure: trajectories of activism and organizational development in decolonizing Vancouver". In M. Tremblay (ed.), *Queer Mobilizations: Social Movement Activism and Canadian Public Policy*, 227–49. Vancouver, BC: UBC Press.

Brydges, T. & M. Hanlon 2020. "Garment worker rights and the fashion industry's response to Covid-19". *Dialogues in Human Geography* 10(2): 195–8.

Brydges, T. & B. Hracs 2019. "The locational choices and interregional mobilities of creative entrepreneurs within Canada's fashion system". *Regional Studies* 53(4): 517–27.

Brydges, T. & J. Sjöholm 2019. "Becoming a personal style blogger: changing configurations and spatialities of aesthetic labour in the fashion industry". *International Journal of Cultural Studies* 22(1): 119–39.

Brydges, T. *et al.* 2021. "Changing geographies of fashion during Covid-19: the Australian case". *Geographical Research* 59(2): 206–16.

Bryson, J. 2007. "Arts, dance, cultural infrastructure, and city regeneration: knowledge, audience development, networks, and conventions, and the relocation of a Royal Ballet Company from London to Birmingham". *Norsk Geografisk Tidsskrift/Norwegian Journal of Geography* 61(3): 98–110.

Buchanan, A. & M. Bastien 2015. "Activating the archive: rethinking the role of traditional archives for local activist projects." *Archive Science* 15: 429–51.

Bull, D. & L. Dickens 2021. "Covid commentaries: London's cultural landscape". *The London Journal* 46: 121–27.

Bunce, S. 2018. "Alternatives to gentrification: exploring community land trusts and urban ecovillage practices". In L. Lees & M. Phillips (eds), *Handbook of Gentrification Studies*, 413–27. Cheltenham: Edward Elgar.

Burgum, S. 2019. "From Grenfell Tower to the home front: unsettling property norms using a genealogical approach". *Antipode* 51(2): 458–77.

Burgum, S. 2020. "This city is an archive: squatting history and urban authority". *Journal of Urban History* 48(3): 504–22.

Burke, P. 1978. *Popular Culture in Early Modern Europe*. New York: Harper & Row.

Butler, J. *et al.* 2016. *Vulnerability in Resistance*. Durham, NC: Duke University Press.

Caillot, M.-A. 2013. *A Company Man: The Remarkable French-Atlantic Voyage of a Clerk for the Company of the Indies*. New Orleans: The Historic New Orleans Collection.

Caldeira, T. 2015. "Social movements, cultural production, and protests: São Paulo's shifting political landscape". *Current Anthropology* 56(S11): S126–36.

Caldeira, T. 2017. "Peripheral urbanization: autoconstruction, transversal logics, and politics in cities of the global South". *Environment and Planning D: Society and Space* 35(1): 3–20.

Calhoun, C. 1992. "The infrastructure of modernity: indirect social relationships, information technology, and social integration". In H. Haferkamp & N. Smelser (eds), *Social Change and Modernity*, 205–36. Berkeley, CA: University of California Press.

Camargo, L. *et al.* 2020. "Fast and ultra-fast fashion supply chain management: an exploratory research". *International Journal of Retail & Distribution Management* 48(6): 537–53.

Campkin, B. 2021. "Queer infrastructures: LGBTQ+ networks and urban governance in global London". In R. Ramos & S. Mowlabocus (eds), *Queer Sites in Global Contexts: Technologies, Spaces, and Otherness*. New York: Routledge.

Capdevila, I. 2015. "Coworking spaces and the localized dynamics of innovation in Barcelona". *International Journal of Innovation Management* 19(3): 1–25.

Carse, A. 2017. "Keyword: infrastructure: how a humble French engineering term shaped the modern world". In P. Harvey *et al.* (eds), *Infrastructures and Social Complexity: A Routledge Companion*, 27–39. London: Routledge.

Carter, P. 2019. "Looking for something real: affective encounters". *Annals of Tourism Research* 76: 200–13.

Castán Broto, V. *et al.* 2021. "Walk the pipeline: urban infrastructure landscapes in Bengaluru's long twentieth century". *International Journal of Urban and Regional Research* 45(4): 696–715.

Castells, M. 2004. *The Network Society: A Cross-Cultural Perspective.* Cheltenham: Edward Elgar.

Caswell, M. 2014. "Seeing yourself in history: community archives and the fight against symbolic annihilation." *The Public Historian* 36(4): 26–37.

Caswell, M. *et al.* 2016. "'To be able to imagine otherwise': community archives and the importance of representation". *Archives and Records* 8(1): 5–26.

Catungal, J.-P. & D. Leslie 2009. "Contesting the creative city: race, nation, and multiculturalism". *Geoforum* 40(5): 701–4.

Caust, J. 2003. "Putting the 'art' back into arts policy making: how arts policy has been 'captured' by the economists and the marketers". *International Journal of Cultural Policy* 9(1): 51–63.

Caust, J. 2021. "Sustainability of artists in precarious times: how arts producers and individual artists have adapted during a pandemic". *Sustainability* 13: 1–15.

Cesio, P. 2017. Ola Urbana: La Iniciativa que Llena con Arte las Periferias en Bolivia. *Aleteia.* https://es.aleteia.org/2017/05/08/ola-urbana-la-iniciativa-que-llena-con-arte-las-periferias-en-bolivia/

Chapman, M. & L. Matthews 2021. "The archive of power: drawings and Wangi Power Station". 37th Annual SAHANZ Conference. www.sahanz.net/conferences/what-if-what-next-speculations-on-historys-futures/

Charlton, E. 2020. "Trashing Johannesburg: Ponte City-as-archive of everyday loss". *Cultural Geographies* 27(2): 277–92.

Chitrakorn, K. 2020. "Fashion's bankruptcy watch list is growing in the US." *Vogue Business.* www.voguebusiness.com/consumers/fashion-bankruptcy-watch-list-is-growing-in-the-us

Chen, T.-T. & H.-R. Ke 2017. "Public library as a place and breeding ground of social capital: a case of Singang Library". *Malaysian Journal of Library and Information Science* 22(1): 45–58.

Chen, X. & A. Kanna (eds) 2012. *Rethinking Global Urbanism: Comparative Insights from Secondary Cities.* New York: Routledge.

Cifor, M. *et al.* 2018. "'What we do crosses over to activism': the politics and practice of community archives." *The Public Historian* 40(2): 69–95.

City of Sydney 2020. "Making space for culture in Sydney: cultural infrastructure study 2020". www.cityofsydney.nsw.gov.au/surveys-case-studies-reports/understanding-the-cultural-sector-research-and-studies

City of Toronto (n.d.) "Tourism". www.toronto.ca/business-economy/industry-sector-support/tourism/

City of Vancouver 2018. "Making space for arts and culture: 2018 cultural infrastructure plan". https://vancouver.ca/files/cov/making-space-for-arts-and-culture.pdf

Clapperton, J. 2010. "Contested spaces, shared places: the Museum of Anthropology at UBC, Aboriginal peoples, and postcolonial criticism". *BC Studies: The British Columbian Quarterly* 165: 7–30.

Clifford, J. 1997. *Museums as Contact Zones.* New York: Routes.

Cohen, A. 1993. *Masquerade Politics.* Berkeley, CA: University of California Press.

Cohendet, P. *et al.* 2011. "Rethinking urban creativity: lessons from Barcelona and Montreal". *City, Culture and Society* 2: 151–8.

Comunian, R. 2011. "Rethinking the creative city: the role of complexity, networks and interactions in the urban creative economy. *Urban Studies* 48(6): 1157–79.

Conolly, L. 2011. *The Shaw Festival: The First Festival.* Oxford: Oxford University Press.

Cooper, D. 2016. "House proud: an ethnography of the BC gay and lesbian archives". *Archival Science* 16(3): 261–88.

Corble, A. & R. Van Melik 2021. "Public libraries in crises: between spaces of care and information infrastructures". In R. Van Melik *et al.* (eds), *Global Reflections on Covid-19 and Urban Inequalities, Volume 3: Public Space and Mobility*, 119–30. Bristol: Bristol University Press.

Courage, C. & A. McKeown 2018. *Creative Placemaking: Research, Theory and Practice*. New York: Routledge.

Creative Industries Council 2021. "Creative industries growth surge continues". www.thecreativeindustries.co.uk/facts-figures/uk-creative-overview-facts-and-figures-employment-figures.

Creative Land Trust (CLT) 2019. "Creative places create value: the impact of creative workspace on local residential property". https://creativelandtrust.org/wp-content/uploads/2021/09/210047_210915_CreativeWorkspace_FinalReport_LowRes_Spreads-1.pdf

Creative Land Trust (CLT) 2022. "About us". https://creativelandtrust.org/about-us/

Creative United (CU) 2016. "Making space: developing and sustaining affordable artists' studios and creative workspaces". https://creativeunited.org.uk/wp-content/uploads/2016/08/Making_Space_Executive_Summary_FINAL.pdf

Crewe, L. 2010. "Wear: where? The convergent geographies of architecture and fashion". *Environment and Planning A* 42(9): 2093–108.

Crewe, L. 2016. "Placing fashion: art, space, display and the building of luxury fashion markets through retail design". *Progress in Human Geography* 40(4): 511–29.

Crewe, L. 2017. *The Geographies of Fashion: Consumption, Space and Value*. London: Bloomsbury.

Cronin, A. 2008. "Urban space and entrepreneurial property relations: resistance and the vernacular of outdoor advertising and graffiti". In A. Cronin & K. Hetherington (eds), *Consuming the Entrepreneurial City: Image, Memory, Spectacle*, 65–84. New York: Routledge.

Cru, J. 2017. "Bilingual rapping in Yucatán, Mexico: strategic choices for Maya language legitimation and revitalisation". *International Journal of Bilingual Education and Bilingualism* 20(5): 481–96.

da Silva, L. 2016. *A Literatura Fora do Lugar: A Constituição de Poetas e Escritores Nos Saraus das Periferias de São Paulo*. Master's thesis, Universidade de São Paulo.

Dale, S. 2021. *Shift Change: Scene from a Post-Industrial Revolution*. Toronto: Between the Lines.

Dameri, R. & P. Demartini 2020. "Knowledge transfer and translation in cultural ecosystems". *Management Decision* 59(9): 1885–907.

Daniels, S. 2011. "Art studio". In J. Agnew & D. Livingstone (eds), *The Sage Handbook of Geographical Knowledge*, 137–48. London: Sage.

Danziger, P. 2020. "Amazon, already the nation's top fashion retailer is positioned to grab even more market share". *Forbes*. www.forbes.com/sites/pamdanziger/2020/01/28/amazon-is-readying-major-disruption-for-the-fashion-industry/?sh=7ae99c3967f3

Daoust Lestage 2018. "La Place des Festivals and La Promenade des Artistes". In B. Ivers (eds), *Staging Urban Landscapes, The Activation and Curation of Flexible Public Spaces*, 88–102. Berlin: Birkhäuser.

Datta, A. & N. Ahmed 2020. "Intimate infrastructures: the rubrics of gendered safety and urban violence in Kerala, India." *Geoforum* 110: 67–76.

Davis, D. 1999. "The power of distance: re-theorizing social movements in Latin America". *Theory and Society* 28(4): 585–638.

De Genova, N. 2017. *The Borders of "Europe": Autonomy of Migration, Tactics of Bordering*. Durham, NC: Duke University Press.

Débord, G. 1970. *The Society of the Spectacle*. New York: Black & Red Press.

DeFilippis, J. *et al.* 2018. "W(h)ither the community in community land trusts?" *Journal of Urban Affairs* 40(6): 755–69.

Derrida, J. 1996. *Archive Fever: A Freudian Impression*. Trans. E. Prenowitz. Chicago, IL: University of Chicago Press.

Deskmag 2019. "Number of coworking spaces and members worldwide". https://coworkingstatistics.com/number-of-coworking-spaces-and-members-worldwide-througout-the-years

Detamore, M. 2010. "The carnal body: representation, performativity, and the rest of us". *Geography Compass* 4(3): 241–54.

Devine, A. & B. Quinn 2019. "Building social capital in a divided city: the potential of events". *Journal of Sustainable Tourism* 27(10): 1495–512.

Devine, K. & A. Boudreault-Fournier 2021. *Audible Infrastructures: Music, Sound, Media*. Oxford: Oxford University Press.

Dickson, L. 2015. "'Ah! Other bodies!' Embodied spaces, pleasures and practices at Glasgow film festival". *Participations: Journal of Audience and Reception Studies* 12(1): 703–24.

Dickinson, P. 2017. "Choreographies of place: dancing in the Vancouver sublime from dusk to dawn". In L. Levin & M. Schweitzer (eds), *Performance Studies in Canada*, 90–114. Montreal & Kingston: McGill-Queen's University Press.

Dodson, J. 2009. "The 'infrastructure turn' in Australian metropolitan spatial planning". *International Planning Studies* 14(2): 109–23.

Dodson, J. 2017. "The global infrastructure turn and urban practice". *Urban Policy and Research* 5(1): 87–92.

Domanski, D. *et al.* 2020. "A comprehensive concept of social innovation and its implications for the local context: on the growing importance of social innovation ecosystems and infrastructures". *European Planning Studies* 28(3): 454–74.

Dourish, P. & G. Bell 2007. "The infrastructure of experience and the experience of infrastructure: meaning and structure in everyday encounters with space". *Environment and Planning B: Planning and Design* 34(4): 414–30.

Dova, E. *et al.* 2022. "A mega-event in a small city: community participation, heritage and scale in the case of Pafos 2017 European Capital of Culture". *European Planning Studies* 30(3): 457–77.

Dovey, J. *et al.* 2016. "The practice of cultural ecology: network connectivity in the creative economy". *Cultural Trends* 25(2): 87–103.

Duxbury, N. & G. Richards 2019. "Towards a research agenda in creative tourism: a synthesis of suggested future research trajectories". In N. Duxbury & G. Richards (eds), *A Research Agenda for Creative Tourism*, 182–92. Cheltenham: Edward Elgar.

Duxbury, N. *et al.* 2008. *Under Construction: The State of Cultural Infrastructure in Canada*. Vancouver: Centre for Expertise on Culture and Communication, Simon Fraser University.

Džupka, P. & M. Gróf 2021. "The influence of the new cultural infrastructure on residential property prices: evidence from Košice ECoC 2013". *Cities* 110(1): 1–13.

Economist 2020. "Flat-white world: even as traditional globalisation has slowed, a new kind has sped up". www.economist.com/international/2020/11/05/even-as-traditional-globalisation-has-slowed-a-new-kind-has-sped-up

Elsner, J. & R. Cardinal 1994. *The Cultures of Collecting*. London: Reaktion.

Escalona-Orcao, A. *et al.* 2020. "Cultural and creative ecosystems in medium-sized cities: evolution in times of economic crisis and pandemic". *Sustainability* 13(1): 49. https://doi.org/10.3390/su13010049

Escobar, A. 1992. "Culture, economics, and politics in Latin American social movements: theory and research". In A. Escobar & S. Alvarez (eds), *The Making of Social Movements in Latin America*, 62–85. New York: Routledge.

Evans, G. 2003. "Hard-branding the cultural city: from Prado to Prada". *International Journal of Urban and Regional Research* 27(2): 417–40.

Falconi, J. 2014. "The Festivals Internacional de Teatro de la Habena (FITH) and the Festival of Mexico (FMX): between place and placelessness". *Latin American Theatre Review* 48(1): 181–193.

Featherstone, M. 1991. *Consumer Culture and Postmodernism*. London: Sage.

Ferreri, M. *et al.* 2017. "Living precariously: property guardianship and the flexible city". *Transactions of the Institute of British Geographers* 42: 246–59.

Filion, P. *et al.* 2019. "Introduction: The scope and scales of suburban infrastructure". In P. Filion *et al.* (eds), *Critical Perspectives on Suburban Infrastructures*, 1–42. Toronto: University of Toronto Press.

Findley, L. 2005. *Building Change: Architecture, Politics and Cultural Agency*. London: Routledge.

Flinn, A. 2007. "Community histories, community archives: some opportunities and challenges". *Journal of the Society of Archivists* 28(2): 151–76.

Florida, R. 2002. *The Rise of the Creative Class: And How It's Transforming Work, Leisure, Community and Everyday Life*. New York: Basic Books.

Florida, R. & M. Seman 2020. *Lost Art: Measuring Covid-19's Devastating Impact on America's Creative Economy*. Washington, DC: Brookings Institute.

Florida, R. *et al.* 2021. "Cities in a post-Covid world". *Urban Studies*. https://doi.org/10.1177/00420980211018072

Foord, J. 2009. "Strategies for creative industries: an international review". *Creative Industries Journal* 1(2): 91–113.

Forkert, K. 2016. "Austere creativity and volunteer-run public services: the case of Lewisham's libraries". *New Formations* 87: 11–28.

Foucault, M. 1966. *The Order of Things: An Archaeology of the Human Sciences*. Trans. A. Sheridan. New York: Vintage.

Freeman, E. 2010. *Time Binds: Queer Temporalities, Queer Histories*. Durham, NC: Duke University Press.

Freeman, L. & N. Blomley 2019. "Enacting property: making space for the public in the municipal library". *Environment and Planning C: Politics and Space* 37(2): 199–218.

Frey, B. 1994. "The economics of music festivals". *Journal of Cultural Economics* 18: 29–39.

Friederici, N. 2018. "Grounding the dream of African innovation hubs: two cases in Kigali". *Journal of Developmental Entrepreneurship* 23(2): 1850012.

Friedmann, J. 1989. "The Latin American *barrio* movement as a social movement: contribution to a debate". *International Journal of Urban and Regional Research* 13(3): 501–10.

Frost-Kumpf, H. 1998. *Cultural Districts: The Arts as a Strategy for Revitalizing our Cities*. Washington: Americans for the Arts.

Furlong, K. 2010. "Neoliberal water management: trends, limitations, reformulations". *Environment and Society* 1(1): 46–75.

Furlong, K. 2020. "Geographies of infrastructure II: concrete, cloud, and layered (in)visibilities". *Progress in Human Geography* 45(1): 190–98.

Gallant, P. 2016. "George Brown's fashion exchange in Regent Park aims to create jobs, help designers". *Yonge Street*. www.yongestreetmedia.ca/civicimpact/georgebrownfashionexchange03302016.aspx.

Gallen, B. 2015. "Night lives: heterotopia, youth transitions and cultural infrastructure in the urban night". *Urban Studies* 52(3): 555–70.

Gandy, M. 2004. "Rethinking urban metabolism: water, space and the modern city". *City* 8(3): 363–379.

Gandy, M. 2011. "Landscape and infrastructure in the late-modern metropolis". In G. Bridge & S. Watson (eds), *The New Blackwell Companion to the City*, 57–65. Chichester: John Wiley.

Gandy, M. 2014. *The Fabric of Space: Water, Modernity, and the Urban Imagination*. Cambridge, MA: MIT Press.

Garbasz, Y. 2021. Personal website: http://yishay.com/.

Garrett, L. *et al.* 2017. "Co-constructing a sense of community at work: the emergence of community in coworking spaces". *Organization Studies* 38(6): 821–42.

Gasch, L. & L. Dickens 2022. "Covid commentaries: London's cultural policy". *The London Journal* 47(2): 135–40.

Gatrell, V. 2013. *The First Bohemians: Life and Art in London's Golden Age*. London: Allen.

Geoghegan, H. 2010. "Museum geography: exploring museums, collections, and museum practices in the UK". *Geography Compass* 4(10): 1462–76.

Getzner, G. 2020. "Urban and rural preferences for cultural policies and infrastructures". *Cultural Trends* 29(5): 378–99.

GhostLight 2020. "About". www.ghostlight.ca/about

Gieseking, J. 2020. "Mapping lesbian and queer lines of desire: constellations of queer urban space". *Environment and Planning D: Society and Space* 38(5): 941–60.

Gill, J. 1997. *Lords of Misrule: Mardi Gras and the Politics of Race in New Orleans*. Jackson, MI: University Press of Mississippi.

Giovanardi, M. *et al.* 2014. "Co-performing tourism places: the 'Pink Night' festival". *Annals of Tourism Research* 44: 102–15.

Glass, M. *et al.* 2019. "Regional infrastructures, infrastructural regionalism". *Regional Studies* 53(12): 1651–6.

Godet, A. 2020. "Behind the masks: the politics of Carnival". *Journal of Festive Studies* 2(1): 1–31.

Golden, H. 2022. "Chewbacchus shortening route due to not enough NOPD officers volunteering for parade". *WDSU*, 4 February. www.wdsu.com/article/chewbacchus-route-change-nopd-officers-parade/38986066

Goodwin, J. *et al.* 2001. "Introduction: why emotions matter". In J. Goodwin *et al.* (eds), *Passionate Politics: Emotions and Social Movements*, 1–24. Chicago, IL: University of Chicago Press.

Graham, S. 2004. "Postmortem city: towards an urban geopolitics". *City* 8(2): 165–96.

Graham, S. & S. Marvin 2001. *Splintering Urbanism: Networked Infrastructures, Technological Mobilities and The Urban Condition*. New York: Routledge.

Graham, S. & S. Marvin 2022. "*Splintering Urbanism* at 20 and the 'infrastructural turn'". *Journal of Urban Technology* 29(1): 169–75.

Graham, S. & C. McFarlane 2015. *Infrastructural Lives: Urban Infrastructure in Context*. London: Routledge.

Greater London Authority 2014. "Artists' workspace study: report and recommendations". www.london.gov.uk/sites/default/files/artists_workspace_study_september2014_reva_web_0.pdf.

Greater London Authority 2018. "Artists' workspace annual data note: cultural infrastructure plan". www.london.gov.uk/sites/default/files/2018-artists-workspace-study-data-note.pdf.

Greater London Authority 2019a. "Creative supply chains study". www.london.gov.uk/sites/default/files/creative_supply_chains_study_final_191011.pdf.

Greater London Authority 2019b. "Cultural infrastructure plan: a call to action". www.london.gov.uk/sites/default/files/cultural_infrastructure_plan_online.pdf

Greater London Authority 2022a. "Culture and good growth". www.london.gov.uk/what-we-do/arts-and-culture/culture-and-good-growth.

Greater London Authority 2022b. "Cultural infrastructure map". www.london.gov.uk/what-we-do/arts-and-culture/cultural-infrastructure-toolbox/cultural-infrastructure-map.

Green, C. 2001. *From Factories to Fine Art*. PhD thesis, University of London.

Green, N. 2020. "The holding option: artists in East London 1968–2020". *Built Environment* 46(2): 229–47.

Gregory, H. & K. Robertson 2018. "No small matter: micromuseums as critical institution". *Racar Special Issue: Critical Curating* 43(2): 89–101.

Gregson, N. & L. Crewe 2003. *Second-Hand Cultures*. Oxford: Berg.

Grodach, C. 2017. "Urban cultural policy and creative city making". *Cities* 68: 82–91.

Guevara, J. 2019. "Colectivos de arte, creación, gestión y comunidad en Los Barrios de Lima (2007–2013): la experiencia de CHOLO, el colectivo, ambre y espacio abierto". *Ensayos Críticos Sobre Arte, Educación Artística y Cultura en El Perú*. ENSABAP.

Gutiérrez Rodríguez, E. 2018. "The coloniality of migration and the 'refugee crisis': on the asylum-migration nexus, the transatlantic white European settler colonialism-migration and racial capitalism". *Refuge: Canada's Journal on Refugees* 34(1): 16–28.

Hae, L. 2011. "Dilemmas of the nightlife fix: post-industrialisation and the gentrification of nightlife in New York City". *Urban Studies* 48(16): 3449–65.

Halberstam, J. 2003. "What's that smell? Queer temporalities and subcultural lives". *International Journal of Cultural Studies* 6(3): 313–33.

Hall, P. 1966. *The World Cities*. London: Weidenfeld & Nicholson.

Hall, P. 1998. *Cities in Civilization: Culture Technology and Urban Order*. London: Weidenfeld & Nicolson.

Hall, S. 2012. *City, Street and Citizen: The Measure of the Ordinary*. London: Routledge.

Hamdi, N. 2010. "The intelligence of informality". In S. Goldsmith & L. Elizabeth (eds), *What We See: Advancing the Observations of Jane Jacobs*, 34–43. Oakland, CA: New Village Press.

Harris, A. 2012. "Art and gentrification: pursuing the urban pastoral in Hoxton, London". *Transactions of the Institute of British Geographers* 37: 226–41.

Harris, E. 2020. *Rebranding Precarity: Pop-up Culture as the Seductive New Normal*. London: Zed.

Hartley, J. *et al.* 2012. *Key Concepts in Creative Industries*. London: Sage.

Hartwick, E. 1998. "Geographies of consumption: a commodity-chain approach". *Environment and Planning D: Society and Space* 16(4): 423–37.

Harvey, D. 2000. *Spaces of Hope*. Los Angeles, CA: University of California Press.

Harvey, D. 2012. *Rebel Cities: From the Right to the City to the Urban Revolution*. London: Verso.

Harvie, J. 2013. *Fair Play: Art, Performance and Neoliberalism*. London: Palgrave Macmillan.

Hawkins, H. 2017. *Creativity*. London: Routledge.

Healy, B. 2020. "7 opportunities thanks to Covid-19 (and, fuck you, Covid-19)". *Canadian Stage*. www.canadianstage.com/cs-grid-blog/read/7-opportunities-thanks-to-Covid-19-and-fuck-you-Covid-19

Heil, T. 2021. "Interweaving the fabric of urban infrastructure: Senegalese City-making in Rio de Janeiro". *International Journal of Urban and Regional Research* 45(1): 133–49.

Hesmondhalgh, D. & A. Pratt 2005. "Cultural industries and cultural policy". *International Journal of Cultural Policy* 11(1): 1–14.

Hetherington, K. 2013. "Rhythm and noise: the city, memory and the archive". *The Sociological Review* 61: 17–33.

Hetherington, K. 1997. "Museum topology and the will to connect". *Journal of Material Culture* 2(2): 199–218.

Higgins, R. 2018. "Memory, archives, and activism in Montreal: a collective quest". *Contemporary French Civilization* 43(3/4): 445–67.

Hill, W. 2017. *Art After the Hipster: Identity Politics, Ethics and Aesthetics*. London: Palgrave Macmillan.

Hillier, B. & T. Abbruzzese 2022. "Smart cities: big data and surveillance". In A. Bail & L. Peake (eds), *Urbanization in a Global Context*. Oxford: Oxford University Press.

Historypin 2010–20. "About". https://about.historypin.org/

Hjalager, A.-M. 2009. "Cultural tourism innovation systems: the Roskilde Festival". *Scandinavian Journal of Hospitality and Tourism* 9(2/3): 266–87.

Holden, J. 2015. *The Ecology of Culture: A Report Commissioned by the Arts and Humanities Research Council's Cultural Value Project*. Arts & Humanities Research Council. https://publicartonline.org.uk/downloads/news/AHRC%20Ecology%20of%20Culture.pdf

Holman, W. 2015. "Makerspace: towards a new civic infrastructure". *Places Journal*. https://doi.org/10.22269/151130

Holston, J. 2008. *Insurgent Citizenship: Disjunctions of Democracy and Modernity*. Princeton, NJ: Princeton University Press.

Howe, C. *et al.* 2016. "Paradoxical infrastructures: ruins, retrofit, and risk". *Science Technology and Human Values* 41(3): 547–65.

Hracs, B. 2009. "Beyond bohemia: geographies of everyday creativity for musicians in Toronto". In N. Edensor *et al.* (eds), *Spaces of Vernacular Creativity: Rethinking the Cultural Economy*, 75–88. London: Routledge.

Hubbard, P. 2016. "Hipsters on our high streets: consuming the gentrification frontier". *Sociological Research Online* 21(3): 106–11.

Hubbard, P. 2017. *The Battle for the High Street: Retail Gentrification, Class, and Disgust.* London: Palgrave Macmillan.

Hughes, T. 1993. *Networks of Power: Electrification in Western Society, 1880–1930.* Baltimore, MD: Johns Hopkins University Press.

Huysmans, F. & N. Palliser 2017. "Community librarians: de Nederlandse praktijk". Cubiss. https://cubiss-longread.nl/community-librarians/.

ICOM 2007. "Museum definition". https://icom.museum/en/resources/standards-guidelines/museum-definition/

ICOM 2018. "Standing committee for museum definition, prospects and potentials". https://icom.museum/wp-content/uploads/2019/01/MDPP-report-and-recommendations-adopted-by-the-ICOM-EB-December-2018_EN-2.pdf

ICOM 2022. "Museum definition". https://icom.museum/en/resources/standards-guidelines/museum-definition/

INCITE! Collective (ed.) 2017. *The Revolution Will Not Be Funded: Beyond the Non-profit Industrial Complex.* Durham, NC: Duke University Press.

Ignatow, G. 2011. "What has globalization done to developing countries' public libraries?" *International Sociology* 26(6): 746–68.

Imrie, R. 2021. *Concrete Cities: Why We Need to Build Differently.* Bristol: Policy Press.

Ivaldi, S. *et al.* 2018. "Coworking(s) in the plural: coworking spaces and new ways of managing". In S. Taylor & S. Luckman (eds), *The New Normal of Working Lives: Critical Studies in Contemporary Work and Employment*, 219–41. Cham: Palgrave Macmillan.

Irwin, R. & S. Springgay 2008. "A/r/tography as practice-based research". In S. Springgay *et al.* (eds), *Being with A/r/tography*, i–xxxiii. Rotterdam: Sense Publishers.

Isador, G. 2022. "How I went broke succeeding in theatre". *The Local.* https://thelocal.to/how-i-went-broke-succeeding-in-theatre/.

Jackson, S. 2011. *Social Works: Performing Art, Supporting Publics.* New York: Routledge.

Jamieson, K. 2004. "Edinburgh: the festival gaze and its boundaries". *Space & Culture* 7(1): 64–75.

Janes, R. & S. Sandell 2019. *Museum Activism.* New York: Routledge.

Jiang, L. & L. Yu 2020. "Consumption of a literary tourism place: a perspective of embodiment". *Tourism Geographies* 22(1): 127–50.

Johnston, J. & S. Baumann 2015. *Foodies: Democracy and Distinction in the Gourmet Foodscape.* London: Routledge.

Jones, A. & J. Murphy 2010. "Theorizing practice in economic geography: foundations, challenges, and possibilities". *Progress in Human Geography* 35(3): 366–92.

Jones, P. *et al.* 2019. *Cultural Intermediaries Connecting Communities: Revisiting Approaches to Cultural Engagement.* Bristol: Policy Press.

Jordan, J. 2016. "Festivalisation of cultural production: experimentation, spectacularisation and immersion". *Journal of Cultural Management and Policy* 6(1): 44–55.

Julien, H. & S. Genuis 2009. "Emotional labour in librarians' instructional work". *Journal of Documentation* 65(6): 926–37.

Kallianos, Y. & M. Fumanti 2021. "The everyday and the evental public space: rethinking the spatio-temporal modalities of radical political events". *Antipode* 53(4): 1104–23.

Khamis, S. *et al.* 2017. "Self-branding, 'micro-celebrity' and the rise of social media influencers". *Celebrity Studies* 8(2): 191–208.

Kanai, J. & S. Schindler 2022. "Infrastructure-led development and the peri-urban question: furthering crossover comparisons". *Urban Studies* 59(8): 1597–617.

Katz, C. 2004. *Growing Up Global: Economic Restructuring and Children's Everyday Lives*. Minneapolis, MN: University of Minnesota Press.

Keil, R. 2009. "The urban politics of roll-with-it neoliberalization". *City* 13(2/3): 230–45.

Kern, L. 2013. "All aboard? women working the spaces of gentrification in Toronto's junction". *Gender, Place & Culture* 20(4): 510–27.

Kern, L. 2015. "From toxic wreck to crunchy chic: environmental gentrification through the body". *Environment and Planning D: Society and Space* 33(1): 67–83.

Ketchum, A. 2020. "Lost spaces, lost technologies, and lost people: online history projects seek to recover LGBTQ+ spatial histories". *Digital Humanities Quarterly* 14(3). www.digitalhumanities.org/dhq/vol/14/3/000483/000483.pdf

Khlystova, O. *et al.* 2022. "The impact of the COVID-19 pandemic on the creative industries: a literature review and future research agenda". *Journal of Business Research* 139: 1192–210.

Kingsbury, P. 2016. "Rethinking the aesthetic geographies of multicultural festivals: a Nietzschean perspective". *Annals of the American Association of Geographers* 106(1): 222–41.

Kim, A. 2020. "Can we design for culture? Paradigms and provocations". *Built Environment* 46(2): 199–213.

Kim, W. 2011. "The viability of cultural districts in Seoul". *City, Culture and Society* 2: 141–50.

Kinder, K. 2016. *DIY Detroit: Making Do in a City Without Services*. Minneapolis, MN: University of Minnesota Press.

Kinser, S. 1990. *Carnival, American Style*. Chicago, IL: University of Chicago Press.

Kleinman, J. 2014. "Adventures in infrastructure: making an African hub in Paris". *City & Society* 26(3): 286–307.

Klinenberg, E. 2018. *Palaces for the People: How to Build a More Equal and United Society*. London: Bodley Head.

Knowles, R. 2017. *Performing the Intercultural City*. Ann Arbor, MI: University of Michigan Press.

Kong, L. 2007. *Singapore's Hawker Centres: People, Places, Food*. Singapore: National Environment Agency.

Kong, L. 2015. "From sushi in Singapore to Laksa in London: globalising foodways and the production of economy and identity". In L. Kong & V. Sinha (ed.), *Food, Foodways and Foodscapes: Culture, Community and Consumption in Post-Colonial Singapore*, 38–58. Singapore: World Scientific.

Korn, M. *et al.* 2019. *Infrastructuring Publics*. Berlin: Springer.

Krätke, S. 2010. "'Creative cities' and the rise of the dealer class: a critique of Richard Florida's approach to urban theory". *International Journal of Urban and Regional Research* 34(4): 835–53.

Krivý, M. 2013. "Don't plan! The use of the notion of 'culture' in transforming obsolete industrial space". *International Journal of Urban and Regional Research* 37(5): 1724–46.

Kruger, L. 2021. "Performance and politics in a time of confinement: virtual stages between South Africa and African America." *Critical Stages* 23. www.critical-stages.org/23/performance-and-politics-in-a-time-of-confinement-virtual-stages-between-south-africa-and-african-america/

Kruger, R. *et al.* 2020. "The production of community in community land trusts". *City & Community* 19(3): 638–55.

Kuebart, A. 2021. "Open creative labs as functional infrastructure for entrepreneurial ecosystems: using sequence analysis to explore tempo-spatial trajectories of startups in Berlin". *Research Policy* 51(9): 1–12.

Kumbier, A. 2014. *Ephemeral Material: Queering the Archives*. Sacramento: Litwin Books.

LA Network 2017. "Latinoamérica Expresa su Vitalidad Con El Arte Urbano". *LA Network*. https://la.network/arte-urbano-en-latinoamerica/.

Lakhani, N. 2016. "Landfill-harmonic: the Mexican music school on the edge of a rubbish dump". *The Guardian*. www.theguardian.com/world/2016/nov/21/mexican-music-school-vicente-guerrero-edge-of-a-rubbish-dump

Landau, F. 2020a. "Cultural infrastructures of vulnerability: reflections on care during and after Covid-19". https://artsoftheworkingclass.org/text/cultural-infrastructures-of-vulnerability

Landau, F. 2020b. "Cultural infrastructures of vulnerability II: cultural institutions in (post-) pandemic exposure". https://artsoftheworkingclass.org/text/cultural-infrastructures-of-vulnerability-ii

Landau, F. 2021. "[Un]grounding agonistic public space: approaching Mouffe's spatial theory via museums". In F. Landau *et al.* (eds), *[Un]Grounding: Post-Foundational Geographies*, 153–73. New York: Columbia University Press.

Landau, F. *et al.* 2021. *[Un]Grounding: Post-Foundational Geographies*. New York: Columbia University Press.

Landau-Donnelly, F. & Y. Garbasz, forthcoming. "Critique beside and beyond institutions: introducing the Women's Walking Museum an exercise of radical dreaming".

Landau-Donnelly, F. & A. Sethi 2022. "Articulating a museum from absence: emptiness in the Conflictorium beyond pandemic times". *Museum International* 73(3/4): 168–79.

Landry, C. 2008. *Creative City: A Toolkit for Urban Innovators*. London: Earthscan.

Landry, C. 2020. "Arts, culture and the city: an overview". *Built Environment* 46(2): 170–81.

Lange, B. 2006. "Landscapes of scenes: socio-spatial strategies of culturepreneurs in Berlin". In T. Terkenli & A.-M. d'Hauteserre (eds), *Landscapes of a New Cultural Economy of Space*, 41–67. Dordrecht: Springer.

Lange, B. 2011. "Professionalization in space: social-spatial strategies of culturepreneurs in Berlin". *Entrepreneurship and Regional Development* 23(3/4): 259–79.

Larkin, B. 2013. "The politics and poetics of infrastructure". *Annual Review of Anthropology* 42(1): 327–43.

Latham, A. & J. Layton 2019. "Social infrastructure and the public life of cities: studying urban sociality and public spaces". *Geography Compass* 13(7): 1–15.

Latham, A. & P. Wood 2015. "Inhabiting infrastructure: exploring the interactional spaces of urban cycling". *Environment and Planning A* 47(2): 300–19.

Lawhon, M. *et al.* 2018. "Thinking through heterogeneous infrastructure configurations". *Urban Studies* 55(4): 720–32.

LaRochelle, L. 2017. "Queering the map". www.queeringthemap.com

Leahy, H. 2016. *Museum Bodies: The Politics and Practices of Visiting and Viewing*. Abingdon: Routledge.

Lees, L. 2003. "Super-gentrification: the case of Brooklyn Heights, New York City." *Urban Studies* 40(12): 2487–509.

Lefebvre, H. 2003. *The Urban Revolution*. Minneapolis, MN: University of Minnesota Press.

Lefebvre, H. 1991. *The Production of Space*. Blackwell: Oxford.

Left Bank Co. 2021. *Making Space for Culture Incubation Program*. www.leftbankco.com/our-projects/2021/11/5-making-space-for-culture-incubation-program

le Grand, E. 2020. "Representing the middle class 'hipster': emerging modes of distinction, generational oppositions and gentrification". *European Journal of Cultural Studies* 23(2): 184–200.

Leitner, H. & E. Sheppard 2016. "Provincializing critical urban theory: extending the ecosystem of possibilities". *International Journal of Urban and Regional Research* 40(1): 228–35.

Lemanski, C. 2018. "Infrastructural citizenship: spaces of living in Cape Town, South Africa". In K. Ward (ed.), *The Routledge Handbook on Spaces of Urban Politics*, 350–60. New York: Routledge.

Lemanski, C. 2020. "Infrastructural citizenship: (de)constructing state-society relations". *International Development Planning Review* 42(2): 115–26.

Lemanski, C. 2022. "Afterword: citizenship and the politics of (im)material stigma and infrastructure". *Urban Studies* 59(3): 663–71.

Leorke, D. *et al.* 2018. "'More than just a library': public libraries in the 'smart city'". *City, Culture and Society* 15(1): 37–44.

Leslie, D. & N. Rantisi 2011. "Creativity and place in the evolution of a cultural industry: the case of Cirque du Soleil". *Urban Studies* 48(9): 1771–87.

Leslie, D. & N. Rantisi 2019. "Deskilling in cultural industries: corporatization, standardization and the deskilling of creativity at the Cirque du Soleil". *Geoforum* 99: 257–66.

Leslie, D. *et al.* 2014. "Crafting an antidote to fast fashion: the case of Toronto's independent fashion design sector". *Growth and Change* 45(2): 222–39.

Leslie, D. *et al.* 2015. "Qualifying aesthetic values in the experience economy: the role of independent fashion boutiques in curating slow fashion". In A. Lorentzen *et al.* (eds), *Spatial Dynamics in the Experience Economy*, 192–7. New York: Routledge.

Levin, L. & K. Solga 2009. "Building utopia: performance and the fantasy of urban renewal in contemporary Toronto." *TDR: The Drama Review* 53(3): 37–53.

Ley, D. 2003. "Artists, aestheticisation and the field of gentrification". *Urban Studies* 40(12): 2527–44.

Lloyd, R. 2010. *Neo-Bohemia: Art and Commerce in the Post-Industrial City*, 2nd edition. New York: Routledge.

Løgstrup, J. 2021. "Museums as contact or conflict zones: the museum as a target for change". *ONCURATING* 50: 1–13.

Low, S. & A. Smart 2020. "Thoughts about public space during Covid-19 pandemic". *City & Society* 32(1). https://doi.org/10.1111/ciso.12260

Mace, A. & F. Volgmann 2018. "The role of Leipzig's narrative of shrinking". *Urban Geography* 39(6): 803–21.

Malmström, M. 2022. "Making and unmaking masculinities in Cairo through sonic infrastructural violence". *Urban Studies* 59(3): 591–607.

Maly, I. & P. Varis 2016. "The 21st-century hipster: on micro-populations in times of superdiversity". *European Journal of Cultural Studies* 19(6): 637–53.

Marche, G. 2012. "Why infrapolitics matters". *Revue française d'études américaines* 131(1): 3–18.

Marcus, M. 2022. "The math of shutdown". *The Musical Stage Company*. https://musicalstagecompany.com/the-math-of-shutdown/

Markusen, A. 2006. "Urban development and the politics of a creative class: evidence from a study of artists". *Environment and Planning A* 38(10): 1921–40.

Markusen, A. 2010. "Organizational complexity in the regional cultural economy". *Regional Studies* 44(7): 813–28.

Markusen, A. 2014. "Creative cities: a 10-year research agenda". *Journal of Urban Affairs* 36(supp. 2): 567–89.

Marshall, T. & T. Bottomore 1992. *Citizenship and Social Class*. London: Pluto.

Martí-Costa, M. & M. Pradel i Miquel 2012. "The knowledge city against creativity? Artists' workshops and urban regeneration in Barcelona". *European Urban and Regional Studies* 19(1): 92–108.

Martins, G. 2018. *O Sol Na Cabeça: Contos*. São Paulo: Editora Schwarcz.

Marwick, A. 2013. *Status Update: Celebrity, Publicity, and Branding in the Social Media Age*. New Haven, CT: Yale University Press.

Massey, D. 1994. *Space, Place and Gender*. Minnesota, MN: University of Minnesota Press.

Massey, D. 2005. *For Space*. London: Sage.

Mathews, V. 2014. "Incoherence and tension in culture-led redevelopment". *International Journal of Urban and Regional Research* 38(3): 1019–36.

Mattson, G. 2016. "Digital project: mapping lost lesbian bars, 2006–2016". https://greggormattson.com/2016/09/17/mapping-lost-lesbian-bars-2006-2016/

Mattern, S. 2014. "Library as infrastructure". *Places Journal.* https://doi.org/10.22269/140609

Mayor of London 2018. "Mayor calls for continued effort to keep artists in London". Greater London Authority. www.london.gov.uk/press-releases/mayoral/mayor-calls-for-protection-of-artists-spaces.

Mbembe, A. 2002. "The power of the archive and its limits". In C. Hamilton *et al.* (eds), *Refiguring the Archive*, 19–27. Dordrecht: Springer.

McClinchey, K. 2008. "Urban ethnic festivals, neighborhoods, and the multiple realities of marketing place". *Journal of Travel & Tourism Marketing* 25(3/4): 251–64.

McCormack, D. 2008. "Geographies for moving bodies: thinking, dancing, spaces". *Geography Compass* 2(6): 1822–36.

McFarlane, C. & J. Rutherford 2008. "Political infrastructures: governing and experiencing the fabric of the city". *International Journal of Urban and Regional Research* 32(2): 363–74.

McFarlane, C. & J. Silver 2017. "Navigating the city: dialectics of everyday urbanism". *Transactions of the Institute of British Geographers* 42(3): 458–71.

McFarlane, C. & A. Vasudevan 2014. "Informal infrastructures". In P. Adey *et al.* (eds), *The Routledge Handbook of Mobilities*, 256–64. New York: Routledge.

McFarlane, C. *et al.* 2017. "Cities within cities: intra-urban comparison of infrastructure in Mumbai, Delhi and Cape Town". *Urban Geography* 38(9): 1393–417.

McGuirk, J. 2014. *Radical Cities: Across Latin America in Search of a New Architecture*. London: Verso.

McKinney, C. 2020. *Information Activism: A Queer History of Lesbian Media Technologies*. Chapel Hill, NC: Duke University Press.

McKinnie, M. 2007. *City Stages: Theatre and Urban Space in a Global City*. Toronto: University of Toronto Press.

McLean, H. 2014. "Digging into the creative city: a feminist critique". *Antipode* 46(3): 669–90.

McRobbie, A. 2016. *Be Creative: Making a Living in the New Cultural Industries*. Cambridge: Polity.

Melosi, M. 2020. "Urban infrastructure and the cultural turn". In S. Haumann *et al.* (eds), *Concepts of Urban-Environmental History*, 145–54. Bielefeld: Transcript.

Merkel, J. 2019. "'Freelance isn't free': coworking as a critical urban practice to cope with informality in creative labour markets". *Urban Studies* 56(3): 526–47.

Mermet, A. 2017. "Global retail capital and the city: towards an intensification of gentrification". *Urban Geography* 38(8): 1158–81.

Merriam-Webster Dictionary 2022. "'Infrastructure': a new word from old roots". www.merriam-webster.com/words-at-play/infrastructure-history-definition

Message, K. 2018. *The Disobedient Museum: Writing at the Edge*. London: Routledge.

Merx, S. 2011. "Public pie performing public space". *Performance Research* 16(2): 132–37.

Meyboom, A. 2009. "Infrastructure as practice". *Journal of Architectural Education* 62(4): 72–81.

Michael, J. 2015. "It's really not hip to be a hipster: negotiating trends and authenticity in the cultural field". *Journal of Consumer Culture* 15(2): 163–82.

Miles, M. 2007. *Cities and Cultures*. London: Routledge.

Miles, S. *et al.* 2021. "After/lives: insights from the Covid-19 pandemic for gay neighborhoods". In A. Bitterman & D. Baldwin Hess (eds), *The Life and Afterlife of Gay Neighborhoods: Renaissance and Resurgence*, 393–418. Cham: Springer.

Molotch, H. 1996. "LA as design product: how art works in a regional economy". In A. Scott & E. Soja (eds), *The City: Los Angeles and Urban Theory at the End of the Twentieth Century*, 225–75. Oakland: University of California Press.

Mommaas, H. 2004. "Cultural Clusters and the post-industrial city: towards the remapping of urban cultural policy". *Urban Studies* 41(3): 507–32.

Monroe, R. 2021. "Ultra-fast fashion is eating the world". *The Atlantic*. www.theatlantic.com/magazine/archive/2021/03/ultra-fast-fashion-is-eating-the-world/617794/

Monstadt, J. 2022. "Urban and infrastructural rhythms and the politics of temporal alignment". *Journal of Urban Technology* 29(1): 69–77.

Montero, S. & G. Baiocchi 2022. "A posteriori comparisons, repeated instances and urban policy mobilities: what 'best practices' leave behind". *Urban Studies* 59(8): 1536–55.

Montgomery, J. 2007. *The New Wealth of Cities: City Dynamics and the Fifth Wave*. Aldershot: Ashgate.

Moreton, S. 2013. "The promise of the affordable artist's studio: governing creative spaces in London." *Environment and Planning A* 45: 421–37.

Morgan, G. 2020. "'Meaning and soul': coworking, creative career and independent co-work spaces". In S. Taylor & D. Luckman (eds), *Pathways into Creative Working Lives*, 139–58. Cham: Springer.

Morrison, C. 2020. "Public art replacement on the Mapocho River: erasure, renewal, and a conflict of cultural value in Santiago de Chile". *Space and Culture* 23(2): 149–63.

Moss, L. 2009. "Strategic cultural nationalism". *Canadian Literature* 200, 6–14.

Moss, T. 2020. *Remaking Berlin: A History of the City Through Infrastructure, 1920–2020*. Cambridge. MA: MIT Press.

Mosselson, A. 2021. "Cities of sanctuary in environments of hostility: competing and contrasting migration infrastructures". *Antipode* 53(6): 1725–44.

Mouffe, C. 2016. "An agonistic conception of the museum". http:/proyectomuseu.org.

Mould, O. 2018. *Against Creativity: Everything You Have Been Told About Creativity is Wrong*. New York: Verso.

Moura, T. *et al.* 2020. "Power from the peripheries: art, culture and masculinities in Rio de Janeiro". In S. Clisby *et al.* (eds), *Theorising Cultures of Equality*, 158–70. London: Routledge.

Moya-Latorre, A. 2022. "Urban celebration in a Brazilian favela: from an art festival to a youth movement". *International Journal of Urban and Regional Research* 46(6): 1035–53.

Müller, K. & C. Schwarz 2018. *Fanning the Flames of Hate: Social Media and Hate Crime*. Centre for Competitive Advantage in the Global Economy.

Mullings, B. & A. Habib 2022. "Urban governance, ethnicity, race, and youth". In A. Bain & L. Peake (eds), *Urbanization in a Global Context*, 256–74. Toronto: Oxford University Press.

Multiculturalism Policy Index 2022. *Multiculturalism Policy Index*. Queens University. www.queensu.ca/mcp/

Muñoz, J. 1996. "Ephemera as evidence: introductory notes to queer acts." *Women & Performance: A Journal of Feminist Theory* 8(2): 5–16.

Nancy, J.-L. 1991. *The Inoperative Community*. Minneapolis, MN: University of Minnesota Press.

Négrier, E. 2015. "Festivalisation: patterns and limits". In C. Newbold *et al.* (eds), *Focus on Festivals: Contemporary European Case Studies and Perspectives*, 18–20. Oxford: Goodfellow.

Nestle, J. 2015. "Who were we to do such a thing? Grassroots necessities, grassroots dreaming: the LHA in its early years." *Radical History Review* 122: 233–42.

Newman, A. 2021. "The afterlives of infrastructure". *City & Community* 33(2): 1–11.

Niinimäki, K. *et al.* 2020. "The environmental price of fast fashion". *Nature Reviews: Earth & Environment* 1(4): 189–200.

Norcup, J. 2017. "'Educate a woman and you educate a generation': performing geographies of learning, the public library and a pre-school parents' book club". *Performance Research* 22(1): 67–74.

Novy, J. & C. Colomb 2013. "Struggling for the right to the (creative) city in Berlin and Hamburg: new urban social movements, new 'spaces of hope'?". *International Journal of Urban and Regional Research* 37(5): 1816–38.

Nurse, K. 1999. "Globalization and Trinidad Carnival: diaspora, hybridity and identity in global culture". *Cultural Studies* 13(4): 661–90.

O'Brien, P. *et al.* 2019. "Funding, financing and governing urban infrastructures". *Urban Studies* 56(7): 1291–303.

O'Connor, J. 2013. "Intermediaries and imaginaries in the cultural and creative industries". *Regional Studies* 49(3): 374–87.

O'Doherty, B. 1999. *Inside the White Cube: The Ideology of the Gallery Space.* Los Angeles, CA: University of California Press.

O'Grady, A. 2015. "Alternative playworlds: psytrance festivals, deep play and creative zones of transcendence". In G. McKay (ed.), *The Pop Festival: History, Music, Media, Culture*, 149–64. London: Bloomsbury.

Ocejo, R. 2017. *Masters of Craft: Old Jobs in the New Urban Economy.* Princeton, NJ: Princeton University Press.

Office for National Statistics (ONS) 2021. *Housing affordability in England.* www.ons.gov.uk/people populationandcommunity/housing/bulletins/housingaffordabilityinenglandandwales/2020

Oswin, N. 2014. "Queering the city: sexual citizenship in Creative City Singapore". In M. Davidson & D. Martin (eds), *Urban Politics: Critical Approaches*, 139–55. London: Sage.

Pacella, J. *et al.* 2021. "Fire, pestilence, and the extractive economy: cultural policy after cultural policy". *Cultural Trends* 30(1): 40–51.

Paddock, C. & D. Partridge 2021. "Creating public value: how buildings can better serve our communities". Future of London. https://creativelandtrust.org/wp-content/uploads/2021/07/1088-FoL-Better-use-of-public-assets-FINAL-DIGITAL.pdf

Palmer, J. 2018. "The resonances of public art: thoughts on the notion of co-productive acts and public art". *City & Society* 30(1): 68–88.

Parker, B. 2008. "Beyond the class act: gender and race in the 'creative city' discourse". In J. DeSena (ed.), *Gender in an Urban World*, 201–32. Bingley: Emerald.

Pateman, J. & J. Vincent 2016. *Public Libraries and Social Justice*, 2nd Edition. London: Routledge.

Pautz, H. 2005. "The politics of identity in Germany: the Leitkultur debate". *Race & Class* 46(4): 39–52.

Peck, J. 2012. "Austerity urbanism: American cities under extreme economy". *City* 16(6): 626–55.

Phillips, M. *et al.* 2015. "Foucault and museum geographies: a case study of the English 'Renaissance in the Regions'". *Social & Cultural Geography* 16(7): 730–63.

Pidduck, J. 2020. "Les conditions et les 'scènes' de visibilité médiatique lesbienne et féministe: l'atelier de photographie plessisgraphe des années 70 et 80". *Recherches féministes* 33(2): 67–88.

Pierce, J. & D. Martin 2015. "Placing Lefebvre". *Antipode* 47(5): 1279–99.

Pieterse, E. 2013. "Grasping the unknowable: coming to grips with African urbanism". In E. Pieterse & A. Simone (eds), *Rogue Urbanism: Emergent African Cities*, 5–23. Cape Town: Jacana Media.

Pilo, F. 2021. "Negotiating networked infrastructural inequalities: governance, electricity access and space in Rio de Janeiro". *Environment and Planning C: Politics and Space* 39(2): 265–81.

Pløger, J. 2010. "Presence-experiences: the eventalisation of city space". *Environment and Planning D: Society and Space* 28: 848–66.

Podmore, J. 2006. "Gone 'underground'? lesbian visibility and the consolidation of queer space in Montréal." *Social & Cultural Geography* 7(4): 595–625.

Podmore, J. 1998. "Rereading the 'loft living' habitus in Montreal's inner city". *International Journal of Urban and Regional Research* 22(2): 283–302.

Polletta, F. & B. Gardner 2015. "Culture and movements". In R. Scott & S. Kosslyn (eds), *Emerging Trends in the Social and Behavioral Sciences.* Hoboken: Wiley.

Pollio, A. *et al.* 2021. "Surviving supergentrification in inner city Sydney: adaptive spaces and make-shift economies of cultural production". *International Journal of Urban and Regional Research* 45(5): 778–94.

Portmann, A. 2020. "International festivals, the practice of co-production and the challenges of documentation in the digital age". In R. Knowles (ed.), *The Cambridge Companion to International Theatre Festivals*, 36–53. Cambridge: Cambridge University Press.

Potts, D. 2020. *Broken Cities: Inside the Global Housing Crisis.* London: Bloomsbury.

Pratt, A. 2008. "Creative cities: the cultural industries and the creative class". *Geografiska Annaler: Series B, Human Geography* 90(2): 107–17.

Pratt, A. 2009. "Urban regeneration: from the arts 'feel good' factor to the cultural economy: a case study of Hoxton, London". *Urban Studies* 46(5/6): 1041–61.

Pratt, A. 2018. "Gentrification, artists and the cultural economy". In L. Lees & M. Phillips (eds), *Handbook of Gentrification Studies*, 346–62. Cheltenham: Edward Elgar.

Pratt, A. 2020. "Covid-19 impacts cities, cultures and societies". *City, Culture and Society* 21: 100341.

Pratt, A. 2021. "Creative hubs: a critical evaluation". *City, Culture and Society* 24(2): 1–7.

Prince, J. 2009. "Du placard à l'institution: l'histoire des Archives Gaies du Québec (AGQ)". *Archivaria* 68: 295–309.

Prince, R. 2012. "Metaphors of policy mobility: fluid spaces of 'creativity' policy". *Geografiska Annaler: Series B, Human Geography* 94(4): 317–31.

Pyati, A. & A. Kamal 2012. "Rethinking community and public space from the margins: a study of community libraries in Bangalore's slums". *Area* 44(3): 336–43.

Quinn, B. 2005. "Arts festivals and the city". *Urban Studies* 42(5/6): 927–43.

Quinn, B. 2021. "Event and public space post Covid 19". Paper presented at the 5th International Conference on Events: Making New Waves in Africa, Cape Town, WC, South Africa.

Quinn, B. & L. Wilks 2013. "Festival connections: people, place and social capital". In G. Richards *et al.* (eds), *Exploring the Social Impacts of Events*, 15–30. Abingdon: Routledge.

Quinn, B. *et al.* 2020. "Festivals, public space and cultural inclusion: public policy insights". *Journal of Sustainable Tourism* 29(12): 1875–93.

Raco, M. *et al.* 2018. "Slow cities, urban politics and the temporalities of planning: lessons from London". *Environment and Planning C: Politics and Space* 36(7): 1176–94.

Radice, M. 2021. "Creativity, sociability, solidarity: new-wave Carnival krewes' responses to Covid-19 in New Orleans". *Anthropologica* 63(1): 1–27.

Radice, M. & A. Boudreault-Fournier 2017. *Urban Encounters: Art and the Public*. Montreal and Kingston: McGill-Queen's Press.

Ramesh, N. 2022. "An experiment with the minor geographies of major cities: infrastructural relations among the fragments". *Urban Studies* 59(8): 1556–74.

Ramos Ochoa, W. 2018. "Lima heterogénea, la periferia urbana y la emergencia del contexto cultural cholo". *Revista UI: Ensayos Sobre Arte y Cultura* 3(4): 56–69.

Rantisi, N. 2002. "The local innovation system as a source of variety: openness and adaptability in New York City's garment district." *Regional Studies* 36(6): 587–602.

Rantisi, N. 2004. "The ascendance of New York fashion". *International Journal of Urban and Regional Research* 28(1): 86–106.

Rantisi, N. 2011. "The prospects and perils of creating a viable fashion identity". *Fashion Theory* 15(2): 259–66.

Rantisi, N. & D. Leslie 2010. "Materiality and creative production: the case of the mile end neighbourhood in Montreal". *Environment and Planning A* 42(12): 2824–41.

Rantisi, N. & D. Leslie 2021. "In and against the neoliberal state? The precarious siting of work integration social enterprises (WISEs) as counter-movement in Montreal, Quebec". *Environment and Planning A: Economy and Space* 53(2): 349–70.

Rao, V. 2009. "Embracing urbanism: the city as archive". *New Literary History* 40: 371–83.

Rapošová, I. 2019. "'We can't just put any belly-dancer into the program': cultural activism as boundary work in the city of Bratislava". *Journal of Ethnic and Migration Studies* 45(11): 2100–17.

Rattu, K. 2018. "Regeneration and growth in outer London: challenges and opportunities". *Journal of Urban Regeneration & Renewal* 12: 14–19.

Ravits, S. 2022. "City can't promise downtown parades won't get shortened this weekend". *Gambit*, 8 February. www.nola.com/gambit/mardi_gras/article_683654e0-890a-11ec-9863-83fce37637fe.html

Reckwitz, A. 2002. "Toward a theory of social practices: a development in culturalist theorizing". *European Journal of Social Theory* 5(2): 243–63.

Redaelli, E. & D. Stevenson 2022. "Arts in the city: debates in the *Journal of Urban Affairs*". *Journal of Urban Affairs* 44(4–5): 456–70.

Reed, S. 1998. "The politics and poetics of dance". *Annual Review of Anthropology* 27: 503–32.

Ren, J. 2022. "A more global urban studies, besides empirical variation". *Urban Studies* 59(8): 1741–8.

Richards, G. & R. Palmer 2010. *Eventful Cities: Cultural Management and Urban Revitalisation*. Kidlington: Elsevier.

Ridout, N. 2013. *Passionate Amateurs: Theatre, Communism, and Love*. Ann Arbor, MI: University of Michigan Press.

Rimes, H. *et al.* 2017. "Exploring the dynamics of volunteer and staff interactions: from satisfaction to conflict". *Nonprofit Management & Leadership* 28(2): 195–213.

Rivano Eckerdal, J. 2018. "Equipped for resistance: an agonistic conceptualization of the public library as a verb". *Journal of the Association of Information Science and Technology* 69(12): 1405–13.

Robinson, J. 2002. "Global and world cities: a view from off the map". *International Journal of Urban and Regional Research* 26(3): 531–54.

Robinson, J. 2016. "Comparative urbanism: new geographies and cultures of theorizing the urban". *International Journal of Urban and Regional Research* 40(1): 187–99.

Robinson, J. 2022. "Introduction: generating concepts of 'the urban' through comparative practice". *Urban Studies* 59(8): 1521–35.

Rodríguez, D. 2017. "The political logic of the non-profit industrial complex". In INCITE! Collective (ed.), *The Revolution Will Not Be Funded: Beyond the Non-profit Industrial Complex*, 21–40. Chapel Hill, NC: Duke University Press.

Rogerson, C. 2016. "Progressive rhetoric, ambiguous policy pathways: street trading in inner-city Johannesburg, South Africa." *Local Economy* 31(1/2): 204–18.

Rojas-Pick, S. 2014. "Street museum without walls: a curatorial mediation on the convergence of street art and digital culture". Doctoral dissertation, OCAD University.

Roodhouse, S. 2006. *Cultural Quarters: Principles and Practices*. Bristol: Intellect.

Ross, S. 2020. "Comparative legal perspectives on cultural land trusts for urban spaces of culture, community, and art: a tool for counteracting displacement". *Milan Law Review* 2: 98–123.

Rutherford, J. 2020. *Redeploying Urban Infrastructure: The Politics of Urban Socio-Technical Futures*. Cham: Palgrave Macmillan.

Rutherford, J. & O. Coutard 2014. "Urban energy transitions: places, processes and politics of socio-technical change". *Urban Studies* 51(7): 1353–77.

Sanders, T. *et al.* 2022. "Trans architecture and the prison as archive: 'don't be a queen and you won't be arrested." *Punishment & Society*. https://doi.org/10.1177/14624745221087058

Santos Cid, A. 2022. "El rap 'underground' enseña los dientes en la Ciudad de México". *El País*. https://elpais.com/mexico/2022-01-15/el-rap-underground-ensena-los-dientes-en-la-ciudad-de-mexico.html

Sassatelli, M. 2008. "European cultural space in the European Cities of Culture: Europeanization and cultural policy". *European Societies* 10(2): 225–45.

Schaller, S. & S. Guinand 2018. "Pop-up landscapes: a new trigger to push up land value?" *Urban Geography* 39(1): 54–74.

Schiermer, B. 2014. "Late-modern hipsters: new tendencies in popular culture". *Acta Sociologica* 57(2): 167–81.

Schindler, S. 2014. "The making of 'world-class' Delhi: relations between street hawkers and the new middle class". *Antipode* 46(2): 557–73.

Schippers, H. 2016. "Cities as cultural ecosystems: researching and understanding music sustainability in urban settings". *Journal of Urban Culture Research* 12: 10–19.

Schloffel-Armstrong, S. *et al.* 2021. "Geographies of the public library: institutions, architectures, interactions". *Geography Compass* 15(10): e12592.

Schmidt, S. 2019. "In the making: open creative labs as an emerging topic in economic geography". *Geography Compass* 13(9): e12463.

Schmidt, S. & T. Brinks 2017. "Open creative labs: spatial settings at the intersection of communities and organizations". *Creativity and Innovation Management* 26(3): 291–99.

Schmidt, S. *et al.* 2018. "Anchoring resilience in and through open creative labs in Amsterdam, Berlin and Detroit". Paper presented at *EGOS conference*, Tallinn.

Schuessler E., S. Svejenova & P. Cohendet 2021. "Organizing creativity for innovation: situated practices and process perspectives". In E. Schuessler, P. Cohendet & S. Svejenova (eds), *Organizing Creativity in the Innovation Journey*, 1–16. Bingley: Emerald.

Schweitzer, M. 2015. *Transatlantic Broadway: The Infrastructural Politics of Global Performance*. Cham: Springer.

Scorese, P. 2022. "Theatre in quarantine: temporality and nostalgia in remediation". In K. Capece & P. Scorese (eds), *Pandemic Performance Resilience, Liveness, and Protest in Quarantine Times*, 77–98. New York: Routledge.

Scott, A. 1996. "The craft, fashion and cultural-products industries of Los Angeles: competitive dynamics and policy dilemmas in a multisectoral image-producing complex". *Annals of the Association of American Geographers* 86(2): 306–23.

Scott, A. 1999. "The cultural economy: geography and the creative field". *Media, Culture and Society* 21(6): 801–17.

Scott, A. 2001. *The Cultural Economy of Cities*. London: Sage.

Scott, A. 2008. *Social Economy of the Metropolis: Cognitive-Cultural Capitalism and the Global Resurgence of Cities*. Oxford: Oxford University Press.

Scott, M. 2017. "'Hipster capitalism' in the age of austerity? Polanyi meets Bourdieu's new petite bourgeoisie". *Cultural Sociology* 11(1): 60–76.

Scott, R. 2018. *Urban Precarity: Affordable Art Studios in Contemporary London*. DPhil thesis, University of Oxford.

Scott, R. 2022. *Artists' Workspace Consultation Report*. London: King's College London.

Sellie, A. *et al.* 2015. "Interference archive: a free space for social movement culture". *Archival Science* 15(4): 453–72.

Sendra, P. 2015. "Rethinking urban public space: assemblage thinking and the uses of disorder". *City* 19(6): 820–36.

Sennett, R. 2018. "The zero-sum game of cultural infrastructure". Theatrum Mundi Working Papers. London School of Economics. https://theatrum-mundi.org/library/the-zerosum-game-of-cultural-infrastructure/.

Serafini, P. & N. Novosel 2021. "Culture as care: Argentina's cultural policy response to Covid-19". *Cultural Trends* 30(1): 52–62.

Sevelius, J. *et al.* 2020. "Research with marginalized communities: challenges to continuity during the Covid-19 pandemic". *AIDS and Behavior* 24(7): 2009–12.

Shaw, K. 2005. "The place of alternative culture and the politics of its protection in Berlin, Amsterdam and Melbourne". *Planning Theory & Practice* 6(2): 149–69.

Shaw, K. 2014. "Melbourne's Creative Spaces Program: reclaiming the 'creative city' (if not quite the rest of it)". *City, Culture and Society* 5(3): 139–47.

Sheffield, R. 2020. *Documenting Rebellions: A Study of Four Lesbian and Gay Archives in Queer Times*. Sacramento, CA: Litwin Books.

Sheller, M. & J. Urry 2004. *Tourism Mobilities: Places to Play, Places in Play*. London: Routledge.

Sheringham, M. 2010. "Archiving". In M. Beaumont & G. Dart (eds), *Restless Cities*, 1–18. London: Verso.

Siemiatycki, M. *et al.* 2020. "The gendered production of infrastructure". *Progress in Human Geography* 44(2): 297–314.

Silver, J. 2014a. "Financing climate change experiments across Cape Town's housing infrastructure". In H. Bulkeley *et al.* (eds), *An Urban Politics of Climate Change: Experimentation and the Governing of Socio-Technical Transitions*, 119–37. London: Zed Books.

Silver, J. 2014b. "Incremental infrastructures: material improvisation and social collaboration across post-colonial Accra". *Urban Geography* 35(6): 788–804.

Simone, A. 2004. "People as infrastructure: intersecting fragments in Johannesburg". *Public Culture* 16(3): 407–29.

Simone, A. 2021. "Ritornello: 'people as infrastructure'". *Urban Geography* 42(9): 1341–8.

Sitas, R. 2020. "Creative cities, graffiti and culture-led development in South Africa: dlala indima ('play your part')." *International Journal of Urban and Regional Research* 44(5): 821–40.

Sizek, J. 2021. "Zombie infrastructure: a legal geography of railroad monstrosity in the California desert." *Environment and Planning D: Society and Space* 39(4): 758–75.

Sizemore-Barber, A. 2017. "Archival movements: South Africa's gay and lesbian memory in action". *Safundi: The Journal of South African and American Studies* 18(2): 117–30.

Sjöholm, J. 2014. "The art studio as archive: tracing the geography of artistic potentiality, progress and production". *Cultural Geographies* 21(3): 505–14.

Sjöholm, J. 2018. "Making bodies, making space and making memory in artistic practice". In L. Price & H. Hawkins (eds), *Geographies of Making, Craft and Creativity*, 31–43. London: Routledge.

Sledge, M. 2022. "New Orleans defends second-line size clampdown as club leaders push back". *NOLA.com*, 8 March. www.nola.com/news/crime_police/article_fefeb794-9f1e-11ec-b6d8-ff6514cfd836.html

Smith, A. *et al.* 2021. "Staging city events in public spaces: an urban design perspective". *International Journal of Events and Festival Management* 12(2): 224–39.

Spinuzzi, C. *et al.* 2019. "'Coworking is about community': but what is 'community' in coworking?" *Journal of Business and Technical Communication* 33(2): 112–40.

Stanley Niaah, S. 2008. "Performance geographies from slave ship to ghetto". *Space and Culture* 11(4): 343–60.

Star, S. 1999. "The ethnography of infrastructure". *American Behavioral Scientist* 43(3): 377–91.

Star, S. & K. Ruhleder 1996. "Steps toward an ecology of infrastructure: design and access for large information spaces". *Information Systems Research* 7(1): 111–34.

Steele, W. & C. Legacy 2017. "Critical urban infrastructure". *Urban Policy and Research* 35(1): 1–6.

Stehlin, J. 2015. "Cycles of investment: bicycle infrastructure, gentrification, and the restructuring of the San Francisco Bay area". *Environment and Planning A* 47: 121–37.

Stern, M. & S. Seifert 2007. "Cultivating 'natural' cultural districts". www.giarts.org/sites/default/files/Cultivating-Natural-Cultural-Districts.pdf

Sternfeld, N. 2018. *Das Radikaldemokratische Museum*. Berlin: De Gruyter.

Stevens, Q. 2007. *The Ludic City: Exploring the Potential of Public Space*. London: Routledge.

Stewart, J. 2022. "I did a ton of Amazon clothing research: these styles will get the most wear". *Who What Wear*. www.whowhatwear.com/amazon-best-womens-clothing

Stoler, A. 2002. "Colonial archives and the art of governance". *Archival Science* 2(1/2): 87–109.

Sublette, N. 2008. *The World that Made New Orleans*. Chicago, IL: Lawrence Hill.

Sullivan, N. & C. Middleton 2020. *Queering the Museum*. New York: Routledge.

Sumi, G. 2020. "Why people are leaving Toronto for greener pastures". *NOW Magazine*. https://nowtoronto.com/lifestyle/why-people-are-leaving-toronto-for-greener-pastures

Sumi, G. 2021. "The great Toronto exodus continues." *NOW Magazine*. https://nowtoronto.com/lifestyle/the-great-toronto-exodus-continues

Sweeney, J. *et al.* 2018. "Assembling placemaking: making and remaking place in a regenerating city". *Cultural Geographies* 25(4): 571–87.

Symonides, J. 1998. "Cultural rights: a neglected category of human rights". *International Social Science Journal* 50(158): 559–72.

Tarrow, S. 1998. *Power in Movement: Social Movements and Contentious Politics*. Cambridge: Cambridge University Press.

Taylor, K. 2021. "Artists helped make Toronto's distillery district cool: now they're being pushed out". *Globe & Mail*, 15 December. www.theglobeandmail.com/arts/article-artists-helped-make-torontos-distillery-district-cool-now-theyre-being/

Taylor, R. 2019. "Invent your own fashion economy: post-growth cultures". *Fashion Practice* 11(3): 397–416.

TBR 2018. *Livelihoods of Visual Artists: 2016 Data Report*. www.artscouncil.org.uk/sites/default/files/download-file/Livelihoods%20of%20Visual%20Artists%202016%20Data%20Report.pdf

Tett, G. 2022. "Many happy returns: the city spaces that bring joy to our correspondents and writers". *Financial Times*, 10 January. www.ft.com/content/0edf3051-623f-45c7-b4ab-7b83b81e22cb

Theatre Passe Muraille 2020. "May I Take Your Arm?" www.passemuraille.ca/20-21-season/mayitakeyourarm/

Theatre Passe Muraille 2021. "Announcing our 21.22 digital transformation project". www.passemuraille.ca/dclmedia/

Theatrum Mundi 2019. "New cultural infrastructure: can we design the conditions for culture?" https://theatrum-mundi.org/library/can-we-design-the-conditions-for-culture/

Thompson, M. 2015. "Between boundaries: from commoning and guerrilla gardening to community land trust development in Liverpool". *Antipode* 47(4): 1021–42.

Thompson, M. 2020. "From co-ops to community land trusts: tracing the historical evolution and policy mobilities of collaborative housing movements". *Housing, Theory and Society* 37(1): 82–100.

Times-Picayune & NOLA.com 2017. "Traditional second-lines charged at least $1,000 more than Mardi Gras krewes to parade." *The Times-Picayune/NOLA.com*. May 2. www.nola.com/news/politics/article_09793941-6f20-583e-9e0b-56acd87c651a.html

Tiwari, R. 2010. *Space-Body-Ritual: Performativity in the City*. Lanham, MD: Lexington.

Toombs, A. *et al.* 2014. "Becoming makers: hackerspace member habits, values and identities". *Journal of Peer Production* 5: 1–8.

Toronto Arts Council 2021. "Impact of Covid-19 on Toronto's non-profit arts sector". Toronto Arts Council. https://torontoartscouncil.org/Covid-19

Toronto Arts Foundation 2018. "Toronto arts facts". Toronto Arts Council. https://torontoartscouncil.org/TAC/media/tac/Advocacy/Toronto-Arts-Facts.pdf

Toupin, S. 2014. "Feminist hackerspaces: the synthesis of feminist and hacker cultures". *Journal of Peer Production* 5: 1–9.

Travkina, E. & P. Sacco 2020. *Culture Shock: Covid-19 and the Cultural and Creative Sectors*. Organisation for Economic Affairs.

Treré, E. 2012. "Social movements as information ecologies: exploring the coevolution of multiple internet aechnologies for activism". *International Journal of Communication* 6: 1–19.

UN HABITAT 2012. *Community Land Trusts: Affordable Access to Land and Housing*. Kenya: United Nations Human Settlements Programme. https://unhabitat.org/sites/default/files/download-manager-files/Community%20Land%20Trusts%20Affordable%20Access%20to%20Land%20and%20Housing.pdf

UNESCO 2009. "Cultural cycle". https://en.unesco.org/creativity/node/747.

UNESCO 2020. *Culture in Crisis: Policy Guide for a Resilient Creative Sector*. https://en.unesco.org/creativity/publications/culture-crisis-policy-guide-resilient-creative

United Nations 1948. Universal Declaration of Human Rights. www.un.org/en/about-us/universal-declaration-of-human-rights

Valli, C. 2015. "A sense of displacement: long-time residents' feelings of displacement in gentrifying Bushwick, New York". *International Journal of Urban and Regional Research* 39(6): 1191–208.

van der Merwe, J. & B. Doucet 2021. "Housing challenges, mid-sized cities and the Covid-19 pandemic". *Canadian Planning and Policy* 2021(1): 70–90.

Van Melik, R. 2020. "From books' library to people's palace". *Geografie* 29(3): 22–4.

Van Melik, R. & M. Merry 2021. "Retooling the public library as social infrastructure". *Social & Cultural Geography*. https://doi.org/10.1080/14649365.2021.1965195

Van Melik, R. & D. van der Schraaf 2020. "Mobile devices and their effect on the sociality of Dutch intercity trains". *Mobilities* 15(3): 380–96.

Van Mil, B. *et al.* 2019. *Evaluatie Wet stelsel openbare bibliotheekvoorzieningen*. The Hague: KWINK groep.

Vårheim, A. *et al.* 2019. "Examining libraries as public sphere institutions: mapping questions, methods, theories, findings and research gaps". *Library and Information Science Research* 41(2): 93–101.

Villalonga-Olives, E., I. Kawachi & I. Hernández-Aguado 2021. "Social capital during the first wave of the Covid-19 outbreak: the case of the island of Menorca". *International Journal of Environmental Research and Public Health* 18(23): 12720.

Virani, T. & R. Gill 2019. "Hip hub? Class, race and gender in creative hubs". In R. Gill *et al.* (eds), *Creative Hubs in Question*, 131–54. Cham: Palgrave Macmillan.

Vivant, E. 2010. "The (re)making of Paris as a bohemian place?" *Progress in Planning* 74(3): 107–52.

Vivant, E. 2013. "Creatives in the city: urban contradictions of the creative city". *City, Culture and Society* 4(2): 57–63.

von Geibler, J. *et al.* 2014. "Exploring the potential of a German living lab research: infrastructure for the development of low resource products and services". *Resources* 3(3): 575–98.

Wade, L. *et al.* 2019. *Downtown Mardi Gras: New Carnival Practices in Post-Katrina New Orleans*. Jackson, MI: University Press of Mississippi.

Wainwright, O. 2017. "Britain has enough land to solve the housing crisis: it's just being hoarded". *The Guardian*, 31 January.

Waitt, G. 2008. "Urban festivals: geographies of hype, helplessness and hope". *Geography Compass* 2(2): 513–37.

Ward, J. & P. Hubbard 2019. "Urban regeneration through culture". In T. Schwanen & R. van Kempen (eds), *Handbook of Urban Geography*, 195–209. Cheltenham: Edward Elgar.

Watermeyer, R. 2012. "A conceptualisation of the post-museum as pedagogical space". *Journal of Science Communication* 11(1): 1–11.

Watson, V. 2003. "Conflicting rationalities: implications for planning theory and ethics". *Planning, Theory & Practice* 4(4): 395–407.

Wynn, J. 2015. *Music City: American Festivals and Place Making in Austin, Nashville and Newport*. Chicago, IL: University of Chicago Press.

Weller, S. 2008. "Beyond 'global production networks': Australian fashion week's trans-sectoral synergies". *Growth and Change* 39(11): 104–22.

Whiting, S. *et al.* 2022. "'Creative city' RIP?". *M/C Journal* 25(3). https://journal.media-culture.org.au/index.php/mcjournal/article/view/2901

Wild, S. 2021. "Canadian stage announces Dream in High Park lineup". *BroadwayWorld.com*. www.broadwayworld.com/toronto/article/Canadian-Stage-Announces-dream-in-high-park-Lineup-20210509

Williams, M. 2018. "Urban commons as more-than-property". *Geographical Research* 56(1): 16–25.

Williams, S. & E. Currid-Halkett 2011. "The emergence of Los Angeles as a fashion hub: a comparative spatial analysis of the New York and Los Angeles fashion industries". *Urban Studies* 48(14): 3043–66.

Wilson, D. & A. Jonas 2021. "The people as infrastructure concept: appraisal and new directions". *Urban Geography* 42(9): 1333–40.

Wilson, E. 2000. *Bohemians: The Glamorous Outcasts*. New Brunswick, NJ: Rutgers University Press.

Wolseth, J. & F. Babb 2008. "Introduction: youth and cultural politics in Latin America". *Latin American Perspectives* 35(4): 3–14.

Wood, E. 2003. *Insurgent Collective Action and Civil War in El Salvador*. New York: Cambridge University Press.

World Cities Culture Forum (WCCF) 2022. *Community Arts Stabilization Trust*. www.worldcitiescultureforum.com/case_studies/community-arts-stabilization-trust

Young, M. 2020. "Leisure pursuits in South Africa as observed during the Covid-19 pandemic." *World Leisure Journal* 62(4): 331–5.

Young, M. 2021. "Now you see it (now you don't): users, maintainers and the invisibility of infrastructure". In M. Nagenborg (ed.), *Technology and the City: Towards a Philosophy of Urban Technologies*, 101–19. Cham: Springer.

Yue, A. 2022. "Conjunctions of resilience and the Covid-19 crisis of the creative cultural industries". *International Journal of Cultural Studies* 25(3/4): 349–68.

Zilberstein, S. 2019. "Space making as artistic practice: the relationship between grassroots art organizations and the political economy of urban development". *City & Community* 18(4): 1142–61.

Zukin, S. 1982. *Loft Living: Culture and Capital in Urban Change*. New Brunswick, NJ: Rutgers University Press.

Zukin, S. 1995. *The Cultures of Cities*. New York: Routledge.

Zukin, S. 2008. "Consuming authenticity: from outpost of difference to means of exclusion". *Cultural Studies* 22(5): 724–48.

Zukin, S. 2010. *Naked City: The Death and Life of Authentic Urban Places*. New York: Oxford University Press.

Zukin, S. 2012. "Competitive globalization and urban change: the allure of cultural strategies". In X. Chen & A. Kanna (eds), *Rethinking Global Urbanism: Comparative Insights from Secondary Cities*. New York: Routledge.

Zukin, S. & L. Braslow 2011. "The life cycle of New York's creative districts: reflections on the unanticipated consequences of unplanned cultural zones". *City, Culture and Society* 2(3): 131–40.

Zukin, S. *et al.* 2009. "New retail capital and neighborhood change: boutiques and gentrification in New York City". *City & Community* 8(1): 47–64.

Zukin, S. *et al.* 2016. "Spaces of everyday diversity: the patchwork ecosystem of local shopping streets". In S. Zukin *et al.* (eds) *Global Cities, Local Streets: Everyday Diversity from New York to Shanghai*, 1–28. New York: Routledge.

Zulli, D. 2018. "Capitalizing on the look: insights into the glance, attention economy, and Instagram". *Critical Studies in Media Communication* 35(2): 137–50.

INDEX

Note: Page numbers in italics denote figures.